U.S.-CHINA ECONOMIC COMPETITION

Gains and Risks in a Complex Economic and Geopolitical Relationship

Howard J. Shatz, Daniel Egel, Editors

Nadia Almasalkhi, Daniel Egel, Aaron B. Frank,
C. Ben Gibson, Timothy R. Heath, Khrystyna Holynska,
King Mallory, Steven W. Popper, Howard J. Shatz,
Alexandra Stark, Tobias Sytsma,
Noosha Uddin, Jessie Wang

Prepared for the Defense Advanced Research Projects Agency
Approved for public release; distribution is unlimited

RAND NATIONAL DEFENSE RESEARCH INSTITUTE

For more information on this publication, visit **www.rand.org/t/RRA1947-1**.

About RAND

The RAND Corporation is a research organization that develops solutions to public policy challenges to help make communities throughout the world safer and more secure, healthier and more prosperous. RAND is nonprofit, nonpartisan, and committed to the public interest. To learn more about RAND, visit www.rand.org.

Research Integrity

Our mission to help improve policy and decisionmaking through research and analysis is enabled through our core values of quality and objectivity and our unwavering commitment to the highest level of integrity and ethical behavior. To help ensure our research and analysis are rigorous, objective, and nonpartisan, we subject our research publications to a robust and exacting quality-assurance process; avoid both the appearance and reality of financial and other conflicts of interest through staff training, project screening, and a policy of mandatory disclosure; and pursue transparency in our research engagements through our commitment to the open publication of our research findings and recommendations, disclosure of the source of funding of published research, and policies to ensure intellectual independence. For more information, visit www.rand.org/about/principles.

RAND's publications do not necessarily reflect the opinions of its research clients and sponsors.

Published by the RAND Corporation, Santa Monica, Calif.

Library of Congress Cataloging-in-Publication Data is available for this publication.

ISBN: 978-1-9774-1506-6

Cover: Illustration by Sara Herbst/RAND, Yevhenii/Adobe Stock and royyimzy/Adobe Stock

About This Report

U.S.-China competition, including economic competition, has come to define U.S. foreign policy since 2017. The two economies are the first- and second-largest national economies in the world, and they are deeply intertwined in all aspects of international exchange. Any changes to the relationship, however necessary, could be costly.

To respond to this challenge, RAND researchers conducted economic and institutional analyses of U.S.-China competition, engaged in a participatory foresight exercise to understand the long-term path for ensuring U.S. economic health, and created two economic competition games exploring the dynamics of multiple countries trying to ensure their economic health while interacting with each other and the private sector. This report, the first of a four-part series, includes the economic and institutional analyses of U.S.-China economic competition. The second report presents the results of a participatory foresight exercise designed to understand the path for ensuring long-term U.S. economic health. The third and fourth reports describe two economic competition games that explore the dynamics of multiple countries trying to ensure their economic health while interacting with each other and the private sector.

This report includes the economic and institutional analyses of U.S.-China economic competition. Individual chapters cover the Chinese concept of economic security; a stocktaking of China-related measures by the United States; empirical and theoretical accounts of how intertwined supply chains are, as well as the advantages and disadvantages of production network assurance strategies and of sanctions on Chinese officials versus more-cooperative modes of engagement; and examinations of specific aspects of U.S.-China competition, including return migration of Chinese nationals from the United States to China, energy and environmental security, how Chinese privately owned enterprises might differ from Western private enterprises and what that means for policy, and potential ways by which to update the rules of international trade to adapt to China's unique system of economic management.

The research reported here was completed in August 2024 and underwent security review with the sponsor before public release.

The views, opinions, and/or findings expressed are those of the authors and should not be interpreted as representing the official views or policies of the Department of Defense or the U.S. government.

RAND National Security Research Division

This research was sponsored by the Defense Advanced Research Projects Agency and conducted within the Acquisition and Technology Policy Program of the RAND National Security Research Division (NSRD), which operates the National Defense Research Institute (NDRI), a federally funded research and development center sponsored by the Office of the Secretary of Defense, the Joint Staff, the Unified Combatant Commands, the Navy, the Marine Corps, the defense agencies, and the defense intelligence enterprise.

For more information on the RAND Acquisition and Technology Policy Program, see www.rand.org/nsrd/atp or contact the director (contact information is provided on the webpage).

Acknowledgments

We thank Whitney Mason, director of DARPA's Microsystems Technology Office, for overall guidance and feedback on this project; Michael Dambach and Paul Dietrich, both of DARPA, for further support; Anne Fischer, formerly deputy director of DARPA's Defense Sciences Office, for guiding an early iteration of this project; Joel Predd of RAND for leading that earlier iteration; and Predd and Caolionn O'Connell, formerly of RAND and now at the Aerospace Corporation, for conceiving of the project. Josh Lipsky of the Atlantic Council and Keith Crane of RAND provided valuable reviews that greatly improved the manuscript. At RAND, Jaron Feldman's expert editing greatly improved the manuscript, and Sara Herbst designed the cover, with early input from Santos Vega. We also include additional acknowledgements from some chapter authors.

Nadia Almasalkhi, the author of Chapter 6, expresses gratitude to the colleagues and mentors who offered resources and insights to support her chapter, including Howard Shatz, Daniel Egel, Lev Navarre Chao, Fiona Quimbre, and Elliot Ji.

Noosha Uddin, the author of Chapter 7, thanks Daniel Egel and Howard Shatz for their careful mentorship and thorough review of the manuscript and for their leadership in this project. Their contributions to the research agenda, suggestions for improvement, and constructive commentary greatly strengthened the chapter. Uddin especially thanks other colleagues from the broader research team for their expertise, guidance, and recommendations: Fabian Villalobos for the section on critical minerals processing and refinement; Steven Popper for the section illustrating potential scenarios of U.S.-China economic strategic interactions; Ben Preston for ensuring that details surrounding current and future nuclear energy capacities for electricity generation were plausible so that potential policy recommendations could be derived from them; Aimee Curtright for ensuring that the discussion on commercial nuclear energy generation included the U.S. Department of Defense's interests and efforts toward transportable nuclear technologies; and Nadia Almasalkhi and other RAND 2023 summer associates for their exceptional encouragement during formal and informal discussions surrounding framing, scenario-building, and other aspects of the research. Finally, Uddin thanks Paasha Mahdavi, Olivia Quinn, and Taylor Trummel of the University of California, Santa Barbara, for their academic expertise regarding U.S. clean energy transition policies and ongoing research support.

Steven Popper, the author of Chapter 8, states that the chapter could not have come into being in its current form without the skillful research assistance of his RAND colleague, Gregory Smith.

All errors of fact and interpretation remain those of the authors.

Summary

U.S.-China competition has come to define U.S. foreign policy attention. Economics is an important component. The two economies are the first- and second-largest national economies in the world, and they are deeply intertwined in all aspects of international exchange, including trade, investment, finance, and even flows of people. This is the first time since at least World War II that the United States' chief geopolitical rival is also an important economic partner.

Completely separating the economies would be costly and might not even be possible. On the other hand, deep levels of engagement might not be beneficial for the United States. With this challenge in mind, the Defense Advanced Research Projects Agency asked RAND the following question: *How can the United States ensure that its economy meets the nation's needs under conditions of coupled, strategic competition?* Answering this question included exploring the proactive steps that can be taken to ensure a healthy U.S. economy over the long term, what such a U.S. economy might look like, and whether ensuring that the U.S economy meets the nation's needs can be done in a way that does not necessarily hamper the Chinese economy but rather provides benefits to all.

The Many Dimensions of U.S.-China Economic Interactions and Competition

We assembled a multidisciplinary team to research a variety of topics:

- China's concept of economic security
- U.S. cooperative and competitive policy measures vis-à-vis China in the 21st century
- how intertwined the economies are and measures to derisk and maintain supply-chain assurance
- theoretical modeling of the effectiveness of U.S. pressure versus cooperative measures
- the human element—consequences for the United States and China of Chinese return migration from the United States
- the energy element—cooperation and competition in energy markets
- what a Chinese private enterprise really is compared with a Western private enterprise and what this means for policy
- measures to safeguard or even improve the rules-based global trading system.

From this work, four core observations emerged.

Observation 1: Conceptual Differences Challenge Effective Policymaking

One of the challenges of creating effective policies to ensure a healthy U.S. economy that meets the nation's needs over the long term and that also takes account of U.S.-China economic exchange is that, in many ways, the U.S. and Chinese economies are strikingly different in how they operate. We explored two conceptual differences: economic security and private enterprises.

China appears to have a much broader conception of economic security than does the United States. China's concept of economic security overlaps with other aspects of national security—such as politics, governance, and the military—and it has become central to the legitimacy of the Chinese Communist Party (CCP). China's economic security concept reflects concerns about subjugation and control by foreign powers and the CCP's reliance on economic growth. It has led to significant involvement of the government and party in the economy and to efforts to shape and lead international rule-setting. Most important, the economic and political security overlap underpins resistance to foreign pressure to change the Chinese economic system.

This government involvement in the economy extends to the realities of private companies in China and how they differ from private companies in the United States and Western, market-oriented economies. Chinese private enterprise merits greater scrutiny because of three factors. The first is the influence on firm behavior exercised by senior decisionmakers in the Chinese government. The second is the omnipresence and univalent political authority of the CCP and the means by which it blurs the line between the party-state and the firm. The third is the sheer scale of resources available to China for subsidies. These conceptual differences mean that an agreed-on set of rules related to the international trading system may have very different consequences for the behavior of Chinese firms versus Western firms, with Chinese firms gaining nonmarket advantage in what appears to be a level playing field but is not.

Observation 2: Understanding of U.S. Policy Approaches to Competition Is Incomplete

Since 2001, particularly following the global financial crisis of 2008–2009, the United States has sought to influence the trajectory of China's economic engagement with the United States and the world. Although initially focused on cooperative economic measures, the United States has relied increasingly on coercive economic measures. Coercive economic measures have been instituted with more frequency since 2018 and include export controls, tariffs, law enforcement against intellectual property theft, and competing industrial subsidies. These tools have shown only limited success in meeting their strategic objectives and have affected the U.S. and allied economies as well. Cooperative measures have not transformed the relationship but have achieved more circumscribed goals and may also have had positive externalities with few costs.

Theoretical modeling can shed more light on the value of coercive versus cooperative measures. An agent-based model created as part of our work on U.S.-China economic competition found that sanctioning a particularly powerful group backfired, further concentrating the power of the group and leading to unfavorable economic results. In contrast, scenarios with cooperative economic interventions that benefited groups more inclined to foster and benefit from international trade were more effective at bringing a more diverse group of elites into positions that could influence Chinese policy. Future work is needed to validate the model and how it represents a large and complex political system, but its results suggest that considering the consequences of policies on different interest groups within China merits attention.

Observation 3: The U.S. and Chinese Economies Are Integrated in Complex Ways Such That Decoupling Comes with Great Costs

One of the challenges of crafting policy related to U.S.-China economic competition is that the U.S.-China relationship is complex, and the level of exchange and interaction is enormous. Researchers on our project team studied different empirical aspects of this relationship: the intertwining of production networks, Chinese students and professionals in the United States and their return migration, and the energy relationship.

The global economy has become increasingly interconnected since the mid-1990s, largely because of an increasing reliance on China as a supplier of inputs for many countries. While China has become a supplier to the world, it has increasingly drawn supplies for its production from South America, Africa, and the Middle East rather than the United States, Asian economies, and the European Union. Despite those trends, the United States and China remain the largest single-country suppliers of inputs worldwide. And although China's rapid growth in relevance for the global economy is unquestioned, the United States still supplies a higher share of foreign value-added required to produce a dollar of global output than does China.

Chinese students in the United States constitute a large share of foreign students, and many of these Chinese students stay to work and contribute to the U.S. economy. But many also go home. Return migration to China could benefit the United States, for example, by strengthening productivity-enhancing economic ties. But return migration can also raise a security concern over intellectual property transfer or theft. Although returnees are competitive in the Chinese labor market, many appear to be discontented with their opportunities there. Returnees also appear to flounder in China's startup scene without support from local partners and networks. In addition, returnees appear to play only a minor role in China's technology transfer efforts. U.S. policy could be directed at retaining highly skilled Chinese immigrants while tailoring the security response to focus on research security and research integrity cases with clear connections to national security or economic espionage. These efforts can support U.S. economic growth and technological advancement and mitigate risks posed by foreign nationals.

Another way that the U.S. and Chinese economies are intertwined is through energy. China is a supplier of green technologies to the United States, while U.S. companies supply liquefied natural gas and petroleum to China. There is also competition, such as when Chinese or U.S. companies compete for oilfield rights or when China or the United States aims to develop critical mineral supplies. With both countries seeking energy security and environmental security, the United States would benefit by building critical mineral processing capabilities at home and in friendly countries and supporting the expansion of the domestic nuclear industry for commercial use but continuing to cooperate with China in selected areas of mutual benefit.

Observation 4: Multilateral Approaches to Meeting the China Challenge Can Mitigate Risks and Enhance Benefits

We paid special attention to two policy areas: production network assurance—or safeguarding supply chains—and measures to rescue the rules-based global trading system. There have been enormous benefits from economic integration but also costs; likewise, there will be costs and benefits of economic de-integration. Investments in technology, trade with allies, and alternative goods are critical to limiting the cost of production network assurance in the long run. Production network assurance is always costly in the short run, but the right kind of investments could lower the cost of production network assurance in the long run. Improving cost competitiveness through production technology, enhancing market access with allies, and increasing opportunities for alternative goods and suppliers as substitutes could help countries transition from a globalization model aimed at cost minimization to one aimed at production network assurance. Beyond just trade policy, this calls for broad-based technological collaborations among allies.

Even with technology advances that change production processes, trade will remain important. Much of the friction in the global trade order stems from the distortions of world trade caused by China's unique system of economic management. One possible improvement is to institute a standalone multilateral competitive neutrality framework. Such a framework would require that firms receiving state aid and that compete with other enterprises disclose all state aid received annually. Enterprises that fail to comply would be subject automatically to a high import tariff surcharge. A somewhat lower automatic surcharge would apply to those in compliance. Enterprises would be able to reduce this surcharge further, along a sliding scale that ends at zero, depending on their ability to document progress along several dimensions related to subsidization. Such a framework is not only country neutral—because many countries provide state aid—but it might also be welcomed by some economic reformers in China who recognize the potentially ruinous outcomes of that country's extensive system of subsidies.

Policy Principles

The U.S. and Chinese economies are deeply intertwined. Although mutual gains from trade and investment are enormous, there are also risks, and the U.S.-China geopolitical and security rivalry threatens to unravel the economic interdependence that has been a hallmark of the past two decades. There is no easy answer to the challenge of maintaining gains from trade and investment while safeguarding U.S. security and reducing tensions. But several principles emerge from this research.

Both Countries Face Risks

The United States relies on China for inputs into its defense industrial production; the exact nature and amount of this dependence is not known. Materials and goods controlled by China are also important for civilian production. China too relies on the United States for inputs, particularly semiconductors based on U.S. designs, semiconductor manufacturing equipment, software, and other forms of intellectual property. China also relies on the United States as a market for its exports—if direct or indirect access to U.S. markets were to be disrupted, unemployment and economic difficulties in China could result, leading to internal unrest.

Recognize the Challenge

China is not a benign player in the international economy. It plays by rules that differ from those of the advanced industrial countries of the West. It ties economic performance to security in a manner that goes well beyond what Western market economies do. By virtue of its economic system, it can damage Western economies, such as by building vast capacity in some industries with subsidies, thereby underpricing Western rivals that must live within market disciplines. Recognizing that China follows different rules means that the terms of its participation in the global system should be adjusted to take account of those differences. Reshaping those terms will require cooperation by the advanced market economies.

Recognize That Separating from the Chinese Economy Will Be Costly

The global system with China at the core of global manufacturing has evolved because China has proved to be an effective producer of goods that are low cost, adjusted for their quality, increasing the overall efficiency of the global economy. But this system may not have properly priced in risk, especially unexpected, disruptive events. Changing the system will impose costs, and there may be a middle ground between full cooperation and full separation. If companies need to move production, they will move to higher-cost or less efficient locations. If companies cease joint innovation activities, they may not innovate as much. If companies need to stop selling certain goods to China, they will have lower profits that may result in less employment, research and development, or investment.

The central, immediate policy challenge will be allocating these costs. Options include federal government subsidies, especially if companies are forced to adjust to safeguard national security, or regulations that in effect impose these costs on companies, either directly or indirectly. There is a potentially larger policy challenge as well, and that is how to envision and guide revised or new economic relationships that will solve the problems brought about by current economic relationships without creating even larger problems.

Choose Carefully

Recognizing that disengaging from China, at least partially, will be costly, the United States and its allies and partners will benefit from being selective in how they engage and how they disengage. Guiding production into lower-cost locations other than China rather than to the United States or other wealthier countries should serve to keep the cost of separation lower than otherwise. It should also serve to build resilience by ensuring that production of important items is not concentrated in one geographic location. Concentrating all production, even in the United States, could be riskier than making sure it is distributed more broadly. And leaving production in China could be efficient if, in the case of disruption, production can be reestablished easily elsewhere within a few weeks. This is to say that the characteristics of the manufacturing processes make a great deal of difference in whether a dominant position in production is efficient and low risk or efficient but high risk.

There is no reason to think that governments, especially when political considerations enter into decisionmaking, will choose actions that are low cost compared with the benefits those actions provide. This suggests that governments should set broad, enforceable principles that can guide private-sector actions and let the private sector determine the best specific courses of action.

Maintain Dialogue and Aim for Ways to Find Mutual Benefit

Tensions between the two biggest single-country economies have not proved beneficial for either. In the face of these tensions, efforts at dialogue have proved useful, not least to forestall relations getting worse. But there may also be points of agreement regarding steps each can take to enhance economic exchange through which economic benefits will exceed security costs.

It Is Not Just About China

Even with slower rates of growth, China will remain an important and highly influential economy with which many countries will want to engage. But while China looms large in global economic discussions, the United States remains the dominant economy in terms of income, wealth, productivity, innovation, and finance—all sources of enormous power. U.S.

economic success will depend not only on how it manages its relationship with China, but on how it creates its own vision for economic success and develops policies to achieve that. Such policies include those related to education and skill-building, the allocation of the federal government budget, fiscal balance, regulatory policy, urban public safety, and energy policy. Domestic U.S. policies can have enormous consequences on U.S. economic performance and, accordingly, on how the United States meets the China challenge.

Contents

Figures and Tables

Figures

Tables

CHAPTER 1

Introduction

King Mallory and Howard J. Shatz

From 1978 to the time of this writing in 2024, China underwent an outstanding economic transformation that lifted hundreds of millions of Chinese citizens out of poverty, allowed China to occupy the position of the world's premier trading nation, and permitted the Chinese economy to grow to become the largest or second largest in the world, depending on how one measures gross domestic product (GDP). That growth was not without geopolitical consequences. Starting in 2012, under the leadership of Chinese Communist Party (CCP) General Secretary Xi Jinping, China began to adopt a more assertive international role designed to protect China's new global interests and to achieve geopolitical influence that is more reflective of China's larger international economic role. China's newfound assertiveness has had both military and economic dimensions:

- China made broad, sweeping territorial claims in the South and East China Seas; significantly expanded its military and nuclear forces; and opened an overseas military base.
- It set up an international development bank to cooperate with—and possibly compete with—the World Bank.
- It launched a multilateral infrastructure initiative to generate business and secure access to markets and raw materials.
- It launched a Made in China 2025 initiative with the goal of achieving self-sufficiency and global market leadership in key emerging technologies.
- It subjected Western companies operating in China to greater scrutiny.
- Where it saw its interests impinged on, China began to engage in acts of economic coercion toward its immediate regional neighbors and countries around the world.

Other countries reacted:

- China's maritime territorial claims were rejected. The Philippines sought arbitration and won an arbitral tribunal judgment against China's claims under the United Nations

Convention on the Law of the Sea, a judgment that China rejected.[1] A coalition of nations subsequently instigated freedom-of-navigation exercises to assert their rights of free passage in the disputed waters.

- Competing infrastructure initiatives were launched.[2]
- New barriers against trade with China were erected, often focusing on advanced technologies.[3]
- Chinese foreign direct investments in sensitive technology sectors began to be scrutinized more closely and—in some cases—blocked.[4]
- Some Western companies ring-fenced their China businesses, diversified their production within their international supply chains to additional countries, or pulled back from new investments in China as defensive measures.[5]
- Some nations began to discuss instituting a multilateral mechanism by which to counter Chinese acts of economic coercion.[6]

In 2017–2018, international reaction to China's assertiveness took on a new dimension. Starting with the United States, both it and China imposed a series of increased tariffs on key imports from the other country. Eventually, almost half of Chinese exports to the United States and more than two-thirds of U.S. exports to China were covered by these increased tariffs. And, because the United States repeatedly blocked the appointment of new members to the World Trade Organization's Dispute Settlement Mechanism's Appellate Body, the international mechanism designed to help resolve such battles was unable to contribute to resolving the standoff. Bilateral relations between China and the United States reached their lowest level in more than 50 years.

---

[1] Caitlin Campbell and Nargiza Salidjanova, "South China Sea Arbitration Ruling: What Happened and What's Next?" U.S.-China Economic and Security Review Commission, issue brief, July 12, 2016.

[2] European Commission, "Global Gateway," webpage, undated; White House, "Fact Sheet: Partnership for Global Infrastructure and Investment at the G7 Summit," May 20, 2023.

[3] Bureau of Industry and Security, "Commerce Implements New Export Controls on Advanced Computing and Semiconductor Manufacturing Items to the People's Republic of China (PRC)," press release, October 7, 2022.

[4] Andreas Rinke and Miranda Murray, "Germany Blocks Chinese Stake in Two Chipmakers over Security Concerns," Reuters, November 9, 2022.

[5] Agatha Kratz and Camille Boullenois, "Irrational Expectations: Long-Term Challenges of Diversification Away from China, Rhodium Group," September 13, 2023.

[6] Group of Seven, "G7 Leaders' Statement on Economic Resilience and Economic Security," May 20, 2023.

The Rationale for This Study

Within this broader context, the Defense Advanced Research Projects Agency's (DARPA's) Strategic Technology Office asked RAND to examine how the United States could ensure that its economy meets the nation's needs under conditions of coupled strategic competition with China. DARPA has since shifted this work to the Microsystems Technology Office.

- RAND's remit from DARPA was not to approach the topic with a zero-sum mentality. Instead, RAND was to consider the premise that there is still space for substantial mutual gains from a less dysfunctional U.S.-China relationship and that there is still space for mutual benefits even under conditions of fierce competition.
- RAND was further to consider the assumption that interdependencies between the United States and China were established facts that both countries have to address and not just sources of risk that had to be completely removed (e.g., by completely decoupling the two economies).

The overall goals were to explore the proactive steps that the United States can take to ensure a healthy U.S. economy over the long term, what that economy might look like, and whether it can do so in ways that do not necessarily hamper the Chinese economy but rather that provide mutual benefits. The study aimed to provide insights about how to think about economic competition with China and identify gaps, new directions, and proactive steps that might be taken to best position the United States.

In response to DARPA's request, RAND engaged a team of 20 researchers spanning a variety of academic disciplines (economics, engineering, information science, international defense research, physics, political science, and sociology). RAND's approach to answering the questions posed by DARPA was organized into three main lines of effort:

1. economic and institutional analysis of U.S.-China economic competition
2. a participatory foresight exercise designed to imagine what a competitive future U.S. economy would look like (and how to get there)
3. two games on economic competition to explore interactions between countries and businesses as China and the United States seek advantage in economic competition and to elucidate possible strategies by which to strengthen or mitigate unintended consequences of proposed policy interventions.

Within each line of effort, differing analytical approaches were employed, sometimes involving multiple methods of analysis. This report provides the results of the first line of effort. It consists of ten chapters organized according to four broad themes:

1. a scene-setting analysis of the historical evolution of the Chinese concept of economic security and its application to both domestic and foreign policy (Chapter 2)
2. a stock-taking of U.S. cooperative and coercive measures targeting China (Chapter 3)

3. two examinations of what modeling and economic theory may tell us about the advantages and disadvantages of production network assurance strategies and of sanctions on Chinese officials versus more-cooperative modes of engagement (Chapters 4 and 5). The first of these chapters (Chapter 4) provides an empirical basis for understanding the relationship by investigating the overall integration of the global economy and the important roles that both the United States and China play. The second (Chapter 5) develops and applies a theoretical model to examine ways to shape the future structure of elite networks when engaging with China.
4. four chapters examining key practical aspects of U.S.-China relations: return migration (Chapter 6), energy and environmental security (Chapter 7), an exploration of how Chinese privately owned enterprises (POEs) might differ from Western private enterprises and what that means for policy (Chapter 8), and potential ways by which the rules of international trade can be updated to adapt to China's unique system of economic management (Chapter 9).

In this chapter, we first review the extent to which the United States and China are economically intertwined. We then introduce the contents of each chapter in the report. In the final chapter (Chapter 10), we cover implications and new directions.

The United States and China as Economic Partners

The United States and China have deep economic relations in both trade and investment, but China is one of many important U.S. trade partners.

Trade in Goods and Services

We consider trade data starting in 2000. For three years, from 2016 through 2018, China was the leading U.S. single-country bilateral partner for trade in goods and services (Figure 1.1). But that was unusual. Except for those three years, Canada was the largest single-country trading partner with the United States through 2023. Mexico was the second largest from 2000 through 2006, and then again in 2019, 2021, 2022, and 2023. In terms of economic blocs—groups of countries whether in a free trade area, customs union, or otherwise unified market—the United States' United States-Mexico-Canada Agreement (USMCA) partners of Canada and Mexico combined have been the leading trade partner every year, followed by the European Union (EU).

China stands out in U.S. imports (Figure 1.2). China became the leading single-country import source in 2009 and had been first through 2022, falling to third (behind Canada and Mexico) in 2023. And as noted in Chapter 4, China's actual share of imports likely is higher because of the Chinese goods that are embedded in imports from other countries. Notably, as with total trade, USMCA and the EU outstrip China in terms of total direct U.S. imports.

FIGURE 1.1
U.S. Trade in Goods and Services

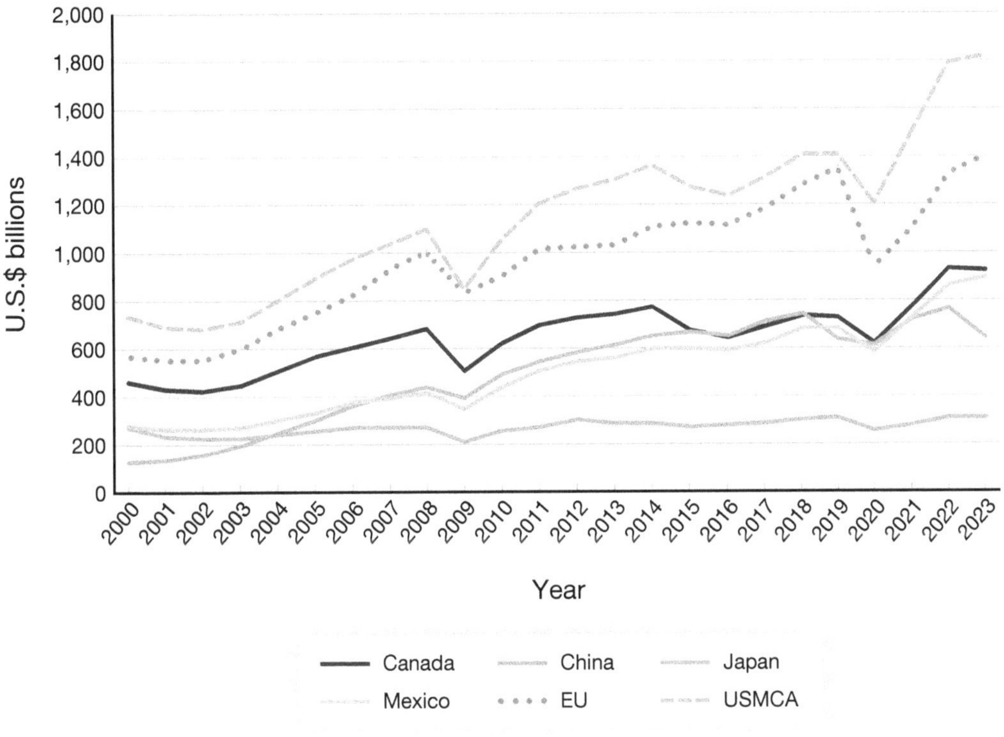

SOURCE: Features information from U.S. Bureau of Economic Analysis, "U.S. Trade in Goods and Services, by Selected Countries and Areas, 1999–Present," spreadsheet, last updated June 6, 2024.

NOTE: Data for Canada and Mexico are shown both independently and as part of USMCA. EU data do not include the United Kingdom starting in 2020.

China has especially dominated in U.S. *goods* imports, and this has caused the most political consternation. As with imports of goods and services, China was the leading single-nation source of U.S. goods imports from 2009 through 2022, taking over from Canada (China was also number 1 in 2007 but lower ranked before that) (Figure 1.3). In 2023, China fell to the number two spot, behind Mexico, but still slightly ahead of Canada. Notably, although USMCA has always been the largest source of goods imports, Chinese goods imports actually were larger than those from the EU every year starting in 2009, except for 2019, 2022, and 2023.[7]

This pattern of China as the leading import source changed dramatically in 2023. Goods imports from Mexico in 2023 totaled $484.5 billion, compared with $427.5 billion for China and $427.3 billion for Canada. This means that among country groupings, USMCA was by

[7] U.S. Bureau of Economic Analysis, 2024.

FIGURE 1.2
U.S. Imports of Goods and Services

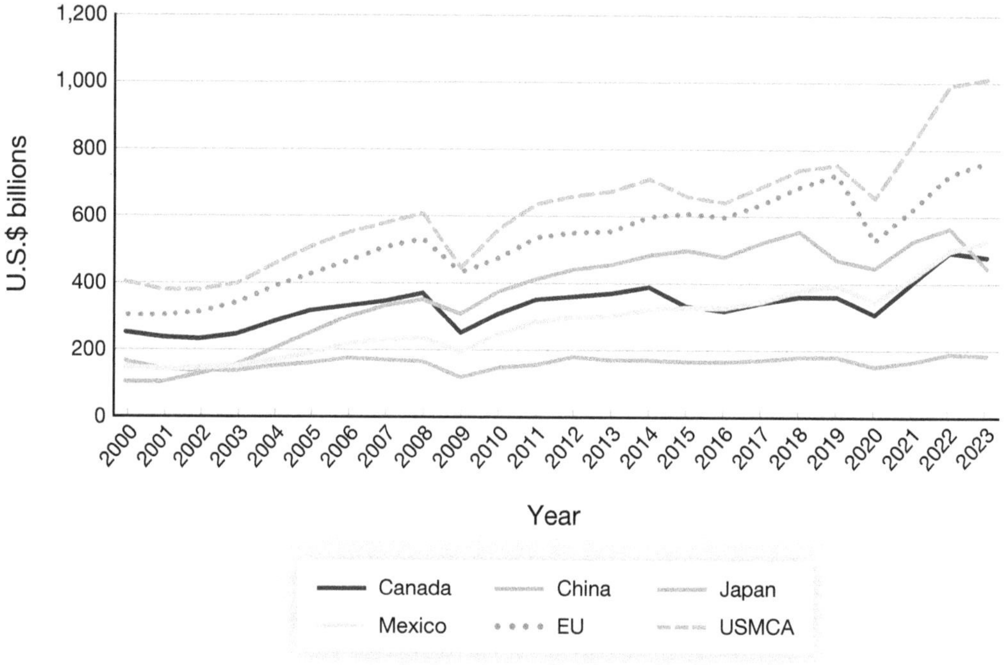

SOURCE: Features information from U.S. Bureau of Economic Analysis, 2024.
NOTE: Data for Canada and Mexico are shown both independently and as part of USMCA. EU data do not include the United Kingdom starting in 2020.

far the leading source, accounting for 29.3 percent of all goods imports in 2023, followed by the EU at $579.5 billion (or 18.6 percent).[8]

The decline in U.S. goods imports directly from China is notable: In 2022, they totaled $537.0 billion, so the 2023 total represents a 20-percent decline. However, as noted in our discussion of goods and services imports, it might be that U.S. imports from China have not dropped quite that much. Rather, some of the imports from Mexico might include Chinese goods shipped indirectly to the United States and Chinese inputs assembled in Mexico that would have previously been assembled in the United States.[9]

8 U.S. Bureau of Economic Analysis, 2024.

9 Chinese authorities recorded a drop in exports to the world (equivalent to world imports from China) from 2022 to 2023, with 2022 exports totaling $3,594 billion and 2023 exports totaling $3,380 billion, a 5.9-percent decline. See General Administration of Customs of the People's Republic of China, "(3) China's Total Export & Import Values by Trade Mode, January–December 2022 (in USD)," webpage, January 8, 2023a; and General Administration of Customs of the People's Republic of China, "(3) China's Total Export and Import Values by Trade Mode, January–December 2023 (in USD)," webpage January 12, 2024a. Chinese data also show exports to the United States totaling $500.3 billion in 2023, down 14.0 percent from exports to the United States of $581.8 billion in 2022. See General Administration of Customs of the Peo-

FIGURE 1.3
U.S. Imports of Goods

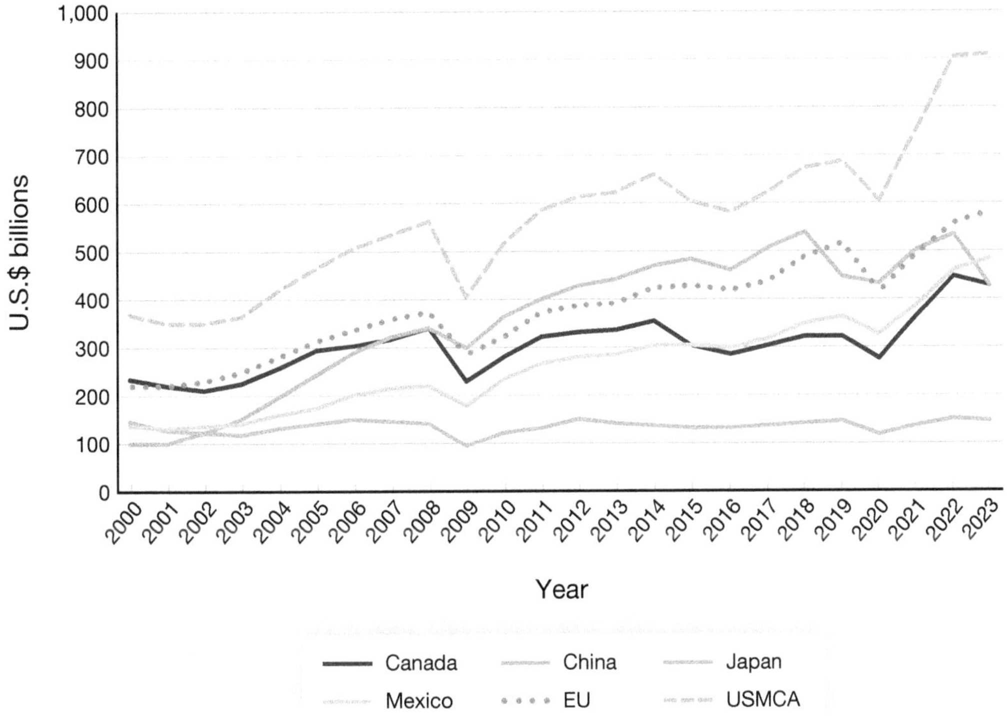

SOURCE: Features information from U.S. Bureau of Economic Analysis, 2024.
NOTE: Data for Canada and Mexico are shown both independently and as part of USMCA. EU data do not include the United Kingdom starting in 2020.

Imports from China by Commodity

U.S. imports from China include all manner of goods, but when commodities are divided into 98 different categories, two in particular dominate: More than 25 percent of all imports from China are either in the category of (1) electrical machinery and equipment, and sound and television recorders and reproducers or (2) machinery and mechanical appliances.[10] Levels are one issue; the extent to which China dominates a sector is another.

ple's Republic of China, "(4) China's Total Export & Import Values by Country/Region, December 2022 (in USD)," webpage, January 8, 2023b; and General Administration of Customs of the People's Republic of China, "(4) China's Total Export & Import Values by Country/Region, December 2023 (in USD)," webpage, January 12, 2024b.

[10] Specifically, these categories are Harmonized Tariff System (HTS) code 85, "Electrical Machinery and Equipment and Parts Thereof; Sound Recorders and Reproducers, Television Image and Sound Recorders and Reproducers, and Parts and Accessories of Such Articles" and HTS code 84, "Nuclear Reactors, Boilers, Machinery and Mechanical Appliances; Parts Thereof." Data are annual from 2018 through 2022 and are from U.S. International Trade Commission, DataWeb, database v.4.7.10, 2023.

The United States imports large amounts of these goods from many countries. In 2021 and 2022, the first two years after the coronavirus disease 2019 (COVID-19) pandemic, China accounted for an average of 31.2 percent of all imports in the electrical machinery and recording category, down from an average of 40.1 percent in the two years before the pandemic, 2018 and 2019. Likewise, in the machinery category, China accounted for 24.3 percent of all U.S. imports in 2021 and 2022, and 27.8 percent of all U.S. imports in 2018 and 2019. Although these are sizable percentages, they indicate that there appear to be numerous other suppliers.

Notably, China has dominance in several lower-skilled commodities. In 2021 and 2022, imports from China accounted for an annual average of 92.0 percent of all U.S. imports in umbrellas, walking sticks, and similar products. Those same years, China accounted for 78.2 percent of all imports in feathers and down, artificial flowers, and articles of human hair and 77.2 percent of all imports of toys, games, and sports equipment.[11]

These data suggest that some trade with China may be of concern—such as if there is a high level of dependence on imports of electrical equipment meant for U.S. defense industries. But trade with China in other sectors is likely to be far more benign and to involve commodities for which the United States does not have the workforce for producing; the interest in producing; or a cost advantage for producing, given U.S. wage rates.

Foreign Direct Investment

In terms of the size of the interaction, trade is the most important way that the United States and China interact economically. The cumulative amount of U.S. foreign direct investment (FDI) in China—investment for the purpose of controlling a company or owning real estate—amounted to $126.1 billion in 2022, or only 1.9 percent of total U.S. direct investment abroad.[12]

But as a manufacturing hub, China has attracted relatively more FDI in certain sectors. In 2022, China accounted for $58.7 billion cumulative U.S. FDI in manufacturing, or 5.8 percent of the U.S. global total. Although the level has risen from the $53.9 billion mark in 2018, the percentage that year was 7.3 percent, much higher than in 2022. Almost three-quarters of this manufacturing investment was in three sectors: chemicals, which includes pharmaceuticals; computers and electronic products; and transportation equipment.

---

[11] Specifically, these three HTS codes (in the order listed) are HTS 66, "Umbrellas, Sun Umbrellas, Walking Sticks, Seatsticks, Whips, Riding-Crops and Parts Thereof"; HTS 67, "Prepared Feathers and Down and Articles Made of Feathers or of Down; Artificial Flowers; Articles of Human Hair"; and HTS95, "Toys, Games and Sports Equipment; Parts and Accessories Thereof" (U.S. International Trade Commission, 2023).

[12] The value presented is direct investment position (U.S. Bureau of Economic Analysis, "U.S. Direct Investment Abroad: Balance of Payments and Direct Investment Position Data," webpage, last updated July 20, 2023a).

The majority of goods and services that the companies that U.S. foreign direct investors control in China are sold to the Chinese market. Considering only majority-owned foreign affiliates, in 2021, 80.1 percent of all goods and services were supplied to buyers in China, and 13.7 percent were supplied to non-U.S. foreign countries.[13] However, this varied by industry. U.S.-owned foreign affiliates in electrical equipment sold 27.3 percent of their goods and services to non-U.S. third countries, suggesting the purchasers were part of multinational production networks, with the final destination of those products either in those third countries or elsewhere, including the United States. In contrast, U.S.-owned foreign affiliates in the transportation industry in China sold fully 91.0 percent of their goods and services to China, suggesting that these affiliates were producing for the local market. Both kinds of investment make economic sense: The first, with high sales to third countries, brings efficiencies in the form of lower costs and a specialized workforce. The second, with high sales to the host country, brings efficiencies in the form of better tailoring the output to the local market and reducing transportation costs to get the goods and services to the final consumer.

Considering FDI in the other direction—from China to the United States—China is a relatively minor player. In 2022, Chinese investors accounted for only 0.5 percent of all FDI in the United States, with investments totaling $28.7 billion.[14] This has declined from 2018, when the value was $35.4 billion, and the percentage was 0.8 percent. These percentages differ by industry, but in 2022, the highest percentage for any individual sector was 1.6 percent for a sector that includes a grab-bag of industries.[15]

It is fair to note that *quantity* is only one issue in considering Chinese investment in the United States. Also at issue is whether such ownership, even of just a few companies, gives China privileged access to technologies and knowledge that may give it a military edge. That issue is one of the many reasons why U.S.-China economic cooperation is not wholly beneficial, even if there are significant benefits.

---

[13] U.S. Bureau of Economic Analysis, "Worldwide Activities of U.S. Multinational Enterprises: Preliminary 2021 Statistics," webpage, last updated November 17, 2023b.

[14] The value presented is direct investment position (U.S. Bureau of Economic Analysis, 2023b). If we consider data by ultimate beneficial owner, the percentage rises to 0.9 percent. Data recorded by ultimate beneficial owner includes investments from China that go through third countries and then to the United States.

[15] Labeled "other industries" in the data, this broad agglomeration includes mining; utilities; construction; transportation and warehousing; administration, support, and waste management; health care and social assistance; accommodation and food services; agriculture, forestry, fishing, and hunting; management of nonbank companies and enterprises; and miscellaneous services.

Other Forms of U.S.-China Economic Interaction

China and the United States interact in numerous ways beyond trade and FDI. For example, as of November 2023, China directly held $782.0 billion worth of U.S. Treasury securities, with Hong Kong holding an additional $211.1 billion.[16] Holdings of U.S. securities are likely higher when one includes (1) debt issued by government-sponsored enterprises or government agencies other than the U.S. Treasury and (2) U.S. Treasury debt held by China in offshore custodians.[17]

Chinese students constitute the largest single foreign-student group at U.S. universities. In the 2022–2023 academic year, there were 289,526 such students, with Indian students the second-largest group at 268,923 students.[18] As discussed in Chapter 6, foreign students bring both benefits and risks to the United States. People and organizations from the two countries engage in research collaborations, register patents at each other's patent offices, co-invest in new ventures, and engage in other forms of economic collaboration that bind the two economies.

With this background to set the stage, we now introduce the contents of each chapter in the report.

Economic and Institutional Analysis of U.S.-China Economic Competition

The U.S.-China economic rivalry had been a growing factor in U.S. international relations even before the release of the December 2017 U.S. National Security Strategy, which identified economics as an important realm of U.S.-China competition.[19] Since then, a large and growing literature on U.S.-China economic competition has emerged.[20] The question therefore emerged as to how we could add to this growing literature.

---

[16] U.S. Department of the Treasury, "Treasury International Capital Data for November—Table 5: Major Foreign Holders of Treasury Securities," January 19, 2024.

[17] Brad W. Setser, "China Isn't Shifting Away from the Dollar or Dollar Bonds," *Council on Foreign Relations* blog, October 3, 2023.

[18] Institute of International Education, *Open Doors 2023: Report on International Educational Exchange*, 2023.

[19] White House, *National Security Strategy of the United States*, December 2017.

[20] Examples in the two years after the release of the 2017 National Security Strategy include C. Fred Bergsten, *China and the United States: Trade Conflict and Systemic Competition*, Peterson Institute for International Economics, Policy Briefs 18-21, October 2018; Chad P. Bown, *The 2018 US-China Trade Conflict After 40 Years of Special Protection*, Peterson Institute for International Economics, Working Paper 19-7, April 2019; Alicia Garcia Herrero, "US-China Economic Competition: Impact on EU-China Relations," *in Panorama: Insights into Asian and European Affairs—Trade and Economic Connectivity in the Age of Uncertainty*, Konrad-Adenauer-Stiftung, 2019; and Charles W. Boustany and Aaron L. Friedberg, *Partial Disen-*

We opted for a bottom-up approach: We selected a set of leading researchers on China, economic competition, and competition more generally and invited them to develop chapters on topics they thought needed more attention in understanding U.S.-China economic competition. Not only were we agnostic regarding the topics, we were also agnostic regarding the methods. The result was a set of chapters reflecting the authors' expertise and judgment and using methods varying from qualitative analysis to economic modeling to a theoretical agent-based model of subnational behavior.

We next introduce this research, chapter by chapter, under several themes.

The Chinese Concept of Economic Security

In the first substantive chapter (Chapter 2), Timothy Heath, a political scientist who specializes on China, analyzes the Chinese concept of economic security and finds the following:

- Spurred by the 1997 Asian financial crisis and the country's integration into the global economy, China defines economic security in terms of its capacity to resist disruptions, both domestic and foreign, to the environments that enable economic growth.
- The concept includes expanding China's right to determine international trade rules.
- Economic security focuses on avoiding mass protests caused by economic disruptions.
- Regional secessionist tendencies take second place as a domestic security threat, followed by energy dependence and climate change.
- Domestically, China seeks to strengthen its competitiveness by stimulating demand, protecting its intellectual property, and launching technology leadership initiatives.
- China also seeks to reduce threats from external sources by strengthening controls on investment, increasing monitoring of private companies, and bolstering financial controls.
- Internationally, China seeks trade and investment dominance, a role as a rule and norm setter, preferential access to markets, and promotion of its model of economic growth—one that prioritizes development over strengthening governance and political institutions.

Heath finds that the economic and security aspects of U.S.-China relations are mutually reinforcing for China. China is likely to become more resistant to U.S. efforts to shape its behavior. China is also unlikely to compromise in a way that preserves U.S. leadership in international economic institutions.

---

gagement: A New U.S. Strategy for Economic Competition with China, National Bureau of Asian Research, NBR Special Report No. 82, November 2019.

Assessing U.S. Measures Against China

Alexandra Stark, a political scientist with an international relations focus, takes stock of U.S. economic measures related to China (Chapter 3). She does so by analyzing cooperative and coercive measures employed by the United States over time and by looking at two case studies: semiconductors and tariffs. Stark finds the following:

- Although initially focused on cooperative economic measures, the United States has relied increasingly on coercive measures with China. Such cooperative measures have not transformed the relationship between the two countries, but they have been more successful in achieving more-circumscribed goals and might also have had positive externalities with few costs.
- The many coercive tools employed (such as competing industrial subsidies, export controls against companies and products, and law enforcement efforts against the theft of intellectual property) have shown only limited success in meeting their objectives.
- These economic policy instruments have also had significant negative secondary and tertiary effects on the U.S. and allied economies.
- U.S. consumers have borne the brunt of the costs of these measures in the form of higher prices.
- Although U.S. actions on semiconductors have had a tangible impact on Chinese national champions, such as Huawei, and it might take a decade for China to catch up in semiconductor production, benefits from this approach are likely over only the short to medium term.
- U.S. tariffs on imports of solar panels, washing machines, steel, and aluminum did not remedy the U.S. trade deficit, had narrow benefits for certain U.S. industries, and had broader negative effects on U.S. producers and consumers.

Empirical Realities and Theoretical Considerations

The next two chapters provide the empirical basis for understanding global economic integration and the important role that both the United States and China play and then ask what theory has to say about modes of engaging China.

In Chapter 4, economists Tobias Sytsma and Jessie Wang examine the integration and deintegration of international production networks or supply chains empirically and theoretically. They find the following:

- The global economy has become increasingly interconnected, and although the United States has increasingly relied on Chinese production, China's reliance on the United States has decreased.
- China has started to rely more on South America, Africa, and the Middle East, and for all major economies, regional (in China's case, Asian, and in the United States' case, Mexican and Canadian) economic relations remain vital to production networks. Even

with the importance of regions, the world's two leading national economies, the United States and China, are leaders in supplying and being supplied by the rest of the world.
- "Friendshoring" can be quite costly and challenging and is less effective if friendly countries continue to trade with China, as they currently continue to do.
- Reducing dependence of foreign suppliers through selective decoupling with clear priorities could cause the least amount of disruption in achieving higher production network assurance.
- Changes in technology could lower the cost of trade-offs. These technology changes—in coordination with allies—could include technology related to production, reductions in trade costs with allies and partners, creation of alternative goods, and the ability to track the reliability of supplier partners.

In Chapter 5, sociologist Ben Gibson, information scientist Aaron Frank, political scientist Khrystyna Holynska, and economist Jessie Wang use agent-based modeling to examine the best ways in which to shape the future structure of elite networks when engaging with China. Using their model, they find the following:

- Cooperation with select groups can achieve a more cooperative bilateral relationship than can pressure, such as a pure sanctions strategy.
- Within a three-tiered network structure of (1) traders and entrepreneurs, (2) state-owned enterprise executives and government ministers, and (3) central party officials and CCP General Secretary Xi Jinping, sanctioning CCP Central Committee members will likely backfire, strengthening the power of those officials.
- Cooperative interventions that benefit groups that are more inclined to protect trade would likely be more effective in shaping the future structure of Chinese elites.

Two interventions of the latter type were tested separately and together: (1) resource injections benefiting traders and entrepreneurs (e.g., through foreign investment) and (2) a switch in modeling those actors' goals from promoting their own individual self-interest to promoting the combined interests of groups of traders and entrepreneurs. In both cases, these examples of strategic cooperation had a greater effect on the structure of political leadership than did more-competitive actions.

Practical Considerations

The next four chapters investigate practical aspects of engaging China: return migration of Chinese students, workers, and entrepreneurs from the United States; energy and environmental security; whether Chinese POEs abide by a similar or different set of rules than Western POEs and what that might mean for economic and trade policy; and how one might set about adjusting the rules of international trade if Chinese enterprises do in fact play by a different set of rules than other enterprises.

In Chapter 6, sociologist Nadia Almasalkhi investigates high-skilled return migration from the United States and China, finding the following:

- More students come to the United States from China than from any other country. Certain departments in some U.S. universities have become quite dependent on the revenues that they obtain from foreign students, including students from China.
- Just over half of all students from China study in the science, technology, engineering, and mathematics (STEM) fields.
- With 666,000 college-educated, Chinese-born workers employed in the United States in 2021, the U.S. education system is a major feeder of Chinese nationals to the U.S. technology workforce.

Almasalkhi outlines the various incentives and push and pull factors involved in a student's decision to return or stay, noting that there has been a 400-percent increase in such return migration in the decade before 2020. Although dominated by masters and MBA students, returnees to China with Ph.D. degrees were concentrated in the STEM fields. The acceleration of return migration among highly educated Chinese immigrants is notable given the shortage of STEM workers in the United States. Almasalkhi recommends addressing these challenges by

- allowing students engaged in Optional Practical Training in the United States to travel overseas and reenter the country (as opposed to current rules that require them to stay in the United States)
- increasing the number of H-1B visas available to Chinese nationals
- increasing the number of green cards available through employment preference categories
- clarifying foreign funding disclosure requirements
- targeting the U.S. security response to Chinese threats more narrowly
- being more careful not to single out individual nationalities during law enforcement actions.

In Chapter 7, political scientist Noosha Uddin examines the topic of U.S.-China energy competition and cooperation with a focus on energy and environmental security, finding the following:

- The two economies are intertwined when it comes to energy; the United States supplies hydrocarbons to China, and China supplies materials and products for solar and wind generation of electricity to the United States.
- China depends on coal for 60 percent of the electricity it generates. It is the biggest consumer and producer of coal and the biggest emitter of carbon dioxide in the world.
- China's commitment to decarbonization wavers. China's leadership has stated that it intends to favor economic development over environmental protection.

- Both China and the United States would like to advance their own production in new energy industries and nuclear energy generation.

Uddin closes by investigating and describing the advantages and disadvantages of five future scenarios of cooperation and competition between the United States and China on energy and environmental security: (1) business as usual, (2) enhanced cooperation, (3) selective delinking, (4) complete delinking, and (5) competition.

In Chapter 8, economist Steven Popper scrutinizes whether Chinese POEs operate under conditions and rules similar to those under which POEs in the market-based, economically advanced countries of the Organisation for Economic Co-operation and Development (OECD) are assumed to operate. He finds that Chinese POEs play by different rules and operate under different constraints. Popper notes significant areas of divergence that call into question whether the rules and policies of both the OECD countries and international regulatory organizations should treat Chinese and OECD POEs the same way. The differences lie in the structure and behaviors of the Chinese private firm, including

- party organizations within the firm
- ownership
- lines of control over management decisions
- incentive structures
- the firm's relationship to state and party
- its market behavior
- the private firm's role as an instrument of the CCP.

He concludes that, because of these differences, "in viewing the Chinese POE, external governments and economic actors are dealing with an organizational form that they believe they understand—but probably do not as well as they should or could. It is worth taking the trouble to improve that understanding."

In Chapter 9, recognizing that Chinese enterprises operate according to a different set of rules, international defense researcher King Mallory examines diplomatic options by which to resuscitate the global trade order by adapting to the distortions of world trade caused by China's unique system of economic management. First, Mallory

- traces the historical emergence of the global trade system
- describes the emergence of China's system of economic management
- details the challenges that it poses to the global trade order.

He then outlines three policy options:

1. do nothing
2. make minor changes
3. make large changes in addition to or in parallel to the existing global trade order.

Mallory finds that the third option will be more successful at reaching a solution in which benefits are spread broadly. He recommends that policymakers consider instituting a competitive neutrality framework—such as that instituted by Australia to eliminate distortions created by Chinese state aid to its enterprises—at the global level. Mallory suggests that such a framework might

- be able to address the systemic distortions of global trade caused by China
- be welcomed by economic reformers in China, the EU, and developing countries
- direct U.S.-Chinese competition into a more constructive channel that provides positive results for all nations involved.

Topics Not Covered: Monetary and Financial Competition

Any collection such as this one will necessarily be incomplete. This does not mean that topics not covered are unimportant but rather that requirements of time, budget, and expertise will result in the inclusion of some subjects and the exclusion of others. Probably the most important area of U.S.-China economic competition excluded is that of monetary and financial competition.

China has approached finance and the international economy in two broad ways, one by turning inward and one by turning outward. Spurred on by the 2008–2009 global financial crisis, China has worked to insulate its banking system from the international economy.[21] China tightened political oversight and financial regulation, including limiting cross-border transactions, focusing the banking system on the domestic economy. This added security has come at a cost—specifically, inefficient capital allocation, a limited role in international rulemaking, and a more limited set of options for savers in China that is less attractive than savers elsewhere in the world have access to.

The outward turn has come in the form of internationalizing the renminbi (China's national currency), increasing its acceptance in international payments, and pushing forward on the development of a central bank digital currency, which can also be used in international payments, helping users avoid the U.S. dollar system.[22] For almost two decades, China has been creating financial coordination mechanisms with other members of the Shanghai Cooperation Organization, leading to greater use of local currencies and to swap lines. Although China does not aim to replace the dollar globally—yet—it aims to make its own currency prominent in use throughout the region and to minimize exchange risk with the dollar.[23]

---

[21] Niels Graham and Josh Lipsky, "Chinese Banking's SVB Resilience," Atlantic Council, March 30, 2023.

[22] The U.S. national security and economic competition implications of a Chinese central bank digital currency are explored in Daniel Egel, Jim Mignano, Sale Lilly, James V. Marrone, Max Rangeley, Charles P. Ries, Jessie Wang, and Dulani Woods, *Central Bank Digital Currencies and U.S. Strategic Competition with China*, RAND Corporation, RR-A2911-1, 2024.

[23] Zongyuan Zoe Liu, "China Is Quietly Trying to Dethrone the Dollar," *Foreign Policy*, September 21, 2022.

Likewise, it has created its own clearing and settlement system, the Cross-Border Interbank Payment System, to enable greater use of the renminbi for trade settlement. This does not represent a complete break from the international financial ecosystem. Although China's system does have a messaging function, it largely relies on the Belgian-based global messaging system Society for Worldwide Interbank Financial Telecommunication for communications between banks.[24] This effort to gain international use for the Chinese currency extends to China's developing central bank digital currency. The People's Bank of China, the central bank, is one of four founding central banks of Project mBridge, a digital currency platform that enables cross-border payments and settlement and that became commercially viable in June 2024.[25] The New York Innovation Center of the Federal Reserve Bank of New York is an observing member, so the United States is also involved in this project.

Finally, as another measure to gain international acceptance for the renminbi, the International Monetary Fund (IMF) agreed in 2015 to bring the renminbi into the basket of currencies making up the IMF's special drawing rights reserve asset, effective 2016, joining the U.S. dollar, the euro, the Japanese yen, and the British pound. The IMF judged that two criteria were met: that China was a major exporter and that its currency was "freely usable," under the IMF's definition.[26] Some questioned this decision and noted that it seemed to be more political than economic, following an effort by China to gain this achievement.[27] And the IMF said the effects of this inclusion on China would "include developing deep and liquid financial markets, achieving a certain degree of openness of the capital account, delivering predictable macroeconomic outcomes, strong and credible institutions, and securing the integrity of the markets—for example by putting in place a reliable rule of law."[28] Many of these effects have not wholly materialized, however. Nonetheless, the measure illustrates one aspect of China's efforts to internationalize the renminbi for its own financial security and to compete with the United States in the international monetary system.

All of these aspects of monetary and financial competition will benefit from further exploration by researchers, the output of which can serve as a companion to the findings in this report.

---

[24] Emily Jin, "Why China's CIPS Matters (and Not for the Reasons You Think)," *Lawfare*, April 5, 2022; Zhang Yan, Winni Zhou, and Ryan Woo, "What Is China's Onshore Yuan Clearing and Settlement System CIPS?" Reuters, February 28, 2022.

[25] Bank for International Settlements, "Project mBridge Reaches Minimum Viable Product Stage and Invites Further International Participation," webpage, last updated June 5, 2024.

[26] IMF, "IMF Adds Chinese Renminbi to Special Drawing Rights Basket," September 30, 2016.

[27] Benjamin J. Cohen, "Crashing the SDR," Project Syndicate, November 19, 2015.

[28] IMF, 2016.

Conclusion

Given the security tensions between the United States and China and the extent to which their economies are intertwined, the United States faces a central question in its conduct of domestic and international economic policy: How can the United States ensure that its economy meets the nation's needs under conditions of coupled, strategic competition?

During the Cold War, the United States' chief geopolitical rival was the Soviet Union, but their economies were almost completely separate. At the same time, in the 1970s and 1980s, the United States' chief economic rival was Japan, but the two countries were security partners and treaty allies. Now, the United States' main geostrategic rival, China, is at once an economic competitor and a participant in a mutually beneficial economic relationship. In fact, during 2017 to 2021, the first major wave of U.S. measures on China, the U.S. public generally viewed China as a military or security threat but also an economic opportunity, and the business community was broadly supportive of the strategic direction of U.S. policy but less comfortable with the tactical measures being taken.[29]

Successfully navigating this complexity will be central to the well-being of the U.S. economy over the short, medium, and long terms. Ideally, there may be proactive steps that the United States can take to ensure a healthy U.S. economy and that bring about mutual gains from trade and investment with all of the United States' economic partners, including China.

The final chapter in this report (Chapter 10), by Daniel Egel and Howard J. Shatz, draws from the preceding chapters to integrate the findings and then lay out essential policy questions to be answered as the United States, and the world, try to move toward greater supply chain assurance and an improved trading system in which all economies can thrive on a basis that is both fair and beneficial. Companion reports in this series cover related topics. Two reports are on economic competition games that were developed specifically for this project and that are designed to explore potential interactions shaping the global economic system and the way that the system interacts with geopolitical realities.[30] A third report looks to the long term, drawing from a participatory foresight process, exploring a vision for a healthy U.S. economy and discussing the steps that will help the United States arrive there.[31]

---

[29] Bonny Lin, Howard J. Shatz, Nathan Chandler, Cristina L. Garafola, Eugeniu Han, Andy Law, King Mallory, and Zev Winkelman, *Bridging the Gap: Assessing U.S. Business Community Support for U.S.-China Competition*, RAND Corporation, RR-A1417-1, 2022.

[30] David R. Frelinger, Jenny Oberholtzer, Stephen M. Worman, and Kate Giglio, *Rising Tide: Designing a Game of International Economic Competition*, RAND Corporation, RR-A1947-3, 2025; David A. Shlapak, Colin Levaunt, and Gregory Smith, *Coupled Competition: A Prototype Game to Explore the U.S.-China Relationship*, RAND Corporation, RR-A1947-4, 2025.

[31] Steven W. Popper, Richard Silberglitt, Fabian Villalobos, Khrystyna Holynska, Krystyna Marcinek, Nadia Almasalkhi, and Jack Lashendock, *Build Thee More Stately Mansions: Participatory Foresight and the Mid-Century U.S. Economy*, RAND Corporation, RR-A1947-2, 2025.

Abbreviations

CCP	Chinese Communist Party
COVID-19	coronavirus disease 2019
DARPA	Defense Advanced Research Projects Agency
EU	European Union
FDI	foreign direct investment
GDP	gross domestic product
HTC	Harmonized Tariff Code
IMF	International Monetary Fund
OECD	Organisation for Economic Co-operation and Development
POE	privately owned enterprise
STEM	science, technology, engineering, and mathematics
USMCA	United States-Mexico-Canada Agreement

References

Bank for International Settlements, "Project mBridge Reaches Minimum Viable Product Stage and Invites Further International Participation," webpage, last updated June 5, 2024. As of September 18, 2024:
https://www.bis.org/about/bisih/topics/cbdc/mcbdc_bridge.htm

Bergsten, C. Fred, *China and the United States: Trade Conflict and Systemic Competition*, Peterson Institute for International Economics, Policy Briefs 18-21, October 2018.

Boustany, Charles W., and Aaron L. Friedberg, *Partial Disengagement: A New U.S. Strategy for Economic Competition with China*, National Bureau of Asian Research, NBR Special Report No. 82, November 2019.

Bown, Chad P., *The 2018 US-China Trade Conflict After 40 Years of Special Protection*, Peterson Institute for International Economics, Working Paper 19-7, April 2019.

Bureau of Industry and Security, "Commerce Implements New Export Controls on Advanced Computing and Semiconductor Manufacturing Items to the People's Republic of China (PRC)," press release, October 7, 2022.

Campbell, Caitlin, and Nargiza Salidjanova, "South China Sea Arbitration Ruling: What Happened and What's Next?" U.S.-China Economic and Security Review Commission, issue brief, July 12, 2016.

Cohen, Benjamin J., "Crashing the SDR," Project Syndicate, November 19, 2015.

Egel, Daniel, Jim Mignano, Sale Lilly, James V. Marrone, Max Rangeley, Charles P. Ries, Jessie Wang, and Dulani Woods, *Central Bank Digital Currencies and U.S. Strategic Competition with China*, RAND Corporation, RR-A2911-1, 2024. As of September 12, 2024:
https://www.rand.org/pubs/research_reports/RRA2911-1.html

European Commission, "Global Gateway," webpage, undated. As of December 21, 2024: https://commission.europa.eu/strategy-and-policy/priorities-2019-2024/stronger-europe-world/global-gateway_en

Frelinger, David R., Jenny Oberholtzer, Stephen M. Worman, and Kate Giglio, *Rising Tide: Designing a Game of International Economic Competition*, RAND Corporation, RR-A1947-3, 2025. As of June 23, 2025:
https://www.rand.org/pubs/research_reports/RRA1947-3.html

Garcia Herrero, Alicia, "US-China Economic Competition: Impact on EU-China Relations," in *Panorama: Insights into Asian and European Affairs—Trade and Economic Connectivity in the Age of Uncertainty*, Konrad-Adenauer-Stiftung, 2019.

General Administration of Customs of the People's Republic of China, "(3) China's Total Export & Import Values by Trade Mode, January–December 2022 (in USD)," webpage, January 8, 2023a. As of September 17, 2024:
http://english.customs.gov.cn/Statics/0e6993a0-fc98-4a26-9f76-021943ab0089.html

General Administration of Customs of the People's Republic of China, "(4) China's Total Export & Import Values by Country/Region, December 2022 (in USD)," webpage January 8, 2023b. As of September 17, 2024:
http://english.customs.gov.cn/Statics/039f4962-4b2f-4087-bcd0-4e6fdd9bf104.html

General Administration of Customs of the People's Republic of China, "(3) China's Total Export & Import Values by Trade Mode, January–December 2023 (in USD)," webpage, January 12, 2024a. As of September 17, 2024:
http://english.customs.gov.cn/Statics/d54988b0-0ae8-429d-88da-9d2a0be71ce3.html

General Administration of Customs of the People's Republic of China, "(4) China's Total Export & Import Values by Country/Region, December 2023 (in USD)," webpage, January 12, 2024b. As of September 17, 2024:
http://english.customs.gov.cn/Statics/e1351568-5e17-4534-affd-c369e3506613.html

Graham, Niels, and Josh Lipsky, "Chinese Banking's SVB Resilience," Atlantic Council, March 30, 2023.

Group of Seven, "G7 Leaders' Statement on Economic Resilience and Economic Security, May 20, 2023.

IMF—*See* International Monetary Fund.

Institute of International Education, *Open Doors 2023: Report on International Educational Exchange*, 2023.

International Monetary Fund, "IMF Adds Chinese Renminbi to Special Drawing Rights Basket," September 30, 2016.

Jin, Emily, "Why China's CIPS Matters (and Not for the Reasons You Think)," *Lawfare*, April 5, 2022.

Kratz, Agatha, and Camille Boullenois, "Irrational Expectations: Long-Term Challenges of Diversification Away from China, Rhodium Group," September 13, 2023.

Lin, Bonny, Howard J. Shatz, Nathan Chandler, Cristina L. Garafola, Eugeniu Han, Andy Law, King Mallory, and Zev Winkelman, *Bridging the Gap: Assessing U.S. Business Community Support for U.S.-China Competition*, RAND Corporation, RR-A1417-1, 2022. As of May 8, 2025:
https://www.rand.org/pubs/research_reports/RRA1417-1.html

Liu, Zongyuan Zoe, "China Is Quietly Trying to Dethrone the Dollar," *Foreign Policy*, September 21, 2022.

Popper, Steven W., Richard Silberglitt, Fabian Villalobos, Khrystyna Holynska, Krystyna Marcinek, Nadia Almasalkhi, and Jack Lashendock, *Build Thee More Stately Mansions: Participatory Foresight and the Mid-Century U.S. Economy*, RAND Corporation, RR-A1947-2, 2025. As of June 23, 2025:
https://www.rand.org/pubs/research_reports/RRA1947-2.html

Rinke, Andreas, and Miranda Murray, "Germany Blocks Chinese Stake in Two Chipmakers over Security Concerns," Reuters, November 9, 2022.

Setser, Brad W., "China Isn't Shifting Away from the Dollar or Dollar Bonds," *Council on Foreign Relations* blog, October 3, 2023.

Shlapak, David A., Colin Levaunt, and Gregory Smith, *Coupled Competition: A Prototype Game to Explore the U.S.-China Relationship*, RAND Corporation, RR-A1947-4, 2025. As of June 23, 2025:
https://www.rand.org/pubs/research_reports/RRA1947-4.html

U.S. Bureau of Economic Analysis, "U.S. Direct Investment Abroad: Balance of Payments and Direct Investment Position Data," webpage, last updated July 20, 2023a. As of February 8, 2024:
https://www.bea.gov/international/di1usdbal

U.S. Bureau of Economic Analysis, "Worldwide Activities of U.S. Multinational Enterprises: Preliminary 2021 Statistics," webpage, last updated November 17, 2023b. As of September 18, 2024:
https://www.bea.gov/worldwide-activities-us-multinational-enterprises-preliminary-2021-statistics

U.S. Bureau of Economic Analysis, "U.S. Trade in Goods and Services, by Selected Countries and Areas, 1999–Present," spreadsheet, last updated June 6, 2024.

U.S. Department of the Treasury, "Treasury International Capital Data for November—Table 5: Major Foreign Holders of Treasury Securities," January 19, 2024.

U.S. International Trade Commission, DataWeb, database, v.4.7.10, 2023. As of December 29, 2023:
https://dataweb.usitc.gov

White House, *National Security Strategy of the United States of America*, December 2017.

White House, "Fact Sheet: Partnership for Global Infrastructure and Investment at the G7 Summit," May 20, 2023.

Yan, Zhang, Winni Zhou, and Ryan Woo, "What Is China's Onshore Yuan Clearing and Settlement System CIPS?" Reuters, February 28, 2022.

CHAPTER 2

China's Economic Security: A Key Driver of Competition with the United States

Timothy R. Heath

Overview

Like many countries, China has adopted the concept of *economic security*, in which economics is viewed as having an important security dimension. China's concept of economic security overlaps with other aspects of national security, such as politics, governance, and the military. Economic security is an idea that is becoming central to the legitimacy of the Chinese Communist Party (CCP). The importance of economic security and the vulnerability of the economy (including to external economic influences) helps underpin key domestic and foreign policies, such as initiatives to dominate frontier technologies, the deployment of military forces abroad, and efforts to revise and lead multilateral trade institutions. Concern for economic security also motivates Beijing to adopt a more aggressive posture regarding disputes involving economics and to resist compromises in disputes that could hamper its growth prospects. At the same time, because economics is so central to China's security and CCP legitimacy, there are hard limits to how much disruption Beijing can afford on economic policy. These limits suggest that Beijing will be reluctant to provoke a major war because of the dislocation that could arise. These limits may also open potential areas for cooperation, especially in areas of international economic institutions.

Like many countries, China's government has adopted the concept of *economic security*, in which economics is viewed as having an important security dimension. China's concept of economic security overlaps with other aspects of national security, such as politics, governance, and the military. Economic security is an idea that has become central to Chinese Communist Party (CCP) legitimacy. At the same time, China's economy has grown more vulnerable to external influences because of its integration with the world economy. The importance of economic security and the vulnerability of the economy help underpin key domestic and foreign policies, including initiatives to dominate frontier technologies, the deployment of military forces abroad, and efforts to revise and lead multilateral trade institutions. Concern for economic security also motivates Beijing to adopt a more aggressive posture regarding disputes involving economics and to resist compromises in disputes that could hamper its growth prospects. At the same time, because economics is so central to China's security and CCP legitimacy, there are hard limits to how much disruption that Beijing can afford on economic policy. These limits suggest that Beijing will be reluctant to provoke a major war because of the dislocation that could arise. These limits may also open potential areas for cooperation, especially in areas of international economic institutions.

To analyze Chinese concepts of economic security, I reviewed Western academic writings on the topic, as well as Chinese-language documents. The latter included speeches by CCP General Secretary Xi Jinping and official documents, such as CCP National Congress reports, plans, and laws. I also examined Chinese scholarly writings and commentary in key journals and news sources, such as *Seeking Truth* [求是], *Outlook* [瞭望], and *People's Daily* [人民日报].

This chapter proceeds in the following manner. In the first section, I outline the general concept of economic security. China is not the first country to adopt that idea, but its approach reflects the country's political system, strategic situation, and economic power. In the second section, I explore China's historical evolution. As refined under Xi, the notion of economic security overlaps and reinforces security concerns across virtually all elements of state power. In the third section, I analyze the application of the idea on domestic policy. In the fourth section, I analyze its application for foreign policy. In the last section, I consider some implications for U.S. policy.

Economic Security: The Concept

Economic security may be broadly understood as the ability of a state to maintain and develop its socioeconomic system of choice and its relative economic power under conditions of international uncertainty.[1] It is an idea that has gained currency with governments around the world since the 2000s. A survey conducted by the Organisation for Economic Co-operation and Development (OECD) in 2016 concluded that many developed nations now view various economic sectors—including energy, telecommunications, and health care—as potentially within the domain of national security.[2] The increasing salience of the concept reflects in part the vulnerabilities that arise from global economic integration. Countries have experienced increases in trade and investment through participation in the global market—but at the cost of surrendering some autonomy. Production is no longer centered in one country but is dispersed around the world. Similarly, capital can now flow rapidly across borders thanks to digital technologies, which open opportunities for more-productive investments but also loosen control by governments over investments in their own countries. The increased salience of economic security may also reflect a decline in the threat posed by conventional military dangers. Despite the Russia-Ukraine war, the incidence of armed conflict between industrialized states has remained at a low level since the Cold War.[3]

The United States has long viewed a strong economy as foundational for national strength, but the 2017 National Security Strategy (NSS) was the first to introduce the term *economic security.* It stated, "Economic security is national security," adding that economic vitality, growth, and prosperity are absolutely necessary for American power and influence.[4] The 2022 NSS did not use the term, but it included a section that discussed measures to "advanc[e] the interests of American workers." [5] The 2022 NSS also included provisions to both strengthen the domestic economy and shape the global economy.

American allies have also adopted policies to promote economic security. A 2020 study by the Hague Center for Strategic Studies identified five common objectives in European definitions of economic security:

1. Preventing trade tensions;
2. Keeping trade routes open;

---

1 Gustaaf Geeraerts and Weiping Huang, "The Economic Security Dimension of the EU–China Relationship: Puzzles and Prospects," in Emil J. Kirchner, Thomas Christiansen, and Han Dorussen, eds., *Security Relationships Between China and the European Union*, Cambridge University Press, 2016.

2 Frédéric Wehrlé and Joachim Pohl, *Investment Policies Related to National Security*, OECD Publishing, 2016.

3 Steven Pinker, *The Better Angels of Our Nature: The Decline of Violence in History and Its Causes*, Viking Books, 2011.

4 White House, *National Security Strategy of the United States of America*, December 2017, p. 17.

5 White House, *National Security Strategy*, October 2022, p. 12.

3. Countering economic (cyber) espionage;

4. Ensuring the supply of energy and raw materials;

5. Safeguarding national security when investments are made or companies are taken over.[6]

In 2022, Japan appointed its first economic security minister, Sanae Takaichi. Prime Minister Fumio Kishida said economic security is "a fundamental requirement" for achieving sustainable economic growth.[7]

Given that all other major economies have adopted some notion of economic security, it should not be surprising that China has done so as well. However, Beijing's approach reflects its own unique political system, strategic situation, and historical experience.

China's Concept of Economic Security and Its Historical Evolution

Chinese leaders have long appreciated the security dimensions of the national economy. For example, in founding the People's Republic of China in 1949, Chinese leaders led by Mao Zedong sought to build an autarkic economy to strengthen the nation's security from the capitalist West. In the 1950s and 1960s, China also advanced economic cooperation with communist states around the world in part to improve its political influence and national security.[8]

However, theoretical analysis and official use of the term *economic security* [经济安全] came much later. Beijing took an important step in this direction in the late 1970s when it abandoned Maoist politics in favor of more pragmatic politics centered on market-friendly reforms. The subsequent improvements in internal stability in the 1980s and 1990s convinced party leaders of the supreme importance of economic growth.[9] However, officials at that time viewed economics as distinctly separate from national security. They viewed economic policy as a largely domestic matter and national security primarily in terms of foreign policy designed to ensure territorial integrity and prevent subversion from hostile external forces.[10]

---

6 Adája Stoetman, Minke Meijnders, and Merel Martens, "Economic Security with Chinese Characteristics," *Strategic Monitor 2019–2020: The Writing on the Wall*, Hague Center for Strategic Studies, January 28, 2020.

7 Toru Fujioka and Yuki Hakiwara, "Japan Will Monitor China, New Economic Security Minister Says," Bloomberg, August 29, 2022.

8 Jonathan Spence, *The Search for Modern China*, W.W. Norton & Company, 1991.

9 Wu Baiyi, "The Chinese Security Concept and Its Historical Evolution," *Journal of Contemporary China*, Vol. 10, No. 27, 2001.

10 Wang Zhengyi, "Conceptualizing Economic Security and Governance: China Confronts Globalization," *Pacific Review*, Vol. 17, No. 4, 2004.

Chinese thinkers began to specify direct linkages between economics and national security when their country deepened its integration into the global economy in the mid-1990s.[11] Zhao Ying, a research fellow at the Institute of Industrial Economic Research of the Chinese Academy of Social Sciences, is widely regarded as one of the first Chinese experts to highlight nonmilitary threats in the post–Cold War world. Zhao authored a study in 1994 titled *Threats to China's Economy*.[12] The book defined economic security in terms of a "country's global economic competitiveness; its capacity to resist disruptions to, threats to, and invasion of its economy; and the domestic and international environments enabling a country's economy to survive and grow continuously."[13] The definition's emphasis on resisting foreign "disruptions to, threats to, and invasion of its economy" highlighted a key political imperative that would continue to characterize Beijing's concept of economic security.

China's interest in economic security increased as it deepened its dependence on international trade and as unrest intensified over time. The 1997 Asian Financial Crisis exposed the depth of China's dependence on international trade and the risks of instability that arose from rapid growth. Reflecting the change in outlook, China's government in 2002 introduced a "new national security" concept that identified threats in the economic as well as military and political domains.[14] Underscoring this point, the government that year also identified unemployment and unrest related to economic growth among top political and security priorities.[15]

Throughout the 2000s, China's rapid development aggravated a variety of domestic and security problems. Inequality soared between rural and urban areas, between provinces, and between the formal and informal sectors of the economy. Moreover, the decentralization of authority to facilitate growth led to problems of economic overheating, segmentation of the national market owing to practices of local protectionism, and local administrative interference and rent-seeking in state-owned enterprise management.[16] Around 2004, authorities began to advocate for a more "scientific" form of development that adequately addressed the political and security problems generated by rapid growth.[17] China subsequently made policy adjustments to reduce unemployment, address inequality, and recentralize some authority.[18]

---

[11] Wang, 2004.

[12] Zhao Ying [赵英], *Threats to China's Economy—Considerations of China's Economic Security* [中国经济面临的危险-国家经济安全轮], Yunnan Renmin Publishing, 1994.

[13] Zha Daojiong, "Chinese Considerations of 'Economic Security,'" *Journal of Chinese Political Science*, Vol. 5, No. 1, March 1999, p. 72.

[14] Wang, 2004.

[15] Jiang Zemin, "Full Text of Jiang Zemin's Report at the 16th Party Congress," Xinhua, November 17, 2002.

[16] Susan L. Shirk, *The Political Logic of Economic Reform*, University of California Press, 1993.

[17] Joseph Fewsmith, "Promoting the Scientific Development Concept," *China Leadership Monitor*, No. 11, July 30, 2004.

[18] Wang, 2004.

Internationally, China's rapid growth deepened the economy's vulnerability to disruptions abroad. For example, in 2006, the country's trade dependence surged to nearly 60 percent of GDP, although it receded slightly thereafter.[19]

The global financial crisis of 2008–2009 added a powerful impetus to Beijing's sensitivity to the vulnerabilities posed by China's integration into the global economy. When the crisis hit, global demand contracted just as the Chinese economy had reached the peak of its dependence on trade for growth. The crisis also accelerated political movements in Western countries in favor of protectionist measures and skepticism about the benefits of international trade.[20]

The compounding effects of manufacturing overcapacity, a contraction in world export markets, and intensifying geostrategic competition over trade highlighted threats to China's internal stability from the international economic order. China's deepening involvement abroad also exposed more citizens and their assets to harm. Accordingly, in 2004, Chinese leaders for the first time assigned to the People's Liberation Army (PLA) the mission to protect the country's development-related interests, such as vital sea lanes and Chinese assets and personnel abroad.[21]

Despite policy adjustments, the economic-related political and stability problems persisted. Alluding in part to the severity of the many difficulties that confronted policymakers, Xi explained in a 2014 speech that China faced a "more complicated internal and external security environment" than "at any other time in history."[22] He stated that China needed to take into account "both domestic and external security issues" and "both traditional and non-traditional security issues" when making decisions on national security.[23] Authorities began to regard economics and security as mutually reinforcing and interdependent. Xi explained in a separate 2014 speech that "development is the foundation of security, and security is the necessary condition for development."[24]

---

[19] Li Cui, "China's Growing External Dependence," *Finance and Development*, Vol. 44, No. 3, September 2007. The trade dependency ratio measures the sum of exports and imports divided by GDP. The higher the ratio, the more a country's economy depends on trade for growth.

[20] Niels Graham and Josh Lipsky, "Chinese Banking's SVB Resilience," Atlantic Council, March 30, 2023; Wenjie Chen, Mico Mrkaic, and Malhar Nabar, "Lasting Effects: The Global Economic Recovery 10 Years Later," *IMF Blog*, October 3, 2018.

[21] Timothy R. Heath, Kristen Gunness, and Cortez Cooper, *The PLA and China's Rejuvenation: National Security and Military Strategies, Deterrence Concepts, and Combat Capabilities*, RAND Corporation, RR-1402-OSD, 2016.

[22] "Xi Jinping: Adhere to the Overall National Security Concept and Follow the Path of National Security with Chinese Characteristics" ["习近平:坚持总体国家安全观 走中国特色国家安全道路"], Xinhua, April 15, 2014.

[23] "Xi Jinping: Adhere to the Overall National Security Concept and Follow the Path of National Security with Chinese Characteristics," 2014.

[24] Xi Jinping, "New Asian Security Concept for New Progress in Security Cooperation," remarks at the Fourth Summit of the Conference on Interaction and Confidence Building Measures in Asia, Ministry of

In 2015, China passed the National Security Law, which defined economic security as the "safeguarding of the basic system of the national economy and the order of the socialist market economy" through the establishment of "structures and mechanisms to prevent and dissolve economic security risks and to safeguard the security of important sectors, crucial areas, focus industries, major infrastructure and major construction programs as well as other economic interests that affect the lifelines of the national economy."[25] This definition makes clear that China regards the nature of its socialist economy as essential to national security, suggesting that Beijing will resist demands for fundamental change. This law also does not restrict policy to only domestic affairs. Instead, it calls for establishing "structures and mechanisms" that "affect the lifelines of the national economy," which authorizes state action in foreign policy and abroad.[26]

In their writings on the topic, Chinese scholars and analysts emphasize the importance of economic self-reliance and freedom from external threats amid conditions of international uncertainty. One definition offered by a 2023 article in *Economics Daily* explained that "stability is the primary characteristic of a country's economic security." It added that achieving such stability required taking action to "reverse the situation of key core technologies being controlled by others."[27]

China's government has carried out actions and policies to strengthen economic security along these terms. In 2013, China formed the National Security Commission, a small leadership group composed of Xi and a handful of Politburo Standing Committee members. According to an *Outlook* report, the commission counts "economic security" among its primary areas of responsibility. Reflecting the considerable overlap of domestic and foreign policy, the report explained that the group is charged with "protecting national industries and China's brands," "gradually reducing China's reliance on foreign energy sources," "gradually advancing the construction of economic cooperation mechanisms in the Asia-Pacific region," "constructing global free trade zones," "actively participating in global economic governance," and "expanding China's right to formulate international trade rules."[28] In explaining China's proposal for a new security architecture for Asia, Xi linked the region's economic prospects to security cooperation, stating that Asia should "foster sound interactions and synchronized progress of regional economic cooperation and security cooperation."[29] This formulation showed that Chinese authorities regarded regional security cooperation as a pre-

---

Foreign Affairs of the People's Republic of China, May 21, 2014.

[25] "National Security Law of the People's Republic of China" ["中华人民共和国国家安全法"], July 1, 2015.

[26] "National Security Law of the People's Republic of China," 2015.

[27] "Firmly Safeguard the Bottom Line of Economic Security" ["牢牢守住经济安全底线"], *Economics Daily* [经济日报], December 12, 2021.

[28] Chen Xiangyang [陈向阳], "Seize the Opportunity to Plan China's National Security Strategy in a New Era" [抓好新时期中国安全的计划机会], *Outlook* [瞭望], December 2, 2013.

[29] Xi, 2014.

condition for greater regional economic cooperation. Building on this point, the 14th Five-Year Plan is the first to prominently feature national security as a consideration in all policy areas, including economics.[30]

The 2015 National Security Law includes economic security as part of a comprehensive view of "national security," which it defines as the "relative absence of international or domestic threats to the state's power to govern, sovereignty, unity and territorial integrity, the welfare of the people, sustainable economic and social development, and other major national interests, and the ability to ensure a continued state of security."[31] The law's definition derives from the "comprehensive security concept" [总体安全观] advanced by Xi in 2014. This concept defines security in extremely broad terms, incorporating (1) political, economic, social, and other aspects of domestic security and (2) security for overseas citizens, corporations, and other interests needed for China's economic development.[32] The comprehensive security concept now comprises 16 security arenas deemed essential to China's development and the party-state's survival by keeping China domestically stable and economically thriving. The concept is closely linked to achieving the "rejuvenation of the Chinese nation" by 2049 and has been encoded in the revised Party Constitution and various party documents and laws.[33]

Xi explained that, to carry out the comprehensive security concept and ensure the country's revitalization, officials had to regard economic security as the "foundation" of national security, with which "military, technological, cultural, and social security" helps avert danger before it materializes. Underscoring the linkages with foreign policy, the comprehensive security concept also requires security for overseas interests.[34] Chinese Foreign Minister Wang Yi explicitly defined overseas economic interests as a vital part of national security when he described China's growing overseas economic presence as an emerging "offshore China," the safeguarding of which he defined as a "core task" of the country's foreign policy.[35] Achieving security in these terms helps uphold political security.[36]

---

[30] "Xi Jinping Stresses in 26th Collective Study Session of Central Committee Political Bureau: Adhere to Systemic Thinking, Establish Great Security Pattern to Provide Strong Support for Building Socialist Modern Country" ["习近平在中央政治局第二十六次集体学习时强调 坚持系统思维构建大安全格局 为建设社会主义现代化国家提供坚强保障"], Xinhua, December 12, 2020.

[31] "National Security Law of the People's Republic of China," 2015.

[32] "Xi Jinping: Adhere to the Overall National Security Concept and Follow the Path of National Security with Chinese Characteristics," 2014.

[33] Sheena Chestnut Greitens, "Internal Security and Grand Strategy: China's Approach to National Security Under Xi Jinping," statement before the U.S.-China Economic and Security Review Commission hearing on "U.S.-China Relations at the Chinese Communist Party's Centennial," January 28, 2021.

[34] "Full Text of Xi Jinping's Report to the 20th Party Congress," Xinhua, October 25, 2022.

[35] Wang Yi [王毅], "China's Foreign Policy Will Hold Dear the Broad Interests of the People, Protect Offshore Interests" ["中国外交将做广大老百姓的贴心人，做海外同胞利益的守护人"], Ministry of Foreign Affairs of the People's Republic of China, March 7, 2022.

[36] "A Major Innovation in China's National Security Theory and Practice" ["中国国家安全理论与实践的重大创新"], *Seeking Truth* [求是], February 28, 2017.

Since its founding, the National Security Commission has invested considerable work on the elaboration of laws, regulations, and policies that address security concerns in all domains, including economics.[37]

Threats to Economic Security

The Chinese government's decision to pursue economic security owed in part to changes in the types and severity of threats to China's economic system and growth prospects. The persistence of social stability challenges, globalized production, information networks, and geopolitical alignments all contributed a sense among Chinese leaders that economic security had become a high-priority issue.

In a 2014 speech to the Politburo, Xi stated that the "current and coming period will be a period prone to all kinds of contradictions and risks in our country, with a marked increase in risk factors, both foreseeable and difficult to foresee."[38] Similarly, in a 2019 speech, Xi outlined the seven most prominent risks to the China dream: politics, ideology, the economy, science and technology, society, the external environment, and party-building. Xi characterized the international situation as "complex and grim."[39]

Buttressing Chen's assessment, China's social stability situation has indeed remained volatile as economic growth has been strong. Since 2010, authorities have spent more on internal security than on the military; research by criminologists suggests that the country continues to face high levels of crime and unrest despite government efforts to suppress such information.[40] Unemployment among urban youth reached record highs in 2023 (above 20 percent).[41] Taiwan continues to resist overtures to unify with China, and Tibet and Xinjiang continue to experience unrest and instability, as noted in a 2019 defense white paper.[42]

Chinese commentators also express distrust and suspicion of U.S. intentions in an escalating competition. After Washington levied tariffs against Beijing and restricted trade in concert with allies, Chinese media stepped up denunciations of the United States as an economic threat. In 2020, the *People's Daily* criticized Washington for adopting a "beggar-thy-neighbor

---

37 Yang Zekun, "Robust National Security Legal System Urged," *China Daily*, April 16, 2024.

38 "Xi Jinping: Explanation on 'CCP Central Committee Recommendation on Formulating the 14th Five-Year Plan on Developing the National Economy and Society and 2035 Long-Term Goals'" ["习近平：关于《中共中央关于制定国民经济和社会发展第十四个五年规划和二〇三五年远景目标的建议》的说明"], Xinhua, November 3, 2020.

39 "Xi Jinping Makes Important Speech at Opening Ceremony of Provincial and Ministerial-Level Major Leading Cadres' Thematic Workshop on Persisting in Bottom-Line Thinking and Concentrating Efforts on Guarding Against, Resolving Major Risks" ["习近平在省部级主要领导干部坚持底线思维着力防范化解重大风险专题研讨班开班式上发表重要讲话"], Xinhua, January 21, 2019.

40 Børge Bakken, *Crime and Control in China: The Myth of Harmony*, Polity Books, 2022.

41 "China's Record-High Youth Unemployment Rate Likely to Worsen," Bloomberg, May 16, 2023.

42 State Council Information Office of the People's Republic of China, *China's National Defense in the New Era*, July 24, 2019.

economic and trade policy," "practicing protectionism and unilateralism," and "wantonly brandishing the bludgeon of sanctions," all of which it called a "serious threat to global economic security."[43] Regarding overseas interests, China's economy has indeed grown more vulnerable to threats around the world. Not only does the country depend heavily on trade, but it has also grown dependent on energy imports. In 2017, China surpassed the United States to become the world's largest importer of oil.[44] Its citizens and enterprises operate on an increasingly global scale as well. According to a 2022 report by the Migration Policy Institute, 10.5 million Chinese citizens live abroad.[45]

In sum, China's concept of economic security reflects the country's growth as a major trading power, as well as long-standing political insecurities about the vulnerabilities raised by China's integration into the global economy. Economic growth has become more critical to the legitimacy of CCP rule, but growth has also become more vulnerable to disruption and to destabilizing influences both within and outside China. Accordingly, authorities have regarded economic policy as increasingly within the domain of security policy. This applies to both domestic and foreign policy.

Domestic Policy Dimension

Economic security carries important implications for China's domestic policy. Many policies reflect the influence of economic security concerns, but they generally share several features. Two broad overarching categories consist of measures to (1) strengthen national competitiveness and (2) reduce threats from external sources. These measures collectively aim to strengthen China's economic self-reliance. A commentary in China's news agency, Xinhua, explained that "China is committed to realizing a high level of self-reliance and self-improvement, defined by the leadership as the most essential characteristic of China's new development paradigm." It justified the pursuit of self-reliance on the grounds that "only by holding core technologies in its own hands can the country ensure economic security, national security and security in other areas."[46]

---

[43] Zhong Sheng [钟声], "Brandishing Bludgeon of Sanctions Poses Threat to Global Economic Security" ["挥舞制裁大棒威胁全球经济安全"], *People's Daily* [人民日报], October 29, 2020.

[44] U.S. Energy Information Administration, "China," webpage, April 2020.

[45] Heidi Østbø Haugen and Tabitha Speelman, "China's Rapid Development Has Transformed Its Migration Trends," Migration Policy Institute, January 28, 2022.

[46] "China Committed to High Level of Self Reliance, Self Improvement," commentary, Xinhua, January 12, 2021.

Measures to Strengthen National Competitiveness

Economic security–related measures to strengthen competitiveness include policies to stimulate domestic demand, protect intellectual property rights (IPR) for Chinese companies, and bolster technology leadership.

Stimulate Domestic Demand

Chinese leaders recognize that China's export sector has played an important role in driving the country's phenomenal growth. Although lucrative, dependence on foreign markets leaves China's economy highly vulnerable to disruption. Accordingly, Beijing has for years sought to bolster domestic demand as a driver of growth. In 2020, the Politburo put forth the concept of "dual circulation," which prioritized efforts to expand its domestic consumer base, as well as maintain its foreign export markets.[47] At the 20th Party Congress, Xi called for implementing policies to promote dual circulation.[48] Authorities have made limited progress in shaping the economy along these lines. Although China's trade dependency ratio declined from 61 percent in 2006 to around 34 percent in 2021, it has made little progress in expanding consumption as a driver of growth, which increased from around 35 percent in 2020 to around 38 percent in 2022.[49] In contrast, domestic investment, especially in real estate, has been the dominant economic driver in recent years.

Protect Intellectual Property Rights for Chinese Companies

Chinese leaders have emphasized the importance of bolstering IPR for Chinese companies. In highlighting indigenous technological development and IPR as key elements of international competition and national security, Xi stated at a 2020 Politburo study session that "intellectual property rights have an increasingly important impact on a country's security in science and technology, economic security as well as security in many other areas."[50] Western observers have subsequently noted a striking shift toward a more protectionist and nationalist stance in China's approach to such issues as IPR protection, foreign investment, and technological development. For example, in a 2022 literature review of China's approach to IPR protection, the authors noted that, although China is itself frequently accused of IPR violations, China's government has supported more-aggressive efforts by Chinese companies to sue foreign companies for IPR infringement.[51] The number of IPR-related lawsuits, they noted, increased more than three times from 2016 to 2020.

---

[47] "Scientifically Understand the New Development Pattern of 'Dual Circulation,'" ["科学认识 '双循环' 新发展格局"], Xinhua, November 9, 2020.

[48] "Full Text of Xi Jinping's Report to the 20th Party Congress," 2022.

[49] Hung Tran, "Dual Circulation in China: A Progress Report," Atlantic Council, October 4, 2022.

[50] Cao Lei [曹磊], "Safeguard National Security in the Area of Intellectual Property Rights" ["在知识产权领域维护国家安全"], *People's Daily* [人民日报], December 3, 2020.

[51] Katrin Muehlfeld and Mei Wang, "Intellectual Property Rights in China—A Literature Review on the Public's Perspective," *Frontiers in Sociology*, Vol. 7, April 11, 2022.

Technology Leadership Initiatives

China's efforts to develop itself into a technological leader also reflect its concept of economic security. In 2015, China announced the Made in China 2025 initiative, aimed at comprehensively upgrading China's industry.[52] The initiative aims to establish Chinese market leadership in advanced manufacturing industries, such as information technology, computerized machines, robots, energy-saving vehicles, medical devices, and high-tech equipment for aviation, maritime, and rail transport. The initiative is expected to generate strong competition for established leaders in advanced technologies, such as the United States and Germany.[53]

China has also sought to strengthen its influence on international standards through industrial policies that strengthen Chinese domestic development. In 2018, China launched China Standards 2035, a strategic scheme overseen by a revamped agency—the Standards Administration of China—to encourage indigenous innovation under Chinese party-state guidance.[54]

Measures to Control External Threats

Measures to control external threats to the domestic economy include those that strengthen controls on foreign investment, increase monitoring of private companies, and bolster financial controls.

Controls on Foreign Investment

China has tightened controls on foreign investment. Inspired by the Committee on Foreign Investment in the United States, since 2010, China's government has adopted review procedures that employ a broad definition of security. According to new procedures announced in 2011, China's national security review covers "transactions involving important agricultural products, energy and resources, infrastructure facilities, transportation services, core technologies, and important equipment manufacturing enterprises."[55] Analysts have noted a vague and inclusive set of factors that could trigger a review, including any deal that could conceivably affect national defense, the stable running of China's economy, social stability, or key technologies involving national security.[56] The 2015 National Security Law not only

[52] State Council of the People's Republic of China, "Made in China 2025," webpage, undated.

[53] Jost Wübbeke, Mirjam Meissner, Max J. Zenglein, Jaqueline Ives, and Björn Conrad, *Made in China 2025: The Making of a High-Tech Superpower and Consequences for Industrial Countries*, Mercator Institute for China Studies, August 12, 2016.

[54] Bjorn Fägerstern and Tim Rühlig, "China's Standard Power and Its Geographic Implications for Europe," Swedish Institute of International Affairs, February 2019.

[55] Ministry of Commerce, "Circular of the General Office of the State Council on the Establishment of the Security Review System for Mergers and Acquisitions of Domestic Enterprises by Foreign Investors" ["關於建立外國投資者併購境內企 業安全審查制度的通知"], February 3, 2011.

[56] Chieh Huang, "China's Take on National Security and Its Implications for the Evolution of International Economic Law," *Legal Issues of Economic Integration*, Vol. 48, No. 2, 2021.

defines what falls into China's national security concerns but also mandates the security review of "foreign investment that jeopardizes, or may jeopardize, national security," including "key materials and technologies," "internet or information technology products and services," "construction projects that implicate national security," and "other major projects or events."[57]

Monitoring Private Companies

For private companies, the increased concern over security has led to expanded government oversight and monitoring. Bureaucracies are required to consider national security at every layer of decisionmaking. Consent can be withdrawn after initial clearance of business activities. Foreign companies face additional risks because Beijing is expanding its retaliatory toolkit to protect China's ever-widening core interests. Multiple laws and regulations now have explicit clauses allowing "reciprocal measures" when state and corporate actions endanger China's "sovereignty, security or development interests."[58]

Strengthening Financial Controls

Chinese officials have bolstered controls to enhance financial security. Explaining the significance of this concept, Xi stated, "Financial security is an important component of national security and important foundation for the stable and healthy development of the economy." He warned that "[i]f there is inadequate financial security, financial risks will be prominent, and economic security will be threatened, which will lead to chaotic economic operations and deteriorating economic situations."[59] For Beijing, financial security entails measures to ensure the independence of the country's financial system and its ability to operate even under adverse market conditions.[60] Relevant policies include measures to expand the use of a state-sponsored digital currency and digital payment systems.[61] China has also invoked "financial security" to justify a tightening of regulatory oversight to reduce risks in the financial system.[62]

---

57 National People's Congress of the People's Republic of China, "Explaining the Introduction to the National Security Law" ["关于中华人民共和国国家安全法(草案的说明"], August 27, 2015.

58 Katja Drinhausen and Helena Legarda, "China's Anti-Foreign Sanctions Law: A Warning to the World," Mercator Institute for China Studies, June 24, 2021.

59 "Safeguarding Financial Security Concerns the Overall Situation" ["维护金融安全事关大局"], *Economics Daily* [经济日报], May 4, 2017.

60 Brian Wong, "How China Must and Can Balance Financial Security and Openness," China-US Focus, June 17, 2022.

61 Robert Greene, "What Will Be the Impact of China's State-Sponsored Digital Currency?" Carnegie Endowment for International Peace, July 1, 2021.

62 Frank Tang, "China's Financial Regulator Vows to Cut 'Blind Spots' and 'Build an Iron Wall' as New Body Takes Shape," *South China Morning Post*, May 18, 2023.

In sum, China's government has revised its approach to domestic economic-related plans, policies, and laws to address national security considerations. This revised approach has meant greater emphasis on protecting Chinese interests, supporting Chinese firms, and limiting foreign access to China's technologies and key markets. But China's economic security also carries important implications for its foreign policy.

Foreign Policy Dimension

China's concept of economic security carries important consequences for its foreign policy. Policies have been deliberately designed to further China's economic interests in part by building China's international leadership in trade. Zhao Ying, a researcher at the Institute of Industrial Economics of the Chinese Academy of Social Sciences, explained that the country's demand for energy, resources, and markets has continued to expand. He notes that economic requirements cannot be separated from international geopolitics, and, therefore, the country's security needs will need to strongly shape its approach to economics.[63]

China's economic security as applied to foreign policy thus involves a tight interweaving of economic and political goals. China also regards economic development and security-related policy as complementary and mutually reinforcing. Economic security as applied to foreign policy thus overlaps considerably with a related concept of *economic diplomacy*, in which China seeks to use diplomacy to advance its economic interests and economics to advance its foreign policy goals.[64] Four broad categories of foreign policy–related economic security measures are (1) trade and investment dominance, (2) norm- and rule-setting, (3) China as a growth model, and (4) protection of overseas interests.

Trade and Investment Dominance

Chinese leaders aim to enhance the country's economic security in part by gaining a dominant position in international trade and investment. A major study carried out by Ministry of Commerce researchers in 2009–2010 concluded that successful reform of China's trade and investment strategy depended in part on China's ability to exercise international influence commensurate with its status as the world's second-largest economy. The study outlined a vision of China as a leader in world trade and investment rather than merely a country that trades in large volumes but passively follows established rules. It used the term "strong trad-

[63] Zhao Ying [赵英], "Why Economic Security is Considered the Foundation of National Security" ["'经济安全' 缘何被视为国家安全基础"], *People's Daily* [人民日报], April 22, 2014.

[64] Timothy R. Heath, "China's Evolving Approach to Economic Diplomacy," *Asia Policy*, Vol. 22, July 2016.

ing power" (贸易强国) to describe this condition, a term that senior leaders subsequently adopted.[65]

Major economic diplomacy initiatives, such as the Belt and Road Initiative (BRI) and the Global Development Initiative (GDI), aim in large part to expand opportunities for Chinese companies. The BRI, announced in 2013, is a potentially $1 trillion initiative to link Eurasia and Africa through Chinese-led infrastructure construction and trade. The initiative has provided an important outlet for Chinese construction and other firms that have saturated the domestic and Western markets.[66] The GDI, announced by Xi in 2021, offers a Chinese-led approach to achieving the Global Sustainable Development goals set by the United Nations. The GDI promotes multilateral cooperation to address such issues as global poverty alleviation, food security, vaccines, climate change, and development finance.[67] The GDI offers significant market opportunities for Chinese green energy and tech companies.

China's pursuit of regional trade initiatives could also enhance its economic security by expanding market access for domestic producers and thereby reduce unemployment. The total population, economic output, and export volume of the 15 member countries in the new Regional Comprehensive Economic Partnership (RCEP) Pacific trade agreement could account for about 30 percent of the global total. The agreement could drive nearly one third of the world's economy to form a large, unified market and enhance the stability of regional economic and trade policies.[68] China's promotion of a Free Trade Area of the Asia-Pacific at a meeting of the Asia-Pacific Economic Cooperation in 2014 could open opportunities for Chinese producers as well.[69] The RCEP and other trade agreements in which China participates also enhance political security by reflecting values and norms that are compatible with China's political system. Scholars have noted that Chinese trade initiatives operate within a paradigm that incorporates political and strategic considerations. For example, Chinese trade deals with countries in the Persian Gulf aim to expand access to energy resources, undertake large-scale infrastructure projects, and demonstrate China's great-power status.[70]

---

65 "Strategic Readjustment and Structural Innovation in China's Foreign Trade Policy in the Post-Crisis Era" ["后危机时代我国对外贸易的战略性天正"], *International Trade* [国际贸易], 2020.

66 Michele Ruta, Matias Herrera Dappe, Somik Lall, Chunlin Zhang, Erik Churchill, Cristina Constantinescu, Mathilde Lebrand, and Alen Mulabdic, *Belt and Road Economics: Opportunities and Risks of Transport Corridor*, World Bank, 2019.

67 Ministry of Foreign Affairs of the People's Republic of China, "Global Development Initiative—Building on 2030 Sustainable Development Goals for Stronger, Greener, and Healthier Global Development (Concept Paper)," June 1, 2024.

68 Wan Wang, "Opportunities and Challenges Facing China's Economic 'External Circulation,'" *China International Strategy Review*, Vol. 4, No. 1, June 2022.

69 Mireya Solís, "China Flexes Muscles at APEC with the Revival of FTAAP," East Asian Forum, November 23, 2014.

70 Mordechai Chaziza, "China's Economic Diplomacy Towards the Gulf Cooperation Council States," *Journal of Contemporary China*, Vol. 34, No. 152, 2025.

Norm- and Rule-Setting

Expanding China's role as a leader of international norms, rules, and standards could pay several benefits for China. First, it could result in preferential access to markets and resources for Chinese firms. It could also disadvantage competitors that follow different norms, rules, and standards. Moreover, strengthening China's leadership role could result in a larger network of friendly partner nations, which might in turn enhance China's sense of security.[71] Through the BRI, China hopes to develop norms for the substantive areas in which it has increased economic and geopolitical interests, concerns, and capacity (e.g., e-commerce, data localization, investment, and infrastructure). Compared with the passive adaptation to the World Trade Organization (WTO) rules, in these areas, China seeks more norm entrepreneurship in international law in terms of promoting Chinese standards and participating in rulemaking.[72]

The BRI, GDI, and other major geoeconomic initiatives undertaken by China underscore its efforts to become a norm and rule setter.[73] In 2013, China announced the BRI.[74] The following year, it also formed the New Development Bank based on the Brazil, Russia, India, China, and South Africa (BRICS) grouping.[75] In 2021, China announced the GDI, further pointing to its ambitions to provide global leadership on development issues.[76] And through the "2035 Standard" project, China has also expanded its leadership role in international bodies that are responsible for setting technology and other standards and rules.[77]

China as a Growth Model

China promotes its political security in part by encouraging more countries to adopt growth policies that mimic its own. The logic of China's growth model is that development-oriented policies create more jobs, reduce poverty, and, thereby, prevent social unrest and ensure state security. This logic justifies development-first policies that prioritize infrastructure and logistics-related projects over the strengthening of governance and political institutions.

---

71 William A. Callahan, "China's 'Asia Dream': The Belt Road Initiative and the New Regional Order," *Asian Journal of Comparative Politics*, Vol. 1, No. 3, September 2016.

72 Heng Wang, "China's Approach to the Belt and Road Initiative: Scope, Character and Sustainability," *Journal of International Economic Law*, Vol. 22, No. 1, March 2019.

73 Manoj Kewalramani, *China as a Rising Norm Entrepreneur*, Institute of Southeast Asia Studies, No. 2, 2024.

74 "Chronology of One Belt, One Road," Xinhua, March 28, 2015.

75 "BRICS Countries Launch New Development Bank in Shanghai," BBC, July 21, 2015.

76 State Council Information Office of the People's Republic of China, "Full Text: A Global Community of Shared Future: China's Proposals and Actions," Ministry of Foreign Affairs of the People's Republic of China, September 26, 2023.

77 Arjun Gargeyas, "China's '2035 Standards' Quest to Dominate Global Standard-Setting," Hinrich Foundation, February 21, 2023.

When countries adopt policies that reflect Beijing's own preferences, they legitimize China's growth model; this in turn can bolster the CCP's legitimacy and sense of security.[78] China's advocacy of this approach is not self-disinterested: It opens new markets for Chinese companies and products as well.

In a 2019 article published in *Seeking Truth*, Xi predicted that the Chinese model would have increasing influence around the world.[79] In a separate speech, he stated that countries can best ensure their own economic security by relying on "both the invisible hand and the visible hand."[80] He explained that China's approach combines the market's ability to allocate resources efficiently with a strong role for the state in controlling key sectors, ensuring equitable social and economic outcomes, stabilizing markets, and solving large-scale problems.

China's model, led by an authoritarian state, is less transparent and thus more attractive to authoritarian regimes. Formal law and formal dispute settlement play reduced roles and are displaced by soft law (set forth in memorandums of understanding) and informal state-to-state and private negotiations to resolve disputes.[81] Several Chinese initiatives illustrate this approach, especially the BRI. Beijing uses the BRI to develop new markets for Chinese products through a trade, investment, and infrastructure network that is governed by a combination of contracts and treaties and is backed by new dispute resolution mechanisms. This network encourages economic integration and dependence on Beijing.[82]

Protect Economic Interests Abroad

Economic security also requires China to protect its citizens and their assets abroad more effectively. At a foreign policy work conference in November 2014, Xi stated that officials should "protect China's overseas interests."[83] Article 78 of China's National Security Law similarly directs all elements of state power to support work to protect national security: "State organs, mass organizations, enterprises, public institutions, and other social organizations shall cooperate with relevant departments in employing relevant security measures as

---

[78] Ilaria Carrozza, "China's Multilateral Diplomacy in Africa: Constructing the Security-Development Nexus," in Daniel Johanson, Jie Li, and Tsunghan Wu, eds., *New Perspectives on China's Relations with the World*, E-International Relations Publishing, 2019.

[79] Xi Jinping, "Several Issues on Adhering to and Developing Socialism with Chinese Characteristics" ["关于坚持和发展中国特色主义的几个问题"], *Seeking Truth* [求是], March 31, 2019.

[80] Xi Jinping, "Working Together to Forge a New Partnership of Win-Win Cooperation and Create a Community of Shared Future for Mankind," Ministry of Foreign Affairs of the People's Republic of China, September 29, 2015.

[81] Tom Ginsburg, "Authoritarian International Law?" *American Journal of International Law*, Vol. 114, No. 2, April 2020.

[82] Nadège Rolland, *China's Eurasian Century? Political and Strategic Implications of the Belt and Road Initiative*, National Bureau of Asian Research, May 23, 2017.

[83] "Xi Eyes More Enabling Int'l Environment for China's Peaceful Development," Xinhua, November 30, 2014.

required by national security efforts."[84] The law makes clear that state authorities bear primary responsibility for national security. The military may play an important role in the protection of overseas interests, but the law does not grant it a leading role in that responsibility.

China's military plays an important role in protecting vital sea lanes and assisting with evacuations of endangered citizens. In the late 2000s, to defend China's economic interests, the PLA began deploying outside the country for the first time. In 2009, the PLA Navy deployed its first task force to the Horn of Africa to protect Chinese merchant ships from the threat of piracy.[85] And in 2011, the PLA carried out its first noncombatant operation to evacuate Chinese nationals in Libya, many of them workers.[86]

Other assets also play an important role in providing security abroad. Chinese companies rely heavily on private security contractors to evade dangers and protect their people and assets. Chinese authorities also cooperate with the security forces provided by host nations to enhance the security of key projects.[87] In Pakistan, for example, China has paid for a 15,000-person force that is responsible for providing security for Chinese workers and their projects.

Implications

China's concept of economic security reflects its maturation as a large, developed economy and the implications of that growth for CCP rule. It also reflects Beijing's belief in the primacy of economic growth as the basis for political and social stability. To achieve domestic security and ensure the perpetuation of CCP rule, Beijing must ensure continued economic growth. To sustain growth, Chinese companies need to outcompete competitors, and the government must minimize disruptions and threats to economic activity. This, in turn, motivates China's government to build robust industrial policies, adopt protectionist trade measures, carry out a more activist security policy abroad, and seek leadership in setting and shaping international trade rules, norms, and standards.

China's adoption of myriad policies to enhance economic security carries several key implications for the United States. The first is that the economic and security dimensions of the U.S.-China relationship will need to be treated as largely mutually reinforcing.[88] This

---

84 "National Security Law of the People's Republic of China," 2015.

85 Alison A. Kaufman, *China's Participation in Anti-Piracy Operations off the Horn of Africa: Drivers and Implications*, Center for Naval Analysis, conference report, July 2009.

86 Gabe Collins and Andrew S. Erickson, "Implications of China's Military Evacuation of Citizens from Libya," *China Brief*, Vol. 11, No. 4, March 10, 2011.

87 Timothy R. Heath, *China's Pursuit of Overseas Security*, RAND Corporation, RR-2271-OSD, 2018.

88 Bonny Lin, Howard J. Shatz, Nathan Chandler, Cristina L. Garafola, Eugeniu Han, Andy Law, King Mallory, and Zev Winkelman, *Bridging the Gap: Assessing U.S. Business Community Support for U.S.-China Competition*, RAND Corporation, RR-A1417-1, 2022.

contrasts with the past, in which U.S. and Chinese leaders treated security and economics as separate domains. In the aftermath of the collision of a U.S. EP-3 electronic signals reconnaissance airplane with Chinese aircraft near Hainan Island in 2001, for example, the two leaders relied on shared interests in economic cooperation to navigate acute political tensions.[89] Such an approach is less likely to work today.

On the contrary, the linkages between economics and security suggests that a worsening in one area is likely to result in a worsening in the other. The mutually reinforcing dynamic will impair efforts to sustain positive momentum in either domain if the other is deteriorating. For example, a worsening of U.S.-China relations over Taiwan will probably not open opportunities to ease tensions through economic engagement but instead will likely aggravate tensions over trade, tariffs, and technology restrictions. If the United States applied economic sanctions against China in regard to a crisis related to Taiwan, for example, China could retaliate with a host of economically punitive measures.[90]

Second, the importance of economic security to CCP legitimacy raises Beijing's sensitivity to potential economic disruptions in a major crisis. China's economy faces vulnerabilities, owing to its dependence on foreign markets and resources, as well as its ownership of large stocks of exposed overseas assets and the many Chinese nationals working in less developed countries with security issues. In a major crisis, fears of severe economic disruptions could have a restraining effect. Disruption or threats to vital inputs or networks—such as oil imports, cyber networks, or maritime shipping—could increase political instability through dramatic increases in prices and unemployment. A reluctance to risk such disruptions provides a strong incentive for Beijing to avoid reckless and rash decisions in a major crisis. This incentive suggests that, in a crisis involving Taiwan or other flash point, Beijing may be open to options to de-escalate tensions. However, this logic holds only so long as Beijing believes its situation can be stabilized. If China's situation were to truly deteriorate to the point that Chinese leaders view restoration of economic growth and prosperity as all but impossible, rational considerations could be thrown aside in favor of bolder and more desperate measures. Similarly, in the extreme scenario in which Chinese leaders decided to risk everything, including total war, to achieve unification with Taiwan, they would in that case likely have little regard for economic costs.

Paradoxically, China will likely become more resistant and less responsive to U.S. efforts to shape Chinese behavior through economic statecraft. Because of the centrality of economic growth to CCP legitimacy, China will likely become more sensitive to vulnerabilities and U.S. measures to exploit China's dependence on the West. Efforts to wield economic policy for punitive reasons will confirm Beijing's belief in the hostile nature of Western countries, as well as the need to achieve national self-reliance. Accordingly, China is likely to respond to

---

[89] Eric Donnelly, "The United States—China EP-3 Incident: Legality and 'Realpolitik,'" *Journal of Conflict and Security Law*, Vol. 9, No. 1, Spring 2004.

[90] Logan Wright, Agatha Kratz, Charlie Vest, and Matt Mingey, *Retaliation and Resilience: China's Economic Statecraft in a Taiwan Crisis*, Atlantic Council, April 1, 2024.

U.S.-imposed sanctions and other punitive economic measures with retaliation rather than compliance. In a 2016 RAND study, David Gompert and Hans Binnendijk concluded that China's economic strength makes efforts to compel behavior through the application of sanctions and other economic measures extremely risky, given China's ability to retaliate and the potential disruption that such measures could pose to the world economy.[91] Beijing's belief in the importance of economic security has only strengthened since then.

Even compromise on trade, investment, and other economic-related issues might become more difficult. China will seek to maximize opportunities for its companies and thus will be reluctant to adopt compromises that are conditioned on sustaining U.S. leadership in international trade institutions. Agreement on rules, norms, and standards are likely to become more difficult as they become politicized. Already, observers have noted that the two countries have moved toward a "more politicized and less judicialized" approach to address national security topics in international economic law.[92]

Despite the securitization of economic policy, there may be hard limits on how much China can afford to escalate tensions. China can ill afford major disruptions to its access to Western markets and imported resources. There may be opportunities to cooperate on shared security concerns that threaten economic activity for both countries. The tentative cooperation between the U.S. and Chinese militaries in the mission to combat maritime piracy near the Horn of Africa could serve as a model for such security cooperation.[93]

China's need for a smoothly functioning global economy also provides potential opportunities for cooperation at the macroeconomic level. China and the United States may find opportunities to coordinate on macroeconomic policy to promote a smoother operation of a global economy on which they both depend.

---

91 David C. Gompert and Hans Binnendijk, *The Power to Coerce: Countering Adversaries Without Going to War*, RAND Corporation, RR-1000-A, 2016.

92 Anthea Roberts, Henrique Choer Moraes, and Victor Ferguson, "Toward a Geoeconomic Order in International Trade and Investment," *Journal of International Economic Law*, Vol. 22, No. 4, December 2019.

93 North Atlantic Treaty Organization, "NATO and China Cooperate to Fight Piracy," January 20, 2012.

Abbreviations

BRI	Belt and Road Initiative
BRICS	Brazil, Russia, India, China, South Africa
CCP	Chinese Communist Party
GDI	Global Development Initiative
GDP	gross domestic product
IPR	intellectual property rights
NSS	National Security Strategy
OECD	Organisation for Economic Co-operation and Development
PLA	People's Liberation Army
RCEP	Regional Comprehensive Economic Partnership

References

"A Major Innovation in China's National Security Theory and Practice" ["中国国家安全理论与实践的重大创新"], *Seeking Truth* [求是], February 28, 2017. As of April 18, 2023: http://www.qstheory.cn/dukan/qs/2017-02/28/c_1120536834.htm

Bakken, Børge, *Crime and Control in China: The Myth of Harmony*, Polity Books, 2022.

"BRICS Countries Launch New Development Bank in Shanghai," *BBC*, July 21, 2015.

Callahan, William A., "China's 'Asia Dream': The Belt Road Initiative and the New Regional Order," *Asian Journal of Comparative Politics*, Vol. 1, No. 3, September 2016.

Cao Lei [曹磊], "Safeguard National Security in the Area of Intellectual Property Rights" ["在知识产权领域维护国家安全"], *People's Daily* [人民日报], December 3, 2020.

Carrozza, Ilaria, "China's Multilateral Diplomacy in Africa: Constructing the Security-Development Nexus," in Daniel Johanson, Jie Li, and Tsunghan Wu, eds., *New Perspectives on China's Relations with the World*, E-International Relations Publishing, 2019.

Chaziza, Mordechai, "China's Economic Diplomacy Towards the Gulf Cooperation Council States," *Journal of Contemporary China*, Vol. 34, No. 152, 2025.

Chen, Wenjie, Mico Mrkaic, and Malhar Nabar, "Lasting Effects: The Global Economic Recovery 10 Years Later," *IMF Blog*, October 3, 2018.

Chen Xiangyang [陈向阳], "Seize the Opportunity to Plan China's National Security Strategy in a New Era" ["抓好新时期中国安全的计划机会"], *Outlook* [瞭望], December 2, 2013.

"China Committed to High Level of Self Reliance, Self Improvement," commentary, Xinhua, January 12, 2021.

"China's Record-High Youth Unemployment Rate Likely to Worsen," Bloomberg, May 16, 2023.

"Chronology of One Belt, One Road," Xinhua, March 28, 2015.

Collins, Gabe, and Andrew S. Erickson, "Implications of China's Military Evacuation of Citizens from Libya," *China Brief*, Vol. 11, No. 4, March 10, 2011.

Donnelly, Eric, "The United States—China EP-3 Incident: Legality and 'Realpolitik,'" *Journal of Conflict and Security Law*, Vol. 9, No. 1, Spring 2004.

Drinhausen, Katja, and Helena Legarda, "China's Anti-Foreign Sanctions Law: A Warning to the World," Mercator Institute for China Studies, June 24, 2021.

Fägerstern, Björn, and Tim Rühlig, "China's Standard Power and Its Geographic Implications for Europe," Swedish Institute of International Affairs, February 2019.

Fewsmith, Joseph, "Promoting the Scientific Development Concept," *China Leadership Monitor*, No. 11, July 30, 2004.

"Firmly Safeguard the Bottom Line of Economic Security" ["牢牢守住经济安全底线"], *Economics Daily* [经济日报], December 12, 2021. As of May 27, 2025: http://www.sasac.gov.cn/n2588025/n2588134/c29624768/content.html

Fujioka, Toru, and Yuki Hagiwara, "Japan Will Monitor China, New Economic Security Minister Says," Bloomberg, August 29, 2022.

"Full Text of Xi Jinping's Report to the 20th Party Congress," Xinhua, October 25, 2022.

Gargeyas, Arjun, "China's '2035 Standards' Quest to Dominate Global Standard-Setting," Hinrich Foundation, February 21, 2023.

Geeraerts, Gustaaf, and Weiping Huang, "The Economic Security Dimension of the EU–China Relationship: Puzzles and Prospects," in Emil J. Kirchner, Thomas Christiansen, and Han Dorussen, eds., *Security Relationships Between China and the European Union*, Cambridge University Press, 2016.

Ginsburg, Tom, "Authoritarian International Law?" *American Journal of International Law*, Vol. 114, No. 2, April 2020.

Gompert, David C., and Hans Binnendijk, *The Power to Coerce: Countering Adversaries Without Going to War*, RAND Corporation, RR-1000-A, 2016. As of September 23, 2024: https://www.rand.org/pubs/research_reports/RR1000.html

Graham, Niels, and Josh Lipsky, "Chinese Banking's SVB Resilience," Atlantic Council, March 30, 2023.

Greene, Robert, "What Will Be the Impact of China's State-Sponsored Digital Currency?" Carnegie Endowment for International Peace, July 1, 2021.

Greitens, Sheena Chestnut, "Internal Security and Grand Strategy: China's Approach to National Security Under Xi Jinping," statement before the U.S.-China Economic and Security Review Commission hearing on "U.S.-China Relations at the Chinese Communist Party's Centennial," January 28, 2021.

Haugen, Heidi Østbø, and Tabitha Speelman, "China's Rapid Development Has Transformed Its Migration Trends," Migration Policy Institute, January 28, 2022.

Heath, Timothy R., "China's Evolving Approach to Economic Diplomacy," *Asia Policy*, Vol. 22, July 2016.

Heath, Timothy R., *China's Pursuit of Overseas Security*, RAND Corporation, RR-2271-OSD, 2018. As of September 24, 2024: https://www.rand.org/pubs/research_reports/RR2271.html

Heath, Timothy R., Kristen Gunness, and Cortez Cooper, *The PLA and China's Rejuvenation: National Security and Military Strategies, Deterrence Concepts, and Combat Capabilities*, RAND Corporation, RR-1402-OSD, 2016. As of September 24, 2024: https://www.rand.org/pubs/research_reports/RR1402.html

Huang, Chieh, "China's Take on National Security and Its Implications for the Evolution of International Economic Law," *Legal Issues of Economic Integration*, Vol. 48, No. 2, 2021.

Jiang Zemin, "Full Text of Jiang Zemin's Report at the 16th Party Congress," Xinhua, November 17, 2002.

Kaufman, Alison A., *China's Participation in Anti-Piracy Operations off the Horn of Africa: Drivers and Implications*, Center for Naval Analyses, conference report, July 2009.

Kewalramani, Manoj, *China as a Rising Norm Entrepreneur*, Institute of Southeast Asia Studies, No. 2, 2024.

Li Cui, "China's Growing External Dependence," *Finance and Development*, Vol. 44, No. 3, September 2007.

Lin, Bonny, Howard J. Shatz, Nathan Chandler, Cristina L. Garafola, Eugeniu Han, Andy Law, King Mallory, and Zev Winkelman, *Bridging the Gap: Assessing U.S. Business Community Support for U.S.-China Competition*, RAND Corporation, RR-A1417-1, 2022. As of May 8, 2025: https://www.rand.org/pubs/research_reports/RRA1417-1.html

Ministry of Commerce, "Circular of the General Office of the State Council on the Establishment of the Security Review System for Mergers and Acquisitions of Domestic Enterprises by Foreign Investors" ["關於建立外國投資者併購境內企 業安全審查制度的通知"], February 3, 2011.

Ministry of Foreign Affairs of the People's Republic of China, "Global Development Initiative—Building on 2030 Sustainable Development Goals for Stronger, Greener, and Healthier Global Development (Concept Paper)," June 1, 2024.

Muehlfeld, Katrin, and Mei Wang, "Intellectual Property Rights in China—A Literature Review on the Public's Perspective," *Frontiers in Sociology*, Vol. 7, April 11, 2022.

National People's Congress of the People's Republic of China, "Explaining the Introduction to the National Security Law" ["关于中华人民共和国国家安全法(草案的说明"], August 27, 2015.

"National Security Law of the People's Republic of China" ["中华人民共和国国家安全法"], July 1, 2015. As of April 18, 2023: http://www.gov.cn/zhengce/2015-07/01/content_2893902.htm

North Atlantic Treaty Organization, "NATO and China Cooperate to Fight Piracy," January 20, 2012.

Pinker, Steven, *The Better Angels of Our Nature: Why Violence Has Declined*, Viking Books, 2011.

Roberts, Anthea, Henrique Choer Moraes, and Victor Ferguson, "Toward a Geoeconomic Order in International Trade and Investment," *Journal of International Economic Law*, Vol. 22, No. 4, December 2019.

Rolland, Nadège, *China's Eurasian Century? Political and Strategic Implications of the Belt and Road Initiative*, National Bureau of Asian Research, May 23, 2017.

Ruta, Michele, Matias Herrera Dappe, Somik Lall, Chunlin Zhang, Erik Churchill, Cristina Constantinescu, Mathilde Lebrand, and Alen Mulabdic, *Belt and Road Economics: Opportunities and Risks of Transport Corridor*, World Bank, 2019.

"Safeguarding Financial Security Concerns the Overall Situation" ["维护金融安全事关大局"], *Economics Daily* [经济日报], May 4, 2017.

"Scientifically Understand the New Development Pattern of 'Dual Circulation'" ["科学认识 '双循环' 新发展格局"], Xinhua, November 9, 2020.

Shirk, Susan L., *The Political Logic of Economic Reform*, University of California Press, 1993.

Solís, Mireya, "China Flexes Muscles at APEC with the Revival of FTAAP," East Asian Forum, November 23, 2014.

Spence, Jonathan D., *The Search for Modern China*, W.W. Norton & Company, 1991.

State Council of the People's Republic of China, "Made in China 2025," webpage, undated. As of May 26, 2023:
https://english.www.gov.cn/2016special/madeinchina2025/

State Council Information Office of the People's Republic of China, *China's National Defense in the New Era*, July 24, 2019.

State Council Information Office of the People's Republic of China, "Full Text: A Global Community of Shared Future: China's Proposals and Actions," Ministry of Foreign Affairs of the People's Republic of China, September 26, 2023.

Stoetman, Adája, Minke Meijnders, and Merel Martens, "Economic Security with Chinese Characteristics," *Strategic Monitor 2019–2020: The Writing on the Wall*, Hague Center for Strategic Studies, January 28, 2020.

"Strategic Readjustment and Structural Innovation in China's Foreign Trade Policy in the Post-Crisis Era" ["后危机时代我国对外贸易的战略性天正"], *International Trade* [国际贸易], 2020.

Tang, Frank, "China's Financial Regulator Vows to Cut 'Blind Spots' and 'Build an Iron Wall' as New Body Takes Shape," *South China Morning Post*, May 18, 2023.

Tran, Hung, "Dual Circulation in China: A Progress Report," Atlantic Council, October 4, 2022.

U.S. Energy Information Administration, "China," webpage, last updated August 8, 2022. As of April 20, 2023:
https://www.eia.gov/beta/international/analysis.cfm?iso=CHN

Wang, Heng, "China's Approach to the Belt and Road Initiative: Scope, Character, and Sustainability," *Journal of International Economic Law*, Vol. 22, No. 1, March 2019.

Wan, Wang, "Opportunities and Challenges Facing China's Economic 'External Circulation,'" *China International Strategy Review*, Vol. 4, No. 1, June 2022.

Wang Yi [王毅], "China's Foreign Policy Will Hold Dear the Broad Interests of the People, Protect Offshore Interests" ["中国外交将做广大老百姓的贴心人，做海外同胞利益的守护人"], Ministry of Foreign Affairs of the People's Republic of China, March 7, 2022.

Wang Zhengyi, "Conceptualizing Economic Security and Governance: China Confronts Globalization," *Pacific Review*, Vol. 17, No. 4, 2004.

Wehrlé, Frédéric, and Joachim Pohl, *Investment Policies Related to National Security: A Survey of Country Practices*, OECD Publishing, 2016.

White House, *National Security Strategy of the United States of America*, December 2017.

White House, *National Security Strategy*, October 2022.

Wong, Brian, "How China Must and Can Balance Financial Security and Openness," China-US Focus, June 17, 2022.

Wright, Logan, Agatha Kratz, Charlie Vest, and Matt Mingey, *Retaliation and Resilience: China's Economic Statecraft in a Taiwan Crisis*, Atlantic Council, April 1, 2024.

Wu Baiyi, "The Chinese Security Concept and Its Historical Evolution," *Journal of Contemporary China*, Vol. 10, No. 27, 2001.

Wübbeke, Jost, Mirjam Meissner, Max J. Zenglein, Jaqueline Ives, and Björn Conrad, *Made in China 2025: The Making of a High-Tech Superpower and Consequences for Industrial Countries*, Mercator Institute for China Studies, August 12, 2016.

"Xi Eyes More Enabling Int'l Environment for China's Peaceful Development," Xinhua, November 30, 2014.

Xi Jinping, "New Asian Security Concept for New Progress in Security Cooperation," remarks at the Fourth Summit of the Conference on Interaction and Confidence Building Measures in Asia, Ministry of Foreign Affairs of the People's Republic of China, May 21, 2014.

Xi Jinping, "Working Together to Forge a New Partnership of Win-Win Cooperation and Create a Community of Shared Future for Mankind," Ministry of Foreign Affairs of the People's Republic of China, September 29, 2015.

Xi Jinping, "Several Issues on Adhering to and Developing Socialism with Chinese Characteristics" ["关于坚持和发展中国特色主义的几个问题"], *Seeking Truth* [求是], March 31, 2019.

"Xi Jinping: Adhere to the Overall National Security Concept and Follow the Path of National Security with Chinese Characteristics" ["习近平:坚持总体国家安全观 走中国特色国家安全道路"], Xinhua, April 15, 2014. As of April 18, 2023: http://www.xinhuanet.com//politics/2014-04/15/c_1110253910.htm

"Xi Jinping: Explanation on 'CCP Central Committee Recommendation on Formulating the 14th Five-Year Plan on Developing the National Economy and Society and 2035 Long-Term Goals'" ["习近平: 关于《中共中央关于制定国民经济和社会发展第十四个五年规划和二〇三五年远景目标的建议》的说明"], Xinhua, November 3, 2020.

"Xi Jinping Makes Important Speech at Opening Ceremony of Provincial and Ministerial-Level Major Leading Cadres' Thematic Workshop on Persisting in Bottom-Line Thinking and Concentrating Efforts on Guarding Against, Resolving Major Risks" ["习近平在省部级主要领导干部坚持底线思维着力防范化解重大风险专题研讨班开班式上发表重要讲话"], Xinhua, January 21, 2019.

"Xi Jinping Stresses in 26th Collective Study Session of Central Committee Political Bureau: Adhere to Systemic Thinking, Establish Great Security Pattern to Provide Strong Support for Building Socialist Modern Country" ["习近平在中央政治局第二十六次集体学习时强调 坚持系统思维构建大安全格局 为建设社会主义现代化国家提供坚强保障"], Xinhua, December 12, 2020.

Yang Zekun, "Robust National Security Legal System Urged," *China Daily*, April 16, 2024.

Zha Daojiong, "Chinese Considerations of 'Economic Security,'" *Journal of Chinese Political Science*, Vol. 5, No. 1, March 1999.

Zhao Ying [赵英], *Threats to China's Economy—Considerations of China's Economic Security* [中国经济面临的危险–国家经济安全轮], Yunnan Renmin Publishing, 1994.

Zhao Ying [赵英], "Why Economic Security Is Considered the Foundation of National Security" ["'经济安全' 缘何被视为国家安全基础"], *People's Daily* [人民日报], April 22, 2014. As of April 20, 2023: http://theory.people.com.cn/n/2014/0422/c40531-24927787.html

Zhong Sheng [钟声], "Brandishing Bludgeon of Sanctions Poses Threat to Global Economic Security" ["挥舞制裁大棒威胁全球经济安全"], *People's Daily* [人民日报], October 29, 2020.

CHAPTER 3

A Stocktaking of Economic Measures Targeting China

Alexandra Stark

Overview

Since 2001, particularly following the global financial crisis, the United States has sought to influence the trajectory of China's economic engagement with the world. Although initially focused on cooperative economic measures, the United States has relied increasingly on coercive economic measures. In this chapter, I provide an initial stocktaking of these measures and an overview of the coercive and cooperative economic tools that the United States has employed in its engagement with China. I then survey existing assessments of the direct effects of these measures on China and the secondary and tertiary effects of these measures on the United States and its allies. Case studies on semiconductor export controls and tariffs provide a more detailed diagnostic of two leading types of coercive economic measures.

Since 2001, particularly following the global financial crisis of 2008–2009, the United States has sought to influence the trajectory of China's economic engagement with the world. Although initially focused on cooperative economic measures, including support for China's entry into the World Trade Organization (WTO), the United States has relied increasingly on coercive economic measures. In this chapter, I aim to take stock of these measures. First, I summarize the types of coercive measures that the United States has taken and how that approach has evolved over time. I also embark on a preliminary analysis of how effective these coercive measures have been, assessing their secondary and tertiary effects on the U.S. domestic economy and on U.S. allies and partners. This framing can help policymakers understand both the potential costs and benefits of such measures and identify whether these measures have been successful in achieving their strategic aims.

In the first section, I provide an overview of findings from the stocktaking exercise. The full timeline of measures, along with their strategic and tactical objectives, relevant legislation, and implementing agencies can be found in the "Supplementary Material" section at the end of this chapter.

The second section includes two case studies, one on the restrictions on semiconductor exports enacted in October 2022 and a second on the U.S. trade tariffs enacted between 2018 and 2020. These two case studies build a framework for identifying the effects of economic measures in terms of both their original objectives and their broader, possibly unanticipated, effects.

Overview of U.S. Economic Measures

U.S. economic engagement with China has evolved significantly since 2000. Initially, the United States supported China's growing involvement in the global economy, believing that, through economic engagement, China could become a "responsible stakeholder" in the international system, whereas coercive measures were likely to damage the U.S. economy as well as China's and antagonize U.S. allies and partners.[1] The U.S.-China Relations Act of 2000 normalized trade relations with China,[2] opening the way for China to become a member

1 Robert Zoellick, "Whither China: From Membership to Responsibility?" remarks to National Committee on U.S.-China Relations, September 21, 2005.

2 Public Law 106-286, Normal Trade Relations for the People's Republic of China, October 10, 2000.

of the WTO in 2001. U.S. Treasury Secretary Henry Paulson described the George W. Bush administration's approach to China as "robust engagement," meaning "intensive dialogue but with resort to WTO dispute settlement and WTO-sanctioned trade remedies if needed," an approach that the Bush administration regarded as "more productive than protectionist policies or legislation."[3]

The Obama administration came into office intending to continue the policy of engagement, upgrading the Bush-era China-U.S. Strategic Economic Dialogue (SED) to the Secretary of State level and expanding its scope to include climate and clean energy priorities.[4] But tensions in the relationship had been developing. Even before the peak of the 2007–2008 global financial crisis, the U.S. Commerce Department had imposed tariffs on Chinese goods, including paper and steel, and the U.S. Congress expressed a keen interest in passing legislation to punish China for currency manipulation.[5] And as China began adopting a more assertive international approach, the United States began to take measures to respond to and constrain Chinese economic influence in the Pacific region. The United States joined negotiations to enter a Pacific free trade agreement known as the Trans-Pacific Partnership in 2008, and the Obama administration's "pivot to Asia," rolled out in 2011, emphasized the need to build a regional counterbalance to China.[6] Cooperation continued alongside these efforts, including through the 2014 Joint Announcement on Climate Change and the Strategic and Economic Dialogue.[7]

At the same time, concern grew among U.S. policymakers about China's manipulation of its currency and Chinese industrial espionage and cyber theft. As the global financial crisis led to an acceleration of the state-led economic growth model in China and raised fears in the United States about China's comparative rate of economic growth, patience about the pace of China's economic and currency liberalization efforts wore thin.[8] In 2018, amid concerns that the United States was falling behind economically, the U.S. Trade Representative released a report outlining U.S. policymakers' concerns that China's state-led economic policies entailed attracting foreign firms to China, stealing their intellectual property, and build-

---

[3] Henry M. Paulson, Jr., *In Advance of the Fourth Cabinet-Level Meeting of the U.S.-China Strategic Economic Dialogue*, transcript of interview with Jessica T. Mathews at the Carnegie Endowment for International Peace, June 10, 2008a.

[4] Dennis Wilder, "The U.S.-China Strategic and Economic Dialogue: Continuity and Change in Obama's China Policy," Brookings Institution, May 15, 2009. The SED was merged with another stream of effort and became the Strategic and Economic Dialogue (S&ED) in April 2009.

[5] Steven R. Weisman, "Paulson's Path to China: Progress, but Miles to Go," *New York Times*, June 11, 2008.

[6] Office of the United States Trade Representative, "Trans-Pacific Partners and United States Launch FTA Negotiations," press release, September 22, 2008. Hillary Clinton, "America's Pacific Century," *Foreign Policy*, October 11, 2011.

[7] White House, "U.S.-China Joint Announcement on Climate Change," press release, November 11, 2014.

[8] See Chapter 9. See also David Dollar, "U.S.-China Trade War Has Its Seeds in the Financial Crisis," Brookings Institution, September 14, 2018.

ing their products in China.[9] With this understanding, the Trump administration took a more coercive approach, aiming to "compel Beijing to cease or reduce actions harmful to the United States' vital, national interests and those of our allies and partners."[10]

The approach of the Biden administration remains focused on the use of coercive measures; the emphasis is on stymying Chinese technological advancements in domains that could erode the United States' military advantage, and cooperative measures appear to be stalled. In late 2022, U.S. policymakers announced a shift in the U.S. approach to global technology competition. In the post–Cold War period, the United States had pursued a *sliding scale* approach, using licensing restrictions to ensure that the United States remained several generations ahead of China and other competitors.[11] However, in the fall of 2022, National Security Advisor Jake Sullivan laid out a new approach, one that called for more-extensive coercive economic measures to not just stay ahead of China but to actively slow or degrade the development of China's technological capabilities.[12] Export controls and investment restrictions are a central component of the new approach.

Competitive industrial policy has also come to the fore: In 2022, the U.S. Congress passed the CHIPS [Creating Helpful Incentives to Produce Semiconductors] and Science Act to support domestic research and manufacturing of advanced semiconductors in the United States and the Inflation Reduction Act, which includes provisions to invest in the domestic clean energy sector.[13] Although these measures also have domestic political and other components, they are seen as a means of leveling the playing field against China's substantial subsidies and investments in its own semiconductor and clean energy industries.

The variety of coercive measures that the United States is employing is summarized in Table 3.1. In addition to an increasing reliance on coercive measures, decisionmakers have extended the set of economic measures that the United States employs. In past decades, the United States tended to rely primarily on financial sanctions as its main tool of economic coercion,[14] but policymakers are increasingly experimenting with a wider array of coercive

[9] Agathe Demarais, "How the U.S.-Chinese Technology War Is Changing the World," *Foreign Policy*, November 19, 2022.

[10] White House, *United States Strategic Approach to the People's Republic of China*, May 26, 2020 (p. 1). The Trump administration also highlighted great-power competition as a priority in its National Security Strategy and National Defense Strategy (White House, *National Security Strategy of the United States of America*, December 2017; U.S. Department of Defense, *Summary of the 2018 National Defense Strategy of the United States of America: Sharpening the American Military's Competitive Edge*, 2018).

[11] Chris Miller, *Chip War: The Fight for the World's Most Critical Technology*, Scribner, 2022, p. 201.

[12] Jake Sullivan, "Remarks by National Security Advisor Jake Sullivan on the Biden-Harris Administration's National Security Strategy," White House, October 12, 2022.

[13] Public Law 117-167, CHIPS and Science Act, August 9, 2022; Public Law 117-169, Inflation Reduction Act of 2022, August 16, 2022.

[14] In this chapter, *sanctions* refers specifically to financial sanctions against Chinese individuals or companies.

TABLE 3.1
Types of Coercive Economic Measures

Measure	Objective	Examples
Export restrictions	• Prevent China from importing high-end, U.S.-manufactured technologies and other goods that could have dual-use applications	• Semiconductor export controls • Export licensing requirements • Adding specific Chinese companies to the Department of Commerce's Entity List
Import restrictions	• Ban U.S. government agencies from importing communications equipment from Chinese firms • Ban imports of goods made by forced labor	• Federal Communications Commission ban on communications equipment • The Uyghur Force Labor Prevention Act (UFLPA)
Trade	• Reduce the U.S. trade deficit • Limit offshoring	• Tariffs on steel and aluminum, solar panels and washing machines
Sanctions	• Prevent human rights abuses • Prevent assistance to Russia's military	• Sanctions on Chinese space technology companies for providing assistance to Russia • Sanctions on Chinese Communist Party officials under the UFLPA
Investment restrictions	• Prevent U.S. investment in Chinese firms or Chinese investment in U.S. firms that poses a national security risk	• Expanded jurisdiction for the Committee on Foreign Investment in the United States Ban on U.S. investment in Communist Chinese military companies
Countermeasures to currency manipulation	• Mitigate unfair trade advantages that China gains through currency manipulation	• Treasury Department currency manipulation designation • Treat currency undervaluation as a subsidy for trade purposes
Law enforcement	• Prevent intellectual property theft • Prevent sanctions evasion	• Justice Department's China Initiative • Huawei indictments
Visa restrictions	• Prevent intellectual property theft • Prevent Chinese military-civil fusion firms from benefiting from U.S. research and education	• Ban on visa for PLA-linked Chinese researchers and graduate students

SOURCES: Author's compilation of information from various sources. See Table 3.3 for specific details.

tools, including tariffs, export controls aimed at specific companies (e.g., Huawei[15]) and products (e.g., semiconductors), and law enforcement measures to prevent the transfer of intellectual property.[16]

[15] Huawei is a technology firm based in Shenzhen, China. It was founded in 1987 by former People's Liberation Army Deputy Regimental Head Ren Zhengfei, and the company designs and produces semiconductors, telecommunications equipment, smart electronic devices, consumer electronics, and other high-end products.

[16] Elizabeth Rosenberg, Peter E. Harrell, and Ashley Feng, *A New Arsenal for Competition: Coercive Economic Measures in the U.S.-China Relationship*, Center for a New American Security, April 2020.

Table 3.2 summarizes the high-level cooperative efforts that the United States has undertaken with China during this same period. These efforts have been far more limited than the coercive measures, especially since 2017, and have been more diffuse in their goals.

Measuring the Effects of U.S. Economic Measures

How should we measure the effects of these economic measures, in terms of both their immediate stated objectives and their potential secondary and tertiary effects? At first glance, many of the economic measures considered here appear to have achieved only limited success in meeting their stated objectives. Some of the coercive measures eventually yielded a negotiated agreement with China, for example, but these agreements are limited in their effects: The tariffs imposed in 2018 and 2019 eventually led to the limited and partially implemented Phase One agreement.[17] At the same time, there is little evidence that most coercive measures have achieved their strategic aims. For many measures, such as the October 2022 semiconductor export controls, it is too early to measure their full effect, although we can estimate what some of the consequences might be.

On the cooperative side, the SED and other such measures are more diffuse in their aims and have outcomes that are more difficult to measure. Although these cooperative measures have not transformed the U.S.-China relationship and tend to be more successful in achieving more-circumscribed goals, they may also have positive externalities and few costs.

At the same time, there is evidence that coercive economic measures have significant secondary and tertiary consequences for the U.S. economy and for allies and partners. The tar-

TABLE 3.2
Types of Cooperative Economic Measures

Measure	Objective	Examples
Normalization of trade relations	Facilitate China's WTO membership	• U.S.-China Relations Act of 2000
Strategic dialogue	Build high-level discussions and "habits of cooperation"	• SED (later S&ED) • U.S.-China Joint Commission on Commerce and Trade
Climate and energy collaboration	Mitigate climate change by cooperating on emissions reductions and clean energy	• U.S.-China Joint Glasgow Declaration on Enhancing Climate Action in the 2020s (2021) • U.S.-China Joint Announcement on Climate Change (2014)
Trade agreement	End disruptive spirals of retaliation	• Phase One agreement on tariffs and trade

SOURCES: Author's compilation of information from various sources. See Table 3.3 for specific details.

[17] Economic and Trade Agreement Between the Government of the United States of America and the Government of the People's Republic of China, January 15, 2020.

iffs damaged both the U.S. and Chinese economies, and a meta-analysis of the effects of these tariffs found that "US consumers of imported goods have borne the brunt of the tariffs through higher prices."[18] The long-term effects of these measures are also unclear: Export controls on semiconductors led to a significant decline in China's imports of these products (and to a large drop in Huawei's annual revenue, for example), but their effectiveness over the long run depends on China's ability to boost its own industrial capacity for research and manufacturing enough to make up the difference. And although some allies and partners are moving closer to the U.S. position on strategic competition with China, many of these measures will still have significant political and economic effects for them: The semiconductor export controls will likely have significant effects on the revenue of firms in Japan, South Korea, Taiwan, and the Netherlands (the countries that are the main producers of semiconductors or semiconductor manufacturing equipment in addition to the United States and China). These measures could also affect nonaligned countries where the United States and China are competing for influence. Although the United States and many key partners have implemented bans on Huawei equipment in their own fifth-generation (5G) telecommunications networks, Huawei has built about 70 percent of Africa's fourth-generation (4G) networks and has an agreement to build 5G networks in South Africa.[19] Globally, Huawei claims to have signed more than 1,000 5G contracts, claiming 30 percent of the total market share.[20]

The effects of these measures on U.S. national security are also more difficult to parse. Coercive economic measures are often justified on narrow and poorly defined national security terms, which makes it more difficult to account for their effects on U.S. national security. On tariffs, for example, the Trump administration's invocation of national security provisions contained in Section 232 of the Trade Expansion Act of 1962 suggested that relying on foreign production of steel and aluminum would leave the United States vulnerable to supply disruptions in the event of a national emergency, but it is not clear that domestic production of aluminum and steel would have a substantial effect on U.S. national security in a modern context.

The following case studies assess two approaches that the United States has taken to coercive economic measures against China. The tariffs imposed by the Trump administration in 2018 and 2019 represented a major shift in the U.S. approach toward more overtly coercive measures. But these measures were also broad and aimed at decreasing interdependence by decreasing imports from and the bilateral trade deficit with China. The semiconductor export controls that were announced in October 2022 are the vanguard of the Biden administration's new targeted approach toward limiting China's indigenous technological capabilities.

---

[18] Pablo D. Fajgelbaum and Amit K. Khandelwal, "The Economic Impacts of the US–China Trade War," *Annual Review of Economics*, Vol. 14, 2022.

[19] Amy Mackinnon, "For Africa, Chinese-Built Internet Is Better Than No Internet at All," *Foreign Policy*, March 19, 2019.

[20] Nicole Sadek, "In Global 5G Race, Telecom Giants Resort to Bribery and Other Alleged Abuses," International Consortium of Investigative Journalists, February 26, 2022.

For each case, I assess the publicly available data on the effects on (1) China's economy, (2) the United States' economy, (3) U.S. allies and partners and their bilateral relationships with the United States, and (4) U.S. national security.

Case Study: Advanced Semiconductor Export Controls, October 2022

On October 7, 2022, the U.S. Department of Commerce's Bureau of Industry and Security (BIS) announced a set of export controls restricting China's ability to import and manufacture advanced computing semiconductor chips. The new rules include

- export restrictions on advanced integrated circuits (or semiconductor chips), products that contain such chips, and certain high-performance computers known as *supercomputers*
- similar restrictions on the tools used to manufacture these chips
- licensing requirements for the transmission of information about these technologies by U.S. persons supporting the production or development of these products
- licensing requirements for sales of these products to 28 entities in China (on the Entity List) that may be using computing facilities to develop products with military applications
- measures to minimize the effects of these restrictions on supply chains in the short term.[21]

Semiconductors, or integrated circuits, are computer chips that can process or store information and are integral components in a wide array of electronic devices. BIS says that these advanced semiconductor chips and related products are used by China to improve military decisionmaking and planning, in autonomous military systems, and to improve weapon design and testing, among other military applications.[22] Earlier export restrictions aimed at semiconductors were designed to keep Huawei from accessing inputs for its 5G base stations (although Huawei was able to purchase semiconductors manufactured in other countries).[23]

[21] These measures include a temporary license that allows for export of the controlled items through April 7, 2023, and a clause grandfathering in products that were already in transit when the regulations were imposed. For the full rule, see BIS, "Implementation of Additional Export Controls: Certain Advanced Computing and Semiconductor Manufacturing Items; Supercomputer and Semiconductor End Use; Entity List Modification," *Federal Register*, Vol. 87, No. 197, October 13, 2022b.

[22] BIS, 2022b.

[23] Chad P. Bown, "How the United States Marched the Semiconductor Industry into Its Trade War with China," *East Asian Economic Review*, Vol. 24, No. 4, 2020.

U.S. officials have also worked with Dutch and Japanese officials to impose similar export restrictions. In March 2023, the Netherlands announced that it would introduce its own restrictions before the summer.[24] Japan is still considering whether to implement its own controls.[25]

Impact on China

According to the Department of Commerce, the aim of these new rules was to restrict China's "ability to both purchase and manufacture certain high-end chips used in military applications."[26] China's semiconductor industry had already experienced significant repercussions from U.S. economic measures even before October 2022. Prior to October 2022, the United States had implemented other restrictions designed to limit China's sale and access to semiconductors, including imposing tariffs on exports of semiconductors from China in 2018, adding the Chinese company Huawei and non-U.S. Huawei affiliates to the Entity List in 2019, and limiting Huawei's access to chips manufactured abroad through the Foreign Direct Product Rule in 2020.[27] As of August 2022, Huawei had the fourth-largest market share of mobile phone vendors worldwide.[28] Huawei's self-reported annual revenue declined by 30 percent in 2021, and annual revenue remained flat from 2021 to 2022 (Figure 3.1). Huawei itself reported that it had entered a "crisis mode" because of the restrictions imposed by the United States but that it was "back to business as usual" by late 2022.[29] The company also began taking steps to build out new business lines to counter the negative effects of U.S. measures on its revenue.

In addition to these various restrictions on Huawei, the United States has blocked other Chinese firms with alleged government ties from acquiring U.S. semiconductor companies. In September 2015, for example, the interagency Committee on Foreign Investment in the

---

[24] Toby Sterling, Karen Freifeld, and Alexandra Alper, "Dutch to Restrict Semiconductor Tech Exports to China, Joining US Effort," Reuters, March 8, 2023.

[25] Dashveenjit Kaur, "Japan Remains in a State of Limbo After the Dutch Join the US in Restricting Chip Exports to China," Techwire Asia, March 7, 2023.

[26] BIS, "Commerce Implements New Export Control on Advanced Computing and Semiconductor Manufacturing Items to the People's Republic of China (PRC)," press release, U.S. Department of Commerce, October 7, 2022a.

[27] BIS, "Addition of Entities to the Entity List," *Federal Register*, Vol. 84, No. 98, May 21, 2019; BIS, "Addition of Huawei Non-U.S. Affiliates to the Entity List, the Removal of Temporary General License, and Amendments to General Prohibition Three (Foreign-Produced Direct Product Rule)," *Federal Register*, Vol. 85, No. 162, August 20, 2020; Bown, 2020.

[28] Statcounter Global Stats, "Mobile Vendor Market Share North America, 2017–2022," webpage, 2022.

[29] Zen Soo, "Huawei Says It's Out of 'Crisis Mode,' Though Revenue Flat," Associated Press, December 30, 2022.

FIGURE 3.1
Huawei Annual Revenue, 2017–2022

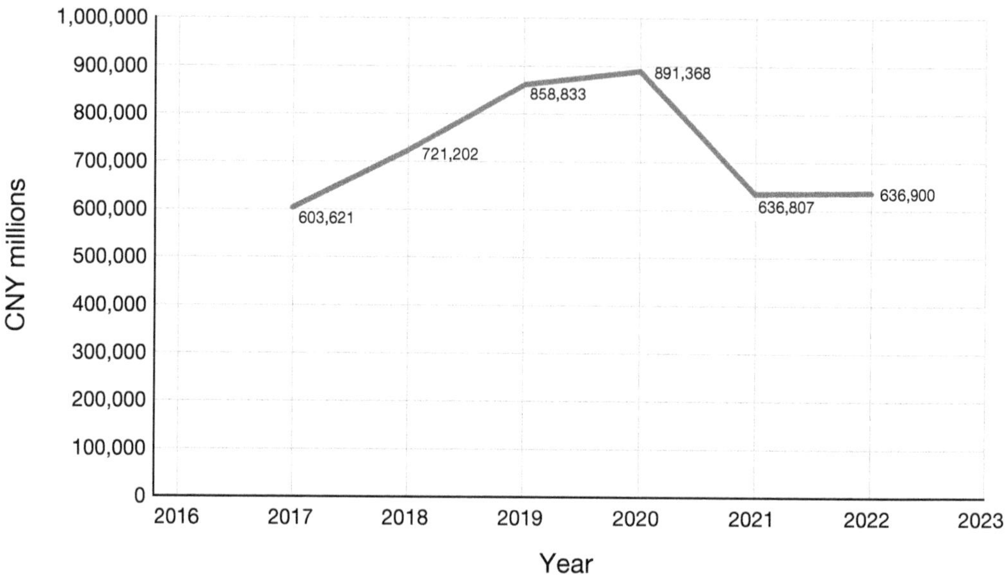

SOURCES: Features information from Huawei Investment and Holding Co., Ltd., *2021 Annual Report*, 2022, p. 9; and Soo, 2022.
NOTE: CNY = Chinese yuan renminbi.

United States initiated an investigation into an offer by Tsinghua Unigroup to buy a stake in Western Digital Corp, effectively killing the deal.[30]

Even so, the newly introduced export restrictions on semiconductors to China appear to have had measurable economic effects in the months since they were introduced. Key firms have already begun to comply with the new rules.[31] China's self-reported imports of integrated circuits declined by 15 percent in 2022 compared with the previous year, the first annual decline since at least 2004.[32] (By contrast, overall imports grew by 17 percent in 2021 and 22 percent in 2020 [Figure 3.2]). On a monthly basis, China's imports of chips declined from $42.1 billion in September 2022 to $33 billion in November 2022.[33]

30 "CFIUS Filing Withdrawn; Deal Abandoned: Unisplendour Corp. and Western Digital Corp.," *The Trade Practitioner* blog, February 24, 2016.

31 Vishnu Kannan and Mubashar Rizvi, "What's in the Commerce Department's Recent Export Controls on Technology Bound for China?" *Lawfare*, November 23, 2022.

32 "China's Imports of ICs Fell in 2022 for First Time Since 2004," Bloomberg, January 14, 2023.

33 Ailing Tan and James Mayger, "China's Imports of Chip-Making Gear Drop to Lowest Since Mid-2020," Bloomberg, December 21, 2022.

FIGURE 3.2
China's Imports of Semiconductors, 2019–2022

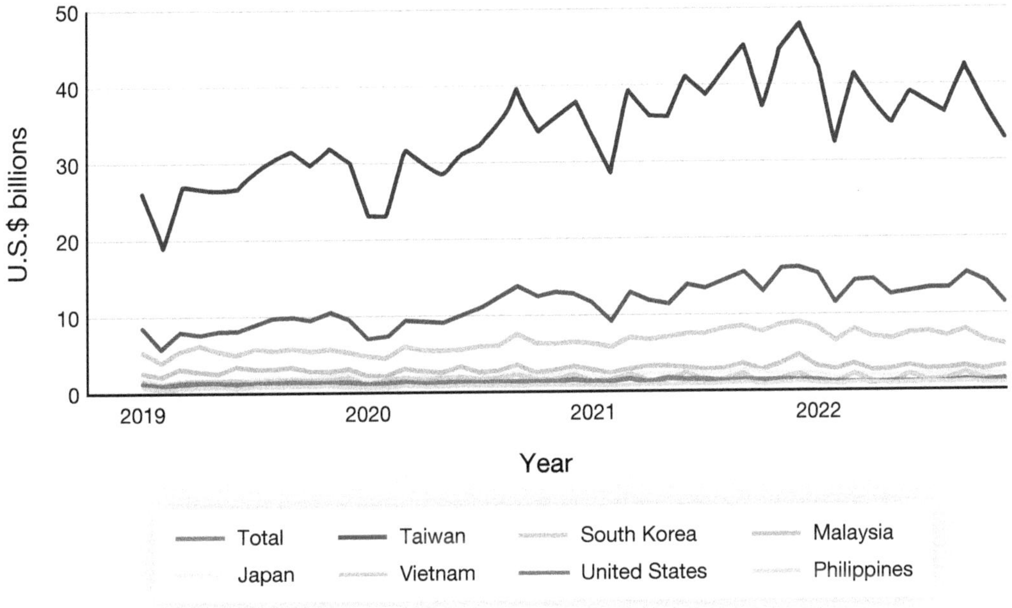

SOURCE: Adapted from Tan and Mayger, 2022, featuring data from China's General Administration of Customs.
NOTE: Data show direct Chinese imports of items under Harmonized System (HS) codes 8541 and 8542.

China's imports of chip-making machines also declined, from about $3.5 billion in September 2022 to $2.3 billion in November 2022 (Figure 3.3).[34]

The export restrictions are targeted at chokepoints in the semiconductor supply chain. Semiconductor supply chains are highly globalized, and several sectors in this supply chain are limited to a small number of producers because of high production costs for some key products and the specialized knowledge and skills needed to produce them (Figure 3.4). For example, companies in the Netherlands and Japan are exclusive providers of certain pieces of equipment required to mass produce high-performing semiconductors. Photolithography tools, the most complex of the semiconductor manufacturing equipment required to make these chips, are highly consolidated: Just one company (ASML, a Dutch company) produces all extreme ultraviolet photolithography tools. Additionally, Chinese companies use parts made by companies based in the United States or in countries allied to the United States. For example, an April 2022 teardown of the Honor X30 Android smartphone found that parts made by U.S. companies comprised 40 percent of the phone's manufacturing cost and

[34] Tan and Mayger, 2022.

FIGURE 3.3
China's Imports of Semiconductor Manufacturing Equipment, 2019–2022

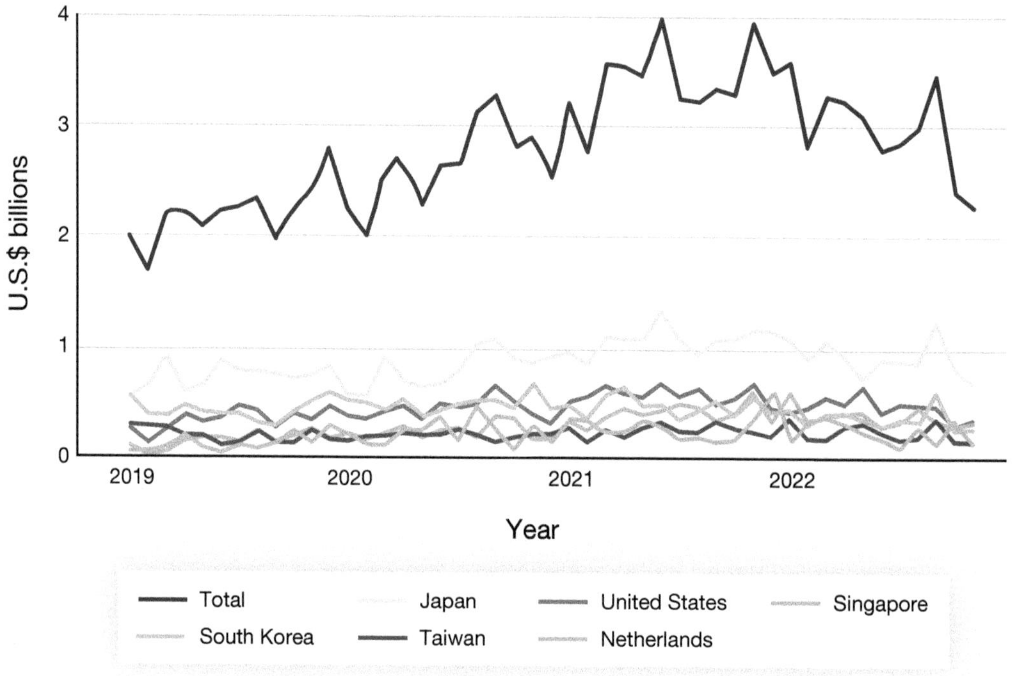

SOURCE: Adapted from Tan and Mayger, 2022, featuring data from China's General Administration of Customs.
NOTE: Data show direct Chinese imports of items under HS code 8486.

that the product included parts made by Qualcomm, Micron, and Qorvo.[35] The specialized nature of the semiconductor supply chain makes it a particularly effective target for export controls.[36]

The concentration of production at different parts of the semiconductor supply chain also means that it will be quite difficult for China to fill the semiconductor gap through domestic production, at least in the short term. Chinese firms lag significantly behind the global leading edge in semiconductor manufacturing equipment. A 2021 study found that the United States, the Netherlands, and Japan collectively held 80 percent to 95 percent of industry share in every subsector of the semiconductor manufacturing equipment industry, whereas China held just 2 percent.[37] In photolithography, the sector in which China lags the furthest behind,

[35] Norio Matsumoto, "Teardown of China Budget Smartphone Honor Reveals Rise in U.S. Parts," Nikkei Asia, April 25, 2022.

[36] Saif M. Khan, *Maintaining the AI Chip Competitive Advantage of the United States and Its Allies*, Center for Security and Emerging Technology, December 2019.

[37] William Hunt, Saif M. Khan, and Dahlia Peterson, *China's Progress in Semiconductor Manufacturing Equipment: Accelerants and Policy Implications*, Center for Security and Emerging Technology, March 2021,

FIGURE 3.4
Market Share by Country in Each Phase of Semiconductor Production

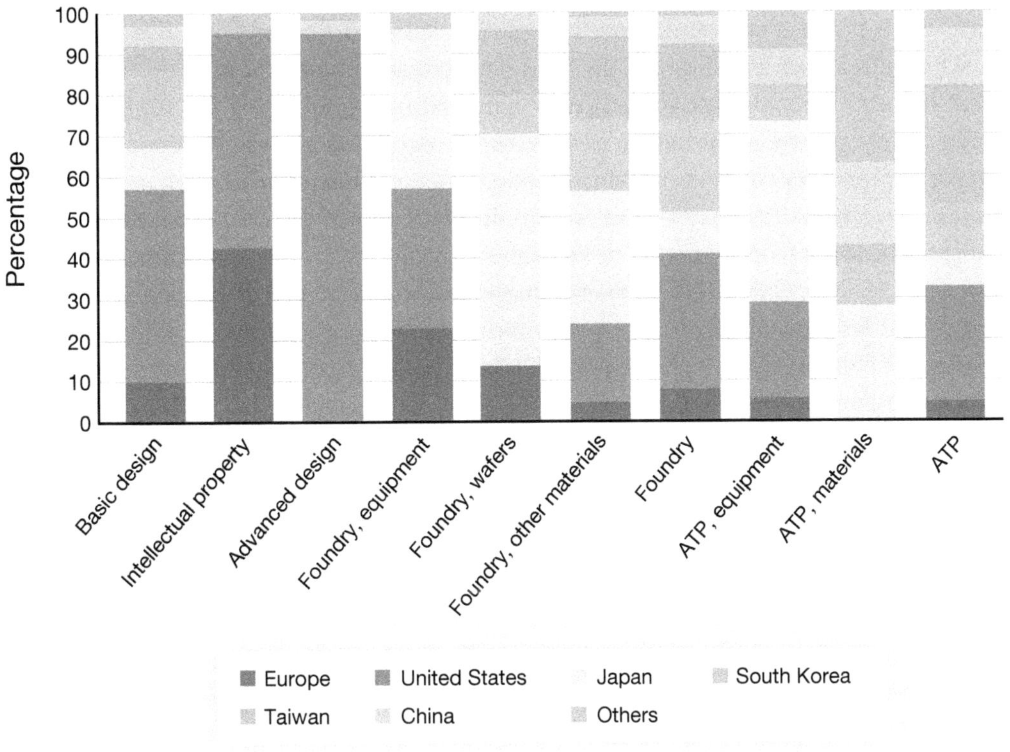

SOURCE: Adapted from Enrique Feás, *The US-China Technology War and Its Effect on Europe*, Real Instituto Elcano, February 28, 2023.
NOTE: ATP = assembly, testing, and packaging.

a 2019 study estimated that it would take China at least one decade to build up a domestic photolithography industry.[38] The export restrictions are regarded by analysts as aggressive and are designed specifically to impede attempts by China to innovate around them.[39]

Measuring the precise effects of these measures on China's economy is difficult. One simulation model found that export restrictions were associated with a decline in China's GDP and welfare but that China's semiconductor industry could ultimately be strengthened.[40]

p. 11.

[38] Khan, 2019, p. 4.

[39] Reva Goujon, Lauren Dudley, Jan-Peter Kleinhans, and Agatha Kratz, "Freeze-in-Place: The Impact of US Tech Controls on China," Rhodium Group, October 21, 2022.

[40] Michael Funke and Adrian Wende, "Modeling Semiconductor Export Restrictions and the US-China Trade Conflict," Bank of Finland Institute for Emerging Economies, BOFIT Discussion Papers 13, November 23, 2022.

In the short term, there is therefore likely little that China can do to circumvent these restrictions. China could take retaliatory measures, such as restricting exports of critical minerals or harassing foreign firms, but these types of measures would not directly address their supply problem and would likely be regarded as escalatory.

China already invests substantially in its domestic semiconductor manufacturing equipment industry through state-owned enterprises and funds, including the largest fund, the National Integrated Circuit Industry Investment Fund (known as the Big Fund), which has invested at least $950 million in China's semiconductor manufacturing equipment industry. China's investment in efforts to develop an indigenous semiconductor industry were already "unprecedented in scope and scale" even before the export restrictions were announced.[41] As part of its Made in China 2025 industrial strategy, China set a goal of meeting 80 percent of its demand for semiconductors through domestic production by 2030.[42] This goal is one of President Xi Jinping's policy priorities and has been backed accordingly by state investment.[43] China is falling well short of this target. In 2021, estimates suggested that China had reached only a self-sufficiency rate in semiconductors of 16 percent despite the massive government investment.[44] This is, in part, because the state-owned funds that have made these investments "tend to be wasteful and risk-averse," and it is not clear that China's semiconductor manufacturing equipment firms are capable of absorbing this funding.[45] These obstacles (and others) mean that even increased state investment in China's semiconductor manufacturing equipment industry may not close the gap.

Over the long term, however, the effectiveness of these restrictions is likely to decline as China gains the capacity to manufacture the relevant tools and products domestically. The restrictions are likely to reinforce Chinese policies to invest in the domestic semiconductor manufacturing equipment industry until domestic firms are potentially able to fill the gap.

Moreover, imposing these restrictions now will have trade-offs for future U.S. policy because, in the future, there will be less leverage in the form of China's dependence on U.S. firms.

Impact on U.S. Domestic Economy

The export restrictions may have substantial effects on U.S. chipmaking firms, but so far, the evidence is mixed. Before the more extensive export controls were announced, a study commissioned by the Semiconductor Industry Association projected that the pre-2022 Entity List restrictions on specific companies would lead to a reduction of 8 percentage points in the

---

[41] Karen M. Sutter, *China's New Semiconductor Policies: Issues for Congress*, Congressional Research Service, R46767, April 20, 2021, p. 3.

[42] Sutter, 2021, pp. 3–4.

[43] "Xi Jinping Picks Top Lieutenant to Lead China's Chip Battle Against U.S.," Bloomberg, June 17, 2021.

[44] Shunsuke Tabeta, "'Made in China' Chip Drive Falls Far Short of 70% Self-Sufficiency," Nikkei Asia, October 13, 2021.

[45] Hunt, 2021, pp. 18–20.

U.S. industry's global market share, amounting to a 16-percent decline in global revenues, or about $36 billion.[46] The association estimated that the ensuing decrease in U.S. research and development would lead to the loss of 40,000 U.S. jobs; notably, however, this model does not account for potential sources of domestic investment, such as the CHIPS and Science Act.[47] The loss of revenue for U.S. firms could hamper domestic innovation because China constitutes a major market, accounting for 32 percent of global semiconductor sales.[48]

However, although U.S. chipmakers argued that the restrictions could harm their bottom line, so far, these firms appear to be making adjustments that have avoided substantial revenue losses. Nvidia, for example, received more than one-fifth of its total revenue from China in 2022 and warned in its 2022 annual report that its "competitive position may be harmed if customers in China do not want to purchase our alternative product offerings. . . . The new requirements may benefit certain of our competitors . . . and encourage customers in China to pursue alternatives to our products."[49] However, Nvidia was able to roll out a modified chip that met the requirements for sale in China, and although its China sales declined, its overall revenue in the compute and networking segment grew by 36 percent.[50]

The restrictions are likely to have longer-term effects on U.S. industry as China moves to source from alternative suppliers, but it is difficult to project these longer-term effects.

Impact on U.S. Relationships with Allies and Partners

The export restrictions have not created a significant rift with U.S. allies and partners, but tensions could emerge depending on the cost-benefit calculations that these allies and partners make about the risks posed by China and the potential costs to their domestic industry. So far, allies and partners have sought exemptions and clarification rather than threatening retaliation.[51] Although the Netherlands and Japan appear to be aligned on this approach for now, their preferences could change over time, especially if the restrictions have a significant economic impact on Dutch and Japanese firms. Other allies will be affected as well; a South Korean firm called the restrictions "painful," for example.[52]

---

[46] Antonio Varas and Raj Varadarajan, *How Restrictions to Trade with China Could End US Leadership in Semiconductors,* Boston Consulting Group, 2020, p. 14.

[47] Varas and Varadarajan, 2020, p. 15.

[48] Virginia Harrison and Martin Farrer, "What Do US Curbs on Selling Microchips to China Mean for the Global Economy?" *The Guardian,* October 18, 2022; Matthew Reynolds, "Assessing the New Semiconductor Export Controls," Center for Strategic and International Studies, November 3, 2022.

[49] Nvidia Corporation, SEC Form 10-K Annual Report for the Fiscal Year Ended January 29, 2023, February 24, 2023, p. 29.

[50] Eliot Chen, "The AI Lockout," *The Wire China,* March 12, 2023.

[51] Alan Beattie, "Biden Goes It Alone in his Trade Assault on China," *Financial Times,* October 20, 2022.

[52] Song Jung-a," SK Hynix Calls US Tech Export Controls to China 'Painful' and Slashes Spending," *Financial Times,* October 26, 2022.

So far, major chipmaking companies' revenues do not appear to have suffered substantially from the restrictions. In the 4th quarter of 2022, the Taiwan Semiconductor Manufacturing Company's (TSMC's) revenue of $19.93 billion surpassed its 2021 revenue of $14.88 billion in the same quarter of 2021.[53] Likewise, the Netherlands' ASML reported in its 2022 annual report that "demand for our systems therefore remains strong. . . . For 2023, ASML expects continued strong growth with a net sales increase of more than 25% and a slight improvement in gross margin, relative to 2022."[54]

U.S. officials tried to get allies on board with implementing similar restrictions prior to its own announcement but were unsuccessful. In addition to negotiations with Japan and the Netherlands, the so-called Chip 4 alliance was created to provide a forum for the United States to coordinate policy decisions with South Korea, Japan, and Taiwan, but this effort has struggled to get off the ground, and the first formal meeting was not held until February 2023.[55] Japan and South Korea have raised concerns about formally coordinating with Taiwan, which China could interpret as a challenge to its One China policy.[56] Additionally, friction between the United States and South Korea over electric vehicle consumer tax credits could complicate coordination efforts.[57] Since its first meeting in February 2023, however, the Chip 4 Alliance has made mixed progress. Japan implemented its own set of chip-related export controls in July 2023, following a similar Dutch ban in June.[58] However, in October 2023, the United States issued waivers to South Korean chipmakers Samsung and SK Hynix, allowing them to ship chip-related equipment to their factories in China indefinitely. As of April 2024, U.S. officials are reportedly still requesting that South Korea adopt its own restrictions.[59]

However, other factors could also potentially disrupt future coordination with allies on semiconductor export controls. Coordination could be disrupted if China decides to retaliate on a bilateral basis against U.S. partners that impose their own bans.[60] Allies and partners could also decide to obey the letter of the law while building around it, learning how to create

---

53 TSMC, "Financial Results—2022Q4," webpage, undated.

54 ASML, "ASML Reports €21.2 Billion Net Sales and €5.6 Billion Net Income in 2022," press release, January 25, 2023.

55 Christian Davies, Song Jung-a, Kana Inagaki, and Richard Waters, "US Struggles to Mobilise Its East Asian 'Chip4' Alliance," *Financial Times*, September 12, 2022; Chang Ai, Novia Huang, and Frances Huang, "Fab 4 Meeting Focuses on Supply Chain Early Warning System: MOEA," Focus Taiwan, February 25, 2023.

56 Davies et al., 2022.

57 Christian Davies and Song Jung-a, "South Korea Complains of Growing Friction with US over High-Tech Trade," *Financial Times*, September 18, 2022.

58 Henry Ridgwell, "Japan Imposes Microchip Export Ban, Angering China," Voice of America, July 28, 2023.

59 Mackenzie Hawkins and Sam Kim, "US Asks South Korea to Toughen Export Curbs on China Chips," Bloomberg, April 2, 2024.

60 Jon Bateman, "Biden Is Now All-In on Taking Out China," *Foreign Policy*, October 12, 2022.

key products without U.S. components that could then be sold to China (assuming that those countries do not enact their own bans).[61]

Ultimately, continued engagement by U.S. allies will play an important role in determining the effectiveness of export restrictions.

Impact on U.S. National Security

The effects of these restrictions on U.S. national security will depend on whether the restrictions are able to prevent China from acquiring advanced semiconductors or building a successful indigenous semiconductor industry (and thereby prevent China from innovating its military capabilities). The effects on national security will also depend on the repercussions that the restrictions have on the U.S. domestic economy and on the U.S. relationship with allies and partners.

Case Study: Tariffs, 2018–2020

In January 2018, the Trump administration imposed tariffs on imports of solar panels and washing machines, adding tariffs on steel and aluminum in March.[62] The tariffs did not discriminate based on origin but were understood to target China (several large economies, including those of Canada and the European Union [EU], were initially exempted). Over several rounds of tit-for-tat retaliation in 2018 and 2019, the Trump administration subsequently added and raised tariffs on goods imported specifically from China. Overall, the United States imposed tariffs on 17.6 percent of 2017 imports throughout 2018 and 2019, corresponding with about 2.6 percent of U.S. GDP.[63] In January 2020, China and the United States signed

---

[61] Eric Levitz, "Biden's New Cold War Against China Could Backfire," *New York Magazine*, November 14, 2022.

[62] David J. Lynch, "Trump Imposes Tariffs on Solar Panels and Washing Machines in First Major Trade Action of 2018," *Washington Post*, January 22, 2018; Scott Horsley, "Trump Formally Orders Tariffs on Steel, Aluminum Imports," NPR, March 8, 2018. The tariff authorities are as follows:

- washing machine and solar cells and modules: Public Law 93-618, Trade Act of 1974; Section 201, Investigation by International Trade Commission, January 3, 1975 (allows the executive to implement tariffs following a U.S. International Trade commission report that the imported goods are causing serious injury to U.S. manufacturers)
- steel and aluminum tariffs: Public Law 87-794, Trade Expansion Act of 1962; Section 232, Safeguarding National Security, October 11, 1962 (allows the executive to implement tariffs following a Commerce Department investigation determining that the imports affect national security)
- China-specific tariffs: Public Law 93-618, Trade Act of 1974; Section 301, Responses to Certain Trade Practices of Foreign Governments, January 3, 1975 (allows USTR to take retaliatory trade action following a USTR investigation into the practices of U.S. trade partners).

[63] Fajgelbaum and Khandelwal, 2022.

the Phase One deal to end the escalatory trade war, but the tariffs remained in place, and the Biden administration chose to keep many of these tariffs in place when it came into office.

Impact on China

The tariffs implemented in 2018 and 2019 that affected China were justified by U.S. officials under both American economic competitiveness terms and national security terms. Announcing the imposition of the China-specific tariffs, U.S. Trade Representative Robert Lighthizer said, "we must take a stand now to uphold fair trade and protect American competitiveness."[64] The Trump administration often framed trade competitiveness in terms of the balance of trade.[65] In this section, I therefore consider the effects of these measures both in terms of the trade deficit and national security.

The tariffs did not remedy the bilateral trade deficit with China. In August 2020, the Department of Commerce reported that the U.S. deficit for trade in goods with China was $83.9 billion, the highest ever recorded, while the overall trade deficit was $67.1 billion.[66] In 2019, a decline in U.S. imports from China was met with a decline in exports to China because of the imposition of retaliatory tariffs (Figure 3.5). However, both exports and imports rose in 2021 and 2022, before imports from China fell 20 percent in 2023. The effects of the tariffs (in addition to other measures, including export controls) varied by product: In 2019, imports of products affected by the tariffs had declined, while imports of products that are unaffected had continued to grow. By four years after the tariffs had been instituted, U.S. imports of certain products—specifically, semiconductors and consumer electronics—had rapidly declined, while imports of such items as furniture, clothing, and footwear also fell. However, imports of other goods, including phones, laptops, and computer monitors, have grown. Although overall imports from the rest of the world have rebounded to pre-pandemic levels, imports from China have not.[67]

Limited data make it difficult to measure the effects of the tariffs on China's economy. The International Monetary Fund projected short-term reductions in China's GDP tied to the tariffs of 0.3 percent to 0.4 percent for 2019 and projected a sustained cost of 0.2 percent of GDP.[68] A 2021 study that used nighttime luminosity to measure changes in GDP found that, although up to 70 percent of China's population was insulated from the effects of the tariffs,

[64] Office of the United States Trade Representative, "USTR Issues Tariffs on Chinese Products in Response to Unfair Trade Practices," press release, June 15, 2018.

[65] Donald J. Trump, "Remarks by President Trump on His Trip to Asia," White House, November 15, 2017.

[66] Doug Palmer, "U.S. Goods Trade Deficit in August Hits Record High," *Politico*, October 6, 2020.

[67] Chad P. Bown, "Four Years into the Trade War, Are the US and China Decoupling?" Peterson Institute for International Economics, October 20, 2022.

[68] Percentages are estimated from the graphs in Scenario Box 1.2 in International Monetary Fund, *World Economic Outlook: Global Manufacturing Downturn, Rising Trade Barriers*, October 2019, pp. 31–33.

FIGURE 3.5
U.S. Imports from and Exports to China Before and After Tariffs

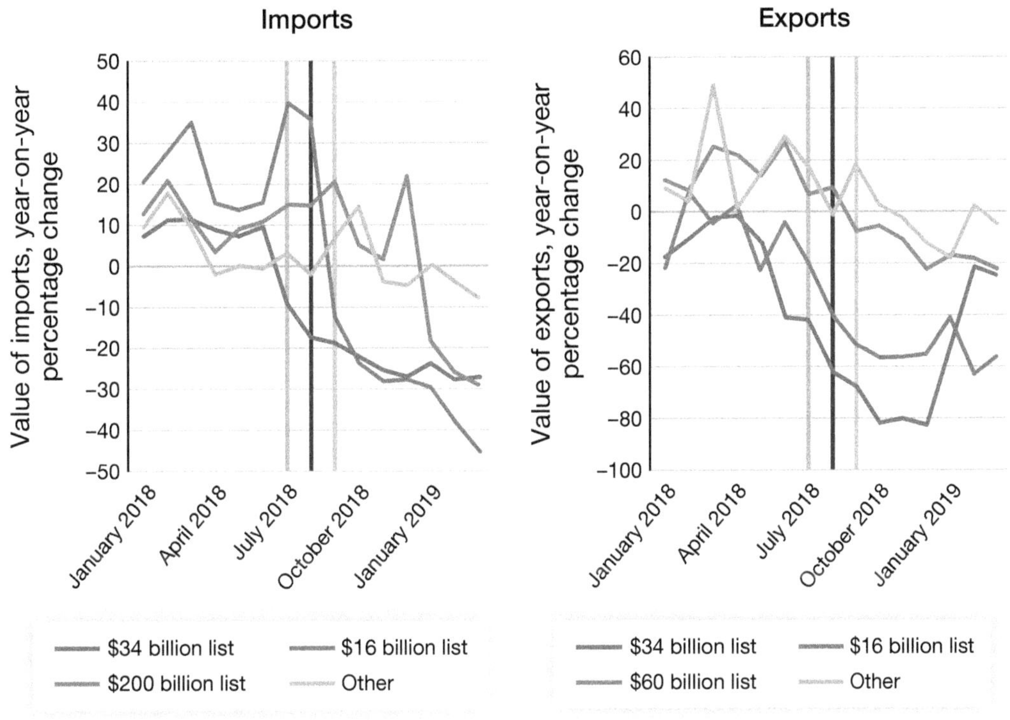

SOURCE: Adapted from Eugenio Cerutti, Gita Gopinath, and Adil Mohammad, "The Impact of US-China Trade Tensions," *IMF Blog*, May 23, 2019, featuring U.S Department of Commerce data and International Monetary Fund staff calculations.

NOTE: Tariff-effective dates for U.S. imports to China are as follows: July 6, 2018, 25 percent on initial $34 billion list; August 23, 2018, 25 percent on $16 billion list; September 24, 2018, 10 percent on $200 billion list, rising to 25 percent on May 10, 2019. Chinese tariff-related dates for U.S. exports to China are as follows: $34 billion list announced on June 16, 2018, effective on July 6, 2018, $16 billion effective on August 23, 2018; and $60 billion effective on September 24, 2018.

the 2.5 percent of the population with greatest exposure experienced a 2.5-percent decrease in income per capita.[69]

Impact on the U.S. Economy

The tariffs may have had narrow benefits in terms of job creation in specific industries, but they had much broader negative effects on U.S. producers and consumers, with most of the cost borne by consumers. The tariffs may have created several thousand new jobs in the industries that were targeted by the tariffs but often at a steep price: A 2020 study found, for example, that the washing machine tariffs may have created about 1,800 domestic jobs at

[69] Davin Chor and Bingjing Li, *Illuminating the Effects of the US-China Tariff War on China's Economy*, National Bureau of Economic Research, Working Paper 29349, October 2021.

the cost of more than $815,000 per job in average annual consumer costs.[70] Estimates from 2019 found that the tariffs imposed costs between about $500 and $1,000 on the average U.S. household.[71] A 2022 meta-analysis found that "US consumers of imported goods have borne the brunt of the tariffs through higher prices," and that tariffs implemented by both the United States and China "lowered aggregate real income" in both countries, "although not by large magnitudes relative to GDP."[72] One model estimated that, by December 2018, early tariffs had cost U.S. consumers and firms $3.2 billion per month in added costs and an additional $1.4 billion in efficiency losses.[73] The combined effects of U.S. and other countries' tariffs raised the price of U.S. manufacturing by an estimated 1 percent.[74] Additionally, the cost of U.S. tariffs was almost completely passed through to domestic prices in 2018.[75] Tariffs may have also contributed to U.S. inflation.[76] Several U.S. business associations, including the Chamber of Commerce and the Information Technology Industry Council, opposed the tariffs.[77] Another model estimated that the trade war caused an overall decline in U.S. well-being of 3.0 percent.[78]

Impact on U.S. Allies and Partners

The steel and aluminum tariffs antagonized key U.S. allies and partners. Although the United States initially granted temporary waivers to Canada, the EU, and Mexico for the steel and aluminum tariffs, it eventually decided not to renew these waivers (South Korea was granted a permanent exemption).[79] Then–President of the European Commission Jean-

[70] Aaron Flaeen, Ali Hortaçsu, and Felix Tintelnot, "The Production Relocation and Price Effects of U.S. Trade Policy: The Case of Washing Machines," *American Economic Review*, Vol. 110, No. 7, July 2020.

[71] Quoctrung Bui and Karl Russell, "How Much Will the Trade War Cost You by the End of the Year?" *New York Times*, September 1, 2019; Taylor Telford, "Trump's Trade War Comes for Consumers: Tariffs Could Cost U.S. Families up to $1,000 a Year, JPMorgan Forecasts," *Washington Post*, August 20, 2019.

[72] Fajgelbaum and Khandelwal, 2022, p. 1.

[73] Mary Amiti, Stephen J. Redding, and David E. Weinstein, "The Impact of the 2018 Tariffs on Prices and Welfare," *Journal of Economic Perspectives*, Vol. 33, No. 4, Fall 2019.

[74] Amiti, Redding, and Weinstein, 2019.

[75] Amiti, Redding, and Weinstein, 2019; Pablo D. Fajgelbaum, Pinelopi K. Goldberg, Patrick J. Kennedy, and Amit K. Khandelwal, "The Return to Protectionism," *Quarterly Journal of Economics*, Vol. 135, No. 1, February 2020.

[76] Weizhen Tan, "Rolling Back U.S.-China Tariffs Would Ease Inflation in the U.S., Former Treasury Secretary Says," CNBC, November 30, 2021.

[77] Eric Martin and Mackenzie Hawkins, "US Firms Renew Plea for Biden to End Trump-Era China Tariffs," Bloomberg, January 19, 2023.

[78] Mary Amiti, Matthieu Gomez, Sang Hoon Kong, and David Weinstein, *Trade Protection, Stock-Market Returns, and Welfare*, National Bureau of Economic Research, Working Paper 28758, revised May 2024.

[79] John Cassidy, "Trump's New Tariffs Are Causing America's Closest Friends to View Him as a Hostile Threat," *New Yorker*, June 1, 2018.

Claude Juncker said that the tariffs were "protectionism, pure and simple," while Canadian Prime Minister Justin Trudeau said it was "insulting and unacceptable" to frame the steel and aluminum tariffs as a national security issue.[80] In response to the 2018 tariffs, several U.S. allies and partners—including the EU, Canada, Turkey, Mexico, India, and South Korea—filed WTO cases against the United States. Several countries also levied their own retaliatory tariffs, including Canada, the EU, Mexico, and Turkey.[81]

The China-specific tariffs also had effects for allies and partners through trade diversion and market segmentation in the cost of traded goods. For example, the $850 million decline in imports from China was almost entirely offset in the United States by a comparable increase in imports from Mexico. Additionally, after China imposed tariffs on soybeans exported to the United States, the price of Brazilian soybeans went up.[82]

Impact on U.S. National Security

The effects of these measures on U.S. national security are more difficult to parse. The Trump administration's invocation of Section 232 of the Trade Expansion Act suggested that relying on foreign production of steel and aluminum would leave the United States vulnerable to supply trade disruptions in the event of a national emergency.[83] Although net import reliance for both steel and aluminum declined slightly following the imposition of the tariffs, both began to climb again after 2020. It is not clear whether these changes are causally linked to the tariffs or to a variety of other factors, including the COVID-19 pandemic. More importantly, it is not clear that increasing U.S. domestic production of steel and aluminum would substantially contribute to national security, even if the tariffs did achieve their stated aims (Figure 3.6).[84]

The effects of tariffs on U.S. national security will also depend on whether they did lasting harm to U.S. relationships with allies and partners and whether they significantly damaged the domestic economy.

---

[80] Cassidy, 2018; Cristiano Limo, "Trudeau: Rationale Behind Trump's Tariffs 'Insulting and Unacceptable' to Canada," *Politico*, June 1, 2018.

[81] Brock R. Williams, Christopher A. Casey, Cathleen D. Cimino-Isaacs, Rachel F. Fefer, Keigh E. Hammond, Vivian C. Jones, Andres B. Schwarzenberg, and Karen M. Sutter, *Trump Administration Tariff Actions: Frequently Asked Questions*, Congressional Research Service, R45529, updated December 15, 2020.

[82] Cerutti, Gopinath, and Mohommad, 2019.

[83] Neil Irwin, "The Real Risks of Trump's Steel and Aluminum Tariffs," *New York Times*, March 1, 2018.

[84] Grady McGregor, "Aluminum Foiled," *The Wire China*, June 4, 2023.

FIGURE 3.6
U.S. Domestic Production of Steel and Aluminum, 2017–2022

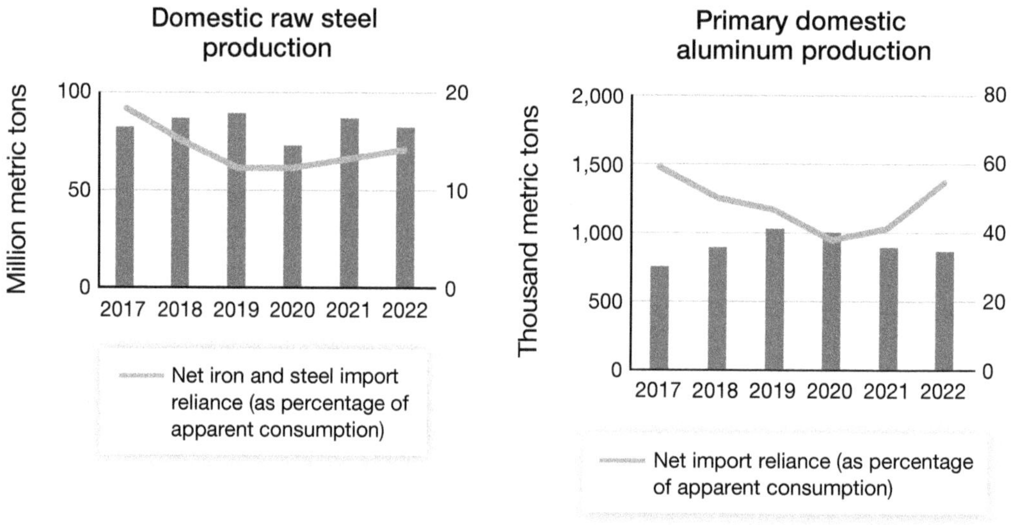

SOURCES: Features information from U.S. Geological Survey, *Mineral Commodity Summaries 2023*, U.S. Department of the Interior, 2023; and U.S. Geological Survey, *Mineral Commodity Summaries 2022*, U.S. Department of the Interior, 2022.

Case Study: Strategic Economic Dialogue

Established in 2006 at the initiative of U.S. Treasury Secretary Henry Paulson, the Strategic Economic Dialogue (SED; renamed the Strategic and Economic Dialogue [S&ED] in 2009) was the most important government-to-government forum for coordinating the U.S.-China economic relationship.[85] The SED was designed to coordinate the bilateral relationship at the highest official level so that issues did not get bogged down in lower-level exchanges and bureaucratic stovepiping.[86] In a broader sense, officials also hoped that the SED would establish "habits of cooperation" that could help steady the relationship "by lessening miscommunication and dispelling misperceptions."[87]

Because both the SED's goals and the means of achieving them were less explicit than some other policy measures, it is difficult to make causal inferences about the SED's efficacy. The SED (and later the S&ED) was associated with some successes, although the successes tended to be either relatively modest in scope or short-lived. The SED and S&ED were also

[85] The S&ED also had an expanded remit that included security and other foreign policy issues in addition to economic issues.

[86] Wayne M. Morrison, *The U.S.-China Strategic and Economic Dialogue (S&ED): Economic Outcomes and Issues,* Congressional Research Service, IF10257, July 14, 2015.

[87] U.S. Department of Treasury, "Remarks by Ambassador Holmer at the Center for Strategic and International Studies on Establishing New Habits of Cooperation in U.S.-China Economic Relations," press release, November 27, 2007.

subject to criticism; several high-level goals failed to be achieved. However, this policy tool had few downsides or costs.

From 2006 through 2008, in the earliest years of the SED, U.S. policymakers pursued the goals of getting China to accelerate the pace of its currency reforms, open and liberalize its domestic markets, improve the business climate for U.S. firms, and address other trade issues, such as intellectual property rights. At the time, China's exchange rate policy was one of the most important issues in the bilateral relationship. When the SED was established, members of Congress were pushing for major tariffs if China did not adjust its pegged exchange rate. Some analysts have argued that the SED and reassurance from Secretary Paulson eased Congress's concerns and avoided a trade war. According to Paulson, "One of the big issues [in 2006] was currency . . . another big issue was the imbalances—China saved so much more than they consumed. We focused on those two [issues] hard and we got results."[88] From September 2006 through January 2009, the renminbi appreciated 13.8 percent against the dollar, and China's current account surplus declined from 10.1 percent of GDP in 2007 to 4.9 percent in 2009.[89] The change in China's exchange rate policy was seen by many as an early achievement of the SED.

SED discussions prior to the 2008 financial crisis were able to achieve agreement on other issues as well, including the Ten-Year Framework for Cooperation on Energy and Environment, a precursor for U.S.-China climate cooperation under the Obama administration. Through the SED, U.S. and Chinese participants also struck agreements on food and product safety inspections and increasing open air travel to and from China. Officials attributed success on these issues to officials' high-level engagement in the SED. For example, the bilateral air-services agreement had stalled out at lower levels before it was concluded at the second SED meeting in May 2007.[90]

The SED was also credited with making the bilateral relationship more constructive in more wide-ranging ways. Bringing multiple high-level cabinet officials into the room together allowed both governments to subvert bureaucracies and speak with one voice to deliver consistent messages.[91] Having an institutionalized forum for bilateral discussion was especially useful when the 2008 financial crisis began; Secretary Paulson credited the SED with helping to steer the U.S.-China relationship through the crisis.[92]

In 2009, newly appointed Secretary of State Hillary Clinton and Secretary of the Treasury Timothy Geithner laid out an agenda for the renamed S&ED that included recovery

---

[88] Paulson Institute, "Paulson on Evolving US-China Relationship," June 29, 2020.

[89] Paulson Institute, 2020.

[90] Henry M. Paulson, Jr., "A Strategic Economic Engagement," *Foreign Affairs*, September/October 2008b.

[91] Taiya M. Smith and Douglas Rediker, "Who Needs a 'G-2'? Here Comes the S&ED," Carnegie Endowment for International Peace, July 26, 2009.

[92] Henry M. Paulson, Jr., "The Benefits of US-China Strategic Economic Dialogue," *Project Syndicate*, December 8, 2007.

from the financial crisis as a top priority.[93] According to a 2021 study that audited the outcomes of the S&ED and their implementation, China and the United States both made and followed through on macroeconomic commitments to stabilize the global economy during this period. China increased its domestic consumption as a share of GDP, and the United States committed to increased savings and temporarily reduced the federal budget deficit.[94] Because these policies had significant domestic benefits, they might have been implemented even without the S&ED. But the existence of the S&ED at least provided a forum to coordinate these policy efforts.

The SED and S&ED have been criticized as a lot of talk accompanied by little action, especially after 2008, when the dialogue yielded fewer tangible achievements to which policymakers could point. Outcome documents tended to rehash what had been agreed at the previous session and were short on specifics about implementation.[95] Political developments periodically halted the dialogue's work. In 2011–2012, the upcoming political transition in Beijing virtually guaranteed that little of substance would be achieved at the intervening meetings.[96] The dialogue was abandoned altogether during the Trump administration. The dialogue was therefore unable to overcome these significant exogenous political obstacles.

The utility of the SED and S&ED rests on several assumptions: (1) that China and the United States have areas of concrete overlap in their economic interests that can be addressed through dialogue; (2) that person-to-person diplomacy and private, high-level conversations among senior leaders who can override their own bureaucracies is a useful model for getting things done; and (3) that habitual cooperation is important for its own sake. For those who agree with these assumptions, the SED and S&ED proved a useful policy tool for maintaining the bilateral economic relationship. For those who do not, the SED and S&ED were little more than window-dressing.

Conclusions

The three case studies presented provide examples of two coercive measures and one cooperative measure. In some ways, all have had the intended effects in the short term. But the coercive measures have come at a cost to the United States, and the longer-term effect of each of these measures appears to be modest, if uncertain.

---

93 Hillary Clinton and Timothy Geithner, "A New Strategic and Economic Dialogue with China," *Wall Street Journal*, July 27, 2009.

94 Tiffany Baron, Rorry Daniels, M. Patrick Hulme, Daniel Jasper, Craig Kafura, and Kacie Miura, *Engagement Revisited: Progress Made and Lessons Learned from the US-China Strategic and Economic Dialogue*, National Committee on American Foreign Policy, September 2021, pp. 55–56.

95 Morrison, 2015.

96 Charles Freeman and Bonnie S. Glaser, "The U.S.-China Strategic and Economic Dialogue," Center for Strategic and International Studies, May 9, 2011.

Export Controls on Semiconductors

After BIS imposed a set of export controls that restricted China's ability to import and manufacture advanced semiconductor chips, China's imports of semiconductors and manufacturing equipment from the United States and its allies declined sharply in 2022. Projections suggest that the restrictions will lead to a decline in the growth rate of China's GDP. China will have difficulty filling the gap in high-end semiconductors through domestic production in the short term. Over the long term, the effectiveness of these restrictions is likely to decline, and they might even strengthen China's semiconductor industry. The restrictions do not appear to have affected the revenues of U.S. firms in the short term, despite the decline in these firms' China exports, because sales to other customers have so far risen. Export restrictions have not created a significant rift with U.S. allies and partners.

Tariffs

Starting in 2018, the United States imposed a series of tariffs on general categories of products and, later, tariffs aimed specifically at China. Modeling suggests that, although up to 70 percent of China's population had negligible exposure to the U.S. tariffs, areas with the largest dependence on exports experienced a decline in output and incomes. By 2023, the tariffs led to an overall decline in U.S. imports from China. In 2019, U.S. exports to China fell because of China's imposition of retaliatory tariffs. However, exports to China rebounded in 2020 and hit an all-time peak in 2022. Independent studies have all found that the costs of the tariffs have been almost entirely borne by U.S. consumers and businesses. Steel and aluminum tariffs annoyed key U.S. allies and partners, leading several to file cases at the WTO.

Strategic Economic Dialogue

The SED is credited with a few early successes, including encouraging China to adjust its exchange rate policy in 2007. It also helped the two countries navigate the aftermath of the 2008 global financial crisis. Proponents argue that the forum established broader "habits of cooperation" in the bilateral relationship. Most of these achievements were either relatively short-lived or small in scope, and the initiative has been criticized as long on talk and short on implementation. However, the SED did achieve some of its economic aims, and appears to have had few unintended downsides or costs to the U.S. economy or the United States' relationships with partners and allies.

Overall Takeaways

The United States has employed a variety of economic measures vis-à-vis China since the U.S.-China Relations Act of 2000.[97] Coercive economic measures have included sanctions,

97 Public Law 106-286, 2000.

tariffs, and law enforcement actions and have been instituted with more frequency since 2018. Case studies of semiconductor export restrictions and tariffs suggest that although such coercive measures can have substantial impact, they can also have negative unintended consequences for the United States' economy and for U.S. allies and partners. In contrast, the effects of cooperative measures (such as the SED) are more diffuse and difficult to measure, but such cooperative measures have been associated with several positive outcomes and have few downsides.

The case studies of export controls and tariffs suggest that it is fairly straightforward to assess the economic effects of coercive measures on the U.S. domestic economy and the global economy, at least in the short term. It is also possible to predict the likely effects of coercive measures on U.S. partners and allies, enabling the United States to determine how best to coordinate with allies and partners in a way that would make these measures more effective and mitigate their costs for the United States, allies, and partners.

There is more to be done to fully assess the strategic impacts of coercive economic measures. These measures are often legally justified in narrow but poorly articulated national security terms. However, the second- and third-order effects of these measures are just as likely to have significant national security impacts as are the measures themselves. It is also more difficult to model the potential long-term effects of coercive measures. For example, whether China is able to build a domestic advanced semiconductor design and manufacturing capacity in the long run is key to the success of semiconductor export control measures. Building a better understanding of how decoupling this supply chain will affect the U.S. economy over time is important.

It is more difficult to assess the causal effects of cooperative measures than of coercive measures, but it is possible to measure their direct effects based on what policymakers say they are intended to do. The SED, for example, is associated with China's more flexible exchange rate policy in 2007, greater bilateral coordination on climate change, and agreements to open air travel to and from China. The SED also failed to accomplish some of its stated goals, such as reaching a bilateral investment treaty agreement. The problem of causal inference with these cooperative measures is that we do not know the counterfactual: For example, were policies adopted by the United States and China to counter the effects of the 2008 financial crisis more successful because of the SED, or would these policies have been implemented even in its absence?

There is more that needs to be known about how cooperative and coercive economic measures interact. For example, are there instances in which implementing coercive measures prevents cooperation on issues that could enhance U.S. national security, such as climate change? Or are there costs to engaging in protracted negotiations as part of cooperative measures and lengthening the timeline before any effects might occur, in contrast to instituting coercive measures that might be more immediately effective?

Supplementary Material

Table 3.3 summarizes major actions taken by either the U.S. Congress, the President, or a Cabinet Secretary to influence U.S.-China economic dynamics.

TABLE 3.3

Timeline of Economic Measures Targeting China

Measure	Date of Implementation	Objective
U.S.-China Trade Relations Act of 2000[a]	2000	Integrate China into the liberal international order
U.S.-China Strategic Economic Dialogue (later Strategic and Economic Dialogue; Comprehensive Economic Dialogue)[b]	2006–2017	Maintain strong and mutually beneficial U.S.-China economic relations
Global financial crisis	2008	–
Copenhagen climate compromise[c]	2009	Enhance global cooperation on climate change through the UNFCC
Cooperation on climate change[d]	2011	Enhance cooperation on climate change, clean energy, and the environment
Secretary Clinton outlines "pivot to Asia"[e]	2011	Increase U.S. engagement in Asia-Pacific region
Joint statement on climate change[f]	2014	Prevent shared challenges to Chinese and U.S. economy from climate change
Trans-Pacific Partnership[g]	2008–2017	Enhance U.S. economic posture vis-à-vis China by enforcing U.S. preferred norms and rules
100-day plan[h]	2017	Mitigate the trade deficit by increasing U.S. exports to China
Foreign Investment Risk Review Modernization Act[i]	2018	Prevent investments in Chinese firms that pose a national security threat
Fiscal Year 2019 National Defense Authorization Act, section 889[j]	2018	Remove and prevent telecommunications equipment made by Chinese firms from being used in U.S. government systems
Tariffs targeting China[k]	2018–2019	Mitigate the trade deficit with China
Justice Department's "China Initiative"[l]	2018–2022	Prevent theft of intellectual property by Chinese firms
Justice Department's Huawei indictment[m]	2019	Punish Huawei and its affiliates for evading U.S. sanctions on Iran
China designated as currency manipulator[n]	2019	Mitigate the trade advantage China gains by manipulating its exchange rate
Phase One trade agreement[o]	2020	U.S.-China trade agreement

Table 3.3—Continued

Measure	Date of Implementation	Objective
Presidential Proclamation 10043[p]	2020	Prevent Chinese students associated with the PLA from accessing U.S. intellectual property
Hong Kong Autonomy Act[q]	2020	Impose sanctions on Hong Kong and Chinese officials
Uyghur Human Rights Policy Act[r]	2020	Impose sanctions on Chinese officials who are abrogating the rights of Uyghurs and other such groups
Holding Foreign Companies Accountable Act[s]	2020	Pressure China to allow the Public Company Accounting Oversight Board (PCAOB) to conduct inspections of Chinese company audits
Executive Order 13959[t]	2020 (expanded 2021)	Bans U.S. investment in "Communist Chinese military companies"
Secretary of State determination that China is committing atrocities in Xinjiang[u]	2021	Pressure China regarding human rights abuses
U.S.-China Joint Glasgow Declaration on Enhancing Climate Action in the 2020s[v]	2021	Advance cooperation on climate change
Secure Equipment Act 2021[w]	2021	Prohibit import of telecoms equipment from Huawei and ZTE
Uyghur Forced Labor Prevention Act[x]	2021	Ban imports of products produced in Xinjiang
CHIPS and Science Act and export restrictions on semiconductors[y]	2022	Support U.S. advanced semiconductor industry and prevent advanced semiconductor exports to China
Inflation Reduction Act[z]	2022	Support U.S. clean energy technology manufacturing

[a] Matt Smith, "Clinton Signs China Trade Bill," CNN, October 10, 2000; Public Law 106-286, 2000.

[b] U.S. Department of Treasury, "U.S.-China Strategic Economic Dialogue (SED)," webpage, last updated March 9, 2009.

[c] United Nations Framework Convention on Climate Change, Copenhagen Accord, December 18, 2009.

[d] White House, "Fact Sheet: U.S.-China Cooperation on Climate Change, Clean Energy, and the Environment," January 19, 2011.

[e] Clinton, 2011.

[f] White House, 2014.

[g] Matthew P. Goodman, "Overcoming the Tragedy of TPP," Center for Strategic and International Studies, September 28, 2021.

[h] Ayesha Rascoe and Michael Martina, "U.S., China Agree to First Trade Steps Under 100-Day Plan," Reuters, May 12, 2017.

[i] U.S. House of Representatives, Foreign Investment Risk Review Modernization Act of 2018, Bill 5841, June 27, 2018.

[j] Public Law 115-232, John S. McCain National Defense Authorization Act for Fiscal Year 2019, August 13, 2018.

[k] Chad P. Bown and Melina Kolb, "Trump's Trade War Timeline: An Up-to-Date Guide," Peterson Institute for International Economics, December 31, 2023.

[l] U.S. Department of Justice, "Information About the Department of Justice's China Initiative and a Compilation of China-Related Prosecutions Since 2018," webpage, last updated November 19, 2021.

Table 3.3—Continued

[m] U.S. Department of Justice, "Chinese Telecommunications Conglomerate Huawei and Huawei CFO Wanzhou Meng Charged with Financial Fraud," press release, January 28, 2019.

[n] U.S. Department of the Treasury, "Treasury Designates China as a Currency Manipulator," press release, August 5, 2019.

[o] Economic and Trade Agreement Between the Government of the United States of America and the Government of the People's Republic of China, 2020.

[p] Proclamation 10043, "Suspension of Entry as Nonimmigrants of Certain Students and Researchers from the People's Republic of China," Executive Office of the President, May 29, 2020.

[q] Public Law 116-49, Hong Kong Autonomy Act, July 14, 2020.

[r] Public Law 116-145, Uyghur Human Rights Policy Act of 2020, June 17, 2020.

[s] Public Law 116-222, Holding Foreign Companies Accountable Act, December 18, 2020.

[t] Executive Order 13959, "Addressing the Threat from Securities Investments That Finance Communist Chinese Military Companies," Executive Office of the President, November 12, 2020.

[u] Michael R. Pompeo, "Determination of the Secretary of State on Atrocities in Xinjiang," U.S. Department of State, January 19, 2021.

[v] U.S. Department of State, "U.S.-China Joint Glasgow Declaration on Enhancing Climate Action in the 2020s," press release, November 10, 2021.

[w] Public Law 117-55, Secure Equipment Act of 2021, November 11, 2021.

[x] Public Law 117-78, Uyghur Forced Labor Prevention Act, December 23, 2021.

[y] Public Law 117-167, 2022.

[z] Public Law 117-169, 2022.

Abbreviations

5G	fifth generation
BIS	Bureau of Industry and Security
CHIPS	Creating Helpful Incentives to Produce Semiconductors
EU	European Union
GDP	gross domestic product
S&ED	Strategic and Economic Dialogue
SED	Strategic Economic Dialogue
WTO	World Trade Organization

References

Ai, Chang, Novia Huang, and Frances Huang, "Fab 4 Meeting Focuses on Supply Chain Early Warning System: MOEA," Focus Taiwan, February 25, 2023.

Amiti, Mary, Matthieu Gomez, Sang Hoon Kong, and David Weinstein, *Trade Protection, Stock-Market Returns, and Welfare*, National Bureau of Economic Research, Working Paper 28758, revised May 2024.

Amiti, Mary, Stephen J. Redding, and David E. Weinstein, "The Impact of the 2018 Tariffs on Prices and Welfare," *Journal of Economic Perspectives*, Vol. 33, No. 4, Fall 2019.

ASML, "ASML Reports €21.2 Billion Net Sales and €5.6 Billion Net Income in 2022," press release, January 25, 2023.

Baron, Tiffany, Rorry Daniels, M. Patrick Hulme, Daniel Jasper, Craig Kafura, and Kacie Miura, *Engagement Revisited: Progress Made and Lessons Learned from the US-China Strategic and Economic Dialogue*, National Committee on American Foreign Policy, September 2021.

Bateman, Jon, "Biden Is Now All-In on Taking Out China," *Foreign Policy*, October 12, 2022.

Beattie, Alan, "Biden Goes It Alone in His Trade Assault on China," *Financial Times*, October 20, 2022.

BIS—*See* Bureau of Industry and Security.

Bown, Chad P., "How the United States Marched the Semiconductor Industry into Its Trade War with China," *East Asian Economic Review*, Vol. 24, No. 4, 2020.

Bown, Chad P., "Four Years into the Trade War, Are the US and China Decoupling?" Peterson Institute for International Economics, October 20, 2022.

Bown, Chad P., and Melina Kolb, "Trump's Trade War Timeline: An Up-to-Date Guide," Peterson Institute for International Economics, December 31, 2023.

Bui, Quoctrung, and Karl Russell, "How Much Will the Trade War Cost You by the End of the Year?" *New York Times*, September 1, 2019.

Bureau of Industry and Security, "Addition of Entities to the Entity List," *Federal Register*, Vol. 84, No. 98, May 21, 2019.

Bureau of Industry and Security, "Addition of Huawei Non-U.S. Affiliates to the Entity List, the Removal of Temporary General License, and Amendments to General Prohibition Three (Foreign-Produced Direct Product Rule)," *Federal Register*, Vol. 85, No. 162, August 20, 2020.

Bureau of Industry and Security, "Commerce Implements New Export Control on Advanced Computing and Semiconductor Manufacturing Items to the People's Republic of China (PRC)," press release, October 7, 2022a.

Bureau of Industry and Security, "Implementation of Additional Export Controls: Certain Advanced Computing and Semiconductor Manufacturing Items; Supercomputer and Semiconductor End Use; Entity List Modification," *Federal Register*, Vol 87, No. 197, October 13, 2022b.

Cassidy, John, "Trump's New Tariffs Are Causing America's Closest Friends to View Him as a Hostile Threat," *New Yorker*, June 1, 2018.

Cerutti, Eugenio, Gita Gopinath, and Adil Mohammad, "The Impact of US-China Trade Tensions," *IMF Blog*, May 23, 2019.

"CFIUS Filing Withdrawn; Deal Abandoned: Unisplendour Corp. and Western Digital Corp.," *The Trade Practitioner* blog, February 24, 2016.

Chen, Eliot, "The AI Lockout," *The Wire China*, March 12, 2023.

"China's Imports of ICs Fell in 2022 for First Time Since 2004," Bloomberg, January 14, 2023.

Chor, Davin, and Bingjing Li, *Illuminating the Effects of the US-China Tariff War on China's Economy*, National Bureau of Economic Research, Working Paper 29349, October 2021.

Clinton, Hillary, "America's Pacific Century," *Foreign Policy*, October 11, 2011.

Clinton, Hillary, and Timothy Geithner, "A New Strategic and Economic Dialogue with China," *Wall Street Journal*, July 27, 2009.

Davies, Christian, and Song Jung-a, "South Korea Complains of Growing Friction with US over High-Tech Trade," *Financial Times*, September 18, 2022.

Davies, Christian, Song Jung-a, Kana Inagaki, and Richard Waters, "US Struggles to Mobilise Its East Asian 'Chip 4' Alliance," *Financial Times*, September 12, 2022.

Demarais, Agathe, "How the U.S.-Chinese Technology War Is Changing the World," *Foreign Policy*, November 19, 2022.

Dollar, David, "U.S.-China Trade War Has Its Seeds in the Financial Crisis," Brookings Institution, September 14, 2018.

Economic and Trade Agreement Between the Government of the United States of America and the Government of the People's Republic of China, January 15, 2020.

Executive Order 13959, "Addressing the Threat from Securities Investments That Finance Communist Chinese Military Companies," Executive Office of the President, November 12, 2020.

Fajgelbaum, Pablo D., Pinelopi K. Goldberg, Patrick J. Kennedy, and Amit K. Khandelwal, "The Return to Protectionism," *Quarterly Journal of Economics*, Vol. 135, No. 1, February 2020.

Fajgelbaum, Pablo D., and Amit K. Khandelwal, "The Economic Impacts of the US–China Trade War," *Annual Review of Economics*, Vol. 14, 2022.

Feás, Enrique, *The US-China Technology War and Its Effect on Europe*, Real Instituto Elcano, February 28, 2023.

Flaaen, Aaron, Ali Hortaçsu, and Felix Tintelnot, "The Production Relocation and Price Effects of U.S. Trade Policy: The Case of Washing Machines," *American Economic Review*, Vol. 110, No. 7, July 2020.

Freeman, Charles, and Bonnie S. Glaser, "The U.S.-China Strategic and Economic Dialogue," Center for Strategic and International Studies, May 9, 2011.

Funke, Michael, and Adrian Wende, "Modeling Semiconductor Export Restrictions and the US-China Trade Conflict," Bank of Finland Institute for Emerging Economies, BOFIT Discussion Papers 13, November 23, 2022.

Goodman, Matthew P., "Overcoming the Tragedy of TPP," Center for Strategic and International Studies, September 28, 2021.

Goujon, Reva, Lauren Dudley, Jan-Peter Kleinhans, and Agatha Kratz, "Freeze-in-Place: The Impact of US Tech Controls on China," Rhodium Group, October 21, 2022.

Harrison, Virginia, and Martin Farrer, "What Do US Curbs on Selling Microchips to China Mean for the Global Economy?" *The Guardian*, October 18, 2022.

Hawkins, Mackenzie, and Sam Kim, "US Asks South Korea to Toughen Export Curbs on China Chips," Bloomberg, April 2, 2024.

Horsley, Scott, "Trump Formally Orders Tariffs on Steel, Aluminum Imports," NPR, March 8, 2018.

Huawei Investment and Holding Co., Ltd., *2021 Annual Report*, 2022.

Hunt, William, Saif M. Khan, and Dahlia Peterson, *China's Progress in Semiconductor Manufacturing Equipment: Accelerants and Policy Implications*, Center for Security and Emerging Technology, March 2021.

International Monetary Fund, *World Economic Outlook: Global Manufacturing Downturn, Rising Trade Barriers*, October 2019.

Irwin, Neil, "The Real Risks of Trump's Steel and Aluminum Tariffs," *New York Times*, March 1, 2018.

Jung-a, Song, "SK Hynix Calls US Tech Export Controls to China 'Painful' and Slashes Spending," *Financial Times*, October 26, 2022.

Kannan, Vishnu, and Mubashar Rizvi, "What's in the Commerce Department's Recent Export Controls on Technology Bound for China?" *Lawfare*, November 23, 2022.

Kaur, Dashveenjit, "Japan Remains in a State of Limbo After the Dutch Join the US in Restricting Chip Exports to China," Techwire Asia, March 7, 2023.

Khan, Saif M., *Maintaining the AI Chip Competitive Advantage of the United States and Its Allies*, Center for Security and Emerging Technology, December 2019.

Levitz, Eric, "Biden's New Cold War Against China Could Backfire," *New York Magazine*, November 14, 2022.

Limo, Cristiano, "Trudeau: Rationale Behind Trump's Tariffs 'Insulting and Unacceptable' to Canada," *Politico*, June 1, 2018.

Lynch, David J., "Trump Imposes Tariffs on Solar Panels and Washing Machines in First Major Trade Action of 2018," *Washington Post*, January 22, 2018.

Mackinnon, Amy, "For Africa, Chinese-Built Internet Is Better Than No Internet at All," *Foreign Policy*, March 19, 2019.

Martin, Eric, and Mackenzie Hawkins, "US Firms Renew Plea for Biden to End Trump-Era China Tariffs," Bloomberg, January 19, 2023.

Matsumoto, Norio, "Teardown of China Budget Smartphone Honor Reveals Rise in U.S. Parts," Nikkei Asia, April 25, 2022.

McGregor, Grady, "Aluminum Foiled," *The Wire China*, June 4, 2023.

Miller, Chris, *Chip War: The Fight for the World's Most Critical Technology*, Scribner, 2022.

Morrison, Wayne M., *The U.S.-China Strategic and Economic Dialogue (S&ED): Economic Outcomes and Issues*, Congressional Research Service, IF10257, July 14, 2015.

Nvidia Corporation, SEC Form 10-K Annual Report for the Fiscal Year Ended January 29, 2023, February 24, 2023.

Office of the United States Trade Representative, "Trans-Pacific Partners and United States Launch FTA Negotiations," press release, September 22, 2008.

Office of the United States Trade Representative, "USTR Issues Tariffs on Chinese Products in Response to Unfair Trade Practices," press release, June 15, 2018.

Palmer, Doug, "U.S. Goods Trade Deficit in August Hits Record High," *Politico*, October 6, 2020.

Paulson, Henry M., Jr., "The Benefits of US-China Strategic Economic Dialogue," *Project Syndicate*, December 8, 2007.

Paulson, Henry M., Jr., *In Advance of the Fourth Cabinet-Level Meeting of the U.S.-China Strategic Economic Dialogue*, transcript of interview with Jessica T. Mathews at the Carnegie Endowment for International Peace, June 10, 2008a. As of March 29, 2023: https://carnegieendowment.org/files/0610_transcript_paulson.pdf

Paulson, Henry M., Jr., "A Strategic Economic Engagement," *Foreign Affairs*, September/October 2008b.

Paulson Institute, "Paulson on Evolving US-China Relationship," June 29, 2020.

Pompeo, Michael R., "Determination of the Secretary of State on Atrocities in Xinjiang," U.S. Department of State, January 19, 2021.

Proclamation 10043, "Suspension of Entry as Nonimmigrants of Certain Students and Researchers from the People's Republic of China," Executive Office of the President, May 29, 2020.

Public Law 87-794, Trade Expansion Act of 1962, October 11, 1962.

Public Law 93-618, Trade Act of 1974, January 3, 1975.

Public Law 106-286, Normal Trade Relations for the People's Republic of China, October 10, 2000.

Public Law 115-232, John S. McCain National Defense Authorization Act for Fiscal Year 2019, August 13, 2018.

Public Law 116-49, Hong Kong Autonomy Act, July 14, 2020.

Public Law 116-145, Uyghur Human Rights Policy Act of 2020, June 17, 2020.

Public Law 116-222, Holding Foreign Companies Accountable Act, December 18, 2020.

Public Law 117-55, Secure Equipment Act of 2021, November 11, 2021.

Public Law 117-78, Uyghur Forced Labor Prevention Act, December 23, 2021.

Public Law 117-167, CHIPS and Science Act, August 9, 2022.

Public Law 117-169, Inflation Reduction Act of 2022, August 16, 2022.

Rascoe, Ayesha, and Michael Martina, "U.S., China Agree to First Trade Steps Under 100-Day Plan," Reuters, May 12, 2017.

Reynolds, Matthew, "Assessing the New Semiconductor Export Controls," Center for Strategic and International Studies, November 3, 2022.

Ridgwell, Henry, "Japan Imposes Microchip Export Ban, Angering China," Voice of America, July 28, 2023.

Rosenberg, Elizabeth, Peter E. Harrell, and Ashley Feng, *A New Arsenal for Competition: Coercive Economic Measures in the U.S.-China Relationship*, Center for a New American Security, April 2020.

Sadek, Nicole, "In Global 5G Race, Telecom Giants Resort to Bribery and Other Alleged Abuses," International Consortium of Investigative Journalists, February 26, 2022.

Smith, Matt, "Clinton Signs China Trade Bill," CNN, October 10, 2000.

Smith, Taiya M., and Douglas Rediker, "Who Needs a 'G-2'? Here Comes the S&ED," Carnegie Endowment for International Peace, July 26, 2009.

Soo, Zen, "Huawei Says It's Out of 'Crisis Mode,' Though Revenue Flat," Associated Press, December 30, 2022.

Statcounter Global Stats, "Mobile Vendor Market Share North America, 2017–2022," webpage, 2022. As of September 7, 2022:
https://gs.statcounter.com/vendor-market-share/mobile/north-america/#yearly-2017-2022

Sterling, Toby, Karen Freifeld, and Alexandra Alper, "Dutch to Restrict Semiconductor Tech Exports to China, Joining US Effort," Reuters, March 8, 2023.

Sullivan, Jake, "Remarks by National Security Advisor Jake Sullivan on the Biden-Harris Administration's National Security Strategy," White House, October 12, 2022.

Sutter, Karen M., *China's New Semiconductor Policies: Issues for Congress*, Congressional Research Service, R46767, April 20, 2021.

Tabeta, Shunsuke, "'Made in China' Chip Drive Falls Far Short of 70% Self-Sufficiency," Nikkei Asia, October 13, 2021.

Taiwan Semiconductor Manufacturing Company, "Financial Results—2022Q4," webpage, undated. As of March 29, 2023:
https://investor.tsmc.com/english/quarterly-results/2022/q4

Tan, Ailing, and James Mayger, "China's Imports of Chip-Making Gear Drop to Lowest Since Mid-2020," Bloomberg, December 21, 2022.

Tan, Weizhen, "Rolling Back U.S.-China Tariffs Would Ease Inflation in the U.S., Former Treasury Secretary Says," CNBC, November 30, 2021.

Telford, Taylor, "Trump's Trade War Comes for Consumers: Tariffs Could Cost U.S. Families up to $1,000 a Year, JPMorgan Forecasts," *Washington Post,* August 20, 2019.

Trump, Donald J., "Remarks by President Trump on His Trip to Asia," White House, November 15, 2017.

TSMC—*See* Taiwan Semiconductor Manufacturing Company.

United Nations Framework Convention on Climate Change, Copenhagen Accord, December 18, 2009.

U.S. Department of Defense, *Summary of the 2018 National Defense Strategy of the United States of America: Sharpening the American Military's Competitive Edge*, 2018.

U.S. Department of Justice, "Chinese Telecommunications Conglomerate Huawei and Huawei CFO Wanzhou Meng Charged with Financial Fraud," press release, January 28, 2019.

U.S. Department of Justice, "Information About the Department of Justice's China Initiative and a Compilation of China-Related Prosecutions Since 2018," webpage, last updated November 19, 2021. As of: February 13, 2024:
https://www.justice.gov/archives/nsd/information-about-department-justice-s-china-initiative-and-compilation-china-related

U.S. Department of State, "U.S.-China Joint Glasgow Declaration on Enhancing Climate Action in the 2020s," press release, November 10, 2021.

U.S. Department of the Treasury, "Remarks by Ambassador Holmer at the Center for Strategic and International Studies on Establishing New Habits of Cooperation in U.S.-China Economic Relations," press release, November 27, 2007.

U.S. Department of the Treasury, "U.S.-China Strategic Economic Dialogue (SED)," webpage, last updated March 9, 2009. As of February 13, 2024:
https://web.archive.org/web/20090617100850/http://www.ustreas.gov/initiatives/us-china/

U.S. Department of the Treasury, "Treasury Designates China as a Currency Manipulator," press release, August 5, 2019.

U.S. Geological Survey, *Mineral Commodity Summaries 2022*, U.S. Department of the Interior, 2022.

U.S. Geological Survey, *Mineral Commodity Summaries 2023*, U.S. Department of the Interior, 2023.

U.S. House of Representatives, Foreign Investment Risk Review Modernization Act of 2018, Bill 5841, June 27, 2018.

Varas, Antonio, and Raj Varadarajan, *How Restrictions to Trade with China Could End US Leadership in Semiconductors*, Boston Consulting Group, 2020.

Weisman, Steven R., "Paulson's Path to China: Progress, but Miles to Go," *New York Times*, June 11, 2008.

White House, "Fact Sheet: U.S.-China Cooperation on Climate Change, Clean Energy, and the Environment," January 19, 2011.

White House, "U.S.-China Joint Announcement on Climate Change," press release, November 11, 2014.

White House, *National Security Strategy of the United States of America*, December 2017.

White House, *United States Strategic Approach to the People's Republic of China*, May 26, 2020.

Wilder, Dennis, "The U.S.-China Strategic and Economic Dialogue: Continuity and Change in Obama's China Policy," Brookings Institution, May 15, 2009.

Williams, Brock R., Christopher A. Casey, Cathleen D. Cimino-Isaacs, Rachel F. Fefer, Keigh E. Hammond, Vivian C. Jones, Andres B. Schwarzenberg, and Karen M. Sutter, *Trump Administration Tariff Actions: Frequently Asked Questions*, Congressional Research Service, R45529, updated December 15, 2020.

"Xi Jinping Picks Top Lieutenant to Lead China's Chip Battle Against U.S.," Bloomberg, June 17, 2021.

Zoellick, Robert, "Whither China: From Membership to Responsibility?" remarks to National Committee on U.S.-China Relations, September 21, 2005.

CHAPTER 4

Production Network Assurance: The Economic Realities of International Integration and De-Integration

Tobias Sytsma and Jessie Wang

Overview

In this chapter, we examine the costs and benefits of economic integration and de-integration between the United States and China, two major players in global production networks. We provide empirical evidence of the increasing reliance of the U.S. economy on Chinese production and the decreasing reliance of China on the U.S. production since 1995. We also develop a theoretical model to (1) examine the relevant costs of reducing and removing economic linkages between countries and (2) evaluate policy proposals, such as friendshoring, that aim to secure the U.S. production network in a context of strategic competition. There is a trade-off between economic benefits and production network assurance. Strategies to reduce the costs of de-integration include investing in production technologies and expanding economic cooperation with allies.

Globalization has been the dominant force shaping the global economy since the end of World War II. It has enabled firms to source inputs from low-cost suppliers across the world, creating complex, interconnected production networks that span countries and regions. These production networks have brought significant benefits, such as lower prices, higher quality, greater variety, and increased productivity.[1]

Globalization has also created challenges and risks that were not fully anticipated or accounted for by its participants and advocates. One of these challenges is the rising political and economic tension between the United States and China, the two largest national economies in the world. This tension has led to the process of *de-integration*, in which connected economic activities are reduced either deliberately or inadvertently, resulting in weaker economic ties between countries. De-integration is a broader concept than *economic decoupling*, which specifically refers to the intentional efforts by policymakers to disentangle the economic ties between nations, often motivated by strategic, political, or security concerns. Although economic decoupling has gained momentum among policymakers and business leaders in both countries as tensions rise between them, we discuss de-integration in this chapter because it is likely a consequence from increasing trade frictions even in the absence of economic decoupling.

In the context of U.S.-China relations, economic decoupling refers to an attempt to break the intricate ties in trade and investment that have developed between the United States and China over decades of market integration. More broadly, decoupling aims to reduce the reliance on foreign suppliers, especially those considered strategic competitors or potential adversaries. The motivation for economic decoupling stems from various concerns and interests.[2] Some of these concerns are related to national security, such as protecting sensitive

---

1 James McNerney, Charles Savoie, Francesco Caravelli, F., Vasco M. Carvalho, and J. Doyne Farmer, "How Production Networks Amplify Economic Growth," *Proceedings of the National Academy of Sciences*, Vol. 119, No. 1, December 21, 2021; Dieter Ernst and Linsu Kim, "Global Production Networks, Knowledge Diffusion, and Local Capability Formation," *Research Policy*, Vol. 31, Nos. 8–9, December 2002; Tobias Sytsma, "Improving Preferential Market Access Through Rules of Origin: Firm-Level Evidence from Bangladesh," *American Economic Journal: Economic Policy*, Vol. 14, No. 1, February 2022; Mary Amiti and Jozef Konings, "Trade Liberalization, Intermediate Inputs, and Productivity: Evidence from Indonesia," *American Economic Review*, Vol. 97, No. 5, December 2007.

2 J. Stewart Black and Allen J. Morrison, "The Strategic Challenges of Decoupling from China," *Harvard Business Review*, May–June 2021; Jeffrey Kucik and Rajan Menon, "Can the United States Really Decouple from China?" *Foreign Policy*, January 11, 2022; A. Michael Spence, "Destructive Decoupling," Council on Foreign Relations, April 4, 2023.

technologies and intellectual property rights. Other concerns are related to economic competitiveness, such as maintaining or enhancing domestic industries, innovation capabilities, and market access in the face of foreign subsidies, dumping, or unfair trade practices. Additional concerns are related to geopolitical influence, such as preserving or advancing strategic alliances, regional stability, and global leadership. Although decoupling does not mean the end of globalization, it is an attempt to reduce reliance on some foreign suppliers that might pose threats or challenges to these concerns and interests.

In this chapter, we examine the concept and implications of economic decoupling from a new perspective. We argue that decoupling is not simply a reversal in globalization but rather a transformation of globalization that requires new objectives and approaches. We propose a new approach to globalization that we call *production network assurance*, which involves managing the risks and uncertainties associated with the production network to ensure that the production process runs smoothly and meets the desired objectives. This approach requires firms and governments to consider not only economic gains and efficiency but also the reliability, security, and stability of their production networks. Prioritizing production network assurance can help mitigate the negative impacts of economic decoupling and enhance the resilience of global production.

Production network assurance differs from supply chain resilience or risk management. Although both share the common goal of mitigating risks and ensuring the continuity of operations, production network assurance specifically focuses on optimizing the reliability and efficiency of the production network in a systematic way. In contrast, supply chain resilience or risk management tends to focus on addressing specific aspects or segments of the supply chain that are vulnerable to disruptions. Production network assurance can enhance supply chain resilience or risk management, but the opposite is not necessarily true.

We offer insights into several aspects of existing and future production networks. First, we evaluate the process of global economic integration since the mid-1990s, focusing on the shift of global production toward China following its entry into the World Trade Organization (WTO) in 2001. Our aim is to provide insights into (1) the extent to which the United States and China have integrated with each other and with other regions and (2) whether China's integration has come at the expense of other countries or regions. To provide answers to these questions, we use the Organisation for Economic Co-operation and Development's (OECD's) Inter-Country Input-Output (ICIO) tables, which provide data on the domestic and international sales of goods and services between sectors.[3] We also create a new economic indicator, the levelized value-added requirements (LVAR), which measures the level of interconnectivity between countries based on their value-added shares in each other's production (see the box titled "Glossary of Economic Terms" for a discussion on this and other economic terms).

To examine the economic implications of severing certain economic connections and de-integrating the globalized economy established over the past three decades, we built a theoretical model that provides insights into strategies designed to strengthen the resilience of

[3] OECD, "Inter-Country Input-Output Tables," dataset, undated.

Glossary of Economic Terms

Input-output (IO) data: A type of economic data that describes the interrelationships among different sectors of an economy. In an IO table, each row represents industry sales, and each column represents industry purchases. The cells in the table show the value of inputs that each industry uses to produce its outputs and the value of the outputs that each industry sells to other industries or final consumers.

Value added: The economic value that an industry or firm creates through its production process after subtracting the cost of its intermediate inputs.

Levelized value-added requirements (LVAR): The foreign value-added required to produce a dollar of output in a country or sector.

Ricardian Trade Model: An economic theory that analyzes international trade based on comparative advantage. The model assumes that countries specialize in producing goods in which they have a lower opportunity cost, and trade occurs to take advantage of the differences in relative costs between countries, resulting in mutual gains from trade.

Friendshoring: The practice of shifting business operations or outsourcing to countries that are considered friendly or closely aligned with a company's home country. It involves establishing partnerships or using services from countries with shared values, cultural affinities, or geopolitical alliances to reduce reliance on riskier trade partners

production networks and reduce the costs of economic decoupling. Our model studies how such strategies as *friendshoring* (i.e., manufacturing and sourcing from geopolitical allies) can reduce the risks associated with the current global production network and their challenges. We explore approaches to identify partners and policy options to enhance production network assurance, and we aim to offer actionable recommendations for managing the economic costs of decoupling and ensuring a more robust global production landscape. We outline our main findings in the following paragraphs.

The global economy has become increasingly interconnected since the mid-1990s, largely because many countries have increasingly relied on China as a supplier. Our empirical analysis suggests that China became a more prominent source of production for many regions in the world between 1995 and 2018, according to the OECD's ICIO dataset. The United States, for example, increased its dependence on Chinese production by almost 13 percentage points over this period. This trend is consistent across regions: The average increase in reliance on Chinese production is 13.1 percentage points. Meanwhile, the United States, the European Union (EU), and other Regional Comprehensive Economic Partnership (RCEP) members (excluding China) saw global reliance on their production decline by an average of 15 percentage points across regions.[4] China, on the other hand, has increased its reliance on production originating in countries in South America, Africa, and the Middle East, offsetting declines in reliance on production from the United States, Asian economies, and the EU.

In a world of global production networks, regional economic relationships remain important. Despite the shifts toward Chinese production in the past two decades, regional economic relationships remain vital to production networks. For example, the United States still relies heavily on production from Mexico and Canada. For China, even though its reliance on production from other Asian economies fell, these economies are still China's largest source of foreign production. The EU relies intensively on production from Middle Eastern and African countries, as well as from the United States. Thus, although globalization has led to more cross-regional integration—especially with China's role in global production networks—regional relationships are still key to production networks.

Such trade strategies as friendshoring can be challenging and costly. Friendshoring, or the practice of shifting trade away from potential adversaries and toward allies, could improve production network assurance by limiting undesirable exposure in the production network. Our theoretical framework suggests that, because the economic linkages between countries are formed by seeking to minimize costs, deviating from those linkages will likely be costly, at least in the short term. The uneven distribution of resources across countries means that achieving the same production costs under new production networks is challenging. We also show that friendshoring is less effective at preventing undesirable exposure to certain countries if friend countries continue trading with them.

Selective decoupling could improve production network assurance at lower cost. Economic decoupling is a costly and complex process, and it affects countries in different ways because countries gain different things from the exchanges in the network. Our model suggests that, by evaluating the relative standing of goods in the production network, countries can identify their strengths and vulnerabilities in trade relationships. Therefore, countries could design clear plans for decoupling to de-integrate only part of the economy and prioritize production network assurance with minimal disruption. However, they should also be aware that potential retaliation from other countries would be equally effective because they have different priorities and interests.

Investments in technology, trade with allies, and alternative goods are critical to limiting the cost of production network assurance in the long run. Our model suggests that production network assurance is always costly in the short run, but the right kind of investments could lower the cost of production network assurance in the long run. Improving cost competitiveness through production technology, enhancing market access with allies, and increasing opportunities for alternative goods and suppliers as substitutes could help countries transition from a globalization model aimed at cost minimization to one aimed at pro-

4 RCEP is a trade bloc formed in 2020 among 15 East Asian, Southeast Asian, and Oceania countries. RCEP includes China, but in our analysis, we exclude the Chinese component of RCEP production.

duction network assurance. This framework also calls for initiatives beyond trade, such as broad-based technological collaborations among allies.

This chapter is organized as follows. In the next section, we discuss the empirical analysis. We start with an overview of the data sources used and a description of our measure of economic interconnection. Then we evaluate differences in interconnectivity across country groups and how it has changed over time for the United States and China. Next, we turn to a theoretical model, which begins with a discussion of the model environment and assumptions and characterizes options for sourcing behavior. We use the model to discuss the costs and challenges of friendshoring, as well as investments that could be made to ease the economic pain of decoupling.

The Evolution of Global Production Networks

In this section, our objective is to assess the transformations that have occurred in global production networks since the mid-1990s. Our primary focus is on examining the changing dynamics between the United States and China, specifically investigating whether there is a balanced level of dependence between the two countries and how their interconnections have influenced their trading relationships with other nations. To address these questions, we develop a measure of economic interconnectivity based on data provided by the OECD. We begin by discussing the data, then describe our measure of connectivity and evaluate how relationships have changed, and conclude with broad lessons from the analysis.

Inter-Country Input-Output Data

The following empirical analysis draws on the OECD's ICIO dataset, which contains cross-country-sector IO data for 1995–2018. The data structure is similar to typical national IO data, which describe the interdependencies between different economic sectors or industries. The data typically consist of a matrix or table that shows the flow of goods and services between industries, typically measured by the monetary value of those transactions. IO data also contain information on the sector's *value added*, the economic value that an industry or firm creates through its production process, after subtracting the cost of its intermediate inputs.

The ICIO dataset goes beyond typical IO datasets by including cross-country and cross-sector linkages, making it possible to track flows of goods and services between industries and countries. By including country-sector trade relationships, the ICIO dataset allows for analyses of global trade and supply chains that extend beyond direct imports. For instance, with ICIO data, it is possible to track intermediate goods imports used in producing other goods. It is also possible to track the value added of intermediate goods trade, separate from gross trade flows. The ICIO data cover 45 industries based on Revision 4 of the International

Standard Industrial Classification.[5] For the purposes of the report, the data are aggregated across countries into eight groups: China, the United States, the then-28 members of the EU (EU 28), Canada, Mexico, RCEP countries (excluding China), other Asian countries, South America, and the rest of world (ROW).

Table 4.1 displays the structure of ICIO data for a simple two-country, three-sector global economy. The data consist of intermediate use transactions (t), which show the value of intermediate input goods and services purchased by the column sector from the row sector; value added (VA), which measures the contribution of labor and capital to production in the column sector and includes industry profits, labor costs, taxes, and subsidies; final demand (f), which is the consumption of final goods by households and governments; and gross output (X), which is the sum of the rows and the sum of the columns. For instance, $t_{B,2}^{A,1}$ is the value of intermediate inputs purchased in Country A's industry 1 from Country B's industry 2, $f_{A,3}^{B}$ is the consumption of goods or services produced in Country A's sector 3 by households in Country B, and $VA^{B,3}$ is the value added in Country B's industry 3. IO data are *balanced*, meaning that everything produced is consumed by some entity. Specifically, the sum of a row produces the same value as the sum of the column. Thus, gross output (X) is shown as both a row and column.

Measuring Production Interdependence

To evaluate the evolving trade dynamics since 1995, we create a standardized measure of production network dependence that is based on the value added required to produce one unit of output. Value added is commonly viewed as a superior metric for assessing a sector's contribution to an economy in comparison with gross production because it accounts for the value contributed by the sector itself.[6] More precisely, value added represents the difference between a sector's gross output and the cost of its intermediate inputs.

We refer to our measure as the levelized value-added requirements (LVAR) of production. LVAR builds off other measures of value-added requirements but is unique in that it focuses specifically on the role of foreign value added.[7] We measure LVAR at the country-by-country level, but it also can be constructed at a more disaggregated level, such as the country-industry–by–country-industry level.

In other words, LVAR measures each country's share of the total foreign value added required to produce a dollar of output in any other country. For example, if it takes a total of $0.50 of foreign value added to produce a dollar of output in the United States, and $0.25 of

[5] Department of Economics and Social Affairs, *International Standard Industrial Classification of All Economic Activities*, 4th rev., United Nations, 2008.

[6] Ronald E. Miller and Peter D. Blair, *Input-Output Analysis: Foundations and Extensions*, 2nd ed., Cambridge University Press, 2009.

[7] Richard Baldwin, Rebecca Freeman, and Angelos Theodorakopoulos, "Horses for Courses: Measuring Foreign Supply Chain Exposure," National Bureau of Economic Research, working paper 30525, September 2022; Miller and Blair, 2009.

TABLE 4.1

ICIO Structure

		Country A			Country B			Final Demand (*f*)		Gross Output (*X*)
		Industry 1	Industry 2	Industry 3	Industry 1	Industry 2	Industry 3	Country A	Country B	
Country A	Industry 1	$t_{A,1}^{A,1}$	$t_{A,1}^{A,2}$	$t_{A,1}^{A,3}$	$t_{A,1}^{B,1}$	$t_{A,1}^{B,2}$	$t_{A,1}^{B,3}$	$f_{A,1}^{A}$	$f_{A,1}^{B}$	$X_{A,1}$
	Industry 2	$t_{A,2}^{A,1}$	$t_{A,2}^{A,2}$	$t_{A,2}^{A,3}$	$t_{A,2}^{B,1}$	$t_{A,2}^{B,2}$	$t_{A,2}^{B,3}$	$f_{A,2}^{A}$	$f_{A,2}^{B}$	$X_{A,2}$
	Industry 3	$t_{A,3}^{A,1}$	$t_{A,3}^{A,2}$	Intermediate Use Matrix (T)		$t_{A,3}^{B,2}$	$t_{A,3}^{B,3}$	$f_{A,3}^{A}$	$f_{A,3}^{B}$	$X_{A,3}$
Country B	Industry 1	$t_{B,1}^{A,1}$	$t_{B1}^{A,2}$			$t_{B1}^{B,2}$	$t_{B1}^{B,3}$	$f_{B,1}^{A}$	$f_{B,1}^{B}$	$X_{B,1}$
	Industry 2	$t_{B,2}^{A,1}$	$t_{B,2}^{A,2}$	$t_{B,2}^{A,3}$	$t_{B,2}^{B,1}$	$t_{B,2}^{B,2}$	$t_{B,2}^{B,3}$	$f_{B,2}^{A}$	$f_{B,2}^{B}$	$X_{B,2}$
	Industry 3	$t_{B,3}^{A,1}$	$t_{B,3}^{A,2}$	$t_{B,3}^{A,3}$	$t_{B,3}^{B,1}$	$t_{B,3}^{B,2}$	$t_{B,3}^{B,3}$	$f_{B,3}^{A}$	$f_{B,3}^{B}$	$X_{B,3}$
Value added (*VA*)		$VA^{A,1}$	$VA^{A,2}$	$VA^{A,3}$	$VA^{B,1}$	$VA^{B,2}$	$VA^{B,3}$			
Gross output (*X*)		$X_{A,1}$	$X_{A,2}$	$X_{A,3}$	$X_{B,1}$	$X_{B,2}$	$X_{B,3}$			

NOTE: Author's depiction of ICIO data (OECD, undated).

the foreign value added comes specifically from China, the United States' LVAR for China is 50 percent.

Calculating LVAR

In matrix notation, LVAR is constructed as

$$LVAR = \left[\left(VA\,\hat{X}^{-1}\right)L - \hat{L}\right]\vec{v}.$$

The steps to calculating the LVAR are as follows. First, the Leontief inverse matrix is calculated from the T matrix and a diagonalized version of the X matrix ($\hat{X}$). Specifically, $L = \left(I - T\hat{X}^{-1}\right)^{-1}$, where each element l measures the value of inputs from the row country/sector required to produce a dollar of output in the column country/sector. The Leontief inverse matrix has the desirable property that it accounts for the total linkages between sectors, including direct and indirect value added that comes through third countries.[8]

Next, using the **VA** matrix and $\hat{X}$, the value added per unit of output is calculated as $VA'\hat{X}^{-1}$, where each element is the value added of a country/sector relative to its gross output. Next, the value-added multiplier matrix is calculated as $VA'\hat{X}^{-1}L$, where each element measures the value-added content of inputs from the row country/sector needed for the column sector to produce a dollar of output. To remove domestic value added, we subtract the diagonal portion of the Leontief inverse matrix ($\hat{L}$), which shows the domestic value added that is required to produce a dollar of output. Finally, we divide each element of the resulting matrix by the column sum. This transforms each element into a percentage. In matrix notation, this last transformation is given by $\vec{v} = (\vec{1}_{n.}\left(\left(VA'\hat{X}^{-1}\right)\right)L - \hat{L}))^{-1}$, where $\vec{1}_{n.}$ is an n-entry row vector of 1s.

The domestic value added that is required to produce a dollar of domestic output is not included in LVAR. However, it plays a critical role in national production. Across countries, domestic value-added requirements make up the vast majority of the total value-added requirements needed to produce output. For instance, in the United States in 2018, approximately 94 percent of the total value added required to produce a unit of output came from domestic sources. The remaining 6 percent came from foreign sources, and this is the portion of the value-added requirements used to construct the LVAR for the United States. The large domestic share is largely driven by the higher value added of service sector activities, which are generally less tradeable than goods.[9]

---

8 The Leontief inverse matrix accounts for indirect trade flows. For example, the Leontief inverse matrix accounts for products that are produced in Country A, used in production of products in Country B, and then sold to Country C. The Leontief inverse matrix accounts for Country A's direct exports to Country B and Country B's direct exports to Country C but also Country A's indirect exports to Country C through Country B. More specifically, the Leontief inverse matrix is equal to $(I - A)^{-1} = I + A + A^2 + A^3 + \ldots + A^n$, where the matrix A reports the observed sectoral linkages.

9 Sébastien Miroudot, Jehan Sauvage, and Ben Shepherd, "Measuring the Cost of International Trade in Services," *World Trade Review*, Vol. 12, No. 4, October 2013.

How Interdependent Were Production Networks in 2018?

Table 4.2 shows the LVAR matrix for 2018. As with Table 4.1, the rows correspond to the exporting country, and the columns correspond to the purchasing country. Each element in the table has been scaled by the total value added required in the column country, making each element a percentage of the total value-added requirements. For instance, according to the data for 2018, the EU contributed 17 percent of the LVAR for China.

Table 4.2 highlights several important aspects of the global economy. First, Chinese and U.S. value added play a relatively outsized role in global production. The last column of Table 4.2 displays the row average value-added requirements, which is the share of LVAR in the average region sourced from the row country. In 2018, 20.8 percent of the average LVAR came from the United States, and 15.7 percent came from China. To put these numbers in perspective, the entire EU 28 contributed 22.6 percent to the average LVAR.

Second, the table highlights the importance of regional economic relationships. For example, RCEP countries make up 33.5 percent of China's LVAR (shown in the China column), and the United States makes up more than 50 percent of Mexico and Canada's LVAR. The regional nature of economic ties is unsurprising given the trade-dampening effect of geographic distance but also suggests that globalization is more regional than typically discussed.[10]

TABLE 4.2
LVAR Matrix for 2018

	Destination Country								
Source Country	China	EU	Canada and Mexico	Other Asia	RCEP	ROW	South America	United States	Average
China	–	12.38	13.43	16.71	24.96	12.84	14.63	15.19	15.73
EU	15.90	–	13.69	18.68	19.30	42.70	25.69	22.07	22.58
Canada and Mexico	2.25	2.91	–	1.54	2.84	2.14	4.43	23.06	5.60
Other Asia	13.02	15.50	3.92	–	12.26	14.03	5.38	7.52	10.23
RCEP	33.51	13.27	10.02	23.41	–	12.31	9.06	14.16	16.53
ROW	20.18	32.46	5.66	27.45	19.66	–	15.45	13.88	19.25
South America	5.45	3.14	2.66	1.85	4.27	3.33	–	4.13	3.55
United States	9.68	20.35	50.62	10.36	16.71	12.65	25.35	–	20.82

SOURCE: Authors' analysis of data from OECD, undated.

NOTE: Country groups are aggregated prior to performing the LVAR calculation. For instance, EU is an aggregate of all EU 28 countries. The LVAR for country groups is computed using external value-added requirements only.

[10] Matias Berthelon and Caroline Freund, "On the Conservation of Distance in International Trade," *Journal of International Economics*, Vol. 75, No. 2, 2008.

How Has Production Interdependence Changed Since the 1990s?

Next, we evaluate how LVARs have changed over time. Table 4.3 displays the LVAR for the United States and China in 1995 and 2018. The first row of the table highlights that, although foreign value added is important, domestic value added (which is not included in LVAR) is also critical. In the United States, LVAR is between 5 percent and 6 percent of total value-added requirements, whereas in China, LVAR accounts for 11 percent of total value-added requirements. The remainder comes from domestic sources.

The indented rows of the table show each foreign region's share of the LVAR for the United States and China. For instance, in 1995, China accounted for 2.5 percent of the foreign value added required to produce a dollar of output in the United States. In 2018, China's share had grown to over 15 percent. This is a 508-percent increase, or an increase of 12.5 percentage points. In China, the United States' share of foreign value added fell by 2.2 percentage points between 1995 and 2018. Notably, even though China has started relying less on U.S. value added, China still relies on more value added from the United States than the United States does from China in absolute terms because of China's larger reliance of foreign value added in general.

TABLE 4.3

LVAR Shares over Time for United States and China

	United States				China			
			Change				Change	
	1995	2018	Level	Percent	1995	2018	Level	Percent
LVAR as percentage of total value-added requirements	5.60	6.30	0.70	12.50	11.10	11.00	−0.10	−0.90
Country share of LVAR								
China	2.50	15.19	12.70	508.00	—	—	—	—
EU	24.40	22.07	−2.30	−9.43	16.20	15.90	−0.30	−1.85
Canada and Mexico	23.60	23.06	−0.50	−2.12	1.93	2.25	0.32	16.58
Other Asia	6.50	7.52	1.02	15.69	21.20	13.02	−8.20	−38.68
RCEP (minus China)	25.90	14.16	−11.70	−45.17	39.80	33.51	−6.3	−15.83
ROW	13.40	13.88	0.50	3.73	7.51	20.18	12.69	168.97
South America	3.73	4.13	0.4	10.72	1.40	5.45	4.05	289.29
United States	—	—	—	—	11.90	9.68	−2.22	−18.66
HHI	2,065.10	1,721.52		−16.64	2,499.62	2,080.57		−16.76

SOURCE: Authors' calculations of data from OECD, undated.

NOTE: This table displays the change in the LVAR for the United States and China between 1995 and 2018. The HHI row displays the Herfindahl-Hirshman Index, which is calculated as the sum of the squared shares.

The last row of Table 4.3 displays the Herfindahl-Hirshman Index (HHI) for LVAR country shares. The HHI is calculated as the sum of the squared shares and is a common measure of market concentration. A higher HHI indicates more market concentration. Although the magnitude of the HHI depends on the level of aggregation across foreign sources, the change in HHI provides evidence of both countries diversifying their foreign value-added sources.

The United States has shifted toward using more Chinese value added in its production processes, and this shift has been offset by a corresponding shift away from RCEP value added. These changes were almost equal in terms of percentage points. It is important to note that RCEP's LVAR for China increased significantly over the same period, suggesting that Chinese value added has become more prevalent in the production processes of many countries, not just that of the United States.

Figure 4.1 shows the change in percentage points of the LVAR for all regions; the rows are the value-added supplying region, and the columns are the sourcing region. Across all regions, China has become a greater source of value added. The shift toward China has largely come at the expense of value added from the EU, RCEP, and the United States. As a result, many products that the United States imports from such regions as RCEP now have greater Chinese value added embodied within them compared with 1995. Moreover, the value added created domestically within RCEP has been declining as production in the region has become more integrated globally. Although the local value-added requirements for the United States and China have remained stable, RCEP's local value-added requirements have decreased by 7 percentage points since 1995, indicating a significant change in the region's production processes.

For China, value-added sourcing has shifted away from RCEP, the United States, and other Asian countries and toward South America and the ROW (primarily Africa and the Middle East). This is likely the result of an increase in China's resource consumption and international efforts to build connectivity with those regions through the Belt and Road Initiative. As shown in Figure 4.1, the ROW and South America have also increased their value-added sourcing from China.

Discussion of Empirical Results

The preceding analysis demonstrates that, not only are the economies of the United States and China intertwined, but all regions of the world are deeply intertwined with each other. Notably, the two leading national economies, the United States and China, are also leaders in supplying and being supplied by the rest of the world. This evolution of the global economy occurred partly by policy choice because of the decline of trade barriers. But more importantly, it occurred because of the decisions of hundreds of thousands of businesses that saw they could use developments in transportation technologies and information and communications technologies to expand internationally and fragment their production to become more efficient than previously. This means that any reversal will also introduce inefficiencies: In other words, it will be costly. However, these businesses likely did not take into account a

FIGURE 4.1
Percentage-Point Change in LVAR Between 1995 and 2018

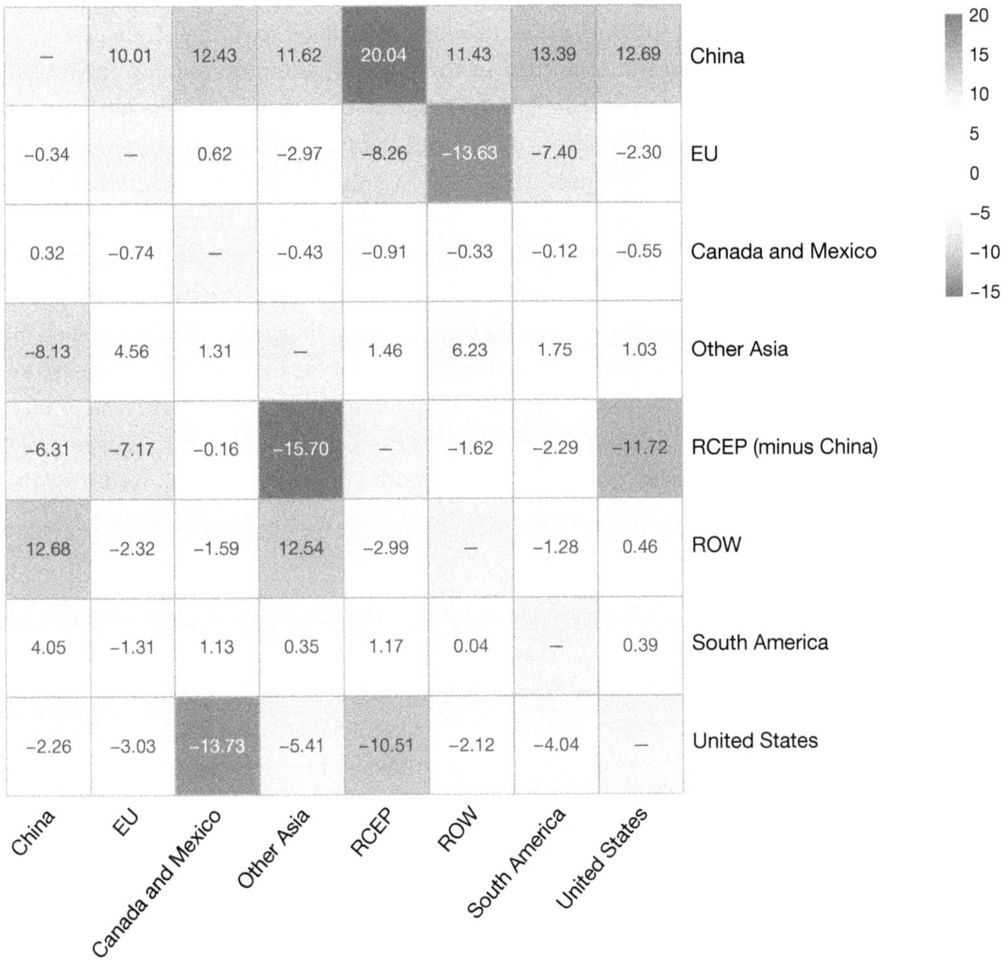

SOURCE: Authors' calculation of data from OECD, undated.

variety of costs, such as firm-specific costs from the risk of political or economic disruptions or risk to the broader economy, that might come from their international engagement. As these risks have manifested, policymakers have focused on how to reverse, to some extent, the developments of these international networks and how to reduce risks to national economies. In the next section, we draw on a new model of the global economy to show the costs and opportunities of mitigating these risks and reducing the level of global exchange.

How to Understand Production Network Assurance in Trade

We set up a model with features from traditional trade models to answer an important question: How do countries pursue production network assurance in trade strategies?[11] The drive for economic gains from trade resulted in the highly interconnected and interdependent global production networks described in the first half of this chapter. The need for production network assurance requires us to consider all the factors we have been studying in trade—such as production capacity, trade costs, and economic gains—and add other factors that are key to the reliability of the network, such as international relationships and risk exposure. We use the model as a framework to assess the channels of risk exposure in the process and interventions that could improve production network assurance. The private sector makes most of the decisions on choosing suppliers, but internalizing risks in such factors as long-term supply chain resilience and national security is intrinsically expensive and does not usually align with profit incentives without interventions. Given these concerns, we abstract from firm-level decisions and describe the framework from a country perspective to derive the optimal strategy for establishing a robust production network with trade.[12]

Model Environment

We model a world with $N + 1$ countries. The United States is country 0 and can choose to trade with countries $n = 1, 2, \ldots, N$. To emphasize the role of international relationships in trade considerations, we rank these countries by the probability that they are friendly enough to the United States to work for mutual gains, with γ_n a variable signifying friendliness, so that $1 \geq \gamma_n \geq 0$ for all n, with 1 being the most friendly. Meanwhile, acknowledging that exogenous interruptions, such as natural disasters, exist domestically without foreign influence and can happen and hinder the production process in any country, we use σ_n to represent the probability that country n is at its normal production capacity, $1 \geq \sigma_n \geq 0$. Then, with probability $\gamma_n \sigma_n$, country n will trade with the United States under mutual agreement and deliver on the completion of production. We also adjust how price is determined to reflect the cost associated with production, trade, and externalities in the economies of scale.

The unit price of goods j produced in country i and sold to country n is

$$p_{ni} = \frac{c_i(j)}{z_i(j)} d_{ni} + \frac{F_i(j)}{\sum_{m=0}^{N} X_{mi}(j)}$$

[11] Specifically, we build off the Ricardian trade model presented in Jonathan Eaton and Samuel Kortum, "Technology, Geography, and Trade," *Econometrica*, Vol. 70, No. 5, September 2002.

[12] A 2021 paper published by the National Bureau of Economic Research also provides a model of international trade in which firms face decisions about where to source intermediate inputs given an exogenous risk of supply disruptions (Gene M. Grossman, Elhanan Helpman, and Hugo Lhuillier, "Supply Chain Resilience: Should Policy Promote Diversification or Reshoring?" National Bureau of Economic Research, working paper 29330, October 2021). Building off a model with constant elasticity of substitution preferences, the authors find that a subsidy for supply chain diversification allows the economy to reach a constrained optimum—again, given that exogenous supply disruptions occur.

where $c_i(j)$ is the cost of resources, such as labor and raw material, as inputs to produce j; $z_i(j)$ is a country- and goods-specific productivity variable; and d_{ni} reflects trade costs between n and i, traditionally measured in trade models.[13] In addition, we include a fixed cost (e.g., infrastructure, technology investment) for country i to produce j, $F_i(j)$. This fixed cost is spread across country i's total production, so the fixed cost that each unit needs to take on depends on the country's total production volume. If $X_{mi}(j)$ is the amount of good j produced in i and sold to m, then $\sum_{m=0}^{N} X_{mi}(j)$ is the amount of j produced in i sold to the entire world, including itself. Note that the pricing equation does not include a term for a producer mark-up, which is commonly included in models of monopolistic competition.[14] Instead, we follow the perfect competition model developed by Jonathan Eaton and Samuel Kortum, in which pricing is determined based on marginal production costs alone.[15] Although our focus on perfectly competitive markets abstracts away from the strategic pricing behavior of firms, it allows us to highlight the key mechanisms through which production network assurance and friendshoring strategies affect trade patterns.

Additionally, our pricing equations include fixed costs, which are not typically included in pricing equations in trade models. Most models set prices to the marginal costs of production or a mark-up over the marginal costs.[16] However, fixed costs in our model play a critical role in capturing the implications of global integration and the externalities from trade. First, if country i already has a large global market share in supplying good j, it has a relatively low average-fixed cost, which gives it a strong price advantage that goes away only when the reduction in exports is sufficiently large. Second, if a country does not already produce a good, the barriers it faces to start production would include a substantial fixed cost that comes from not having the associated infrastructure and not having access to the global market. This describes the externalities from global integration: Once integration happens, there will be positive externalities associated with such specialization and economies of scale from the resulting global production network, and deviation from such a production network will incur costs to override both the production advantage and the externalities. Although we focus on trade on a global scale, the same logic applies to integration in the domestic market. Economic gains have been the main driver of integration—with relatively few disruptions from social, political, and environmental shocks until recent decades—and production network assurance has not been a policy focus until recently. The result is a highly intertwined production network that lacks assurance in the face of uncertainty and risks, and the desire for a more secure, dependable, and selective trade environment emerged.

---

13 For an in-depth discussion of trade costs, see James E. Anderson and Eric van Wincoop, "Trade Costs," *Journal of Economic Literature*, Vol. 42, No. 3, September 2004.

14 For example, see Marc J. Melitz, "The Impact of Trade on Intra-Industry Reallocations and Aggregate Industry Productivity," *Econometrica*, Vol. 71, No. 6, November 2003.

15 Eaton and Kortum, 2002.

16 For an example of marginal costs of production, see Eaton and Kortum (2002); for mark-up over the marginal costs, see Melitz (2003).

Friendshoring is one of the strategies born from this desire for higher production network assurance. To capture the idea of choosing trade partners and trade volumes with concerns besides immediate economic gains, we deviate from the traditional setting that chooses the cheapest product to maximize profit.[17] Instead, we take into account the reality that sourcing from countries with the cheapest price or sourcing from a small number of countries might result in the lack of production network assurance. We thus allow a country to employ a more complicated strategy by considering both the cost of sourcing and the reliability of the resulting production network. One example of such a strategy is to determine with whom we are willing to trade based on how secure we want the supplier to be, before picking the cheapest source within the preapproved list (in other terms, friendshoring). In the most extreme version of this strategy, production occurs only at home and products are not traded internationally. To reflect this type of strategy, we allow a nested partner selection strategy to show the price we face under different scenarios:

- **Strategy 1:** Source only from home, and the price is the cost of production at home. The probability of delivery is σ_0, eliminating possible production network disruption from other countries.[18]
- **Strategy 2:** Source from allies—that is, countries with relationship scores higher than $\gamma^*(j)$. Here, the cutoff value of relationship score $\gamma^*(j)$ is a function of j because this cutoff value is goods specific. The more secure that good j needs to be for noneconomic considerations, the higher this cutoff value should be. This is essentially friendshoring.
- **Strategy 3:** Source from any country, and the price is the lowest global price. This is the scenario for free trade.

$$P_0(j) = \begin{cases} P_0^1(j) = p_{00}(j) = \dfrac{c_0(j)}{z_0(j)} + \dfrac{F_0(j)}{\sum_{m=0}^{N} X_{m0}(j)} & \textit{under strategy } 1 \\ P_0^2(j) = \min\{p_{0i}(j) \mid \gamma_i \geq \gamma^*(j), i \leq N\} & \textit{under strategy } 2 \\ P_0^3(j) = \min\{p_{0i}(j) \mid i \leq N\} & \textit{under strategy } 3 \end{cases}$$

where $P_0(j)$ is the price country 0 pays to obtain good j. Under these strategies, for all j, $P_0^1(j) \geq P_0^2(j) \geq P_0^3(j)$, and the higher $\gamma^*(j)$ is, the higher $P_0^2(j)$ is.

We also show this nested strategy visually in Figure 4.2. When sourcing from all suppliers, any country would source from the lowest-cost supplier, country E. But because countries

---

[17] As was used in Eaton and Kortum (2002).

[18] For countries with a low σ_0, however, this strategy might lead to lower production network assurance. If a country is particularly prone to domestic production risks, the interpretation of the implications from this model would be different. For the context of this analysis, we want to focus on risks associated with international trade, so we assume that the United States and the countries that we are examining have relatively high σ_0 values so that the reason to source inputs from other countries (allies or anyone else) is high production costs.

D and E are not in the friend circle, friendshoring would exclude them as a potential trade partner, and sourcing has to come from countries A, B, and C or home, all of which have higher production costs.

This points directly to one of the costs of friendshoring: The more exclusive a country is in choosing trade partners based on noncost considerations, the more likely it is that countries with low production costs are removed from the friendly partner list, and the more expensive it is to obtain the good. We will discuss additional considerations of friendshoring in the next section.

It is important to recognize that country 0 may need to consider sourcing good *j* from several countries with slightly different prices.[19] When demand for good *j* is high, one partner might not be able to fulfill the entire order. Also, when σ_n is not high enough for existing trade partner *n*, the ability to rely on other trade partners would be especially important because, with probability $1 - \sigma_n$, partner *n* cannot deliver. In other words, with any price $p_{0i}(j)$, the

FIGURE 4.2

Friendshoring and Cost of Sourcing

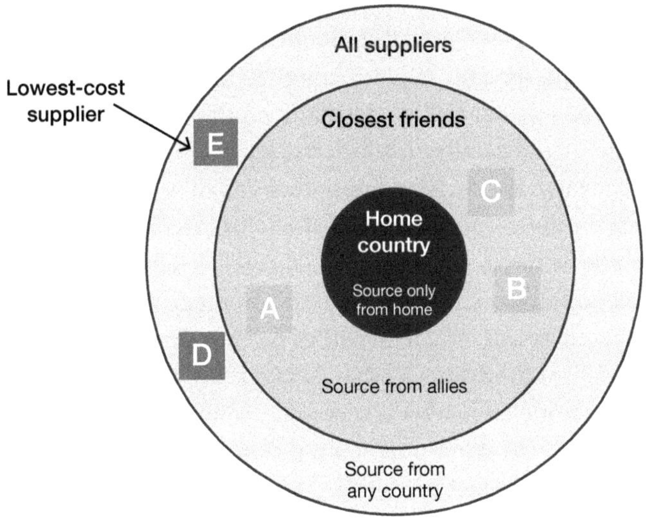

NOTE: This figure displays nested sourcing strategies. Countries A, B, and C are allies of the home country, while countries D and E are not. Country E is the lowest-cost supplier of the good in question but not part of the home country's friendsourcing strategy. This implies that the cost of the good will be higher if the home country excludes Country E from its sourcing strategy.

[19] The Eaton-Kortum model of trade assumes that, in a perfectly competitive global market, all consumers (importers) source goods from the cheapest global producer (exporter). This process results in a de facto *law of one price*, in which profits are competed away, markets clear, and, given the homogeneity of the goods in question, price is equal to marginal cost. Our modifications to this model of trade include nonmonetary costs that can elevate the price of the producer with the lowest marginal production cost, resulting in consumers switching to higher-price producers.

probability that good j can be delivered with this price is $\gamma_i \sigma_i$. Another reason to have more than one trade partners for any good is the reality that goods and services are not supplied inelastically. When country 0's most preferred partners simply do not have enough production capacity to meet the demand, resorting to more partners is inevitable.

Friendshoring Can Be Challenging and Costly

Although friendshoring can partially address the concern of the lack of production network assurance from free trade, the framework showcases the challenges with this strategy and the reasons it could be costly. Our model highlights each of the three main challenges outlined in a 2022 analysis by the International Institute of Strategic Studies: uneven distribution of resources, trade-off between security and access to markets, and fluid trust among countries.[20] In addition, the model also reveals the risk of friendshoring given the current geographic proximity of allies and the limitation of friendshoring without consensus among friends.

Uneven Distribution of Resources

Several factors lead to large variations in the cost of production for countries. One way that we reflect this in our model is through the idea that both total cost $c_i(j)$ and productivity $z_i(j)$ are country- and goods-specific. When a country has limited resources of any kind (material or labor) that are necessary in the production of j—that is, $c_i(j)$—the cost of production is higher relative to that of country i, which has relatively more generous endowments of the resources. Consequently, the decision to produce j at all or produce more of good j can have significant effects on the economy. The most obvious example here is labor. As a country's population ages, the working-age population shrinks.[21] Replacing manufacturing jobs from abroad would put additional strain on domestic production because it can exacerbate labor shortages and drive up prices. The high cost of production can be amplified if the country is not currently efficient at producing j—that is, $z_i(j)$ is low relative to other goods produced in the country. When the global market is accessible, comparative advantage and specialization will steer the country away from producing j, as well as from developing the technologies and skills necessary to manufacture the product. As a result, if economic gains are no longer the priority and the production of j is deemed necessary or of strategic importance, a disproportionately high level of resources would be required to allow such production and reach a desirable production capacity.

These differences in production costs can prove friendshoring challenging if country 0's friends face similar total cost constraints. For example, many countries are aging, albeit at

[20] International Institute of Strategic Studies, "The 'Friend-Shoring' of Supply Chains," *Strategic Comments*, Vol. 28, December 2022.

[21] David E. Bloom, David Canning, and Günther Fink, "Population Aging and Economic Growth," in Michael Spence and Danny Leipziger, eds., *Globalization and Growth: Implications for a Post-Crisis World*, Commission on Growth and Development, 2010.

different rates; all these countries are likely to face labor shortage in the foreseeable future. Starting labor-intensive production in any of these countries will add to labor shortages. A country's friends may face similar strengths in production; for example, they may have a similar comparative advantage in technology-heavy industries, so it may be harder to develop complementary production portfolios with friends.

Trade-Offs Between Assurance and Access to Markets

Just like with anything else that is desirable, production network assurance comes at a cost. When a country excludes risky trade partners, it loses access to their productive capacity, and it could also lose access to their consumers as a result of retaliatory measures. This is particularly true when the countries being excluded are as big as China, a major global exporter and importer. In this model, the nested strategy clearly shows how the price of good j increases as the level of assurance desired increases. The most secure option, producing the good at home (strategy 1), is also the most expensive option. Friendshoring may offer slightly lower prices, but it depends on which countries are considered friends. When a high level of assurance is desired, strategy 2 takes a higher γ^* value, which means a smaller friend circle. Unless these friends already have a place in the global market through their existing comparative advantage, they are highly unlikely to be able to offer a competitive price without making substantial investments to lower their cost of production. As a result, the fewer countries are considered friends, the higher the resulting price will be. In addition to higher import prices, loss of access to large global markets means a loss in exports. The economies of scale component of the price of production ($\frac{F_0(j)}{\sum_{m=0}^{N} X_{m0}(j)}$) increases as total output ($\sum_{m=0}^{N} X_{m0}(j)$) decreases. When a reduction in export is large in magnitude, the impact could be consequential to the industries affected.

Fluid Trust Among Countries

Friendshoring relies on trustworthy friends, but friends can change, especially if they are marginally friendly. The uncertainty in international relationships needs to be acknowledged in the design of friendshoring as an underlying risk. In the friendshoring strategy (strategy 2) in the model, the desired trust level of a partner, $\gamma^*(j)$, depends on how much value good j holds in domestic consumption and production. However, considering that relationships are dynamic, it is obvious that countries with $\gamma \geq \gamma^*$ can change over time. This is especially true for marginally friendly countries with values close to γ^*.

Consequently, when designing friendshoring strategies, a country should first draw up a trade framework that can internalize patterns and trends in international relationships. Although uncertainty will always exist in the way that countries interact with one another, the level of uncertainty can be reduced if it is carefully considered, predicted, and exploited. Second, friendshoring is as much about shoring as about making friends. On the one hand, keeping a close, tight circle of friends could be beneficial: Relying on more-robust allies means higher costs in the short run, but less uncertainty might pay off in the long run. On the other hand, a larger friend circle is likely to yield lower prices and more options—this speaks to the importance of seeking cooperative relationships on a global scale.

Friends in Trade, Friends in Crisis

When friends in trade become friends in crisis, the blow to the production network suffers much bigger losses without the buffer of a global market. Although a high relationship score, γ_n, guarantees that country n will deliver when the production goes as planned, this happens when and only when its production capacity is not affected by exogenous shocks. The actual probability that the delivery happens is $\gamma_n \sigma_n$, and a low σ_n can significantly reduce this probability.

Although friendshoring may reduce uncertainty in global markets, external shocks can still cause widespread disruptions. With climate change, more and more countries are experiencing frequent weather events that could result in loss in productive capacity and output, all contributing to a lower σ. Meanwhile, different regions have different types of climate-related risks, and places in geographic proximity are more likely to suffer from the same weather event. Having a broad production network can mitigate the risk to some degree by sourcing from a diverse set of destinations. In the context of friendshoring, one weather event can hit many friends at once, straining the network. This showcases the importance of diversity of friends in friendshoring, an added layer of complexity when it comes to choosing trade partners. It also means that a country that desires friendshoring needs to have a systematic review of the production risks—both structural and incidental—that it faces, its friends face, and the rest of the world faces before designing and employing friendshoring as a strategy for production network assurance.

Are Friends of Friends Also Friends?

The fixed cost component of the price highlights the externality from global trade: If country i already specializes in good j, it has a significant advantage through its dominant place in the global market. When i is not in the friend circle of country 0, the friendshoring strategy requires consensus among all friends of country 0 to avoid ineffective friendshoring outcomes. For example, if friend country n simply purchases good j or key components of good j from country i and then resells it to country 0, the production network is not more assured, because the strategy simply adds an intermediary and additional transactional cost. For another example, without the main consumer countries of good j agreeing to stop buying from country i, country i will likely keep its dominance in the global market, making any entry attempt of a new producer in the market suffer from a steep price disadvantage. The limitation of friendshoring through this "friends of friends" mechanism can be seen playing out, for example, as China moves production to such countries as Mexico.[22] In general, countries with geopolitical ties and risks would be exposed to economic costs associated with

[22] Niels Graham and Mondrita Rashid, "Is 'Friendshoring' Really Working?" Atlantic Council, July 25, 2023.

trade fragmentation.[23] In the context of friendshoring, eliminating certain trade partners would, at the same time, effectively eliminate countries that are close to them—for example, countries that are close to China politically, such as Vietnam, might be forced to trade only in the same network with China.

To avoid these scenarios, friendshoring needs a high level of consensus (at minimum within the friend circle) to scrutinize and adjust everyone's production network to effectively improve assurance. Unfortunately, friends of friends are not necessarily friends, and with the intricacy of current production networks, the level of consensus required for effective production network assurance through friendshoring might be out of reach. This limitation of friendshoring should be highlighted because it deeply discounts the benefit of this strategy in production network assurance; more work needs to be done to understand this limitation.

Selective Decoupling in Production Network Assurance

Moving toward greater economic independence is painful, and economic decoupling is no different. However, because each country has a unique place in the global market, the decoupling process will not be completely symmetric or representative. This gives space for a well-thought-out plan with clear priorities that would cause the least amount of disruption in achieving higher production network assurance. The strategies associated with how to source good j depend on how much value j carries in production and consumption relative to other goods in consideration. Certain characteristics recommend higher assurance, and, thus, if current suppliers are deemed risky, investment in replacing partners can be prioritized. Our model suggests the following as some examples of characteristics that one might consider:

- goods that are important for national security, economic stability, and social welfare and whose shortage would impose significant costs on the economy and society
- goods that are in high demand
- goods that are currently much more expensive to produce domestically
- goods that cannot be produced domestically
- goods for which it is expensive or takes time to scale up production.

Evaluating the relative standing of goods in the production network helps identify the priority, vulnerability, and strength of the trading relationship. The asymmetry in which goods are priorities for a country suggests that costs are high for all countries that engage in such acts as trade decoupling. Because goods that are high on the priority list are usually different for each county, targeted policies will usually be effective and consequential, but the same is true for retaliation.

[23] Shushanik Hakobyan, Sergii Meleshchuk, and Robert Zymek, "Divided We Fall: Differential Exposure to Geopolitical Fragmentation in Trade, International Monetary Fund," WP/23/270, December 2023.

Technology Matters and Might Be the Ultimate Solution

Replacing existing partners with other partners or with domestic production has an underlying cost to global production and all the countries involved. In the end, resources are limited, everywhere. Any country producing the replacement goods needs to steer resources away from some other goods and services. The general equilibrium implication of moving away from the current production profile for the sole purpose of replacing existing suppliers might have a profound impact on the economy and its structure. Although the reallocation of resources might be painful and might be necessary for production network assurance, it is costly and requires careful implementation and preparation for potential fallouts. One way to prepare for such fallouts is to invest in specific types of technologies.

Many of the challenges described in this chapter come from the limitations of current production technologies and consumption patterns. Overcoming these challenges requires trade-offs, and potentially the only way to avoid such trade-offs is to change the technological landscape. In this section, we outline some of the ways that technological changes can improve production network assurance for a good j that is currently sourced from a risky partner.

Invest in Production

The first and most obvious solution is to invest in the technology to produce j. As discussed earlier, the main repercussion associated with this strategy is cost: If country 0 does not currently produce enough j, it means the cost of production is higher than the import price (i.e., high $\frac{c_0(j)}{z_0(j)}$), and country 0 does not currently have a price advantage from economies of scale (i.e., high average fixed cost $\frac{F_0(j)}{\sum_{m=0}^{N} X_{m0}(j)}$). To change this state of affairs, country 0 can invest in domestic production technology so that $z_0(j)$ is higher and the average production cost is lower, or country 0 can heavily subsidize the industry by lowering $F_0(j)$, removing part of the price disadvantage from the absence of economies of scale. Although both options will be effective in lowering costs in the short run, in the long run, investing in production technology could provide higher returns. New technology is more likely to have positive spillover effects through convergence and dispersion, whereas industry-specific subsidies could introduce inefficiencies and losses for society, or in technical terms, more welfare losses.

Invest in Trade with Allies

Friendshoring, or strategy 2 presented in this model, offers a good balance between cost and production network assurance. For a country n with a robust relationship score, $\gamma_n > \gamma^*(j)$, reducing its production cost (i.e., lowering $\frac{c_n(j)}{z_n(j)}$), reducing its trade cost (i.e., lowering d_{0n}), and enhancing its global market advantage could all effectively reduce the cost of friendshoring. Because every country has limited resources, friendshoring is, in general, a second-best strategy compared with free trade for the efficient allocation of resources. In this scenario, investing in the production technology in allies becomes almost as important as investing domestically. Such a strategy calls for more broad-based technological cooperation among allies.

Reductions in trade costs can come from investment in cross-country transportation systems. Considering how transportation-related technologies have driven global trade, the next generation of transportation-related technologies might well define the next trade era. Such technologies should reduce the cost of transportation, allow the process to come under the full control of allies, and ensure these routes are resilient to disruptions. Improvements in interoperability among global customs agencies would help firms determine their exposure to less-friendly countries in the global production network. Such technologies as blockchain could facilitate interoperability among customs agencies worldwide in this context by enabling the secure exchange of data and by streamlining customs procedures. This interoperability would expedite the movement of goods, reduce administrative burdens, and lower trade costs, ultimately benefiting friendshoring initiatives.

Reducing trade costs through market access agreements can help alleviate some of the additional costs associated with friendshoring. Expanding market access by granting preferential tariffs where possible and reducing non-tariff trade barriers (e.g., rules of origin and other technical barriers to trade) could reduce costs of trade among friends.

Invest in Alternative Goods

Technology may also fundamentally change what a country needs and consumes. If good j becomes less essential and replacements exist, a country does not have to achieve a high level of production network assurance, which is costly. This is not always possible but should be considered carefully as part of the solution in the long run. After identifying current vulnerabilities (i.e., in this model, goods that are crucial and sourced from countries with unreliable delivery), it is important to identify which goods could be optional for production under a more advanced technology.

There are two main reasons why this is a path worth pursuing even though developing production capacities takes time and money. First, the trade-off between production network assurance and economic gains from trade will always exist, as long as the good is considered a necessity for consumption, investment, or national security. One way to avoid this costly trade-off is to always steer away from needing such a good. Second, limited resources mean limited production, so any good that is absolutely necessary for any purpose is, by itself, a risk, regardless of how it is sourced. Even the option with the highest level of assurance, producing at home, does not have full assurance because production can be halted for unforeseeable reasons. A recent incident at a black powder factory in Louisiana, which accidentally exploded in 2021 and has been shut down ever since, highlights how risk is present regardless of whether production occurs abroad or at home.[24] The impact of halted production at the factory is relevant because it is the sole domestic source of an explosive used in mortar shells, artillery rounds, and Tomahawk missiles. The flexibility to not have to rely on something

---

[24] Gordon Lubold, "The U.S. Military Relies on One Louisiana Factory. It Blew Up." *Wall Street Journal*, April 26, 2023.

very specific will decrease the level of production network assurance needed and will ultimately lower the trade-off cost associated with it.

Invest in Components of Assurance

A trade agreement with country n is realized with probability $\gamma_n \sigma_n$. As a result, understanding the values of these two parameters and how they might change in the future is crucial for production network assurance and planning. Technologies that can track, predict, and even influence these parameter values would increase the likelihood for successful trade outcomes and gains from trade substantially. Relationship parameters γ are endogenous and can be boosted by fostering good relationships with important existing and future strategic partners. But even with a very high relationship parameter, γ_n, if production is at risk (i.e., low σ_n), the probability of a realized trade agreement is still low. This calls for investment in the robustness against production shocks for a country seeking production network assurance and for its trade partners.

Conclusion

In this chapter, we analyzed the concept and implications of economic decoupling between the United States and China, the two largest national economies in the world. We argue that decoupling is not simply a reversal or an end of globalization but rather a transformation of globalization that requires new objectives and approaches. We propose a new approach that we call *production network assurance*, which involves managing the risks and uncertainties associated with the production network to ensure that the production process runs smoothly and meets the desired objectives.

Using data from the OECD's ICIO dataset to assess the extent of global economic integration since the mid-1990s—and focusing on the shift of global production toward China following its entry into the WTO in 2001—we find that China has become a more prominent source of production for many regions in the world over this period. At the same time, other regions experienced a decline in global reliance on their production. We also find that regional economic relationships remain important despite the shifts toward Chinese production in the past two decades.

We built a theoretical model that provides insights into potential investment strategies aimed at reducing the costs of decoupling and strengthening the resilience of production networks. The model indicates that selective decoupling by prioritizing goods based on their importance, demand, domestic production capability, and scalability could improve production network assurance. Investment in technology, trade with allies, and alternative goods are critical to limiting the cost of production network assurance.

This chapter has some limitations that should be acknowledged and addressed in future research. One limitation is the lack of more-current data. The data used in this report are based on the OECD's ICIO dataset, which covers the period from 1995 through 2018. Although this is a comprehensive and reliable source of data, it might not reflect the most recent changes and developments in the global economy, such as the impact of the COVID-19 pandemic or the trade tensions between the United States and China.

A second limitation is the simplification of the theoretical framework. Our model can demonstrate the basic mechanism of how production network assurance could play a role in trade decisions, but to fully demonstrate the effects of such strategies as friendshoring, a more comprehensive quantitative model is necessary. Features of the model, such as the relationship parameters and shock parameters, require empirical examination and analysis to provide more-specific policy recommendations.

Abbreviations

EU	European Union
HHI	Herfindahl-Hirshman Index
ICIO	Inter-Country Input-Output
IO	input-output
LVAR	levelized value-added requirements
OECD	Organisation for Economic Co-operation and Development
RCEP	Regional Comprehensive Economic Partnership
ROW	rest of world
WTO	World Trade Organization

References

Amiti, Mary, and Jozef Konings, "Trade Liberalization, Intermediate Inputs, and Productivity: Evidence from Indonesia," *American Economic Review*, Vol. 97, No. 5, December 2007.

Anderson, James E., and Eric Van Wincoop, "Trade Costs," *Journal of Economic Literature*, Vol. 42, No. 3, September 2004.

Baldwin, Richard, Rebecca Freeman, and Angelos Theodorakopoulos, "Horses for Courses: Measuring Foreign Supply Chain Exposure," National Bureau of Economic Research, working paper 30525, September 2022.

Berthelon, Matias, and Caroline Freund, "On the Conservation of Distance in International Trade," *Journal of International Economics*, Vol. 75, No. 2, 2008.

Black, J. Stewart, and Allen J. Morrison, "The Strategic Challenges of Decoupling from China," *Harvard Business Review*, May–June 2021.

Bloom, David E., David Canning, and Günther Fink, "Population Aging and Economic Growth," in Michael Spence and Danny Leipziger, eds., *Globalization and Growth: Implications for a Post-Crisis World*, Commission on Growth and Development, 2010.

Department of Economics and Social Affairs, *International Standard Industrial Classification of All Economic Activities*, 4th rev., United Nations, 2008

Eaton, Jonathan, and Samuel Kortum, "Technology, Geography, and Trade," *Econometrica*, Vol. 70, No. 5, September 2002.

Ernst, Dieter, and Linsu Kim, "Global Production Networks, Knowledge Diffusion, and Local Capability Formation," *Research Policy*, Vol. 31, Nos. 8–9, December 2002.

Graham, Niels, and Mondrita Rashid, "Is 'Friendshoring' Really Working?" Atlantic Council, July 25, 2023.

Grossman, Gene M., Elhanan Helpman, and Hugo Lhuillier, "Supply Chain Resilience: Should Policy Promote Diversification or Reshoring?" National Bureau of Economic Research, working paper 29330, October 2021.

Hakobyan, Shushanik, Sergii Meleshchuk, and Robert Zymek, "Divided We Fall: Differential Exposure to Geopolitical Fragmentation in Trade," International Monetary Fund, WP/23/270, December 2023.

International Institute of Strategic Studies, "The 'Friend-Shoring' of Supply Chains," *Strategic Comments*, Vol. 28, No. 9, December 15, 2022.

Kucik, Jeffrey, and Rajan Menon, "Can the United States Really Decouple from China?" *Foreign Policy*, January 11, 2022.

Lubold, Gordon, "The U.S. Military Relies on One Louisiana Factory. It Blew Up." *Wall Street Journal*, April 26, 2023.

McNerney, James, Charles Savoie, Francesco Caravelli, Vasco M. Carvalho, and J. Doyne Farmer, "How Production Networks Amplify Economic Growth," *Proceedings of the National Academy of Sciences*, Vol. 119, No. 1, December 21, 2021.

Melitz, Marc J., "The Impact of Trade on Intra-Industry Reallocations and Aggregate Industry Productivity," *Econometrica*, Vol. 71, No. 6, November 2003.

Miller, Ronald E., and Peter D. Blair, *Input-Output Analysis: Foundations and Extensions*, 2nd ed., Cambridge University Press, 2009.

Miroudot, Sébastien, Jehan Sauvage, and Ben Shepherd, "Measuring the Cost of International Trade in Services," *World Trade Review*, Vol. 12, No. 4, October 2013.

OECD—*See* Organisation for Economic Co-operation and Development.

Organisation for Economic Co-operation and Development, "Inter-Country Input-Output Tables," dataset, undated. As of May 31, 2023:
https://www.oecd.org/en/data/datasets/inter-country-input-output-tables.html

Spence, A. Michael., "Destructive Decoupling," Council on Foreign Relations, April 4, 2023.

Sytsma, Tobias, "Improving Preferential Market Access Through Rules of Origin: Firm-Level Evidence from Bangladesh," *American Economic Journal: Economic Policy*, Vol. 14, No. 1, February 2022.

CHAPTER 5

Shaping Elite Networks: Strategic Cooperation with China

C. Ben Gibson, Aaron B. Frank, Khrystyna Holynska, and Jessie Wang

Overview

Systemic studies of international relations traditionally rely on empirically falsifiable core assumptions, such as the unity of states as rational actors. However, recent policy-oriented research emphasizes the need to move beyond these assumptions and consider bureaucratic constituencies, individual and group psychology, and the concept of a *selectorate* influencing policymaking within states. In this chapter, we build on the selectorate idea by using agent-based modeling to examine the maneuvering of representative elites to shape the policy agenda and the potential impact on both domestic transformation and elite power structures within China.

An equilibrium was reached in the network after a burn-in period, reproducing in broad strokes China's power system: central party officials occupying the center of a core periphery network and forming a hierarchy of power with these members on top. A simulated scenario sanctioning central party officials backfired, further concentrating the power of the group. Scenarios with cooperative economic intervention that benefited groups that are more inclined to protect international trade were more effective at bringing a more diverse group of elites into positions that could influence Chinese policy. This initial proof-of-concept agent-based model and its counterintuitive results suggest the ability to inform policy decisions aimed at strategically engaging with specific groups within China to shape U.S.-China relations.

Systemic studies of international relations have rested on a set of core assumptions intended to isolate the effects of the distribution of power among states from other considerations, such as their geographic location, regime type, or national or political culture. These core theoretical approaches, most commonly referred to as *realism*, *liberalism*, and *constructivism*, have rested on the core assumptions that (1) states behave as unified actors (i.e., their internal organization has no effects on their external behavior) and (2) the international system is fundamentally a self-help, anarchic one (i.e., there is no independent authority to which states may turn to in order to settle disagreements or enforce commitments).[1] These theories have provided general, though often different, insights into structural and historical pressures for states to cooperate and compete, but they rarely offer insights into the policy choices of states given the limits of their abstraction. Indeed, although international relations scholars have often provided policy advice grounded in their specific theoretical orientation, they have also noted the important difference between developing and testing theories of the international systems versus theories of foreign policy.[2]

Modeling State Behavior

Policy-oriented research in international relations has started to unpack visions of the state as a singular, unified actor and examine decisionmaking in terms of bureaucratic constituencies and processes, including providing considerations of the psychological characteristics of individual leaders and groups, and the internal competition for power among political elites.[3]

---

[1] Kenneth N. Waltz, *Theory of International Politics*, McGraw Hill, 1979; Alexander Wendt, *Social Theory of International Politics*, Cambridge University Press, 1999; Robert Jervis, "Realism, Neoliberalism, and Cooperation: Understanding the Debate," *International Security*, Vol. 24, No. 1, Summer 1999; James E. Dougherty and Robert L. Pfaltzgraff Jr., *Contending Theories of International Relations: A Comprehensive Survey*, 5th ed., Pearson, 2000; Robert O. Keohane and Joseph S. Nye Jr., *Power and Interdependence*, Pearson, 2011).

[2] Waltz, 1979, pp. 71–72.

[3] Andrew W. Marshall, *Problems of Estimating Military Power*, RAND Corporation, P-3417, August 1966; Graham T. Allison and Morton H. Halperin, "Bureaucratic Politics: A Paradigm and Some Policy Implications," *World Politics*, Vol. 24, No. S1, Spring 1972; Irving L. Janis, *Groupthink: Psychological Studies of Policy Decisions and Fiascoes*, 2nd ed., Cengage Learning, 1982; Roger Hilsman, "International Environment, the State, and Intelligence," in Alfred C. Maurer, Marion D. Tunstall, and James M. Keagle, eds., *Intelligence: Policy and Process*, Westview Press, 1985; Graham Allison and Philip Zelikow, *Essence of Deci-*

Recent models of policymaking within states has emphasized the need to avoid the unitary actor assumption by emphasizing the need to consider a governing coalition, specifically the relationship between a singular leader and a *selectorate* (i.e., a group whose approval the leader needs in order to maintain power).[4] The selectorate may be broad and diffuse, spanning the public, such as in democracies, or narrow and concentrated among such groups as a handful of government ministers, party bosses, or tribal elders in which autocratic command is constrained only by the consent of small circle of elites.

In this chapter, we build on the notion of a selectorate but do so from a different strand of social theory. Rather than directly model the selection of foreign policies based on the relative power and preferences of groups, often modeled as the result of a bargaining process in which factions maximize their expected utility of policy positions, we model the maneuvering of representative elites seeking to position themselves in a network of political alliances to have the opportunity to set the policy agenda.[5] Thus, rather than trying to predict which policies may be selected given a set of preferences, we seek to predict the types of agents who will be positioned to partake in the policymaking process, from which additional inferences about acceptable or unacceptable policy choices may flow. This allows us to shift the analytic focus away from the arrangement of elites on specific issues at specific times toward a dynamic model in which being in position to shape the policy agenda itself is contested.

In addressing this research project's core question (*How can the United States ensure that its economy meets the nation's needs under conditions of coupled, strategic competition?*), the model of elite networks in this chapter explores whether a pathway exists through which mutual exchange with China can provide the United States with economic security. The theory and model present a more nuanced assessment of the nature of exchange and mutualism that has failed to produce unequivocal success through engagement and emergence

---

sion: Explaining the Cuban Missile Crisis, 2nd ed., Addison Wesley Longman, 1999; John D. Steinbruner, *The Cybernetic Theory of Decision: New Dimensions of Political Analysis*, Princeton University Press, 2002; Robert Jervis, *Perception and Misperception in International Politics*, new ed., Princeton University Press, 2017b; Robert Jervis, *How Statesmen Think: The Psychology of International Politics*, Princeton University Press, 2017a).

4 Bruce Bueno De Mesquita, Alastair Smith, Randolph M. Siverson, and James D. Morrow, *The Logic of Political Survival*, MIT Press, 2005; Bruce Bueno de Mesquita and Alastair Smith, *The Dictator's Handbook: Why Bad Behavior Is Almost Always Good Politics*, PublicAffairs, 2011.

5 There is a large class of formal *spatial bargaining* models in the field of political economy that seek to identify positions in a multidimensional space at which each agent maximizes its expected utility given its relative power in a zero-sum game. This model is further extended to consider the potential that states may not only reject the other's position but may prefer to risk war than compromise and maintain peace. See James D. Fearon, "Rationalist Explanations for War," *International Organization*, Vol. 49, No. 3, Summer 1995; James D. Fearon, "Bargaining, Enforcement, and International Cooperation," *International Organization*, Vol. 52, No. 2, Spring 1998; Andrew H. Kydd, *Trust and Mistrust in International Relations*, Princeton University Press, 2007; and Andrew H. Kydd, *International Relations Theory: The Game-Theoretic Approach*, Cambridge University Press, 2015.

of shared interests.[6] Indeed, earlier perspectives assumed that trade and exchange created constituencies for more trade and exchange, thus compelling domestic transformation by becoming an end in and of itself. In such a model, heterogeneity within China was expected to emerge and be rewarded through the feedback of exchange.

In the following sections of this chapter, we describe and report the results of using an agent-based model (ABM) to analyze how to use the heterogeneity within China to maximize the policymaking position of those interested in international exchange. The model presented here starts from the assumption that China is internally heterogeneous, and, as a result, trade and exchange may create and empower a constituency for increasing political and economic liberalization, but it may also enrich those elites already occupying privileged positions in the policy network, solidifying their control over the policymaking process by widening the gap in relative power within the country.

Agent-Based Models and Policy Networks

ABMs are computational simulations of individual agents—actors who possess the ability to make choices autonomously—interacting in an environment according to a set of rules. Collectively, the interactions of agents can produce systemic or macroscopic outcomes that cannot be predicted by analyzing the individual agents in isolation. Agents typically represent individuals but can also represent groups, institutions, or other collectives. Using a set of rules, constraints, and principles guiding decisionmaking—combined with endogenous and exogenous features—ABMs are intended to gain insight into the relationship between the behavior of individuals and the structure of the system (i.e., they link agents between microscopic actions and macroscopic outcomes).[7] ABMs also enable simulation of potential interventions in the system, making them attractive tools for policy analysis because they allow for the examination of the consequences of choices and actions that actors might take, incorporating the adaptive responses of agents who continue to pursue their objectives.[8] The flexibility of ABMs in modeling behavior has attracted researchers who seek to build fundamental theories of behavior by reproducing components of observed social systems.[9]

---

6 White House, *A National Security Strategy of Engagement and Enlargement*, February 1995, p. 29; Robert O. Keohane, *After Hegemony: Cooperation and Discord in the World Political Economy*, revised ed. Princeton University Press, 2005.

7 Joshua M. Epstein and Robert L. Axtell, *Growing Artificial Societies: Social Science From the Bottom Up*, Brookings Institution Press and MIT Press, 1996; Robert Axelrod, "Advancing the Art of Simulation in the Social Sciences," *Complexity* Vol. 3, No. 2, November 1997; John H. Miller and Scott E. Page, *Complex Adaptive Systems: An Introduction to Computational Models of Social Life*, Princeton University Press, 2007.

8 Robert Lempert, "Agent-Based Modeling as Organizational and Public Policy Simulators," *Proceedings of the National Academy of Sciences*, Vol. 99, Suppl. 3, May 14, 2002.

9 Henrik Skaug Sætra, "Exploring the Use of Agent-Based Modeling (ABM) in Mixed Methods Research," *Barataria: Revista Castellano-Manchega de Ciencias Sociales*, No. 22, 2017.

A canonical ABM contains several core components:

1. *A population of agents that represents autonomous actors with the ability to make decisions according to a set of rules and goals.* Agents may be homogeneous and only vary with respect to their local environments and historical experiences, such as ants in a colony. Agents may be heterogeneous, such as firms and customers in a marketplace that each have unique preferences regarding the production and consumption of goods. Goals may be highly complex (and include balancing multiple objectives) or simple (such as maintaining bonds of friendship within a network).[10]
2. *An environment in which agents interact.* Environments may enable access to resources, such as information or physical goods (e.g., food or building materials). Environments may also impose structure on the options for interactions between agents, such as representing geographic distance or social networks in which distinctions arise associated with the meaning of *local* that affect what interactions are possible and preferred.[11]
3. *A set of individual states and systemic metrics that are tracked to measure the dynamics of the system as a whole.* Such measures seek to connect how the aggregated actions of the agents relate to systemic or societal outcomes. For example, one of the first ABMs was developed by Thomas Schelling to show how individual preferences for living in racially mixed neighborhoods could nevertheless aggregate to produce highly segregated populations.[12]

An Agent-Based View of International Relations

Because international relations often depend on the internal mechanisms of policy formation, it is important to understand the within-country structure of influence over decision-making.[13] One measure of influence is through a positional analysis of agents in a larger social network. The representation of individuals as components of a larger network allows for the analysis of node-level metrics (e.g., aspects of an individual's position within the broader system). At the node level, network analysis can reveal the concentration of links on select individuals or their position within or between subgroups. Node-level metrics encom-

---

[10] Per Block, Christoph Stadtfeld, and Tom A. B. Snijders, "Forms of Dependence: Comparing SAOMs and ERGMs from Basic Principles," *Sociological Methods & Research*, Vol. 48, No. 1, February 2019.

[11] Duncan J. Watts and Steven H. Strogatz, "Collective Dynamics of 'Small-World' Networks," *Nature*, Vol. 393, No. 6684, June 4, 1998; Alison J. Heppenstall, Andrew T. Crooks, Linda M. See, and Michael Batty, eds., *Agent-Based Models of Geographical Systems*, Springer, 2011.

[12] Thomas C. Schelling, "Models of Segregation," *American Economic Review*, Vol. 59, No. 2, May 1969; Thomas C. Schelling, "Dynamic Models of Segregation," *Journal of Mathematical Sociology*, Vol. 1, No. 2, 1971.

[13] Valerie M. Hudson, "Foreign Policy Analysis: Actor-Specific Theory and the Ground of International Relations," *Foreign Policy Analysis*, Vol. 1, No. 1, March 2005.

pass measures of influence and power, including degree (number of ties belonging to a single node) and more-complex indices, such as Bonacich power centrality, which measures the extent to which nodes are connected to other powerful nodes.[14]

We can also analyze aspects of the larger network. For example, we can measure the stability of the network (i.e., the ability for changes in endogenous or exogenous factors to shift the structure of links between agents reflecting alternative power-sharing and decisionmaking structures). Some elite networks have slow-changing institutional support, such as democracies; others, notably autocracies, rely on a small group of elites.[15] The propensity of political effects resulting from changing the behavior or resources of elites may be more affected in autocracies than in democracies based on differences in how elite pluralism affects network centralization. Specifically, the centralization of the network around a relatively small number of individuals may represent a more malleable system because changes to a small number of people would have large repercussions for the broader network. Some researchers have emphasized other networkwide metrics, such as the ability for information to efficiently pass through network ties to reach the population of actors or span distinct subgroups.[16] Network structures that may prohibit such diffusion include the formation of tight-knit subgroups that do not interact. Such subgroups could also represent competing factions within a political influence network, revealing a potential opportunity for outside influence to affect the system. Network-level metrics include centralization, degree distributions, and clustering metrics. We describe these metrics in greater detail in a subsequent section.

In the next section, we outline the use of network-based ABMs on China's modern political elite. Here, we focus on the distribution of power within heterogeneous elements of Chinese elites and on the unity of elites as operating under one umbrella or central authority. We thus measure the relative influence or power across sectors of Chinese elites, the centralization of the network onto a small number of nodes, and the hierarchical organization of elites in the network. After building an initial network, we seek interventions to enhance the power of individuals interested in international exchange, decrease centralization of the network onto legacy elites, and, potentially, produce competing factions that may represent the beginnings of an internal epochal change in the policymaking processes.

Modeling China's Political Elite

The ABM of China's political elite represents key political constituencies through archetypal agents that reflect key social and economic sectors with distinct political interests and resources. The elite network is composed of multiple, heterogeneous agents who interact with

[14] For more details on Bonacich power centrality, see the "Supplementary Material" section at the end of this chapter.

[15] Bueno de Mesquita et al., 2005; Bueno de Mesquita and Smith, 2011.

[16] Matthew O. Jackson, *Social and Economic Networks*, Princeton University Press, 2008.

one another by "trading" political capital to achieve their desired goals. As political networks emerge, their structural properties are measured using graph-theoretic and social network analysis methods that provide a sense of the leadership's political orientation based on the overall arrangement of the leadership's members and their ideologies.

Agents representing elites have numerous attributes, and each agent can make decisions based on different political strategies. Elite attributes affect how agents make decisions, how other agents perceive their identities and position, and what material or ideological resources are at their disposal. Within the model, elites extract resources of different types and convert those resources into political capital. That political capital is then converted into maintaining existing political affiliations, allowing each elite to develop new relationships with other elites. Political strategies available to elites include the following:

- **Self-interest:** Elites seek to improve their individual position within the national network of elites, constantly using their resources to align with other agents of higher levels of influence.
- **Group-interest:** Elites seek to improve the overall positioning of their individual ethnic, regional, religious, or economic bloc relative to other blocs.
- **Revolutionary:** Elites seek to build alternative centers of power and influence around those agents that lie on the fringes of the network at the beginning of the simulation.
- **Reactionary:** Elites seek to consolidate power amongst the most central agents at the start of the simulation. These agents attempt to push those agents on the periphery of the network further from the center into isolation.

Agents are not confined to a single strategy. For instance, some agents may be 75 percent self-interested, 20 percent group-interested, and 5 percent revolutionary. Their linked preferences are ranked based on a weighted sum of their strategy mix, linking with others that maximize their strategic objectives.[17]

With preferences for links in place, agents then extract resources to form networks. Resources are split into four primary groups: (1) extractive resources, (2) trade, (3) technology, and (4) ideology, information, and security (IIS). Each agent owns a share of these resources, and each resource base varies in its total political value. Using their resource base, agents "purchase" ties to other agents, and those ties' "costs" scale based on the Bonacich power index; more powerful ties are more costly to develop.

Each agent draws political capital from its proximity to other well-connected agents, affording access and prestige to shape policy agendas and to participate in the policy process, whether formally or informally. If an agent cannot afford to make a tie, it will go down the list to its next-ranked choice until it can afford to make a tie.

[17] See the supplementary material at the end of this chapter for a more complete description of elites in the network.

To provide an initial test of the model, RAND's China subject-matter experts produced a set of agent population parameters and agent types and with varying resource bases and strategy mixes that represent elites in China.[18] China's political elite were divided into different agent archetypes, each with different distributions of strategies, group membership, and access to resources. These archetypes were as follows:

- **Xi Jinping:** a unitary leader and singular agent in the model
- **Central party officials:** leaders of the Chinese Communist Party (CCP) whose positions and interests are largely developed and perceived around personal and ideological ties to the central party and Xi.
- **Central government ministers:** leaders of the government's bureaucracy who implement policy
- **Regional leaders (central):** leaders of the regional provinces within China who are centrally located geographically
- **Regional leaders (coastal):** leaders of the regional provinces within China who are located on the coast
- **Regional leaders (Central Asian border):** leaders of the regional provinces within China who are located on the border with Central Asia
- **State-owned enterprise (SOE) leaders (interior):** leaders of SOEs in China that are not on the coast
- **SOE leaders (coastal):** leaders of SOEs on China's coast
- **Entrepreneurs:** leaders of commercial enterprises who primarily develop wealth through the generation of new businesses, technologies, and services
- **Traders:** leaders of commercial enterprises who primarily develop wealth through international trade.

In addition to producing a set of agents, we also built an initial network based on the propensity of different archetypes to be politically connected, which is then modified across time steps until we reach an equilibrium.

The remainder of this section is divided into two parts. First, we make initial evaluations on the behavior of the system as a check on whether the system operates within expectations. We determine whether the system equilibrates to a stable state; we then determine how power

[18] In this version of the agent population, our experts divided the government elites into two groups of people representing the core party elite (central party officials) and senior government officials (central government ministers) occupying the top positions in the bureaucracy. This model presents a coarse view of China's political and economic elite, and, with the exception of Xi Jinping (who occupies a singular place in the political network), group labels may not directly correspond with the formal positions or titles of real-world individuals. For example, in future iterations, regional leaders and state-owned enterprise leaders can be further differentiated into party leaders and government of enterprise leaders. As this stage, this exploratory research is primarily concerned with the merits of network-based representations and strategies for engagement. Increasing representational accuracy is desired but only if the initial experiments performed in this work prove the merits of the network-based approach to strategic cooperation.

is distributed across archetypes. The second section is an exploration of interventions in the system. We explore a punitive intervention in which international sanctions are imposed on central party officials; we then explore three cooperative interventions in which we aim to support archetypes that are more likely to have policy preferences that align with preserving the stability and prosperity of the existing international order.

Initial Evaluation

In this section, we present an initial analysis of the model's dynamics based on the configuration developed by RAND's China subject-matter experts. The model's general process is as follows:

1. At each time step, each agent converts their resources into political capital that is used to update its political links that determine the agent's position in the overall network of elites.
2. Each agent's existing links may be dropped with a given probability, allowing for the agent to revisit the value of making such a commitment.
3. Agents use their available political capital to pay upkeep costs associated with their political links.
4. Agents use their remaining political capital and their individual political strategy to evaluate and rank possible links they can form with other agents to further their political goals.
5. Agents attempt to form links based on their preferences, creating and paying for new links.

One challenge to the use of ABMs is to establish whether emergent structures match what we expect given the empirical data. In this initial building of an ABM, we present a series of measures to test the reasonableness of the network that is generated using this model. These measures include network density, centralization, and the distribution of power across the agent population that represents China's political elite. These measures are a check against *degeneracy* (i.e., a breakdown of network structure that differs from what we would regard as a plausible real-life representation of the status quo). We also measure the *stability* of the system (i.e., when network structure converges on a set of statistics that appear to match those we would expect from the Chinese political system). In the absence of a real, empirical political influence network, we rely on heuristics drawn from expert input and observations.

Figure 5.1 shows a visual representation of the elite political networks at the end of an initialization time series. The top panel shows the composition of archetypes across the network; nodes are colored according to archetypes within the elite network. The core-periphery structure appears to follow a simple three-tiered structure, with traders and entrepreneurs along the same tier as the medium-powerful nodes that include SOE leaders and central government ministers.

FIGURE 5.1

A Core-Periphery Network and Embedded Hierarchical Rings of Relative Power

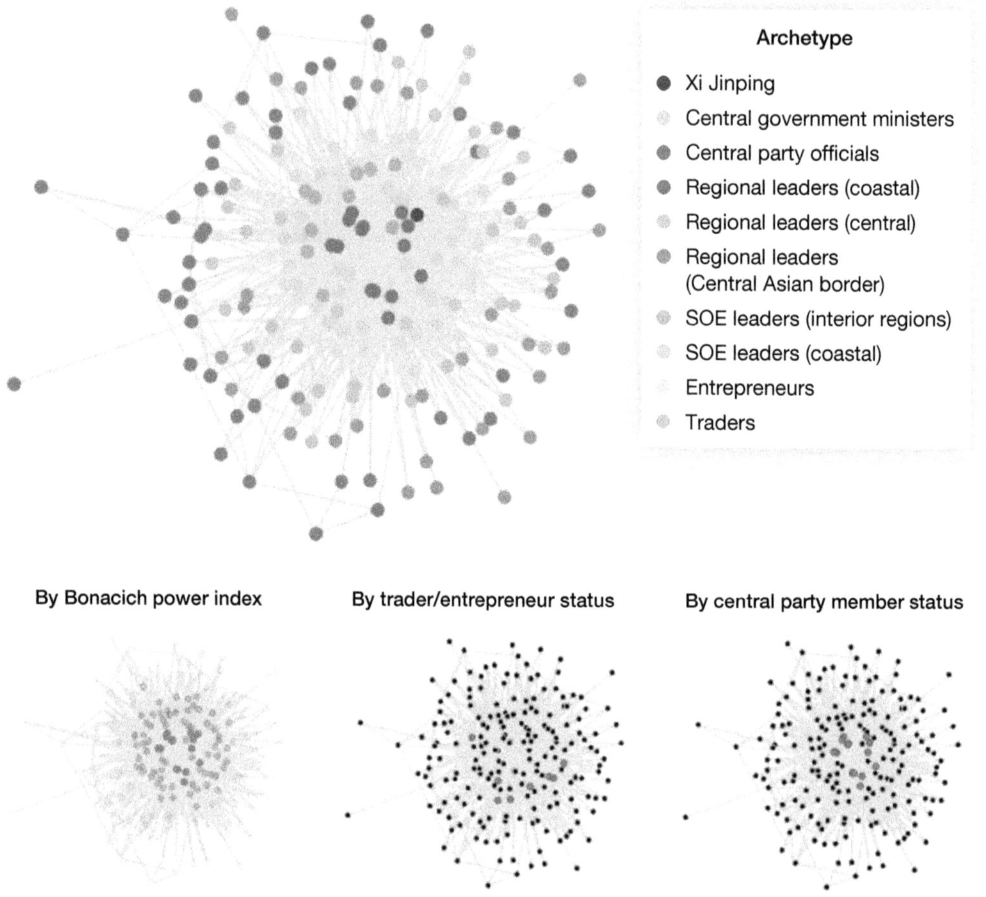

NOTE: This figure shows an ABM-produced political network with a core-periphery structure, as indicated by the varying Bonacich power measures of nodes shaded from light to deep red (bottom left). The top panel and the bottom left panel show that the central core comprises such powerful figures as central party officials and Xi Jinping, while less influential elites, such as regional leaders and SOE heads, form the periphery. The bottom center and right panel highlight the positions of traders and entrepreneurs and central party officials to further show their relative positions in the elite network.

The networks in the bottom panel are identical to the top; the coloring of the nodes is changed only to highlight institutional differences regarding relative position and power in the network. The bottom left panel shades the nodes from light to deep red according to the estimate of their Bonacich power measure in the network. Nodes toward the center of this network are shaded deeper red because they are connected to other, highly connected nodes in the network. Those on the periphery of the network are less connected to more powerful nodes, which lowers their power score. In the center and right panel, agents representing traders and entrepreneurs and central party officials are highlighted to show their respective positions and placement in the core-periphery network structure.

The network-level statistics over time offer additional insights into the evolution of the core-periphery network structure. Comparing the statistics of Bonacich centrality across archetypes confirms the three-tiered power structure of Chinese elites in this ABM. Along the top (average Bonacich centrality of 2.6), central government ministers and Xi Jinping are clearly the most powerful elites. A middle-range tier (average Bonacich centrality of 1.1) consists of SOE leaders, central government ministers, traders, and entrepreneurs. A bottom tier (representing agents who hold the least amount of influence and power) consists of regional leaders of central, coastal, and central Asian border regions.

Figure 5.2 shows the convergence and stability of the Chinese elite ABM over time. To do so, we observe the shift in statistics across an initialization process that *burns in* the network (i.e., executes the ABM for enough time steps until it reaches a stable state). The figure shows this shift from our starting point to the network after 300 time steps. Stability in the ABM is desirable for two major reasons. First, we observe that the Chinese political elite system, like many social systems, is essentially stable; a stable ABM thus approaches a more realistic picture of the system we are attempting to model. Second, when testing network interventions, stability allows us to pinpoint the intervention itself as the likely cause of any observed changes to the network. We thus calibrate the model to reach an equilibrium that appears consistent with the system as we understand it.

In the top panel of Figure 5.2, we see that, after an initial process of equilibration, the centralization, mean degree, and mean Bonacich power index remain stable across time. In the final, burned-in network, centralization—a measure of the concentration of centrality onto a small number of nodes—is lower than our initial network but remains high (0.227 versus 0.029 across 100 random networks with similar density). Mean degree remains about the same as the initial network, although more mixing occurs in the equilibration process as ties are initially gained and lost in rapid succession while agents settle in to stable relationships. The mean power index—a measure of connectedness to those who are well-connected—remains at about 1 across the time series, indicating a stable distribution of power across the time series.

The second and third panels show the convergence of the shared partner distribution over the burn-in period. Shared partners represent the number of dyads shared by pairs of tied nodes. For example, if nodes A and B are tied, and both A and B are tied to node C, dyad A-B have a shared partner C. The shared partner distribution is a measure of clustering; a higher number of shared partners represents a network with tie clusters that is consistent with many social systems.[19] Our initial network simulates a random network conditional on mixing matrices between and within archetypes (see the "Supplementary Material" section at the end of this chapter for more details). Because edge weights do not impose clustering by default, any clustering that occurs in the network is a product of the ABM. Here, we show

[19] The clustering of social systems can be driven by many mechanisms. For example, *triadic closure*—the tendency for friends-of-friends to become friends—has often been explored (Mark S. Granovetter, "The Strength of Weak Ties," *American Journal of Sociology*, Vol. 78, No. 6, May 1973).

FIGURE 5.2

Network Structure Measures over Time Show Emergent, Centralized Structure After Burn-In Period

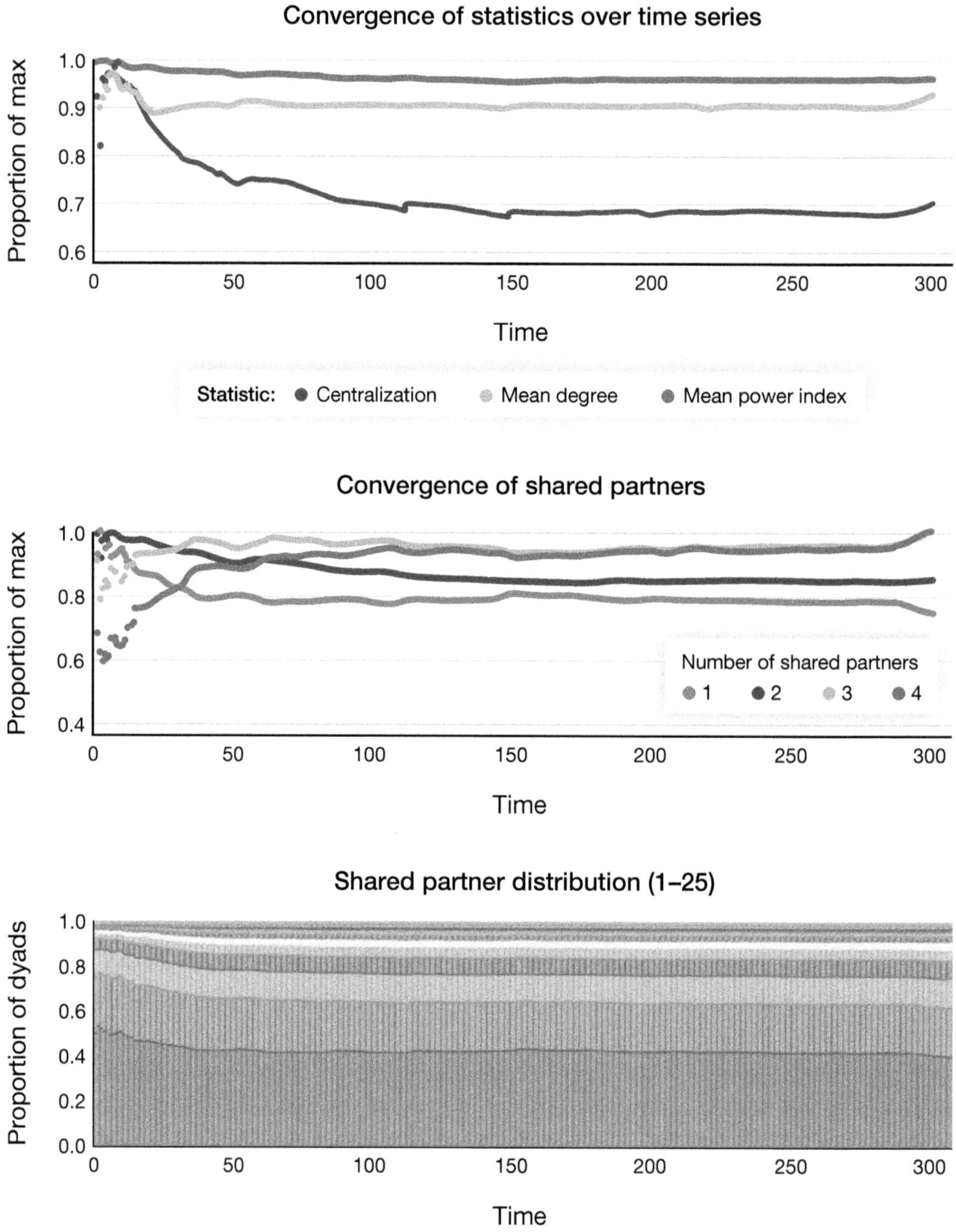

NOTE: This figure shows the stability of centralization, mean degree, and mean Bonacich power index in a network over 300 timesteps, with centralization decreasing but remaining relatively high. The shared partner distribution (the number of ties each pair of connected nodes have in common), demonstrates a significant increase in shared partners overall, indicating the emergence of organic clustering driven by agent behavior, as reflected in a decline in edges with one shared partner and an 80-percent rise in dyads with four shared partners.

that clustering occurs organically as a function of the behavior of the agents; the number of shared partners rises much higher than in our initial network. For example, the number of dyads with one shared partner declines approximately 40 percent over the burn-in period; the number of dyads with four shared partners rises 80 percent.

Structural equivalence is a way to measure whether two nodes occupy a similar position in the network. In a classic hierarchical structure, structural equivalence would be a situation in which two people occupy the same (equivalent) position in the hierarchy. We use structural equivalence to get a matrix of distances between all agents in the network. We then run hierarchical clustering on these equivalence values to determine whether there is a hierarchical structure in the network, with powerful nodes on top and less powerful nodes below. Nodes can be arranged in a hierarchical sequence if they are closely connected in the network but have differences in their relative power. If they are closely connected by differences in power, the higher-powered nodes will be placed above lower-powered nodes in a hierarchical sequence.

Figure 5.3 shows the results of the hierarchical clustering algorithm on the ABM network. As we may expect, senior central party ministers lie on top of the hierarchy (blue nodes on the bottom of the top panel have lines that trace to the top of the plot, representing a higher position on the network). The first cut of structural equivalence shows, essentially, a re-creation of clustering along the lines of the elite archetypes specified by our experts. However, in the initial run, elites appear to have two distinct hierarchical trees, led by different segments of the group of central party officials. In our interventions, we observe how this hierarchy changes given the policy actions taken to affect the network.

Strategic Interventions Within the ABM

To answer this project's core research question (*How can the United States ensure that its economy meets the nation's needs under conditions of coupled, strategic competition?*), we tested a series of scenarios that explored how U.S. policies affecting access to resources and strategies of Chinese elites may influence the structure of China's political networks. We compared the impact of competitive and cooperative interventions on the change in network power structure, hierarchical organization, and network statistics. Together, these changes offer hints as to whether actions taken on the part of the United States (or other exogenous actors) can alter which elites (and therefore which interests) may have influence over political agenda-setting within China. To do so, we first explored the effects of an intervention representing the imposition of sanctions on elite party members. We next tested three cooperative interventions, building the resource base of groups that were more amenable to international exchange.

Given the computational costs of the simulation, and given the available project time, the following scenarios represent the results of single model runs applying the policy intervention. Although ABMs are stochastic models whose results should be generalized only after significant statistical testing, our intuition of the model's general tendencies and its macroscopic stability developed over months of verification and validation lead us to believe that

FIGURE 5.3

Hierarchical Clustering Results on the ABM Network Show a Two-Tier Segmentation of Political Elites Centered on Different Segments of Central Party Officials

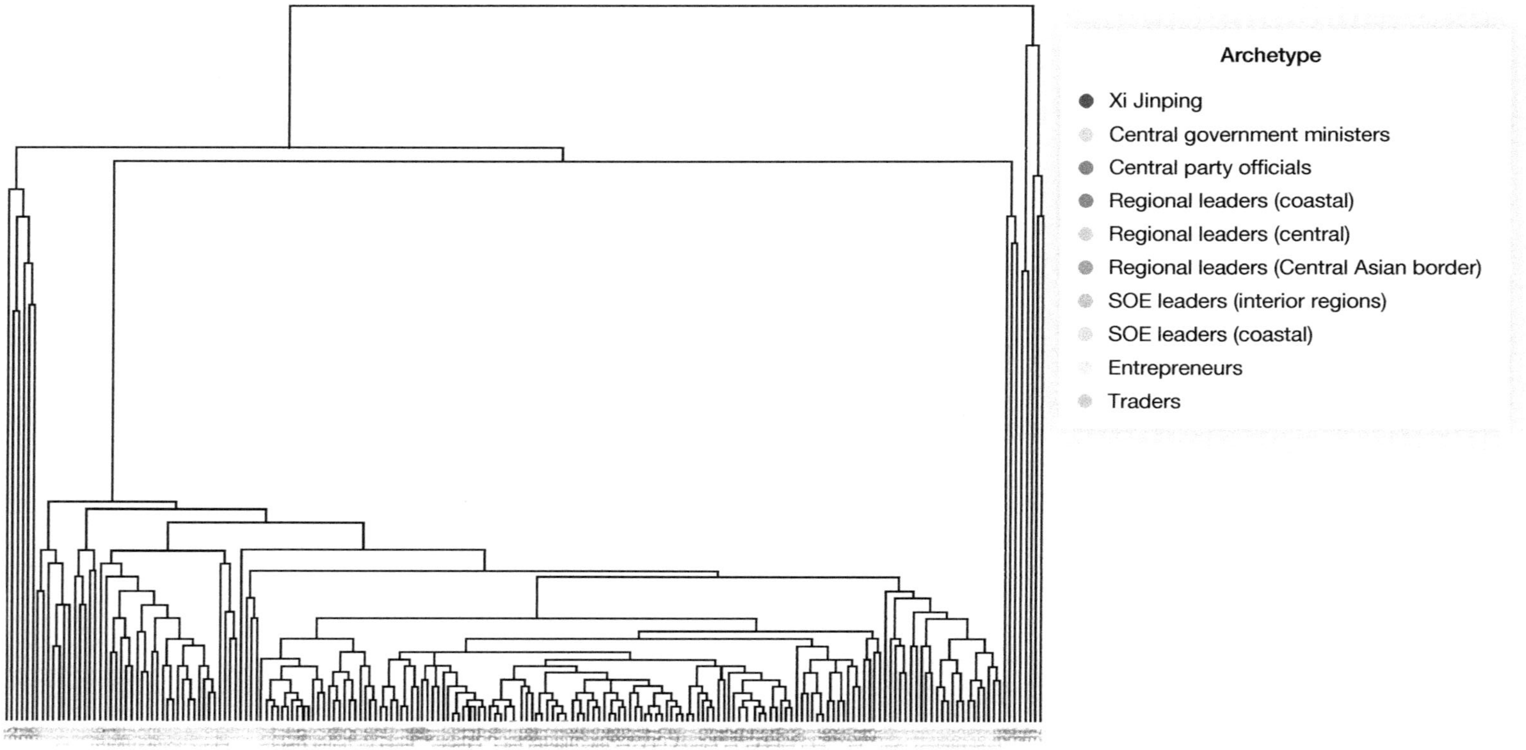

NOTE: This figure shows hierarchical clustering results on the ABM network, revealing central party officials at the top of the hierarchy and lower-level actors below them. Hierarchical clustering attempts to position nodes according to their relative power in the network, and results were produced from their calculated power index. All nodes lie on the bottom, and their lines can be traced to the node's relative position in the network's hierarchy. Elites exhibit two distinct hierarchical trees led by different segments of central party ministers, but interventions in the network later alter this hierarchy.

the single run results discussed below provide typical qualitative macroscopic responses to the proposed policy interventions. Although uncertainties remain regarding the quantitative effect sizes that policy interventions might have, the general directions of the effects observed below are likely to generalize and be confirmed by additional simulation runs. To better characterize (1) quantitative effect sizes and distributions at the system level and (2) microscopic, agent-level effects on elites would require additional simulation runs and model instrumentation to verify. Thus, in the following discussion, we focus on the direction and types of changes that policy actions have on the policy network, leaving more-detailed analysis for future research.

Scenario 1: Sanctioning Elite Party Members

In this scenario, we introduce an exogeneous shock to the resource base of central party officials, the most powerful agents in the ABM, consistent with the application of international sanctions on their resources. The question here is whether a reduction in resources negatively affects these agents' control over decisionmaking, as measured by their relative position within the network. We first run the ABM to establish a structural baseline, reaching an equilibrium after a 300 time-step burn-in period. We then target members of the central party minister archetype with a one-time, 25-percent reduction in resources to promote shifts in power among elites.

After 100 time steps, the imposition of sanctions on central party officials has an effect that is the opposite from what was intended: The central party officials cut ties with lower-priority nodes while maintaining and building new ties with one another, as shown in Figure 5.4. The resulting response is a 37.9-percent increase in the Bonacich power index for this group and a 21-percent to 33-percent reduction in power for all other groups. Instead of encouraging realignment, nonparty groups lose their existing attachments to the strong party core and drift further to the periphery. In this intervention into the network of China's political elite, an international sanction backfires by reducing the influence of other groups and increasing the power of the sanction's targeted group.

Simulated sanctions also changed the organization of structural equivalence in the network. Compared with the baseline sequence shown in Figure 5.3, in which central party members coalesced into two separate hierarchical groups, the imposition of sanctions resulted in the party members forming a single overarching group, as shown in Figure 5.5. Although party members are at baseline structurally equivalent in both the baseline and sanctioned conditions, we see shifts in the hierarchical clustering of nodes. In the baseline, party members are split into two separate trees, representing distinct sections of elites. In the new scenario version, the hierarchical clustering procedure shows the central party member nodes arranged into a single tree.

These findings extend other analyses that have focused on the vulnerabilities of China's political elite to the imposition of sanctions, particular those targeted at individuals and their families. A 2023 study identified vulnerabilities in the Chinese elite where the United States

FIGURE 5.4

The Resulting Political Network After the Sanctioning of Party Ministers Results in a More Concentrated Core Cluster and a Weaker Periphery

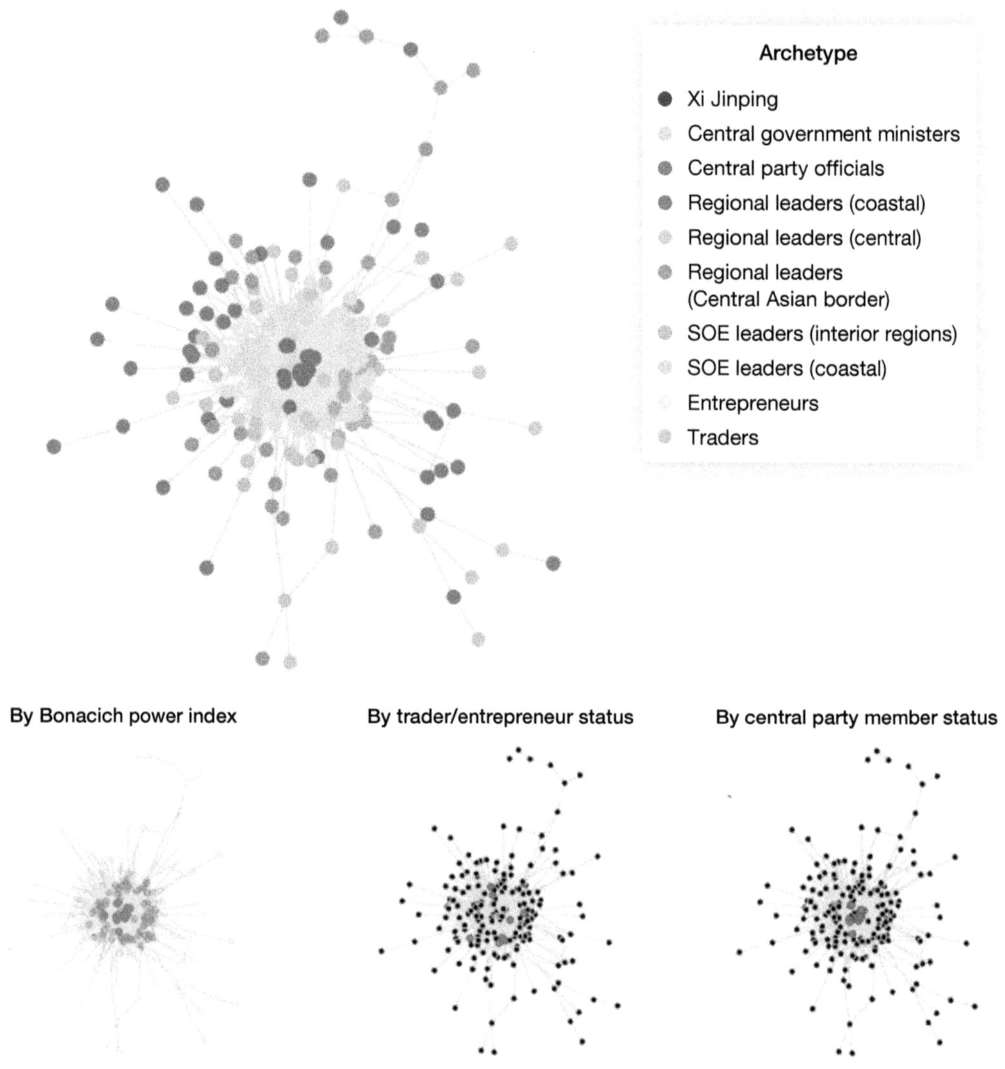

NOTE: This figure shows the resulting network after sanctioning party ministers. The sanctioned archetype strengthens internal tie structure, resulting in a 37.9-percent increase in the Bonacich power index while other groups experience a 21-percent to 33-percent reduction in power, indicating a backfire of the international sanction event. Central party members remain at the center of the network with others on the periphery.

FIGURE 5.5

The Hierarchy of Structural Equivalence in the Network Shifts as Central Party Members Coalesce into a Single Unified Block in Response to Sanctions

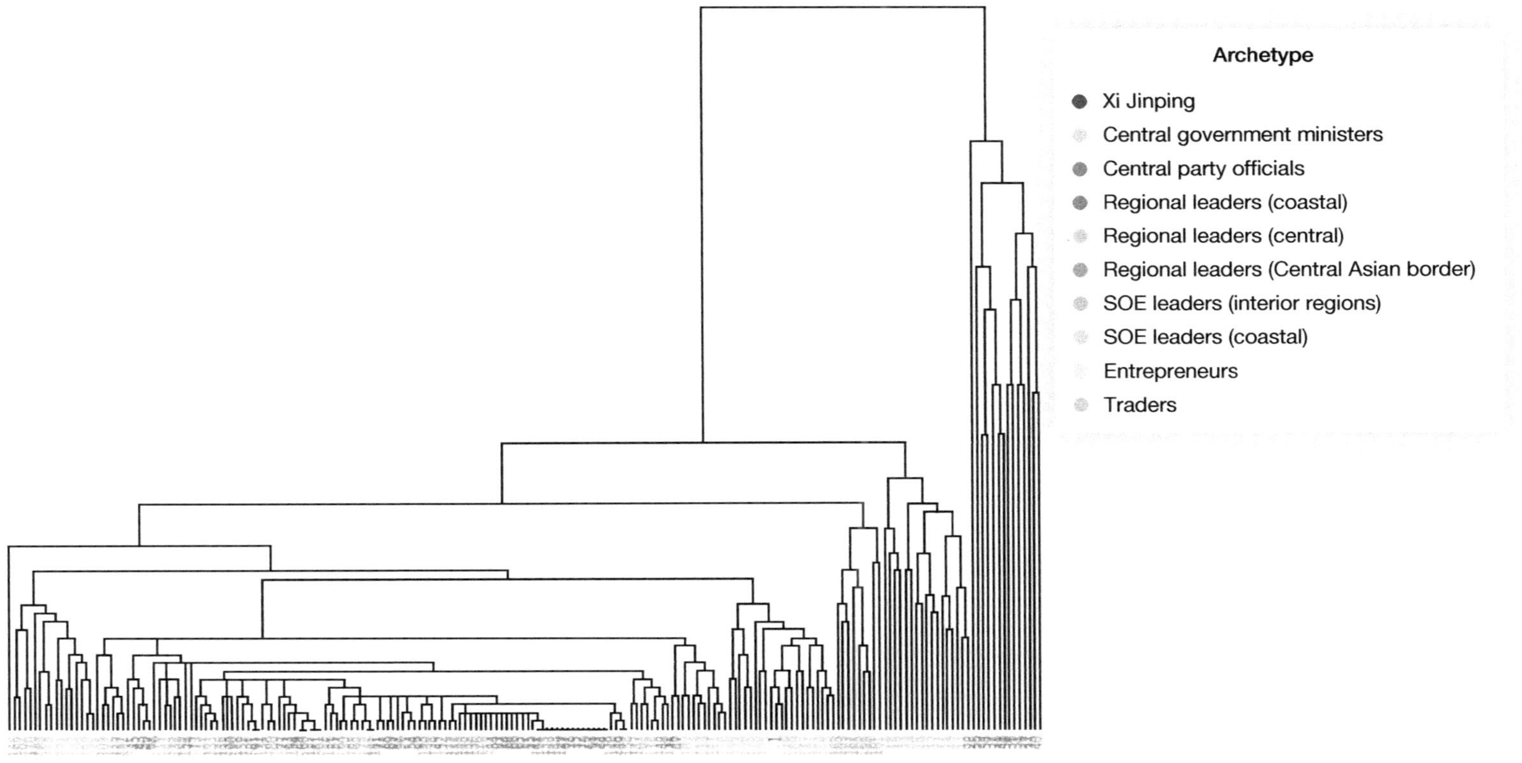

NOTE: This figure shows the hierarchy of structural equivalence in the network shifting as central party members—initially in two separate hierarchies ruling different elite sections—coalesce into a single overarching hierarchy.

may apply financial sanctions to deter or punish Chinese aggression.[20] The findings from our simple model suggest the possibility that efforts to exploit such financial vulnerabilities may indeed impose costs on the elites, but they may also create new opportunities for others to influence policy as much as cause the entrenched leadership to circle the wagons and further limit the participation in agenda-setting and decisionmaking.

Scenario 2: Resource Injection for Traders and Entrepreneurs

In this scenario, we impose a contrasting scenario in which, instead of imposing sanctions on party ministers, we introduce an exogeneous increase of resources available to traders and entrepreneurs in the model. This is consistent with the strategic objective of seeking strategic opportunities to cooperate with China to meet the needs of creating a prosperous and secure U.S. economy. As in Scenario 1, we take a network that has reached an equilibrium state and simulate an intervention in which traders and entrepreneurs experience a one-time, 25-percent increase in resources. This is a rough approximation of a policy action to inject capital through foreign investment or other means. Our intuition is that those elites with access to new or more valuable resources increase their power in the network because they can afford access to a greater number of powerful nodes.

In contrast to Scenario 1, the resulting model's response to increasing resources is consistent with the policy motivation of altering the structure of the political network, elevating the position of agents outside the core party elite, as shown in Figure 5.6. In Scenario 2, traders and entrepreneurs increase their power in the network by 59 percent and 44 percent, respectively, suggesting new opportunities for them to influence policy. In addition, all other groups suffer a loss in power, although only slightly for central party officials (2.6 percent). Even though traders and entrepreneurs remain less resourced than central party members, the sudden increase in resources brings traders and entrepreneurs to approximately the same average power of agents representing the central party. Thus, we see a relatively efficient gain in power for this group relative to the scale of resource growth that it experienced in the model.

The injection of resources also results in a change in the hierarchical organization and concentration of power in the network. The centralization of the network—a measure of concentration of power onto a few nodes—decreased more than in any other scenario simulated in this chapter; the concentration of power was reduced by 82.7 percent over the time series. The number of edges—the total number of ties in the network—was also reduced; the average degree (the number of ties per ego) declined by 71 percent. Figure 5.7 shows, in contrast with the baseline, a much sparser network as the political exchange network is shaken up by the injection of resources to a previously less-powerful group. Although traders and entrepreneurs are not clustered in the top tier, the power of central party members is much reduced with the traders and entrepreneurs gaining the most in power.

---

[20] Charlie Vest and Agatha Kratz, *Sanctioning China in a Taiwan Crisis: Scenarios and Risks*, Atlantic Council and Rhodium Group, June 2023.

FIGURE 5.6

Resource Injection into the Political System Decreases Centralization and Increases the Relative Power of Traders and Entrepreneurs

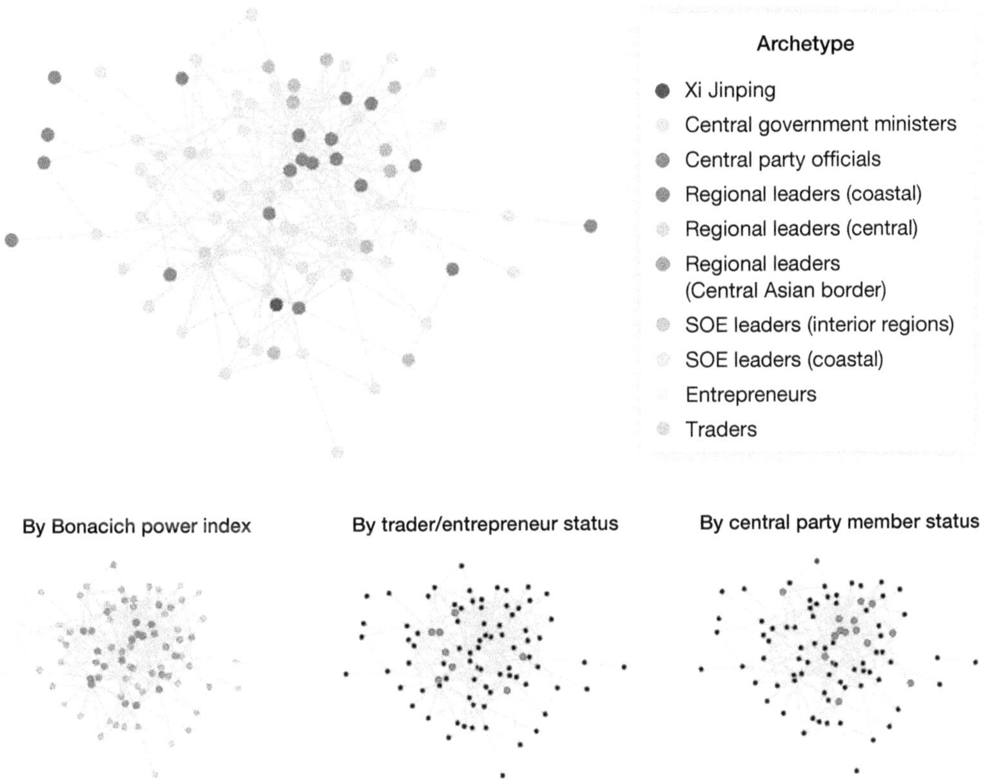

NOTE: This figure shows the results of a resource injection for traders and entrepreneurs. The overall centralization decreases while traders and entrepreneurs substantially increase their relative power.

Scenario 3: Change in Strategy for Traders and Entrepreneurs

For Scenario 3, we took a slightly different approach from the first two scenarios. Instead of altering the resource base of sectors of Chinese elites, we altered the *agent strategies* of sectors that are more likely to be internationally cooperative. This scenario simulated the effects of entrepreneurs and traders acting in a more coordinated fashion, employing the group-interested strategy rather than the self-interested one used in the default model parameterization. These agents' strategies were changed to seek to maximize the influence of their entire groups (i.e., entrepreneurs sought to increase the collective centrality of entrepreneurs as a class of elites, and traders sought to increase the collective centrality of traders as a class of elites). This scenario is consistent with increased cooperation among sectors of elites that are most threatened by international conflict and reduced opportunities for international exchange. The scenario occurs in the same way as Scenarios 1 and 2: We imposed a shift in strategic interests for all traders and entrepreneurs after a burn-in period and observed the network evolution over 100 time steps.

FIGURE 5.7

Hierarchical Organization Becomes Less Defined and Power Is More Widely Distributed as a Result of Injecting Resources into the Political Network

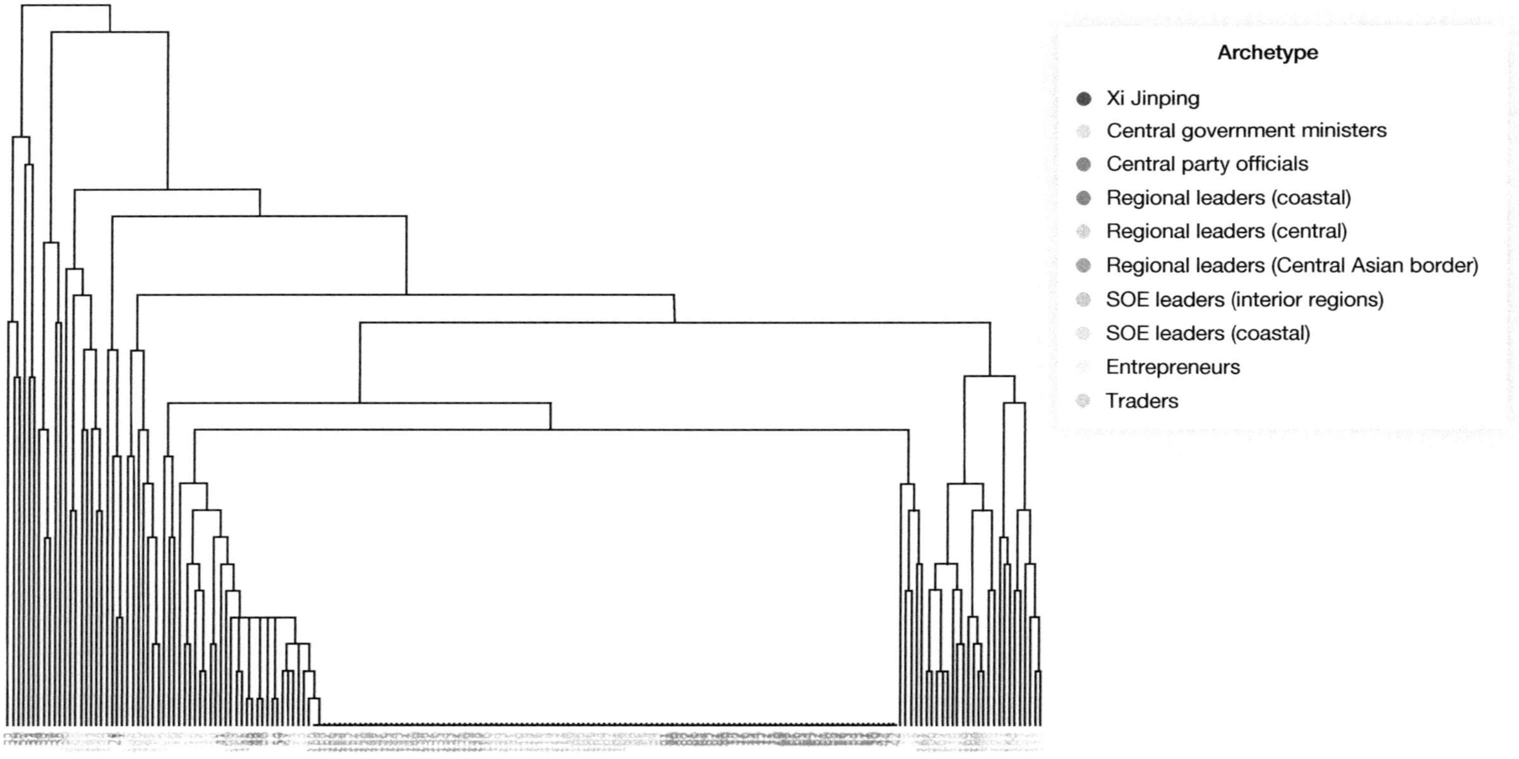

NOTE: This figure shows hierarchical organizing becoming less defined; traders and entrepreneurs gain more power in part because of the dispersal of overall power distribution.

Similar to the results from Scenario 2, traders and entrepreneurs increased their power in the network by 64 percent and 59 percent, respectively, providing them new opportunities to influence policymaking, as shown in Figure 5.8. In addition, all other groups experienced a loss in power, and Central Party Officials experienced more loss than in Scenario 2 (18.6 percent). Without changing the resource base of the agents, the change in strategy allowed traders and entrepreneurs to enter into network positions of power that are approximately equivalent to those held by central party officials. Moreover, the centralization of the network decreased in Scenario 3 slightly less than Scenario 2; the number of edges was again reduced, and average degree declined by 68 percent.

Traders and entrepreneurs also experienced a shift in their relative position in the hierarchy, and a select few of this group rose to one of the top levels of the hierarchy, as shown in Figure 5.9. Power is dispersed; central party officials and traders and entrepreneurs share power in the top echelons of the hierarchy.

FIGURE 5.8

Changing the Strategies of Traders and Entrepreneurs from Self-Interested to Group-Interested Results in Splitting the Elite Network

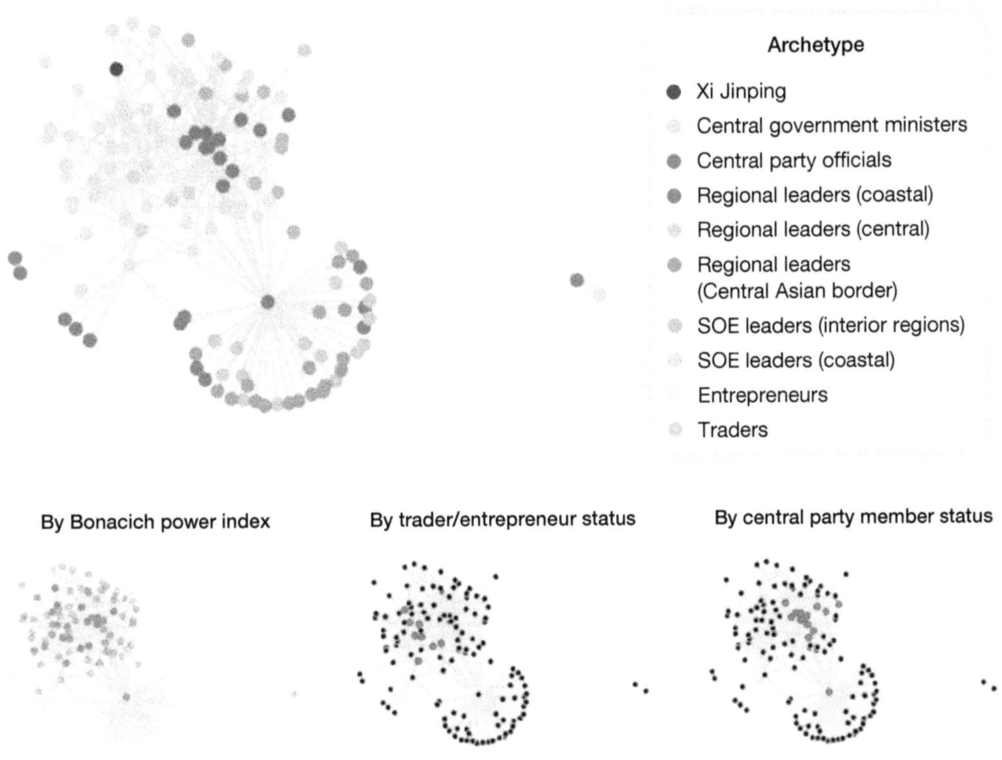

NOTE: In the strategy-driven scenario shown in this figure, traders and entrepreneurs increase their power in the network by 64 percent and 59 percent, respectively, while other groups experience power losses. Traders and entrepreneurs and central party members appear to lie on opposite sides of the central mass, indicating a potential split in the network.

FIGURE 5.9
Traders and Entrepreneurs Enter into Power-Sharing Positions with Central Party Officials

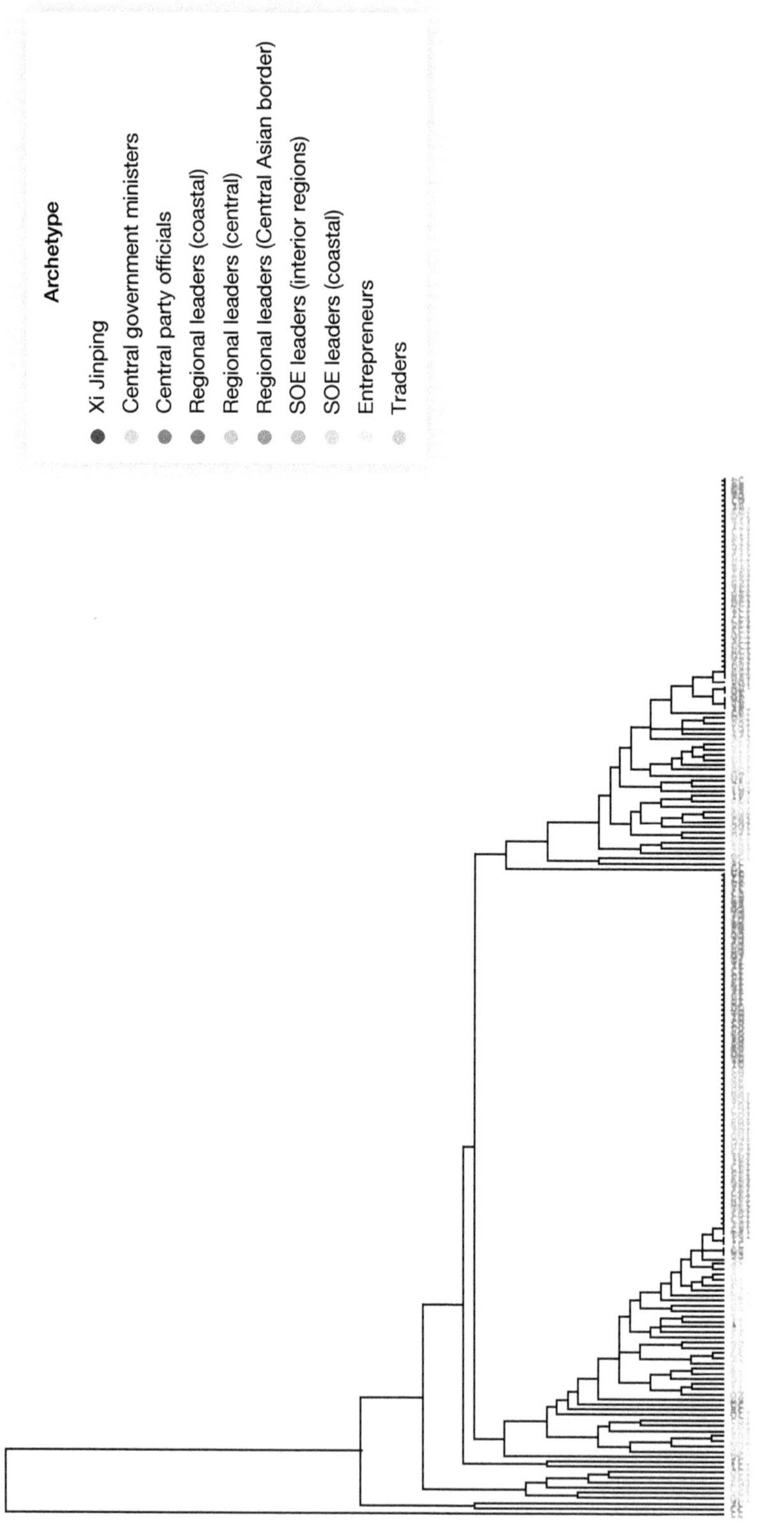

NOTE: This figure shows traders and entrepreneurs entering into power-sharing positions with central party members, resulting from a strategy change.

Scenario 4: Combining Resource Injection and Strategy Change for Traders and Entrepreneurs

For this final scenario, we combined the increased support of additional resources in Scenario 2 with the changes in strategy from Scenario 3.

The resulting network remains in favor of traders and entrepreneurs at the cost of lower power for other groups, as well as decreases in centralization and average degree. However, a key difference occurs. In Figure 5.10, we see a visual split in the network; traders cluster on one side and central party members on the other. On the trader and entrepreneur side, we see central government ministers, coastal and Asian border regional leaders, and Xi Jinping. On the central party minister side, we see interior regional leaders and SOE leaders.

In the structural equivalence clustering in Figure 5.11, we see two main branches led by each group: one by traders and entrepreneurs, the other by central party officials. This scenario appears to have increased the power of traders and entrepreneurs as a group and also to have significantly affected the broader structure of the political network, splitting the elites into two approximate, equally powered leadership camps.

Discussion

We presented an ABM of Chinese elites. The model established archetypes of agents, a resource base for each archetype, and a ranked link preference system based on each agent's strategic goals. After a burn-in period, the resulting network formed by the ABM reached an equilibrium point that reasonably reproduced the status quo power structure within China. Using analytic tools from social network analysis, we found that the ABM placed central party members at the center of a core-periphery network and other agents at various points under them in a hierarchy.

The series of scenarios that we simulated aimed to investigate the impact of exogenous shocks and interventions on the power dynamics and structural organization of Chinese elites. Although the results of the single-run scenarios that we presented must be validated with additional simulation runs, their preliminary results offer insights into how computational modeling of elite dynamics can assist in answering this project's core research question (*How can the United States ensure that its economy meets the nation's needs under conditions of coupled, strategic competition?*) in a way that does not place the United States and China into zero-sum competition.

In Scenario 1, we simulated the imposition of international sanctions on central party members that were intended to reduce the group's influence in the elite network. Rather than diminishing the power of the targeted group, the central party officials responded by strengthening their internal ties and cutting connections with lower-priority nodes. This response resulted in a 37.9-percent increase in the Bonacich power index for the central party members, while other groups experienced 21-percent to 33-percent reductions in power. The

FIGURE 5.10

Shifting Entrepreneur and Trader Strategies to Group-Interested and Providing Greater Access to Resources Produces a Structural Division in the Elite Network

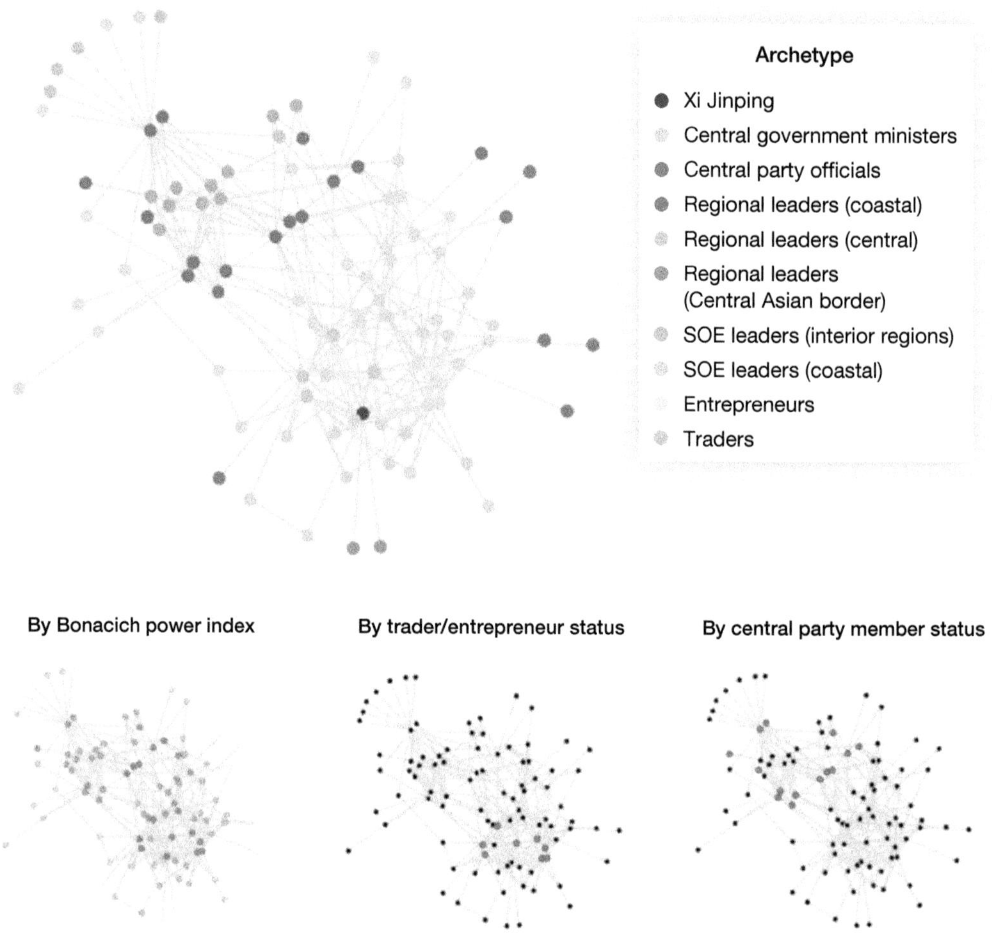

NOTE: This figure shows that shifting strategies and increasing their resource base favors traders and entrepreneurs in terms of power. A notable difference emerges with a visual split in the network (delineating traders on one side and central party members on the other), leading to a structural division in the elite network, with distinct leadership camps formed by traders and entrepreneurs and central party officials.

hierarchical clustering analysis revealed a consolidation of central party officials into a single overarching hierarchy, indicating an unintended reinforcement of their influence.

In Scenario 2, we opted for a cooperative intervention, injecting resources into the groups that might be more open to peaceful conflict resolution and international cooperation as a way to protect international trade. As a result of a 25-percent increase in their resources, traders and entrepreneurs demonstrated a 59-percent and 44-percent increase in power, respectively, while other groups experienced slight losses in power. The network's level of central-

FIGURE 5.11

Traders and Entrepreneurs Become Structurally Equivalent to Central Party Officials, Creating a Separate Cluster of Elites Capable of Setting Policy Agendas

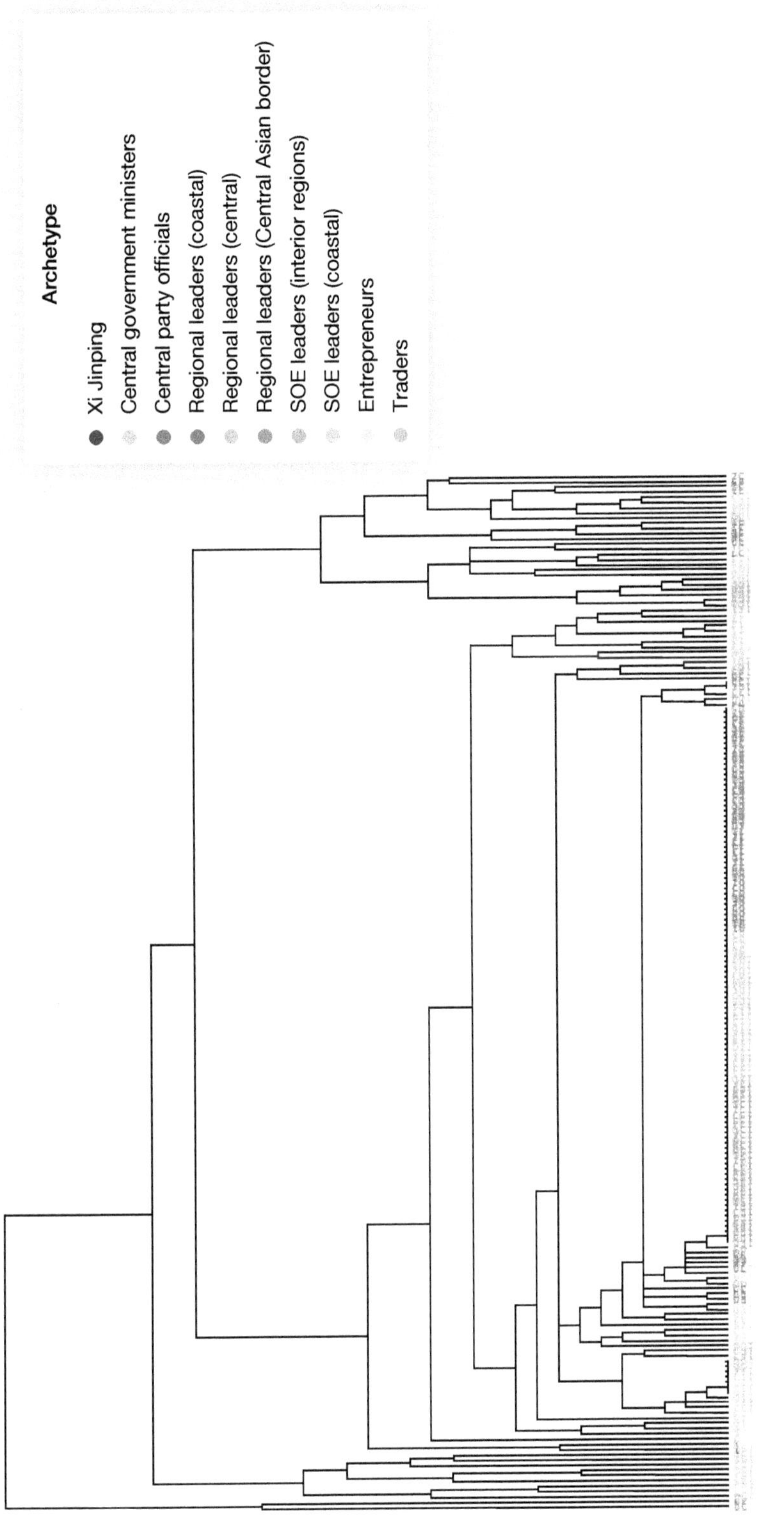

NOTE: In the scenario shown in this figure, traders and entrepreneurs operate structurally equivalent to central party members but lead a separate set of elites in the network.

ization decreased (82.7 percent), and the hierarchical structure shifted, placing traders and entrepreneurs on a higher tier, approaching equivalence with central party officials despite being less resourced overall. This intervention successfully disrupted the existing power dynamics, leading to a network that was more influenced by traders and entrepreneurs.

Scenario 3 introduced a strategic shift among traders and entrepreneurs, emphasizing group interests over self-interest for every agent in these groups. This change in strategy resulted in a 64-percent and 59-percent increase in power for traders and entrepreneurs, respectively. Although the hierarchical organization of the network remained relatively stable, centralization decreased, suggesting a shift toward a more decentralized distribution of power. This scenario highlights the significant impact of altering strategic behaviors on power dynamics within the elite network.

Scenario 4 combined increased resource support and a shift in strategic goals. Traders and entrepreneurs gained power, leading to a visual split in the network, forming apparently distinct camps of leadership. The scenario resulted in a power shift that favored traders and entrepreneurs, realigning the network into two hierarchical branches resembling a competing power structure with central party officials.

In this chapter, we produced a proof-of-concept ABM for assessing the potential consequences of competitive and cooperative interventions in the elite network of China. The sensitivity of the network to changes in resource allocation and strategic behaviors implies that interventions may have intended or unintended consequences. In the competitive scenario, power became entrenched in existing forms; in cooperative interventions, networks shifted to power structures that reflected potentially positive policy outcomes. U.S. policymakers should consider the complex, adaptive nature of elite networks when formulating strategies, recognizing that outcomes might deviate from initial expectations. This analysis is exploratory; however, we lay the groundwork for further research and refined policy analysis in complex social systems.

Future Research

The ABM described here is a proof-of-concept representation of a networked system of elite influence that begins with a material resource base and builds into a larger, dynamic, complex system in which the exchange of political capital indicates the ability to set policy agendas. The actors described were drawn from interviews with subject-matter experts, but additional verification of the network dynamics would be useful to verify that the ABM indeed reflects what is known about Chinese political elites who occupy formal and informal positions of power. For example, additional expert input into the resulting dynamics could help refine, or reimagine, the behavioral rules implied by the model. Additionally, the elite population used in this analysis could be further refined to more precisely represent differentiated groupings—both official and unofficial—within China, further extending the exploratory research presented here regarding strategic cooperation and engagement into a more focused and robust study of China's political dynamics.

Although one-to-one scale models of political elites—in which each individual agent is expected to behave according to the agent's real-world counterpart—are more fiction than science, case studies of the rise and fall of specific elites and political institutions could serve as a powerful means for establishing the validity of the model of macroscopic and microscopic scales based on the ability to replicate different classes of dynamics and outcomes that have been observed empirically.[21] For example, reconstructing the rise of elites in the party hierarchy using empirical data could verify that the ABM is predictive of future influence and power.

Another avenue for future research is the development and refinement of additional rules for characterizing agent behavior. In China, we observe that some party members seem to be abruptly removed from office, either through a purge described as combating corruption or efforts by top elites to exert more control over the political process. The imposition of the ability for top elites to remove threatening agents may be of use to policymakers who are interested in changing the resources or goals of individuals in the network. Importantly, the model we examined in this chapter assumed that all resource types that elites accessed were qualitatively similar (i.e., once converted to political capital, they enabled and constrained behavior in the same way). However, real-world political systems, and the power of elites within them, contain qualitatively different dimensions of power, some of which are coercive, in which the use—or threatened use—of power can limit the political options and choices of others. Thus, agents in our current model may be underconstrained with respect to their strategies choices, potentially overestimating the political value of their resources. A more nuanced and complex representation of resources can aid in answering such questions as the following: Can agents' goals shift toward a more favorable view of the United States if they are at more risk of removal from the political system? Can some agents remain unthreatening even after a shift in policy views? Are some agents attractive or necessary to link to even when their position or identity is not preferred?

Expanding the experimental designs for using the ABM is needed to build effective policy analysis theory. Modeling the rise in economic sectors, which differentially influence elite archetypes, could forecast the rise of certain groups without any intervention framework. U.S. domestic policy on imports of certain products, imposition of international standards on labor or product quality, or other such smaller interventions that avoid direct confrontation with China could also be assessed and quantified. Additional input from experts would be welcome to imagine potential policy shifts. Such an expansion, however, would require new data collection tools for mapping empirical observations and expert beliefs into the model's representation of the political world and would require additional investments in the model's computational architecture to enable more-efficient use of computing resources.

---

[21] Robert L. Axtell and Joshua M. Epstein, "Agent-Based Modeling: Understanding Our Creations," *Bulletin of the Santa Fe Institute*, Vol. 9, No. 2, Winter 1994.

Supplementary Material: Policy Network Technical Implementation

Elite agents were split into sectors that represent the Chinese elite across the country. We split elites into archetypes that represent the internal political and economic structure of China, as described by our experts. Elites are split into several groups. Central government ministers (13 percent of elites) represent elites within the central government and are responsible for implementation of policies across the executive administration. Central party officials (7 percent) are elites within the CCP leadership. Regional leaders (coastal, 25 percent; central, 17 percent; Central Asian border, 17 percent) are elites of regional administrative bodies across China. Economic elites—such as SOE leaders (interior, 5 percent; coastal, 11 percent), entrepreneurs (2 percent), and traders (2 percent)—are also included. Xi Jinping is treated as a unique, single actor in the network.

Influence in the network is measured by the Bonacich's power centrality, defined as

$$CBP\alpha, \beta = \alpha I - \beta A - 1A1$$

where β is an "attenuation" metric, α is a value acting as a scaling parameter, and A is the graph adjacency matrix. The concept of this power metric is to measure the quantity of each node's (ego's) power by the sum of the power held by *alters*—the nodes to which an ego is connected. The attenuation parameter β is the extent to which the power measure is a function of steps outside the immediate alter neighborhood. These *ties-of-ties*, by which we mean the nodes tied to each ego's alters, extend the power measure only slightly outside the range of the immediate alters, with ties-of-ties representing one-tenth of the calculation compared with immediate alters. Bonacich's power centrality is advantageous in two ways:

1. Compared with such alternatives as eigenvector centrality and pagerank, Bonacich power centrality was stable throughout our simulation steps, allowing for a measure that tracked network changes via exchange that was macroscopically stable yet responsive to microscopic, agent-level, change over the time series.
2. Eigenvector centrality and pagerank are difficult to interpret; Bonacich power centrality is interpretable as the aggregation of the power of an ego's ties.

Agents have a weighted sum of strategies in line with their preferences for power. Some agents are mostly self-interested; others have preferences in line with a group interest or preserving or changing the existing power structure entirely. Political strategies available to elites include

- self-interest, *CBPi*, where i is the node. Elites seek to improve their individual position within the national network of elites, constantly using their resources to align with other agents of higher levels of influence. This strategy orders preferences by which ties would most improve their individual Bonacich power.

- group-interest, $\Sigma CBPgi$, where gi are nodes that belong to an ingroup of ego i. Elites seek to improve the overall positioning of their individual ethnic, regional, religious, or economic bloc relative to other blocs. This strategy orders preferences by which ties would most improve the overall group power.
- revolutionary, $-CBPj$. Elites seek to build alternative centers of power and influence around those agents who lie on the fringes of the network at the beginning of the simulation. This strategy orders preferences by the reverse rank-ordering of the current power (or the power of some time point in the past).
- reactionary, $CBPj$. Elites seek to consolidate power among the most central agents at the start of the simulation. These agents attempt to push those agents on the periphery of the network further from the center into isolation. This strategy orders preferences by the rank-ordering of the current power (or the power of some time point in the past).

Each agent has a weighted sum of preferences that is in line with the strategy mix they employ. For example, traders and entrepreneurs are 75-percent self-interested, 20-percent group interested, and 5-percent revolutionary. Potential ties are ranked from 1 to n according to each strategy; low rankings mean high preference for i connecting to j, and high ranking means low preference. Each ranking is multiplied by the strategy weight and summed. For example, if an agent is split 80 to 20 percent between self- and group-interested, rankings for each are calculated; then multiplied by 0.8 and 0.2, respectively; and then summed for a final preference ranking.

With preferences in place, agents then extract resources to form networks. Resources are split into four primary groups: (1) extractive resources, (2) trade, (3) technology, and (4) ideology, information, and security (IIS). Resource allocation is split between members of groups (see Table 5.1). Because groups "share" resources, the amount of resources drawn is split between all members of the group. An initial network is defined and calculated according to mixing matrices (see Table 5.2). This matrix provides a snapshot of the initial probability that an agent from one archetype may be connected to an agent of another archetype. Each tie between agents has a cost that scales with the Bonacich power index of each person. Tie costs are normalized by the average ego resources divided by ego (Freeman) degree, starting with the initial network. This cost is updated each step, scaling the cost of each tie according to their importance, and helps to keep degree stable.

TABLE 5.1

Demographics, Strategies, and Resource Base for ABM Archetypes

	Demographics			Strategies				Resources (Percentage Own)			
Agent Archetype	Region	Institution	Percentage of Elites	Self-Interest	Group-Interest	Rev	Reac	Extractive	Trade	Technology	IIS
Xi Jinping	Beijing	Central government	1	50			50		5	5	80
Central government ministers	Beijing	Central government	13	50	25		25		18	10	10
Central party officials	Beijing	Central government	7	50	25		25		37	48	10
Regional leaders (coastal)	Provinces (coastal)	Regional government	25	25	75			8	4	4	
Regional leaders (central)	Provinces (central)	Regional government	17	25	75			8	5	4	
Regional leaders (Central Asian border)	Provinces (Central Asian)	Regional government	17	25	75			5	4	4	
SOE leaders (interior regions)	Provinces (central)	SOE	5	75	25			15	10	9	
SOE leaders (coastal)	Provinces (coastal)	SOE	11	75	25			15	10	9	
Entrepreneurs	Provinces (coastal)	Technology	2	75	20	5			2	5	
Traders	Provinces (coastal)	Trade	2	75	20	5			5	2	

NOTE: Reac = Reactionary; Rev = Revolutionary. Strategies describe the logic used by agents for linking with other agents: Self-interested agents seek to maximize their personal centrality (Bonacich power index); group-interested agents seek to maximize the total power index of their respective, salient group identity; revolutionary agents seek to maximize the centrality of agents who start the simulation on the network's periphery while minimizing the centrality of those who are start in the core; reactionary agents seek to increase the centralization of the network around the initial core and push those on the periphery into further isolation. Resource types were divided into four broad categories: (1) Extractive resources included natural and agricultural resources; (2) trade included exchange with actors external to China by importing or exporting of goods and services; (3) technology included access and control over industrial and commercial technologies; (4) IIS included control over national ideology, news, information technology and content, and domestic, military, and intelligence services.

TABLE 5.2
Initial Mixing Matrix of the ABM

Initial Connections	Xi Jinping	Central Government Ministers	Central Party Officials	Regional Leaders (Coastal)	Regional Leaders (Central)	Regional Leaders (Central Asian Border)	SOE Leaders (Interior Regions)	SOE Leaders (Coastal)	Entrepreneurs	Traders
Xi Jinping	1									
Central government ministers	0.3	0.2								
Central party officials	0.3	0.2	0.2							
Regional governors (coastal)	0.05	0.1	0.15	0.2						
Regional governors (central)	0.07	0.06	0.18	0.08	0.15					
Regional governors (Central Asian border)	0.05	0.05	0.1	0.07	0.07	0.2				
SOE leaders (interior regions)	0.1	0.1	0.2	0.01	0.25	0.1	0.15			
SOE leaders (coastal)	0.1	0.15	0.25	0.2	0.1	0.05	0.1	0.15		
Entrepreneurs	0.01	0.01	0.01	0.02	0.02	0.05	0.07	0.08	0.25	
Traders	0.01	0.02	0.02	0.02	0.2	0.06	0.06	0.06	0.3	0.25

NOTE: Values in the mixing matrix provide a probability that an agent with a given archetype (row) will have an initial link to other agents of the corresponding archetype (alter).

Abbreviations

ABM	agent-based model
CCP	Chinese Communist Party
IIS	ideology, information, and security
SOE	state-owned enterprise

References

Allison, Graham T., and Morton H. Halperin, "Bureaucratic Politics: A Paradigm and Some Policy Implications," *World Politics*, Vol. 24, No. S1, Spring 1972.

Allison, Graham, and Philip Zelikow, *Essence of Decision: Explaining the Cuban Missile Crisis*, 2nd ed., Addison Wesley Longman, 1999.

Axelrod, Robert, "Advancing the Art of Simulation in the Social Sciences," *Complexity*, Vol. 3, No. 2, November 1997.

Axtell, Robert L., and Joshua M. Epstein, "Agent-Based Modeling: Understanding Our Creations," *Bulletin of the Santa Fe Institute*, Vol. 9, No. 2, Winter 1994.

Block, Per, Christoph Stadtfeld, and Tom A. B. Snijders, "Forms of Dependence: Comparing SAOMs and ERGMs from Basic Principles," *Sociological Methods & Research*, Vol. 48, No. 1, February 2019.

Bueno de Mesquita, Bruce, and Alastair Smith, *The Dictator's Handbook: Why Bad Behavior Is Almost Always Good Politics*, PublicAffairs, 2011.

Bueno de Mesquita, Bruce, Alastair Smith, Randolph M. Siverson, and James D. Morrow, *The Logic of Political Survival*, MIT Press, 2005.

Dougherty, James E., and Robert L. Pfaltzgraff, Jr., *Contending Theories of International Relations: A Comprehensive Survey*, 5th ed., Pearson, 2000.

Epstein, Joshua M., and Robert L. Axtell, *Growing Artificial Societies: Social Science from the Bottom Up*, Brookings Institution Press and MIT Press, 1996.

Fearon, James D., "Rationalist Explanations for War," *International Organization*, Vol. 49, No. 3, Summer 1995.

Fearon, James D., "Bargaining, Enforcement, and International Cooperation," *International Organization*, Vol. 52, No. 2, Spring 1998.

Granovetter, Mark S., "The Strength of Weak Ties," *American Journal of Sociology*, Vol. 78, No. 6, May 1973.

Heppenstall, Alison J., Andrew T. Crooks, Linda M. See, and Michael Batty, eds., *Agent-Based Models of Geographical Systems*, Springer, 2011.

Hilsman, Roger, "International Environment, the State, and Intelligence," in Alfred C. Maurer, Marion D. Tunstall, and James M. Keagle, eds., *Intelligence: Policy and Process*, Westview Press, 1985.

Hudson, Valerie M., "Foreign Policy Analysis: Actor-Specific Theory and the Ground of International Relations," *Foreign Policy Analysis*, Vol. 1, No. 1, March 2005.

Jackson, Matthew O., *Social and Economic Networks*, Princeton University Press, 2008.

Janis, Irving L., *Groupthink: Psychological Studies of Policy Decisions and Fiascoes*, 2nd ed., Cengage Learning, 1982.

Jervis, Robert, "Realism, Neoliberalism, and Cooperation: Understanding the Debate," *International Security*, Vol. 24, No. 1, Summer 1999.

Jervis, Robert, *How Statesmen Think: The Psychology of International Politics*, Princeton University Press, 2017a.

Jervis, Robert, *Perception and Misperception in International Politics*, new ed., Princeton University Press, 2017b.

Keohane, Robert O., *After Hegemony: Cooperation and Discord in the World Political Economy*, revised ed., Princeton University Press, 2005.

Keohane, Robert O., and Joseph S. Nye Jr., *Power and Interdependence*, Pearson, 2011.

Kydd, Andrew H., *Trust and Mistrust in International Relations*, Princeton University Press, 2007.

Kydd, Andrew H., *International Relations Theory: The Game-Theoretic Approach*, Cambridge University Press, 2015.

Lempert, Robert, "Agent-Based Modeling as Organizational and Public Policy Simulators," *Proceedings of the National Academy of Sciences*, Vol. 99, Suppl. 3, May 14, 2002.

Marshall, Andrew W., *Problems of Estimating Military Power*, RAND Corporation, P-3417, August 1966. As of September 23, 2024:
https://www.rand.org/pubs/papers/P3417.html

Miller, John H., and Scott E. Page, *Complex Adaptive Systems: An Introduction to Computational Models of Social Life*, Princeton University Press, 2007.

Sætra, Henrik Skaug, "Exploring the Use of Agent-Based Modeling (ABM) in Mixed Methods Research," *Barataria: Revista Castellano-Manchega de Ciencias Sociales*, No. 22, 2017.

Schelling, Thomas C., "Models of Segregation," *American Economic Review*, Vol. 59, No. 2, May 1969.

Schelling, Thomas C., "Dynamic Models of Segregation," *Journal of Mathematical Sociology*, Vol. 1, No. 2, 1971.

Steinbruner, John D., *The Cybernetic Theory of Decision: New Dimensions of Political Analysis*, Princeton University Press, 2002.

Vest, Charlie, and Agatha Kratz, *Sanctioning China in a Taiwan Crisis: Scenarios and Risks*, Atlantic Council and Rhodium Group, June 2023.

Waltz, Kenneth N., *Theory of International Politics*, McGraw Hill, 1979.

Watts, Duncan J., and Steven H. Strogatz, "Collective Dynamics of 'Small-World' Networks," *Nature*, Vol. 393, No. 6684, June 4, 1998.

Wendt, Alexander, *Social Theory of International Politics*, Cambridge University Press, 1999.

White House, *A National Security Strategy of Engagement and Enlargement*, February 1995.

CHAPTER 6

U.S.-China High-Skilled Return Migration: Implications for Strategic Economic Competition

Nadia Almasalkhi

Overview

In this chapter, I consider how the migration and return migration of highly skilled Chinese nationals between China and the United States may affect U.S.-China strategic economic competition. I highlight the significant role of Chinese migrants in the U.S. science, technology, engineering, and mathematics (STEM) workforce and provide background on trends in return migration to China. I then examine the implications of high-skilled return migration on the Chinese economy and come to three conclusions: (1) Although returnees are competitive in the Chinese labor market, many are discontented with their opportunities in China; (2) although the Chinese Communist Party has hailed returnees as the driving force behind China's mass entrepreneurship strategy, they tend to flounder in China's start-up scene without support from local partners and networks; and (3) although returnees appear to facilitate technology transfer from developed countries to Chinese small and medium enterprises, they play only a minor role in China's technology transfer efforts. In the final section, I consider the implications of Chinese high-skilled return migration for the United States, discuss how high-skilled return migration may create the potential for U.S.-China cooperation and mutual benefit, and make policy recommendations for retaining high-skilled immigrants in STEM fields.

As the United States seeks to secure its economic competitiveness, dynamism, and leadership in the global economy over the long term, it must engage in strategic competition and cooperation with China, the world's second-largest economy. A signature feature of the globalized economy in which this competition and cooperation takes place is the movement of people, labor, and expertise across borders. As the United States considers its future relationship with China, it will need to include its relationship to Chinese people who migrate between the two countries and forge transnational connections between them.

The migration of high-skilled Chinese students, workers, and entrepreneurs between the United States and China could affect bilateral economic competition in many ways. The presence of high-skilled Chinese scholars and workers can help ensure that the U.S. economy meets the nation's needs. Attracting and retaining such high-skilled students and workers benefits the United States while depriving China of their skills, giving the United States an advantage. In many ways, the migration avenues allowing flows of high-skilled Chinese people to the United States is a source of U.S. strength.

On the other hand, Chinese migrants who come to the United States are not bound to remain there; in fact, U.S. regulations often make it difficult to stay. Their return migration to China provides economic benefits to China; China's economy benefits from their skills. However, return migration can be beneficial to both the United States and China, for example, by strengthening ties between industries in both countries and encouraging fruitful cross-border collaborations. It is also possible, though, that the return of high-skilled Chinese migrants to China after gaining experience and expertise in the United States can strengthen China as a strategic competitor. Return migration can also be a cause for concern over intellectual property transfer or even theft. Accordingly, migration of high-skilled Chinese workers and students to the United States and back has implications for competition between China and the United States.

In this chapter, I examine the role of high-skilled Chinese return migration in U.S.-China strategic economic competition. To acquaint the reader with the pool of potential U.S.-to-China return migrants, in the next section, I present statistics and background information on high-skilled Chinese migrants in the United States. In the section after that, I examine the phenomenon of U.S.-to-China return migration, the role of high-skilled return migrants in the Chinese economy, the motivations driving return migration, the impact of return migration on the Chinese economy, and the strategic concerns posed by Chinese return migration from the U.S. perspective. In the final section, I focus on policy options for optimizing the trade-offs that are inherent in high-skilled Chinese return migration.

Profiles of Chinese Students and High-Skilled Workers in the United States

In this section, I provide an overview of the population of high-skilled students and workers from China in the United States. These statistical profiles serve as entry points to understanding the pool of potential high-skilled return migrants from the United States to China. I begin by providing current and historical data on Chinese international students at U.S. postsecondary institutions and then proceed to present data on college-educated foreign-born Chinese workers who are employed in the United States, especially focusing on those working in the technology sector.

Chinese Post-Secondary Students in the United States

China has been the largest sender of international students to U.S. universities. In the 2021–2022 academic year, there were 290,086 Chinese international students in the United States, making up 30.6 percent of the U.S. international student population.[1] This was 1.9 percent of the entire U.S. post-secondary student population.[2] Chinese international students in the United States include undergraduates, graduate students, nondegree-seeking students, and those engaged in optional practical training (OPT). In the 2021–2022 academic year, approximately 42 percent of Chinese international students were enrolled in graduate degree programs, 38 percent in undergraduate degree programs, 2 percent in nondegree-granting programs, and 18 percent in OPT, as shown in Figure 6.1.[3]

The distribution of Chinese international students across academic levels has shifted in recent decades. In the early 2000s, undergraduates constituted only about 15 percent of the Chinese international student population enrolled in degree-granting programs; as of 2022, nearly 50 percent of Chinese degree-seeking students were undergraduates. This trend has brought Chinese international student trends in line with those of international students from other countries, as shown in Figure 6.2.

[1] Institute of International Education, *Open Doors 2022: Report on International Educational Exchange*, 2022. These statistics refer to international students whose place of origin is mainland China, excluding Taiwan and Hong Kong.

[2] National Center for Education Statistics, "Undergraduate Enrollment," webpage, Institute of Education Sciences, U.S. Department of Education, last updated May 2023.

[3] Institute of International Education, 2022.

FIGURE 6.1
Chinese International Students in the United States by Academic Level, 2021–2022

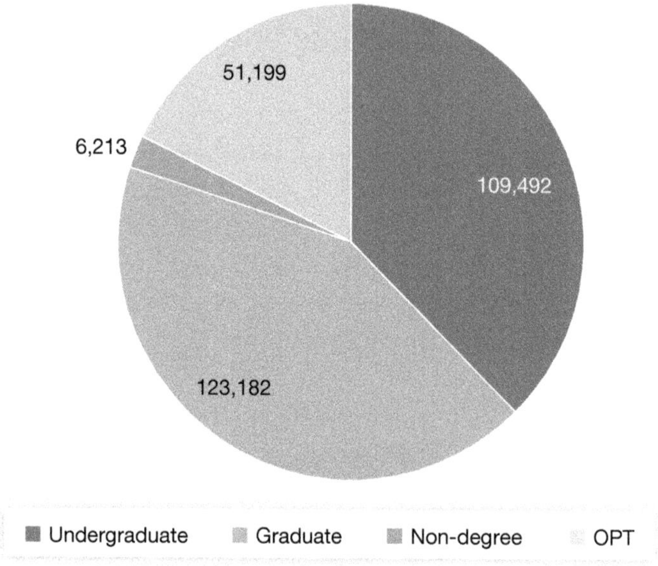

SOURCE: Features information from Institute of International Education, 2022.

The increase in undergraduate Chinese international students over time, displayed in Figure 6.3, is of consequence to the U.S. public higher education system. The majority of Chinese international students at the graduate and undergraduate levels attend public universities, but how Chinese international students fund their education differs across the two levels.[4] Among undergraduate Chinese international students who attended public universities, 86 percent had their undergraduate education funded by their families,[5] and only 9.3 percent received any kind of scholarship or tuition waiver. These statistics indicate that the vast majority of undergraduate Chinese international students pay tuition at public U.S. universities. The increase in the number and share of undergraduate Chinese international students is part of an important trend in which U.S. public universities have actively recruited international students at the undergraduate level and grown increasingly reliant on revenue from

[4] National Center for Science and Engineering Statistics, "National Survey of College Graduates: 2021," dataset, National Science Foundation, NSF 23-306, 2022b.

[5] National Center for Science and Engineering Statistics, 2022b. This statistic includes students who received gift aid from family, as well as those who received loans from family. The denominator includes foreign-born Chinese individuals with college degrees in the United States who first moved to the United States with a student visa and earned their first bachelor's degree at a public U.S. postsecondary institution before February 2021.

FIGURE 6.2
Undergraduate Share of International Student Population in U.S. Degree Programs

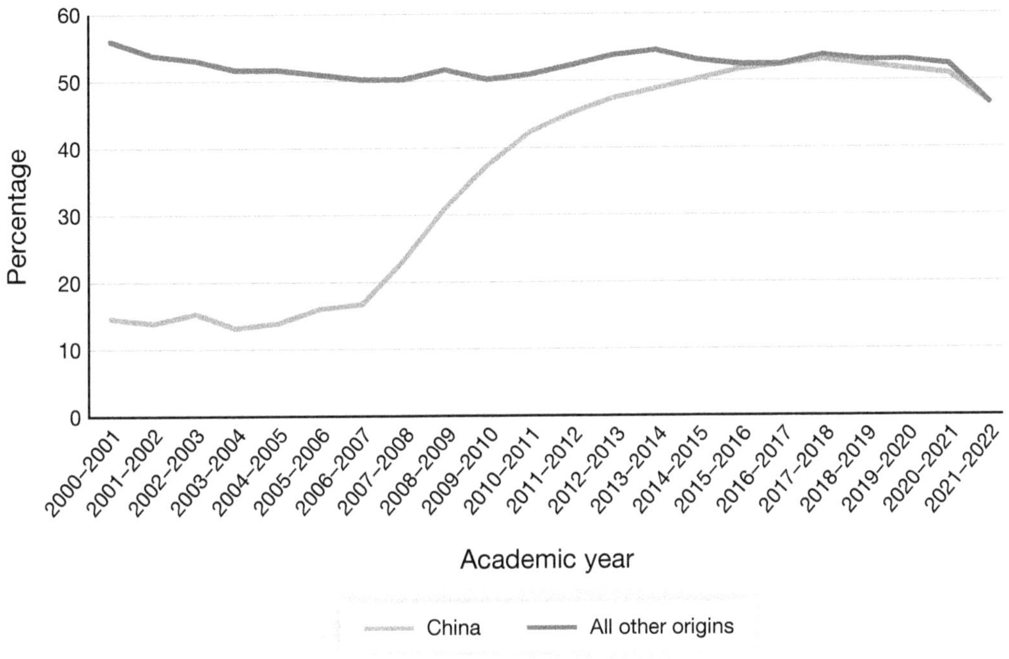

SOURCE: Features information from Institute of International Education, "Open Doors Historical Data, 2000–2022," data file, 2023.

international student tuition.[6] In contrast, 58.6 percent of Chinese international students at the graduate level received grants, fellowships, scholarships, or tuition waivers to fund their graduate education at U.S. public universities; less than one-third received gifts or loans from their families.[7]

The participation of Chinese international students in OPT has risen. OPT allows international students to work in the United States in a position directly related to their field of study, typically following graduation. OPT provides a simpler and more flexible method of gaining temporary work authorization; OPT authorizations are not subject to numerical caps and do not require employer sponsorship, in contrast to H1-B work visas. International students are generally eligible for 12 months of work authorization through the OPT program,

6 Karin Fischer and Sasha Aslanian, "The U.S. Attracts Fewer International Students, Loses Billions in Revenue. Here's Why," NPR, August 9, 2021.

7 National Center for Science and Engineering Statistics, 2022b. The denominator includes foreign-born Chinese individuals in the United States who first moved to the United States with a student visa, whose highest degree is at the graduate level, and who earned their highest degree at a public U.S. university before February 2021.

FIGURE 6.3

Chinese International Student Population in U.S. Degree Programs over Time and by Academic Level

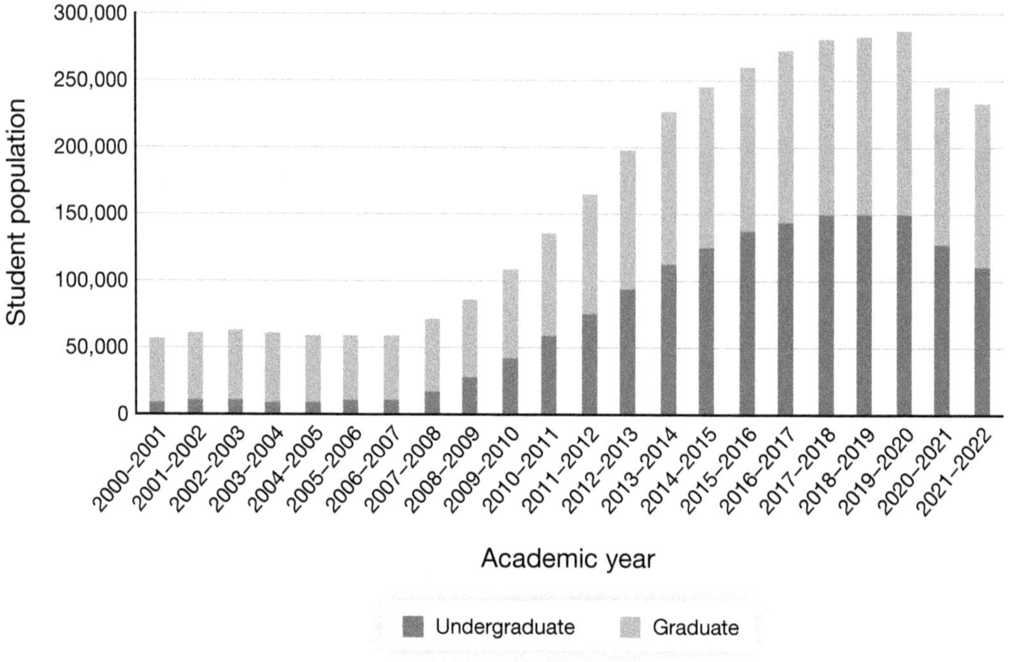

SOURCE: Features information from Institute of International Education, 2023.

but students in science, technology, engineering, and mathematics (STEM) fields are eligible for extensions of their OPT status. The OPT extension for STEM students was introduced in 2008 and lengthened in 2016. Today, STEM students are eligible for a total of 36 months of work authorization through the OPT program. Figure 6.4 shows how the number of Chinese international students in OPT has risen since 2006. The extent to which this rise represents an increase in the number of Chinese international students interested in staying in the United States after graduation is unclear; much of the rise could be attributed to increased lengths of stay among a smaller subset of Chinese international students who are granted the STEM OPT extension.

The majority (51.6 percent) of Chinese international students are concentrated in STEM fields, which are marked with an asterisk in Figure 6.5.[8] For comparison, only about 35 percent of students who are U.S. citizens or permanent residents seek degrees in STEM fields.[9] The trend of Chinese international students pursuing STEM degrees is particularly visible at

[8] Institute of International Education, 2022.

[9] National Science Board, *Science and Engineering Indicators 2022: The State of U.S. Science and Engineering*, National Science Foundation, NSB-2022-1, 2022, p. 8.

FIGURE 6.4
Chinese International Students in Optional Practical Training During Academic Year

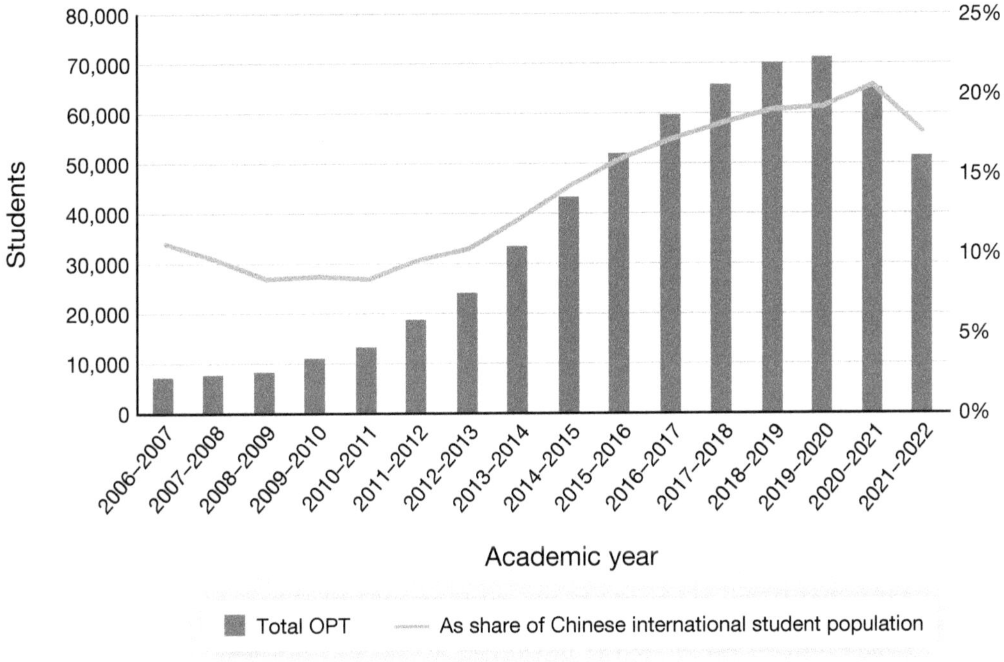

SOURCE: Features information from Institute of International Education, 2022.

the doctoral level; Chinese international students accounted for 11.8 percent of all U.S. doctoral degrees awarded in 2021 but 13.4 percent of doctoral degrees in science and engineering fields.[10]

In summary, the number of Chinese international students in the United States had risen steadily over the past 15 years until a decline since the onset of the COVID-19 pandemic. Undergraduate students and students choosing to stay in the United States after graduation for OPT have driven much of this growth. The high concentration of Chinese international students in STEM fields, coupled with the expanded opportunities for OPT for STEM stu-

[10] National Center for Science and Engineering Statistics, *Doctorate Recipients from U.S. Universities: 2021*, National Science Foundation, NSF 23-300, 2022a. These statistics include Hong Kong as part of China, whereas data from the Institute of International Education designates Hong Kong separately. This figure also includes social science disciplines. Data from the 2021 National Survey of College Graduates yield a similar figure while excluding individuals from Hong Kong and excluding doctorates in social sciences (National Center for Science and Engineering Statistics, 2022b). Those data indicate that individuals born in China (excluding Macao, Hong Kong, and Taiwan) who first moved to the United States with student visas account for 13.6 percent of U.S. doctorates awarded between 2020 and February 2021 in STEM fields (excluding social sciences) and 9.3 percent of doctorates awarded in all fields.

FIGURE 6.5
Percentage Distribution of Chinese International Students Across Fields of Study, 2021–2022

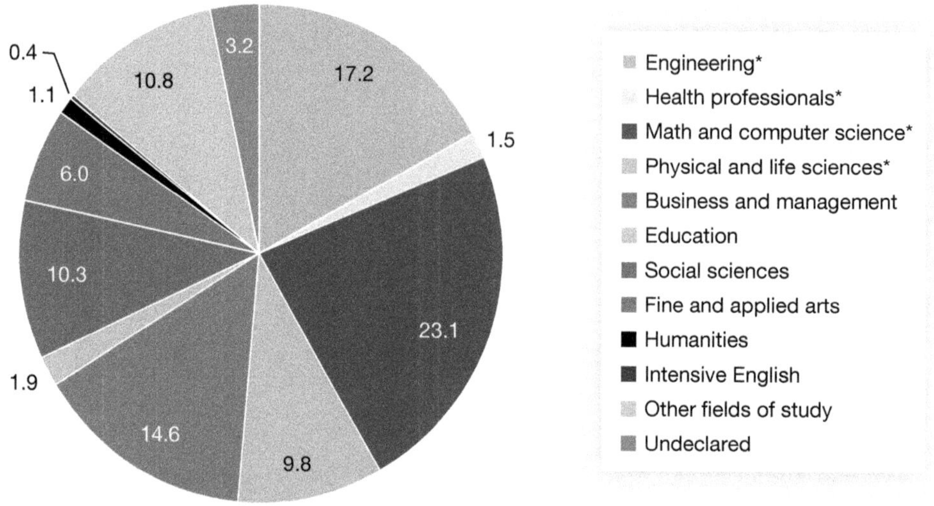

SOURCE: Features information from Institute of International Education, 2022.
NOTE: Asterisks indicate STEM fields.

dents, has aided this growth, as well as provided an avenue for Chinese international students to transition into the U.S. high-skilled workforce.

Chinese High-Skilled Workers in the United States

According to the 2021 National Survey of College Graduates, there are approximately 666,000 college-educated workers born in mainland China and employed in the United States.[11] Figure 6.6 shows the breakdown of these workers by occupations. About 46 percent of them work in science and engineering (S&E) occupations, and half of those work specifically as computer and information scientists.

The H-1B visa program is an important immigration path through which highly skilled foreign nationals gain temporary, renewable work authorization in the United States. H-1B visas are especially important for foreign nationals working in the technology sector; more than 68 percent of all approved H-1B petitions in fiscal year (FY) 2021 were for computer-related occupations.[12] Publicly available data do not indicate how many Chinese nationals with approved H1-B petitions are in each occupational category, but Chinese nationals are the second-largest group of H-1B visa beneficiaries by country of origin, behind Indian

[11] National Center for Science and Engineering Statistics, 2022b.

[12] U.S. Citizenship and Immigration Services, *Characteristics of H-1B Specialty Occupation Workers: Fiscal Year 2021 Annual Report to Congress*, U.S. Department of Homeland Security, 2022.

FIGURE 6.6
College-Educated Chinese Workers Employed in United States by Occupation

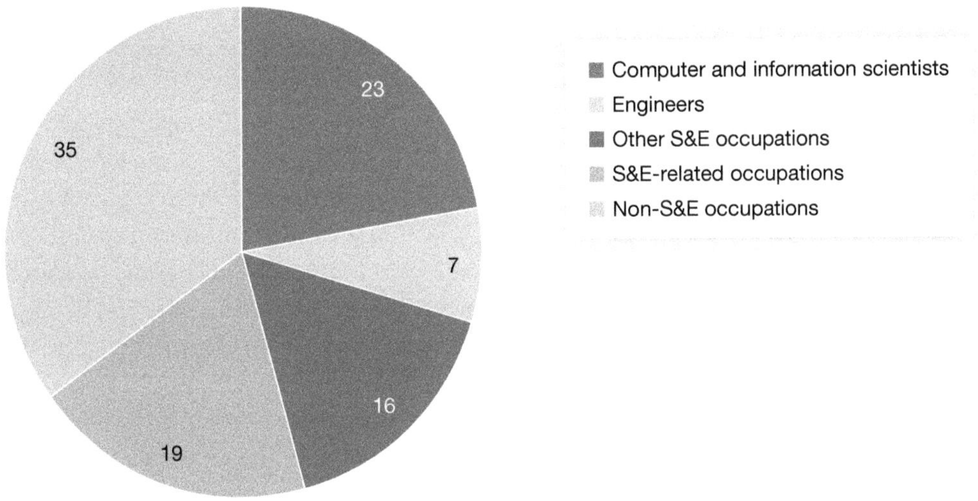

SOURCE: Features information from National Center for Science and Engineering Statistics, 2022.

nationals. In FY 2021, 12.4 percent of approved H-1B petitions were for Chinese beneficiaries, while 74.1 percent were for Indian beneficiaries.[13] Out of the 50,328 Chinese nationals with approved H-1B petitions in FY 2021, 18,770 were for initial employment, and 31,558 were for continuing employment (including applications for renewals, amendments, and transfers to new employers). H-1B visas for initial employment are subject to a numerical cap, but H-1B visas for continuing employment are not, which is part of the reason for the imbalance. Among all approved H-1B petitions for initial employment in FY 2021, more than 60 percent were for individuals who were already residing in the United States with another visa, such as a student visa.[14] The 18,770 Chinese nationals with approved initial H-1B visas in FY 2021 therefore likely included a mix of new Chinese immigrants and other Chinese nationals choosing to stay and work in the United States, while the 31,558 Chinese nationals with approved petitions for continuing H-1B employment include workers wishing to extend their stay in the United States, as well as those changing their employment in the United States without requesting an extension.

[13] U.S. Citizenship and Immigration Services, 2022.

[14] U.S. Citizenship and Immigration Services, 2022.

Computer Scientists

As of 2021, approximately 22.4 percent of college-educated foreign-born Chinese individuals employed in the United States worked in computer and information science occupations.[15] Foreign-born Chinese individuals make up between 3.5 percent and 4.1 percent of all college-educated computer scientists in the United States.[16]

Two segments of the technology sector that are highly strategically important are those that develop artificial intelligence and advanced semiconductors. An estimated 113,668 Chinese-born individuals with at least a bachelor's degree work in these U.S. industries, according to the 2021 Current Population Survey.[17] Chinese immigrants thus make up 3 percent of these industries' educated workforce of 3,823,690 people. The only group by national origin (defined by country of birth) that outnumber Chinese workers in these industries are foreign-born Indian workers, who make up 15.8 percent of this workforce, and U.S.-born workers, who make up two-thirds of this workforce.[18]

Chinese-born computer scientists working in the United States migrate through many paths, as shown in Figure 6.7. More than half of them first came to the United States on student visas, whereas only 15 percent first migrated through work visas, such as the H-1B visa.[19] These statistics indicate that the U.S. educational system is a major feeder pipeline through which Chinese nationals enter the U.S. technology workforce.

Trends over Time

The number of college-educated workers in the United States who were born in mainland China has risen 170 percent over the past two decades. Figure 6.8 shows the growth of this workforce from 2003 to 2021, as well as its distribution across occupation types. There are two notable trends immediately apparent in the figure. The first is that, although the Chinese-born workforce in S&E occupations has more than doubled in size during this period, growth has been greatest in S&E-related occupations, which includes health care professionals, architects, kindergarten through 12th grade teachers of math and science, technologists, and more. The second is that the population of college-educated Chinese workers in the United States grew steadily from the early 2000s into the 2010s but appears to have stalled with the onset

[15] National Center for Science and Engineering Statistics, 2022. The 2021 Current Population Survey with Annual Social and Economic Supplement estimates that 18.5 percent of college-educated people born in China and employed in the United States work in computer and information science occupations.

[16] Sarah Flood, Miriam King, Renae Rodgers, Steven Ruggles, J. Robert Warren, and Michael Westberry, "Integrated Public Use Microdata Series, Current Population Survey: Version 10.0," dataset, IPUMS, 2022; National Center for Science and Engineering Statistics, 2022.

[17] Flood et al., 2022. The artificial intelligence and semiconductor industries are defined as those in Industry Codes 3365, 3390, and 7380 in the Current Population Survey. These industry codes correspond to NAICS codes 5415, 3344, and 3341.

[18] Flood et al., 2022.

[19] National Center for Science and Engineering Statistics, 2022b.

FIGURE 6.7

College-Educated Chinese Computer Scientists Employed in United States by First Visa Status

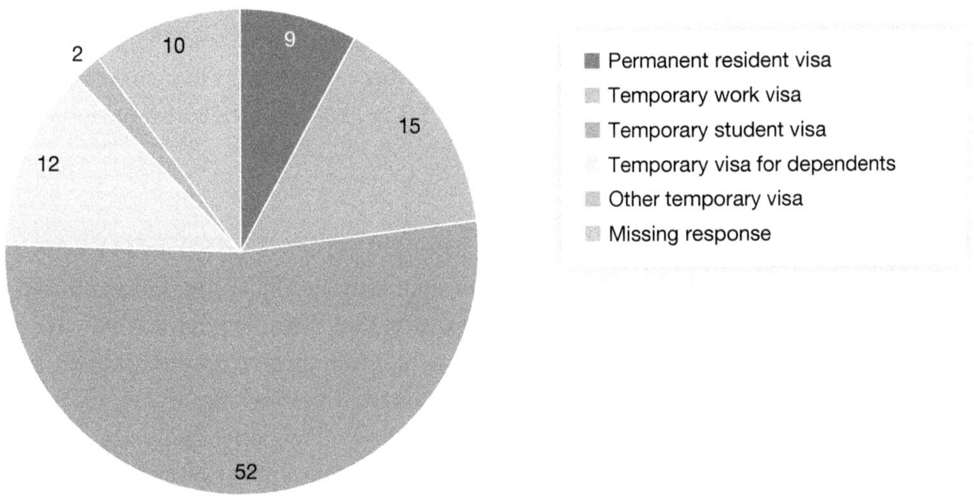

SOURCE: Features information from National Center for Science and Engineering Statistics, 2022.

FIGURE 6.8

College-Educated Chinese Workers in the United States by Occupation Type

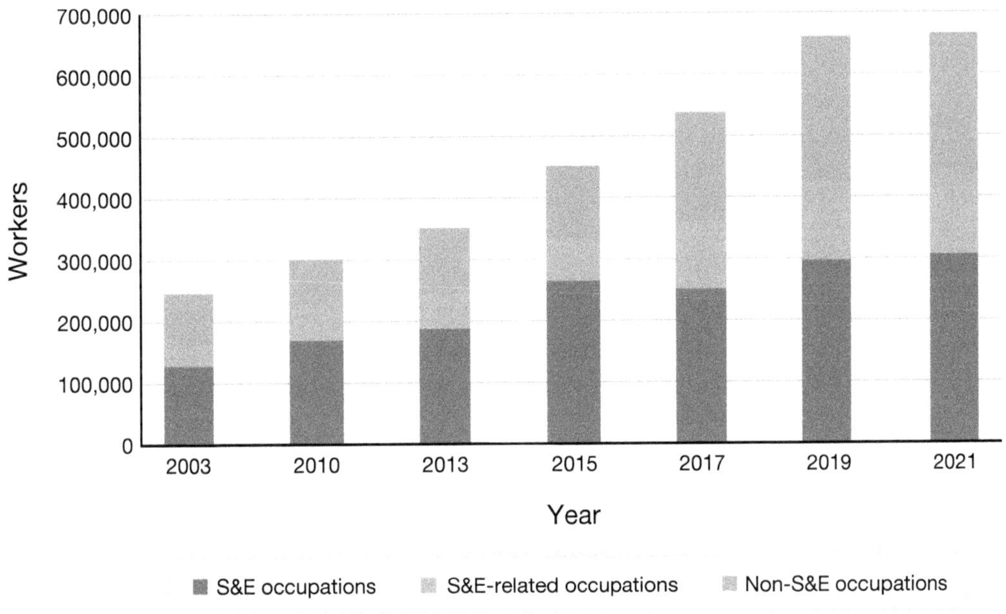

SOURCE: Features information from National Center for Science and Engineering Statistics, 2022.

of the COVID-19 pandemic, which limited international mobility. Whether the population trend will resume its prepandemic course in the coming years remains to be seen.

The Chinese-born share of the college-educated S&E workforce in the United States climbed from 2.8 percent in 2003 to a peak of 4.2 percent in 2015. Since 2015, however, the Chinese-born share of the workforce has fallen slightly and remained steady between 3.8 percent and 4.0 percent. The fact that the Chinese-born share of this workforce has fallen even as their total numbers continue to grow reflects the faster growth of the S&E workforce from other countries of origin.

Conclusion

From the perspective of the United States, these data indicate that Chinese migrants constitute a significant share of the U.S. STEM workforce, and Chinese international students constitute a major pipeline of professional STEM talent. From the perspective of China, these data indicate that the Chinese population in the United States includes many people who have studied strategically important disciplines and have work experience in critical sectors, making the U.S. Chinese community a valuable pool of human capital from which to recruit.

Return Migration

In this section, I address the return migration of Chinese students and high-skilled workers to China. I first detail the push and pull factors driving return migration. I then estimate the number of return migrants to China and the share of Chinese immigrants to the United States who return to China. In the "Who Returns?" subsection, I describe the characteristics of return migrants, including their educational backgrounds, levels of professional experience, and transnational ties. I subsequently discuss the effects of return migrants on the Chinese economy.

Drivers of Return Migration

The decision regarding whether to return to China from the United States is a function of three factors: incentives to stay in the United States, push factors driving Chinese migrants to leave the United States, and pull factors attracting overseas Chinese to return to China. I will review each type of factor in turn.

Staying in the United States is attractive to Chinese international students and high-skilled workers for a variety of reasons. The higher salaries available in the United States are the most significant motivator for remaining in the United States, particularly among Chinese Ph.D. students in STEM fields.[20] For some Chinese students in the United States, politi-

[20] Robert Zeithammer and Ryan P. Kellogg, "The Hesitant 'Hai Gui': Return-Migration Preferences of U.S.-Educated Chinese Scientists and Engineers," *Journal of Marketing Research*, Vol. 50, No. 5, October 2013;

cal, social, and academic freedoms provide strong reasons to stay.[21] Others set down roots while on temporary visas and are reluctant to uproot their households,[22] especially when it means moving their children to an education system they view unfavorably.[23] These are some of the prominent reasons motivating Chinese international students to remain in the United States permanently or indefinitely.

On the other hand, many Chinese international students express strong interest in working *temporarily* in the United States post-graduation. U.S. work experience is perceived to be a valuable asset in the Chinese labor market, so Chinese students often plan to begin their working careers in the United States before later returning to China.[24] Furthermore, gaining U.S. legal permanent residence status or citizenship can be valuable for return migrants; it can provide an insurance policy against unfavorable conditions in China by leaving open the option to re-emigrate while also potentially increasing a worker's market value in China.[25] Chinese students and workers are thus motivated to extend their stays in the United States to facilitate their successful return to China later.

The U.S. context also provides several push factors that drive Chinese students and high-skilled workers to return to China. The first push factor driving Chinese return migration is difficulty finding employment in the United States.[26] The second push factor is immigration policy. The expiration of a visa, the inability to find an employer willing to sponsor a visa petition, or the rejection of a visa petition forces Chinese students and workers to leave the United States and, in most cases, return to China.[27] U.S. immigration processes can discourage Chinese migrants from even attempting to extend their stay in the United States because

---

Wan Yu, "To Stay or to Return? Return Intentions and Return Migrations of Chinese Students During the Transition Period in the United States," *Papers in Applied Geography*, Vol. 2, No. 2, 2016, p. 207. For evidence that lower-paid H-1B workers are more likely to return to China, see Briggs Depew, Peter Norlander, and Todd Sørensen, "Flight of the H-1B: Inter-Firm Mobility and Return Migration Patterns for Skilled Guest Workers," Institute of Labor Economics, Discussion Paper No. 7456, June 2013.

21 Alan Chi Keung Cheung and Li Xu, "To Return or Not to Return: Examining the Return Intentions of Mainland Chinese Students Studying at Elite Universities in the United States," *Studies in Higher Education*, Vol. 40, No. 9, 2015.

22 Several studies of Chinese international students find correlations between being married and intending to remain in the United States. Zeithammer and Kellogg, 2013; Wei Li, Shengnan Zhao, Zheng Lu, Wan Yu, and Xiaojie Li, "Student Migration: Evidence from Chinese Students in the US and China," *International Migration*, Vol. 57, No. 3, June 2019; Robyn Iredale, Fei Guo, and Santi Rozario, eds., *Return Migration in the Asia Pacific*, Elgar Publishing, 2003.

23 Cheung and Xu, 2015; Lisong Liu, "Return Migration and Selective Citizenship: A Study of Returning Chinese Professional Migrants from the United States," *Journal of Asian American Studies*, Vol. 15, No. 1, February 2012.

24 Li et al., 2019; Cheung and Xu, 2015; Zeithammer and Kellogg, 2013; Yu, 2016.

25 Liu, 2012; Yu, 2016.

26 Cheung and Xu, 2015.

27 Yu, 2016.

chances to win the H-1B lottery appear slim and because certain migration statuses impose prohibitive, unappealing conditions, such as the inability to travel abroad for the duration of the OPT period.[28] Escalating anti-Asian sentiment since the COVID-19 pandemic, along with greater scrutiny of Chinese Americans' loyalties in light of U.S.-China competition, has led many to feel unwelcome or unsafe in the United States, pushing them to consider return migration.[29]

Pull factors attracting high-skilled overseas Chinese individuals to return include personal, professional, and policy incentives. One of the most consistently and highly referenced reasons for return migration is to reunite with family.[30] As a result of China's now-ended one-child policy, a significant share of young Chinese individuals living abroad are the only children in their families and thus feel a personal responsibility to live near and take care of their parents.[31] Another common personal reason for return migration is a preference for China's culture.[32] As for professional incentives, economic growth in China has made return migration more attractive,[33] especially as salaries for university graduates have been rising and incomes for overseas graduates have remained higher than for domestic graduates.[34] Returnees to China are also motivated by the desire to advance into managerial roles, an opportunity that many feel is restricted in the United States; career progression and promotion are perceived to happen faster in China.[35] Nonetheless, returnees express worry about China's low salaries and competitive labor markets, as well as their own difficulties with adapting to Chinese workplaces and establishing professional networks.[36]

---

[28] For example, those in OPT cannot leave and reenter the United States, meaning that they cannot visit home for the duration of their OPT employment.

[29] Yu Xie, Xihong Lin, Ju Li, Qian He, and Junming Huang, "Caught in the Crossfire: Fears of Chinese–American Scientists," *Proceedings of the National Academy of Sciences,* Vol. 120, No. 27, July 4, 2023.

[30] LinkedIn China [领英中国], *2022 Insight Report on Overseas Students Returning to China to Seek Employment* [2022中国留学生归国求职洞察报告], 2022, p. 28; Cheung and Xu, 2015; Li et al., 2019; Yu, 2016, p. 208; Chen Siyu, Feng Dan, and Sun Wei, "Data Analysis Report on the Group of Returned Overseas Students," in Wang Huiyao and Miao Lu, eds., *Annual Report on the Development of Chinese Students Studying Abroad (2020–2021),* China: Social Sciences Academic Press, 2021; Center for China and Globalization and Zhaopin.com, *Report on Employment & Entrepreneurship of Chinese Returnees 2017,* 2017, p. 14.

[31] Yixi Lu, Li Zong, and Bernard Schissel, "To Stay or Return: Migration Intentions of Students from People's Republic of China in Saskatchewan, Canada," *International Migration and Integration,* Vol. 10, No. 3, August 2009; Li et al., 2019.

[32] Li et al., 2019.

[33] LinkedIn China, 2022, p. 28; Li et al., 2019; Patrick Gaulé, "Who Comes Back and When? Return Migration Decisions of Academic Scientists," *Economics Letters,* Vol. 124, No. 3, September 2014.

[34] Cao Chen and Zhang Lin, "The Analysis of the Development of Overseas Students After Graduating for Three Years," in Wang Huiyao and Miao Lu, eds., *Annual Report on the Development of Chinese Students Studying Abroad (2020–2021),* Social Sciences Academic Press, 2021.

[35] Iredale, Guo, and Rozario, 2003; Cheung and Xu, 2015.

[36] LinkedIn China, 2022, p. 28; Center for China and Globalization and Zhaopin.com, 2017.

The Chinese government has developed "talent programs" and "entrepreneurship zones" for returnee students, scholars, and entrepreneurs; the specific intention is "to attract more overseas students to go back to China to start their own businesses."[37] However, the changing composition of returnees in the 21st century has undercut this effort because a greater share of returnees have master's and bachelor's degrees and wish to enter the labor market rather than become self-employed entrepreneurs.[38] Nonetheless, in 2014, the policy goal of encouraging overseas students "to become the driving force of mass entrepreneurship and innovation" was affirmed.[39] To support this goal, entrepreneurship parks for overseas returnees have been established, along with incentive programs by both the central Chinese government and local governments to promote entrepreneurship by returnees and to attract returnee talent in general. These incentives include financial incentives, such as tax-free car purchases, housing allowances, and start-up capital, as well as administrative aid for enrolling returnees' children in school and changing one's *hukou* registration, the registration system that gives a person certain rights when living in a specifically designated area.[40] However, only about 20 percent of returnees have a good understanding of such policies,[41] and only 8 to 14 percent say that such policies factor into their return migration plans.[42]

How Many Return?

Over the past 15 years, there has been an increase in the number of overseas students who have returned to China each year from around the world. In the decade preceding the COVID-19 pandemic, the annual number of returnees to China increased by over 400 percent.[43] A new record was set in 2021, when 1.05 million overseas students returned to China.[44] There has therefore been a rise in the supply of foreign-educated human capital in the Chinese market, as well as a rise in awareness that the quality of education gained abroad varies; together, these factors have led to a drop in the prestige associated with foreign degrees.

---

[37] Overseas Study Service Center, *2015 Blue Book for Employment in China after Returning from Study Abroad* [中国留学回国就业蓝皮书2015], Ministry of Education of the People's Republic of China, 2016.

[38] Overseas Study Service Center, 2016.

[39] Overseas Study Service Center, 2016.

[40] Wang Huiyao and Miao Lu, eds., *Annual Report on the Development of Chinese Students Studying Abroad (2020–2021)*, Social Sciences Academic Press, 2021; LinkedIn China, 2022; Emily S. Weinstein, "Chinese Talent Program Tracker," webpage, Center for Security and Emerging Technology, November 2020.

[41] Center for China and Globalization and Zhaopin.com, 2017.

[42] LinkedIn China, 2022; Center for China and Globalization and Zhaopin.com, 2017, p. 14.

[43] National Bureau of Statistics of China, "Statistics on Graduate Students and Students Studying Abroad," in *China Statistical Yearbook 2021*, China Statistics Press, 2021.

[44] He Huifeng, "More of China's Overseas Graduates Head Home, Lured by Jobs and Convenience: Survey," *South China Morning Post*, February 13, 2023.

In part, the growth of the returnee population can be attributed to the growth of the overseas student population, which makes it important to examine the rate of return in addition to the volume of return. There are several ways to measure the rate of return migration (as shown in Table 6.1), such as by comparing the number of Chinese students who have ever completed education abroad to the number of Chinese students who have ever returned. This is the approach taken by Chinese government sources, which have reported return rates of up to 87 percent in recent years—a far cry from the roughly 25 percent return rate they were reporting in 2006.[45] If Chinese sources are to be believed, an increasing proportion of overseas students are returning to China rather than settling abroad, particularly since the 2008 financial crisis.

TABLE 6.1

Comparison of Statistics on Prevalence of Chinese Student Return Migration

Measuring What?	Source	Year	Chinese Student Population	Rate (%)
Intention to return immediately after graduation	LinkedIn[a]	2022	All overseas	32
			In the United States	25
		2020	All overseas	29
	Chinese private education provider[b]	2021	All overseas and domestic students intending to study abroad	31
	Peer-reviewed article[c]	2014	In the United States	25.8
Intention to return eventually	Peer-reviewed article[c]	2014	In the United States	65.5
Actual, eventual return after graduation	Chinese government[d]	2019	All overseas who completed their studies abroad since 1978	86.28
		2006		25.03
Intention to **stay** in the United States immediately after graduation	U.S. National Science Foundation[e]	2020	Graduating Ph.D. students in the United States	80.1
			Graduating Ph.D. students in the United States in S&E fields	81.7
Definite plans to **stay** in the United States after graduation	U.S. National Science Foundation[e]	2020	Graduating Ph.D. students in the United States in S&E fields	59.7

[a] LinkedIn China, 2022.

[b] "New Oriental's '2021 China Study Abroad White Paper' Officially Released: Undergraduate and Above Study Abroad Groups are Mainstream, High School Intention Groups Rise in Percentage" ["新东方《2021中国留学白皮书》正式发布：本科及以上留学群体是主流，高中意向群体占比上升"], Sohu, May 21, 2021.

[c] Li et al., 2019.

[d] Ministry of Education of the People's Republic of China, 2020 (for 2019 data); Wong, 2020 (for 2006 data).

[e] National Center for Science and Engineering Statistics, *Doctorate Recipients from U.S. Universities: 2020*, National Science Foundation, NSF 22-300, 2021.

---

[45] Ministry of Education of the People's Republic of China, "Statistics on Chinese Learners Studying Overseas in 2019," press release December 15, 2020; Matthew Wong, "More Chinese Students Returning Home after Overseas Study," China.org.cn, April 5, 2020.

Another way to gauge the rate of return migration is through surveys of Chinese overseas students' intentions to return to China after graduation. The results of multiple surveys converge with around 30 percent of respondents reporting that they intend to return to China immediately after graduation (see Table 6.1 and Table 6.5 in the supplementary materials section for details).[46] Among Chinese students in the United States specifically, the share intending to return appears to be around the same as or lower than it is for overseas Chinese students more broadly, hovering around 25 percent.[47] Among Chinese students in the United States graduating with Ph.D.'s, only about 20 percent report intending to leave the United States after graduating.[48]

There is clearly a large difference between the results of surveys on return intentions compared with other reports on the rate of realized return migration. A few explanations could account for this discrepancy. First, intentions to return to China or stay abroad might not be predictive of actual migration. Those who report intending to stay overseas after graduation may not receive the necessary visas or employment offers to make their intention a reality, and thus may return to China despite not initially having the intent to return. For example, about 22 percent of Chinese STEM Ph.D. students who graduated from U.S. universities in 2020 reported intending to remain in the United States but not having definite employment or postdoctoral study plans; without such commitments, they may end up returning involuntarily.[49] Second, the high return rates produced by Chinese sources claim to reflect the share of overseas Chinese who return at any point in time, but the surveys on return intentions ask about the intention to return to China immediately after graduation. It is possible that, although only around 25 to 30 percent of overseas Chinese students opt to seek their first job post-graduation in China, a larger share prefers to gain work experience abroad and then eventually return to China. One survey of Chinese international students in the United States found that, although only about 26 percent of respondents planned to return to China immediately after graduation, 66 percent planned to return after working abroad for a few years.[50] Thus, the share of Chinese international students who return to China, even from the United States, may be well above half among recent graduates and early-career professionals.

---

[46] LinkedIn China, 2022; "New Oriental's '2021 China Study Abroad White Paper' Officially Released: Undergraduate and Above Study Abroad Groups are Mainstream, High School Intention Groups Rise in Percentage," 2021.

[47] LinkedIn China, 2022; Li et al., 2019.

[48] National Center for Science and Engineering Statistics, 2021, Table 53.

[49] National Center for Science and Engineering Statistics, 2021, Figure 29.

[50] Li et al., 2019.

Who Returns?

Educational Profile

In this subsection, I review (1) how educational attainment is related to the likelihood of return migration from the United States and (2) the educational profile of returnees to China overall.

College-educated Chinese immigrants to the United States used to be more likely to stay in the United States than those with less education, but that trend has reversed in the 21st century.[51] The correlation that existed in the late 20th century between having high educational attainment and staying in the United States may have been due in part to U.S. policies in the early 1990s that granted immigration benefits to Chinese university students. These policies, established by Executive Order 12711 in 1990 and the Chinese Student Protection Act in 1992, removed the legal barriers that prevented Chinese university students from remaining in the United States and cleared a path for their expedited acquisition of U.S. employment-based green cards, without requiring employer sponsorship.[52] Over 54,000 Chinese nationals obtained U.S. green cards through the 1992 act.[53]

However, since the 2000s, return migration has been most prevalent among those who had a college degree or higher and lowest among those who had a high school education or less.[54] As shown in Figure 6.9, the rate of outmigration from the United States is highest among the most-educated Chinese immigrants. It is estimated that almost one-third of

---

[51] Arturo A. Aguilar Esteva, "Stayers and Returners: Educational Self-Selection Among U.S. Immigrants and Returning Migrants," Institute of Labor Economics, Discussion Paper No. 7222, February 2013.

[52] Executive Order 12711, "Policy Implementation with Respect to Nationals of the People's Republic of China," Executive Office of the President, April 11, 1990; Public Law 102-404, Chinese Student Protection Act of 1992, October 9, 1992. Executive Order 12711 applied to Chinese nationals and their dependents who were in the United States at some point between June 5, 1989, and April 10, 1990; it prevented their nonimmigrant visas from expiring, deferred their deportation proceedings, waived the requirement for them as international students to leave the United States for two years after the end of their studies, and granted them work authorization. The Chinese Student Protection Act of 1992 allowed the same population to apply for permanent residence in the United States through the employment-based preference category, but it waived the requirements for labor certification, certain credentials applicable to immigrant health care professionals, and unexpired documentation. It also exempted these Chinese nationals from the annual per-country numerical limit on the issuance of employment-based green cards.

[53] Lei Zhang, "The Chinese Student Protection Act of 1992: Student Immigration and the Transpacific Neoliberal Model Minority," *Journal of Asian American Studies*, Vol. 24, No. 3, October 2021, p. 443.

[54] Aguilar Esteva, 2013, pp. 19, 49. Aguilar Esteva (2013) analyzed data from the immigration cohort of 1995–2000 and estimated how many of them had return migrated by 2010. I extend this analysis using data from the American Community Survey (ACS), accessed through IPUMS (Steven Ruggles, Sarah Flood, Matthew Sobek, Danika Brockman, Grace Cooper, Stephanie Richards, and Megan Schouweiler, "IPUMS USA: Version 13.0," dataset, IPUMS, 2023). Specifically, I compared (1) the educational attainment data from respondents to the 2011 ACS, 1-Year Sample, whose birth country is China, whose age was between 30 and 40 at the time of survey in 2011, and whose year of immigration is between 2005 and 2010 with (2) the educational attainment data from respondents to the 2021 ACS, 1-Year Sample, whose birth country is China, whose age was between 40 and 50 at the time of survey in 2021, and whose year of immigration is between 2005 and 2010. I examined changes in population sizes and distributions of educational attainment across the two time points to estimate rates of return and educational selectivity of return. The ACS is not

FIGURE 6.9

Percentage of Chinese Immigrants from Migration Cohort of 2005–2010 Who Left the United States Between 2011 and 2021, by Educational Attainment

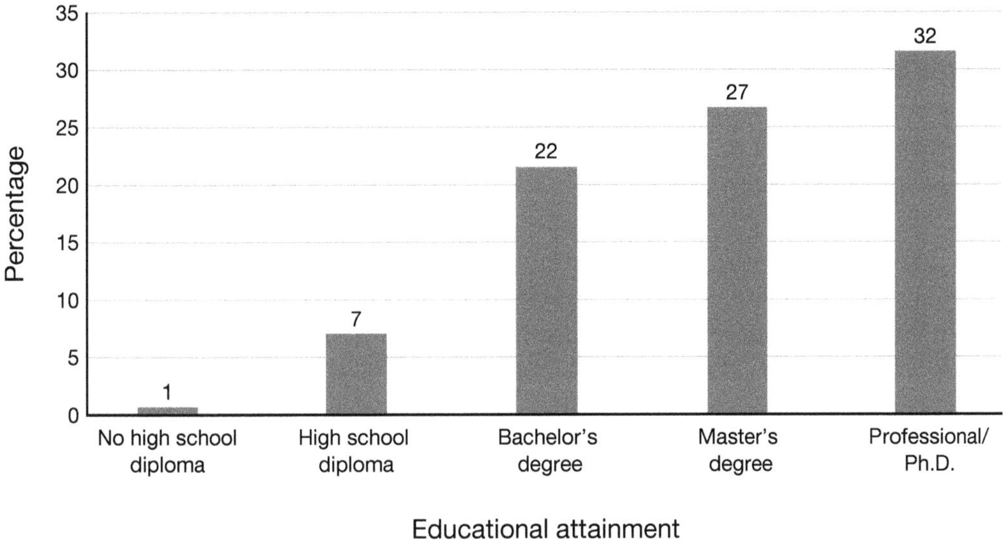

SOURCE: Author's analysis of data from the 2011 and 2021 ACS (Ruggles et al., 2023).

NOTE: The data in this figure are based on the weighted population estimates for people in the United States in each educational attainment category whose birth country is China, whose year of immigration is between 2005 and 2010, and whose age was between 30 and 40 at the time of the 2011 ACS or whose age was between 40 and 50 at the time of the 2021 ACS. The difference in population sizes across the two time points is interpreted as the number of out-migrants over the ten-year period.

Chinese people in the United States in 2011 who had professional or doctoral degrees and who had immigrated to the United States between 2005 and 2010 had returned to China by 2021. Although there were estimated to be 17,591 Chinese immigrants from this cohort with doctorates in 2011, that population shrunk to 12,025 by 2021. These statistics suggest that 31.6 percent of the original population present in 2011 left the United States by 2021.[55] The apparent association between high educational attainment and out-migration, illustrated in Figure 6.9, casts doubt on the theory that return migration is most prevalent among those who are underqualified and uncompetitive in the U.S. labor market.

---

a longitudinal survey, however, so these two samples do not represent a true cohort but rather a "synthetic cohort" (Aguilar Esteva, 2013, p. 3).

[55] Ruggles et al., 2023. See the previous footnote for details on how these estimates were calculated. The difference between the population sizes in 2021 and 2011 is interpreted as representing the number of people from the 2011 population who return migrated by 2021. It is possible that some of the difference is attributable to out-migration to third countries. Another possibility is that a large portion of this population died between 2011 and 2021, but given that this cohort would be no older than 50 years old in 2021, it is reasonable to assume that death is not the main driver of this population's decrease in size.

The returnee population in China is dominated by those who earned master's degrees abroad, particularly in the disciplines of business and economics.[56] The plurality of returnees to China studied abroad in the United Kingdom; the United States tends to be the second-most common country of study.[57] The United States is the largest sender of returnees with Ph.D.'s, however.[58] Unlike their counterparts with bachelor's and master's degrees, returnees with Ph.D.'s appear to be concentrated in STEM fields.[59] Studies conducted by researchers in China report that doctorate-holders account for 3 to 13 percent of the returnee population.[60] (See Tables 6.6 and 6.7 in the supplementary materials section for summaries of data from Chinese-produced studies of returnees.)

Overseas Chinese students who earned their undergraduate degrees in China appear more likely to return than those who earned their undergraduate degrees in the United States. Three-quarters of returnees had completed their undergraduate education in China before studying abroad, whereas only one-fifth of returnees had studied abroad after completing high school in China.[61] Thus, it appears that Chinese students who study abroad at the undergraduate level are underrepresented among returnees.[62] There may be a higher rate of return among those who delayed studying abroad until after completing their bachelor's degree compared with those who studied abroad after completing high school. This could be because those who attend college in China spend more of their formative years in China and develop stronger roots and networks there, which later attract them to return.

Professional Experience

Approximately half of returnees have had full-time work experience abroad.[63] However, returnees tend to return very early in their careers. One survey of returnees found that, among those with full-time work experience abroad, half had worked abroad for less than one

[56] Overseas Study Service Center, 2016; Center for China and Globalization and Zhaopin.com, 2017; Chen, Feng, and Sun, 2021.

[57] Overseas Study Service Center, 2016; Center for China and Globalization and Zhaopin.com, 2017; Chen, Feng, and Sun, "2021.

[58] Overseas Study Service Center, 2016.

[59] Overseas Study Service Center, 2016.

[60] Overseas Study Service Center, 2016; Center for China and Globalization and Zhaopin.com, 2017; Chen, Feng, and Sun, 2021.

[61] Center for China and Globalization and Zhaopin.com, 2017

[62] Data from the United States and the United Kingdom, two top recipients of Chinese international students, indicate that between 40 to 50 percent of Chinese international students are studying at the undergraduate level (Higher Education Statistics Agency, "Where Do HE Students Come From?" webpage, January 31, 2023; Institute of International Education, 2022).

[63] Chen, Feng, and Sun, 2021; Center for China and Globalization and Zhaopin.com, 2017, p. 12. See Table 6.7 in the supplementary materials section for details.

year.[64] There is little-to-no data on the industries or occupations in which returnees worked prior to returning to China.

Academic scientists who return to China also tend to be junior scholars.[65] When high-performing, senior scholars return, they tend to be "part-time" returnees, leading binational lives.[66] China's talent programs appear to recognize the difficulty of attracting high-level talents to live and work in China full-time; several talent programs targeting established scholars and professionals require only part-time residence in China.[67] In terms of the disciplinary backgrounds of returning academics from the United States, about 40 percent belong to the life sciences, 40 percent to mathematics and physical science disciplines, 15 percent to engineering and computer science, and 4 percent to social sciences.[68]

Transnational Ties

Some returnees establish enduring long-term ties to another country before return migrating. This is sometimes an intentional strategy; U.S. permanent residency or citizenship can help one garner higher salaries in China's private sector.[69] Citizenship or permanent residence status in another country also allows returnees to mitigate risks because it provides an escape route in case adverse conditions develop in China.[70] Although holding a foreign citizenship can make working in China complicated given that China does not allow dual citizenship, some Chinese returnees adopt the "two systems, one family" strategy to mitigate risks while avoiding complications; in this strategy, one spouse obtains citizenship in another country while the other maintains Chinese citizenship.[71] In some cases, this strategy may entail family separation while one spouse remains in the United States or elsewhere to meet the residency requirement for naturalization and the other spouse returns to China to work.[72] Not all transnational ties include obtaining immigration status or family separation. Another way that transnational ties are established is by buying property abroad; this method

---

[64] Center for China and Globalization and Zhaopin.com, 2017, p. 12. See Table 6.7.

[65] Gaulé, 2014; Yu et al., 2023.

[66] David Zweig, Kang Siqin, and Wang Huiyao, "'The Best Are Yet to Come': State Programs, Domestic Resistance and Reverse Migration of High-Level Talent to China," *Journal of Contemporary China*, Vol. 29, No. 125, 2020.

[67] Weinstein, 2020.

[68] Derived from Yu et al., 2023, "Supplementary Materials 4: Trends in Migration of Chinese-American Scientists from the US to China," Table S6.

[69] Liu, 2012.

[70] Liu, 2012.

[71] Liu, 2012.

[72] Liu, 2012.

is sometimes employed by Chinese citizens to safeguard their assets.[73] In sum, transnational ties encompass immigration status in another country, family remaining in another country, or owning property in another country.

A minority of returnees have strong transnational ties to the country in which they lived prior to returning. A 2019 survey of returnees found that 9.8 percent had obtained permanent resident status abroad before returning to China, while 6.2 percent owned property in their former country of residence, and 11.3 percent had relatives still living in the former country of residence.[74] Among entrepreneurs and high-level talents, transnational ties are more common. A 2008 survey of returnee entrepreneurs from the United States found that one-third held U.S. green cards or citizenship.[75] A 2000 survey of returnee entrepreneurs found that less than half lived in China full time.[76] Entrepreneurs and high-level talents are more likely to have transnational ties because these returnees typically spend longer lengths of time abroad before returning. This is reflected in the requirements of high-level talent recruitment programs, which often allow those recruited to split time between countries and often do not require Chinese citizenship.[77] However, the ability to maintain transnational ties and lead binational lives might be less feasible today than it was in the 2000s; tensions between the United States and China have increased, and transnational ties have increasingly become cause for suspicion. There is anecdotal evidence that researchers in the Thousand Talents Program are opting to make a complete move to China in light of U.S. scrutiny of American researchers who have ties to China.[78]

Implications of Return Migration for China

The Chinese government's official statements about returnees frame them as competitive in the Chinese labor market, exceptionally skilled (especially in STEM fields), and having the potential to be the driving force in China's mass entrepreneurship strategy. Official government publications laud China's overseas students and returnees as having "a competitive edge in strategically important fields" and claim that they are highly sought after in China's labor

---

[73] Tanza Loudenback, "Middle-Class Chinese People Are Buying Property in the US as a 'Safe Harbor' for Their Money," *Business Insider*, January 11, 2019.

[74] Chen, Feng, and Sun, 2021.

[75] Vivek Wadhwa, AnnaLee Saxenian, Richard B. Freeman, Gary Gereffi, and Alex Salkever, *America's Loss Is the World's Gain: America's New Immigrant Entrepreneurs, Part IV*, March 2009.

[76] Cited in Liu, 2012.

[77] Weinstein, 2020. It should be noted, though, that high-level talent programs tend not to recruit returnees or ethnically Chinese individuals exclusively.

[78] Ellen Barry and Gina Kolata, "China's Lavish Funds Lured U.S. Scientists. What Did It Get in Return?" *New York Times*, February 6, 2020.

market.[79] Official government publications also highlight that return migration of overseas students has increased since the 18th National Congress of the Chinese Communist Party (CCP) in 2012, when Xi Jinping rose to the position of General Secretary of the CCP. Xi is quoted as saying that in the face of "fierce international competition, only the innovator wins" and that overseas student-returnees should be "at the forefront of innovation."[80] Similarly, other national bodies have prioritized encouraging the return of overseas Chinese students, seeing them as the engine of future innovation and entrepreneurship.[81] The Chinese government clearly envisions an important strategic role for returnees in developing the national economy; whether they have lived up to this expectation is unclear.

In this section, I address five questions about the role of returnees in the Chinese economy:

1. To what extent are returnees engaging in entrepreneurship?
2. Are returnees filling jobs in strategically important fields?
3. Are returnees highly competitive in the Chinese labor market?
4. Is their expertise improving the performance of Chinese firms?
5. Are returnees enabling technology transfer?

Entrepreneurship

Returnees have higher entrepreneurship rates than domestic graduates, but they still fall far short of driving a "mass entrepreneurship" boom. According to one study, 1.8 percent of overseas returnees from the class of 2016 had started their own business by 2019, which was higher than the rate of entrepreneurship reported for their domestic graduate counterparts (0.5 percent).[82] In surveys of graduating overseas Chinese students intending to return migrate, between 3 and 5 percent of respondents expressed the intent to start their own business.[83] A separate 2017 survey of returnees at large found that 7.9 percent had started their own business.[84] (For comparison, 10.2 percent of the U.S. labor force was self-employed in 2022.[85]) Although 7.9 percent could be an overestimate of how many returnees start businesses, the rate of entrepreneurship among all returnees is likely higher than the entrepreneurship rate or intention rate of recently graduated returnees (which falls between 1.8 percent and 5 percent).

---

79 Ministry of Education of the People's Republic of China, "Brief Report on Chinese Overseas Students and International Students in China 2017," March 31, 2018; Overseas Study Service Center, 2016.

80 Quoted in LinkedIn China, 2022, p. 54.

81 Overseas Study Service Center, 2016.

82 Cao and Zhang, 2021, Figure 5.

83 Overseas Study Service Center, 2016; LinkedIn China, 2022, p. 22.

84 Center for China and Globalization and Zhaopin.com, 2017.

85 Flood et al., 2022.

Entrepreneurs in general face many difficulties in China. The failure rate of start-ups in China is high. The average lifespan of a Chinese start-up is three years.[86] Venture capital is limited, and venture capitalists tend to be conservative, investing in more-mature firms rather than early-stage start-ups.[87] As a result, most entrepreneurs, including returnee entrepreneurs, rely on their own or their families' funds.[88] Even several government-sponsored start-up funds require a start-up to have already amassed a significant sum of capital from other sources before applying for state-sponsored support.[89] Returnees in particular suffer from a lack of government connections, lack of networks, lack of familiarity with the local market, and cultural differences.[90]

Placement of Returnees in Chinese Labor Market

Returnees tend to work in the private sector. Overseas returnees are employed in private and foreign-owned enterprises at higher rates than their domestic graduate counterparts and are much less likely than domestic graduates to work in state-owned enterprises, government agencies and research institutes, and other public institutions.[91] Although foreign-funded enterprises are not the top employer of returnees, they are returnees' top preference, as shown in Table 6.2. Although returnees as a whole tend to find jobs in the private sector, returnees with doctorates are more likely to work at universities and state-run institutions.[92]

Returnees tend to be concentrated in the financial and technology industries. There are no data on the industries of returnees from the United States specifically, but given the distribution of degree fields across countries of study abroad, it is likely that returnees from the United States concentrate more heavily in the technology industry, while the large number of returnees from the United Kingdom, who largely studied business and related disciplines, tilt returnee averages toward the financial industry (Table 6.3).

Because of the different methodologies of the surveys represented in Table 6.2, they should not be compared with one another to understand trends over time. However, the 2022 survey

---

[86] Wu Feiyi, Niu Xiao, and Yang Jingguang, "New Features of Returnee Entrepreneurship in the New Era," in Wang Huiyao and Miao Lu, eds., *Annual Report on the Development of Chinese Students Studying Abroad (2020–2021)*, Social Sciences Academic Press, 2021.

[87] Yun-Chung Chen, "The Limits of Brain Circulation: Chinese Returnees and Technological Development in Beijing," *Pacific Affairs*, Vol. 81, No. 2, Summer 2008.

[88] Center for China and Globalization and Zhaopin.com, 2017, p. 28; Wu, Niu, and Yang, 2021.

[89] LinkedIn China, 2022.

[90] Wu, Niu, and Yang, 2021; Wei Sun, "The Productivity of Return Migrants: The Case of China's 'Sea Turtles,'" *IZA Journal of Development and Migration*, Vol. 2, No. 1, December 2013; Daomi Lin, Jiangyong Lu, Peter Ping Li, and Xiaohui Liu, "Balancing Formality and Informality in Business Exchanges as a Duality: A Comparative Case Study of Returnee and Local Entrepreneurs in China," *Management and Organization Review*, Vol. 11, No. 2, June 2015; Chen, 2008; Center for China and Globalization and Zhaopin.com, 2017.

[91] Cao and Zhang, 2021.

[92] Overseas Study Service Center, 2016.

TABLE 6.2

Comparison of Survey Results on Returnees' Preferred and Actual Employers

Type of Employer	Percentage of Returnees Preferring Sector, 2015[a]	Percentage of Returnees Preferring Sector, 2022[b]	Percentage of Returnees Employed in Sector, 2017[c]	Percentage of Returnees Employed in Sector, 2019[d]	Percentage of Recent Graduate Returnees Employed in Sector, 2017–2019[e]
Private sector	49	85	74.9	50.5	68
Private enterprises (Chinese-owned)	17	9	39.5	23.4	38.2
Self-employment	3	5	7.9	15.7	1.8
Foreign enterprises (fully or jointly owned)	29	71	27.5	9.8	28
Nonprofits, nongovernmental organizations, and social organizations	—	—	—	1.6	0
Public sector	45	14	21.1	46.9	31
State-owned enterprises	20	10	15.9	17.8	23
Government, public institutions, and universities	25	4	5.2	29.1	9
Other or not reported	6	1	4	1.4	1
Unemployed	—	—	—	1.1	—

[a] Overseas Study Service Center, 2016.

[b] LinkedIn China, 2022.

[c] Center for China and Globalization and Zhaopin.com, 2017.

[d] Chen, Feng, and Sun, 2021.

[e] Cao and Zhang, 2021.

by LinkedIn China is part of a series of periodic surveys, and the trends across those surveys indicate that the technology and finance industries are consistently the top-choice industries for returnees, while a relatively recent trend is the increased interest in working in the health and pharmaceutical industry. The share of returnee respondents interested in the health and pharmaceutical industry rose from 1 percent of returnee respondents in 2020 to 17 percent in 2022.[93]

93 LinkedIn China, 2022, pp. 37–38.

TABLE 6.3

Comparison of Survey Results on Returnees' Industries

Type of Employer	Percentage of Returnees Preferring Industry, 2015[a]	Percentage of Returnees Preferring Industry, 2022[b]	Percentage of Returnees Employed in Industry, 2017[c]	Percentage of Returnees Employed in Industry, 2019[d]	Percentage of Recent Graduate Returnees Employed in Industry, 2017–2019[e]
Finance	30.0	38	14.6	17.4	18.5
Technology	6.7	58	15.5	11.1	14.0
Electronic manufacturing	–	12	–	–	7.5
Manufacturing	–	13	9	7.4	–
Education	9.9	18	–	–	13.7
Education, research institutes, state agencies, and universities				28.2	
Professional and consulting services	–	10	–	–	8.4
Accounting and financial firms	–	–	–	5.6	–
Construction and real estate	–	7	–	6.5	–
Trade and retail	–	14	9.4	4.6	–
Energy	–	3	–	2.2	–
Culture and media	7.8	–	9.9	5.9	–
Health and pharmaceutical	–	17	–	5.4	
Social organizations	–	–	–	1.4	–
Other or not reported	54.4	18	41.6	4.3	37.9

NOTE: The percentages in the second column on returnee preferences do not add up to 100 because respondents were permitted to pick more than one preferred industry.

[a] Overseas Study Service Center, 2016.

[b] LinkedIn China, 2022.

[c] Center for China and Globalization and Zhaopin.com, 2017.

[d] Chen, Feng, and Sun, 2021.

[e] Cao and Zhang, 2021.

Certain industries have higher demand for returnees than others. Returnees are in high demand for education- and translation-related roles, whereas there is an oversupply of returnees seeking roles in senior management, finance, and accounting positions.[94] According to an analysis of data from a Chinese talent recruitment website, 38 percent of new hires in the education industry in 2019 were returnees, compared with 14 percent in the professional services industry (e.g., consulting, accounting, human resources), 11 percent in the technology industry, 6 percent in the financial industry, and 3 percent in the insurance industry.[95]

The distribution of returnees across occupations, in addition to sectors and industries, also provides insight into returnees' roles in the Chinese economy. Among overseas returnees from the classes of 2014, 2015, and 2016 three years after graduation, 22.1 percent worked in finance- and accounting-related occupations, 9.3 percent worked in "computer and data processing," and 7.5 percent worked in software and internet application development.[96] In a 2022 survey by LinkedIn China, 32 percent of respondents were pursuing positions in technology research and development, and 27 percent were pursuing data analyst positions.[97] These data illustrate that returnees in general are concentrated in finance- and technology-related positions but that a significant share of those concentrated in technology-related positions—especially those coming from the United States, where most LinkedIn users are—may be in data analysis or data science roles. Although data analysis and data science can provide important insights on a variety of topics, technology research and development are of greater strategic importance.

Competitiveness in the Labor Market

The competitive edge in the Chinese labor market of an overseas education compared with a domestic education has been diminishing.[98] This is likely related to the increased supply of returnees with overseas degrees and the expanded set of foreign universities at which returnees study, which may not all be held in high esteem by Chinese employers. Still, leaders in some Chinese companies express that returnees are highly competitive and make up a significant share of their workforce, for example in global marketing firms.[99]

---

[94] Chen Xiaoxiao and Liu Xinyao, "Survey on the Employment of Chinese Returned Overseas Students in 2019," in Wang Huiyao and Miao Lu, eds., *Annual Report on the Development of Chinese Students Studying Abroad (2020–2021)*, Social Sciences Academic Press, 2021; Statista, "Business Sectors with the Highest Share of Overseas Returnees Recruitment in China in 2019," webpage, December 2019; Center for China and Globalization and Zhaopin.com, *Report on Employment & Entrepreneurship of Chinese Returnees 2019*, 2019; Center for China and Globalization and Zhaopin.com, 2017.

[95] Statista, 2019; Center for China and Globalization and Zhaopin.com, 2019.

[96] Cao and Zhang, 2021, Figure 4.

[97] LinkedIn China, 2022, p. 38.

[98] LinkedIn China, 2022, p. 25; Mia Nulimaimaiti, "China's Returning Overseas Graduates Hit in the Pocket, Face Harsh Reality of Job Market," *South China Morning Post*, May 21, 2024.

[99] LinkedIn China, 2022.

Returnees earn higher salaries than their domestic counterparts, but their salaries still fall far below their expectations.[100] Historically, returnees' salaries are approximately 30 percent higher than those of their domestic counterparts.[101] However, fewer than one in four returnees holds realistic salary expectations.[102] The starting salary for fresh graduates employed in first-tier cities is around 7,000 yuan per month, and the average job posting on Zhaopin.com—a popular Chinese job-searching platform—advertises a salary of around 10,000 yuan per month.[103] However, more than half of newly graduating returnees expect to make at least 18,000 yuan per month, an expectation that is far higher than the actual average salaries of returnees.[104] In a 2019 survey, 63 percent of returnees described their salaries as below or far below expectations; 34 percent said their salaries matched their expectations, and only 3 percent said their salaries exceeded expectations.[105]

Returnees sometimes struggle to find jobs that match their field of study. Domestic graduates are more likely to report that their job is aligned with their degree field than returnees are.[106] As shown in Table 6.4, several surveys of returnees have found that about one-quarter of returnees feel that their degrees earned abroad are not at all relevant or related to their job in China. This suggests that returnees may struggle to obtain the positions they want and that returnees may be less familiar with—and less prepared for—the demands of the Chinese job market compared with domestic graduates.

Economic Performance of Returnees

Returnees bring valuable skills to the Chinese market, but they struggle because of their lack of networks, government connections, and familiarity with the local market and regulatory environment. As a result, they fail to make an impact in large and hierarchical organizations, and their performance in entrepreneurial ventures is mixed. Returnees appear to have the most impact when they work in conjunction with non-returnees, especially in small and medium enterprises.

Returnees and returnee-founded firms tend to perform worse in some respects. Returnee-founded firms in Zhongguancun Science Park (ZSP)—China's Silicon Valley—tend to have

---

[100] Cao and Zhang, 2021; Chen and Liu, 2021; Nulimaimaiti, 2024.

[101] Cao and Zhang, 2021, Figure 6; "Chinese Students Back to China to Seek Jobs Hit a Record High in 2022: Survey," *Global Times*, February 14, 2023; Cheng Si, "Recruiting Salaries Creep Up in 2022," *China Daily*, January 5, 2023.

[102] LinkedIn China, 2022.

[103] Wu Bingcong, "Only 6.1% of Recent Undergraduates Start at More Than $10,000, and Very Happy but Underpaid Jobs Are Popular" ["仅6.1%应届本科生起薪过万，很幸福但工资不高的工作受欢迎"], Sohu, February 26, 2023; Nulimaimaiti, 2024; Cheng, 2023.

[104] LinkedIn China, 2022, pp. 43–44. Salary expectations are similar across those graduating with bachelor's degrees, master's degrees, and doctorates.

[105] Chen and Liu, 2021.

[106] Cao and Zhang, 2021.

TABLE 6.4

Comparison of Survey Results on Relevance of Returnees' Degrees to Their Jobs

Source	Highly Relevant (%)	Somewhat Relevant (%)	Not Relevant (%)
Center for China and Globalization and Zhaopin (2017)[a]	16.9	54.5	28.6
Beijing Institute of Economic and Social Development (2019)[b]	49.5	27.8	22.7
Center for China and Globalization and Zhaopin (2019)[c]	34	39	27

[a] Center for China and Globalization and Zhaopin.com, 2017.

[b] Chen, Feng, and Sun, 2021.

[c] Chen and Liu, 2021.

lower overall sales and fewer employees.[107] Returnee venture capitalists underperform compared with their non-returnee counterparts because they lack government ties and familiarity with Chinese regulations and business practices. As a result, not only are returnee venture capitalists' offers viewed as less competitive by promising entrepreneurs, but returnee venture capitalists are unable to secure preferential treatment for the start-ups in which they invest and are unable to provide important guidance to entrepreneurs.[108] Similarly, new ventures with boards composed mostly or entirely of returnees tend to perform worse in the stock market; returnee board members are less able to provide guidance and connections that are relevant to the local market or regulatory environment.[109]

Returnees perform better in other respects. Returnee-founded small and medium enterprises in ZSP register more patents in the Chinese Patent Office and are more export-oriented than comparable firms.[110] Although patents registered with the Chinese Patent Office may be derivative of innovations made elsewhere, export activity is a signal that a firm's product is competitive. Firms that combine returnee and domestic talent and that are flexible enough

[107] Haiyang Li, Yan Zhang, Yu Li, Li-An Zhou, and Weiying Zhang, "Returnees Versus Locals: Who Perform Better in China's Technology Entrepreneurship?" *Strategic Entrepreneurship Journal*, Vol. 6, No. 3, September 2012.

[108] Sun, 2013

[109] Ya-Hui Lin, Chung-Jen Chen, and Bou-Wen Lin, "The Dual-Edged Role of Returnee Board Members in New Venture Performance," *Journal of Business Research*, Vol. 90, September 2018.

[110] Xiaohui Liu, Jiangyong Lu, Igor Filatotchev, Trevor Buck, and Mike Wright, "Returnee Entrepreneurs, Knowledge Spillovers and Innovation in High-Tech Firms in Emerging Economies," *Journal of International Business Studies,* Vol. 41, No. 7, September 2010; Igor Filatotchev, Xiaohui Liu, Trevor Buck, and Mike Wright, "The Export Orientation and Export Performance of High-Technology SMEs in Emerging Markets: The Effects of Knowledge Transfer by Returnee Entrepreneurs," *Journal of International Business Studies*, Vol. 40, No. 6, August 2009.

to learn from returnee employees are able to benefit from returnees' skills. In firms that have flexible organizational cultures, the presence of returnees in the top managerial team is associated with higher domestic sales growth.[111] Firms founded by non-returnees in industries that have a high density of returnee workers gain technology from abroad.[112] New ventures that have a mix of returnees and non-returnees on their boards have better stock price performance than ventures that have all-domestic or all-returnee boards.[113] The combination of returnee and non-returnee workers in one firm allows for leveraging returnees' strengths while compensating for their weaknesses.

The findings discussed here should be taken with some caution. The extant research on the economic performance of returnees is based on data from before 2012. Since 2012, there have been changes in the CCP's leadership, in the profile and number of returnees, and in the policy landscape for returnee entrepreneurs. The conclusions reached in this subsection might not hold true for the present day.

Technology Transfer

The primary avenues of technology transfer in China do not rely on returnees. The Chinese government facilitates technology transfer and intellectual property theft through "opaque and discretionary administrative approval processes, joint venture requirements," and other mechanisms.[114] Chinese administrative procedures sometimes require foreign companies that wish to operate in China to disclose their trade secrets. Joint venture requirements mandate that foreign companies collaborate with a Chinese-owned business in order to operate in China; Chinese business partners thus hold significant leverage over foreign companies, which they can use to compel technology transfer.[115] Small and medium Chinese enterprises, however, are unlikely to gain access to foreign technology through this mechanism and are thus more reliant on recruiting employees who have knowledge of foreign technology.[116]

Returnees play a role in technology transfer from more developed countries to China. One way to measure technology transfer is through the number of patents registered with the Chinese Patent Bureau. This is because patents registered with the Chinese Patent Bureau

---

[111] Pao-Lien Chen, Danchi Tan, and Ruey-Jer "Bryan" Jean, "Foreign Knowledge Acquisition Through Inter-Firm Collaboration and Recruitment: Implications for Domestic Growth of Emerging Market Firms," *International Business Review*, Vol. 25, No. 1, February 2016.

[112] Liu et al., 2010.

[113] Lin, Chen, and Lin, "2018.

[114] Office of the United States Trade Representative, *Findings of the Investigation into China's Acts, Policies, and Practices Related to Technology Transfer, Intellectual Property, and Innovation Under Section 301 of the Trade Act of 1974*, Executive Office of the United States Trade Representative, March 22, 2018, p. 5.

[115] Sean O'Connor, *How Chinese Companies Facilitate Technology Transfer from the United States*, U.S.-China Economic and Security Review Commission, May 6, 2019. Joint venture requirements have relaxed in recent years in certain industries.

[116] Chen, Tan, and Jean, 2016.

are more likely to be derivative of existing technologies; China has historically incentivized the submission of low-quality patents by offering subsidies to apply for "utility model and industrial design patents" in addition to "invention patents."[117] Meanwhile, novel innovations originating in China—especially those with market applications—are better proxied by Chinese-origin patents registered with the World Intellectual Property Organization or foreign patent offices. Returnee-founded firms register more patents in the Chinese Patent Bureau than non-returnee–founded firms, and non-returnee–founded firms in industries that have a high density of returnee workers are also more likely to register patents with the Chinese Patent Bureau.[118] This indicates that returnees transfer technology from elsewhere and contribute to knowledge spillover in their industry. However, the movement of workers from multinational corporations within China to local Chinese firms also has a large impact on local firms acquiring Chinese patents, and the impact of worker mobility between multinational corporations and local firms on acquiring Chinese patents is even larger than the impact of returnee entrepreneurs.[119]

The Chinese government uses talent programs and scholarships to promote technology transfer through the recruitment of human capital, with mixed results. For example, some Chinese government scholarships for graduate students require students to return to China after graduating; however, few of the students graduating with Ph.D.'s appear to abide by those contracts.[120] Approximately 3 percent of people successfully recruited to China through the Thousand Talents Program work as Chinese government scientists, but 6 percent work for U.S.-owned firms in China.[121]

Conclusion

Returnees are hailed by the CCP as the driving force behind China's mass entrepreneurship strategy. Although returnees tend to flounder in China's start-up scene without support from local partners and networks, they are assets to China's small and medium enterprises and promote growth in China's private sector. Returnees are an important facilitator of technology transfer to China's small and medium enterprises, although they play only a minor role in the greater scope of China's technology transfer efforts. Returnees continue to be viewed as competitive by Chinese employers, as shown by their higher salaries, but returnees still experience significant disappointment in the labor market as the economic opportunities available fail to meet their expectations.

[117] Alex He, "What Do China's High Patent Numbers Really Mean?" Centre for International Governance Innovation, April 20, 2021.

[118] Liu et al., 2010.

[119] Liu et al., 2010.

[120] Ryan Fedasiuk, "The China Scholarship Council: An Overview," Center for Security and Emerging Technology, July 2020.

[121] Barry and Kolata, 2020.

Implications for U.S.-China Competition and Cooperation

There has been an acceleration of return migration among highly educated Chinese immigrants, including academic scientists, during the past decade. This is problematic for the United States for three reasons. First, the United States has a shortage of STEM workers. Chinese immigrants and students in the United States are concentrated in STEM fields. The United States could address the STEM worker shortage by retaining more Chinese immigrant workers and international students. Second, return migration among academic scientists narrows the U.S. STEM talent pipeline by prompting the relocation of entire laboratories and depriving U.S. universities of teachers and mentors to future students. Third, returnees can help Chinese firms and even the Chinese government advance in important fields and eventually pose a greater economic and national security threat to the United States.

Potential Avenues for Cooperation and Mutual Benefit

However, return migration may provide benefits as well. Historically, the return migration of high-skilled workers from the U.S. technology industry to parts of Asia has benefited the technology industry in both the United States and in the returnees' home countries.[122] Many Taiwanese engineers who studied and worked in Silicon Valley returned to Taiwan in the 1980s and 1990s. They facilitated the development of Taiwan's high-technology industrial region in Hsinchu and supported the development and growth of Silicon Valley. A complementary division of labor developed between Hsinchu and Silicon Valley, in which Silicon Valley took the lead on designing technological products and Hsinchu specialized in the fabrication of advanced technological equipment that the products required.[123] This generated economic growth and high-paying jobs in both places.

Could mainland Chinese returnees similarly facilitate a mutually beneficial relationship between ZSP—China's high-technology industrial region—and Silicon Valley? The answer is likely no.[124] Unlike Hsinchu, ZSP is not characterized by cooperative interfirm relationships involving interfirm knowledge spillover and resource-sharing, nor by strong transnational ties with Silicon Valley, nor by a highly developed domestic venture capital industry.[125] Furthermore, Hsinchu firms became leaders in a niche technology that fits into a global supply chain (i.e., semiconductors), but ZSP firms tend to take an import substitution approach by

---

[122] AnnaLee Saxenian, *The New Argonauts: Regional Advantage in a Global Economy*, Harvard University Press, 2006.

[123] Saxenian, 2006.

[124] Chen, 2008.

[125] Chen, 2008; Yu Zhou and Jinn-Yuh Hsu, "Divergent Engagements: Roles and Strategies of Taiwanese and Mainland Chinese Returnee Entrepreneurs in the IT Industry," *Global Networks*, Vol. 11, No. 3, July 2011.

creating domestic versions of foreign technology for the local market.[126] This approach has led to an antagonistic relationship between ZSP and Silicon Valley, in which ZSP firms have little to offer Silicon Valley because they tend not to develop specialized products that could benefit or fill a gap for other firms.

What the case of Taiwanese returnees can teach us is that transnational connections and collaborations among STEM innovators can be mutually beneficial when all actors have incentives to create and share new knowledge and tools. Interfirm knowledge spillover and resource-sharing in Taiwan and Silicon Valley made it possible for firms to quickly build on each other's innovations to develop more-specialized products and advance the field as a whole, whereas firms in industrial regions in which secrecy is the norm wasted resources on replicating the efforts of other firms and became less competitive.[127]

Academic science is a field that provides incentives for innovation and knowledge-sharing. International collaborations among academic scientists with different strengths are thus more likely to produce collective benefits by advancing collective knowledge. China is the United States' largest scientific research partner in the world, and vice versa.[128] China-based scientists contribute significant strengths and resources to complement those of U.S.-based scientists; in some fields (e.g., research involving embryonic stem cells), many U.S. researchers have difficulties conducting research without the help of Chinese partners.[129] Returnee scientists can facilitate mutually beneficial international research partnerships, especially in areas of nonsensitive, basic scientific research.

Another way that the United States can engage in economic competition with China while producing benefits for both countries is by retaining high-skilled Chinese students and workers. China is clearly invested in attracting human capital, including returnees, from the United States, but there may be an opening for U.S.-China collaboration on this issue given China's current high youth unemployment. In July 2023, Chinese statistics reported that youth unemployment was at 21.3 percent, but some scholars claimed that a more accurate estimate would be 46.5 percent.[130] The CCP has found this state of affairs to be so troublesome that it decided to suspend the release of youth unemployment statistics for months, before ultimately adopting a new methodology for calculating youth unemployment and pub-

[126] Chen, 2008; David Zweig, Siu Fung Chung, and Wilfried Vanhonacker, "Rewards of Technology: Explaining China's Reverse Migration," *Journal of International Migration and Integration*, Vol. 7, No. 4, September 2006; Zhou and Hsu, 2011.

[127] AnnaLee Saxenian, *Regional Advantage: Culture and Competition in Silicon Valley and Route 128*, Harvard University Press, 1996; Chen, 2008.

[128] Karen Hao and Sha Hua, "The U.S. Is Turning Away from China, Its Biggest Scientific Partner, at a Precarious Time," *Wall Street Journal*, August 16, 2023.

[129] Hao and Hua, 2023; Kirstin R. W. Matthews and Daniel Morali, "Can We Do That Here? An Analysis of US Federal and State Policies Guiding Human Embryo and Embryoid Research," *Journal of Law and the Biosciences*, Vol. 9, No. 1, January–June 2022.

[130] "China Halts Publication of Youth Unemployment Report as Numbers Hit Record High," Voice of America, August 16, 2023.

lishing adjusted statistics that place youth unemployment at around 15 percent.[131] Although returnees constitute too small of a share of the youth population to significantly shift the state of youth unemployment in China, the presence of returnees in the current labor market is problematic for the CCP given that returnees have very high job and salary expectations (as discussed previously). Historically, when large populations of educated youth with high expectations are unable to find suitable jobs, social unrest follows.[132] If the United States were to retain and employ a greater number of would-be returnees, that could relieve some pressure for China's government by employing those who are most likely to become disaffected with the CCP. At the same time, the United States would benefit from employing and retaining these migrants; they can help fill the U.S. STEM labor shortage and maintain economic growth at a time when much of the U.S. population is aging into retirement.

U.S. Response So Far

In recent years, some U.S. government actors have viewed the transnational ties and mobility of Chinese migrants in the United States with suspicion, and much of the U.S. security response to these concerns has targeted Chinese students and researchers. Presidential Proclamation 10043 barred the entry of Chinese students and researchers—especially those on Chinese government scholarships—who are connected to any entity in China that implements or supports the military-civil fusion strategy of China.[133] Since 2017, federal grantmaking agencies, such as the National Institutes of Health, began opening investigations into grantees who had allegedly falsified grant forms, particularly those suspected of having received funding from China.[134] The China Initiative, launched by the U.S. Department of Justice (DOJ) in late 2018 and terminated in early 2022, was initially intended to investigate and prosecute economic espionage and national security threats perpetrated to benefit China; however, research integrity cases eventually came to dominate their caseload.[135]

Whether these efforts have produced a net benefit for the United States is debatable. Research security investigations by grantmaking agencies have uncovered failures to dis-

---

[131] "China Halts Publication of Youth Unemployment Report as Numbers Hit Record High," 2023; Amanda Lee and Orange Wang, "China's Youth-Unemployment Picture Still Blurry, Social and Economic Risks Remain Even as Jobless Rate Returns," *South China Morning Post*, January 17, 2024.

[132] International Institute for Labour Studies, *World of Work Report 2013: Repairing the Economic and Social Fabric*, International Labour Organization, 2013; Henrik Urdal, "A Clash of Generations? Youth Bulges and Political Violence," *International Studies Quarterly*, Vol. 50, No. 3, September 2006.

[133] Proclamation 10043, "Suspension of Entry as Nonimmigrants of Certain Students and Researchers from the People's Republic of China," Executive Office of the President, May 29, 2020.

[134] U.S. Government Accountability Office, *China: Efforts Underway to Address Technology Transfer Risk at U.S. Universities, but ICE Could Improve Related Data*, GAO-23-106114, November 2022.

[135] Eileen Guo, Jess Aloe, and Karen Hao, "The US Crackdown on Chinese Economic Espionage Is a Mess. We Have the Data to Show It," *MIT Technology Review*, December 2, 2021.

close foreign funding sources.[136] Counterintelligence measures, such as Presidential Proclamation 10043, focus on applicants for temporary visas for postgraduate study or research, but research security investigations tend to find that violations are committed by principal investigators (i.e., permanent university employees) rather than by doctoral students or visiting scholars.[137] Research integrity investigations under the China Initiative reached guilty verdicts or plea bargains in the majority of those few cases that were pursued to the end, although the conviction rate has been significantly lower for China Initiative cases than for all other DOJ-prosecuted cases.[138] This indicates that these investigations are uncovering violations. However, the relevance of most research security and integrity cases to economic espionage, national security, or technology transfer appears weak, especially given that federally funded research is to be published openly, meaning that there is no need to illicitly transmit the research. Many cases appear to stem from misunderstandings between law enforcement and academic communities, unclear directions on federal forms, and vague rules regarding researchers' financial disclosures.[139] These investigations and proclamations also come at a cost to the United States; they engender a climate of fear among Chinese-descendant academics, accelerate the exit of Chinese-descendant scientists from the United States, and hurt the United States' ability to recruit top scientists and graduate students from abroad.[140]

The United States has taken some positive steps to address the shortcomings of previous research security efforts. The China Initiative was terminated in early 2022, and DOJ officials acknowledged that it appeared to be racially discriminatory.[141] The White House issued guidance on disclosing foreign research funding and instructed federal grantmaking agencies to adapt their forms accordingly.[142] The U.S. Department of Commerce launched an Academic Outreach Initiative to provide guidance to universities on how they and their researchers

---

[136] U.S. Government Accountability Office, 2022.

[137] U.S. Government Accountability Office, 2022.

[138] Guo, Aloe, and Hao, 2021.

[139] Guo, Aloe, and Hao, 2021; Aruna Viswanatha and Sha Hua, "The U.S. Pursued Professors Working with China. Cases Are Faltering.," *Wall Street Journal*, December 20, 2021; Ellen Barry and Katie Benner, "U.S. Drops Its Case Against M.I.T. Scientist Accused of Hiding China Links," *New York Times*, January 20, 2022; Ellen Nakashima and David Nakamura, "China Initiative Aims to Stop Economic Espionage. Is Targeting Academics over Grant Fraud 'Overkill'?" *Washington Post*, September 15, 2021.

[140] Xie et al., 2023.

[141] Evan Perez, "Justice Department Ends Trump-Era China Initiative Following Bias Concerns," CNN, February 23, 2022.

[142] National Science and Technology Council, *Guidance for Implementing National Security Presidential Memorandum 33 (NSPM-33) on National Security Strategy for United States Government-Supported Research and Development*, January 2022.

may be affected by export control regulations.[143] These steps to overcome the gap between academia and law enforcement and build trust between the two are positive developments.

Recommendations

The United States should enhance its efforts to retain highly skilled Chinese immigrants, particularly those in STEM fields, and should narrowly tailor its security response to internal threats by China to avoid creating a chilling effect on academic researchers and graduate students. Together, these efforts can support U.S. economic growth and technological advancement, mitigate risks posed by foreign nationals, and avoid creating antagonism between Chinese immigrants and U.S. authorities that could ultimately benefit the CCP.

Retain Chinese STEM Talent

The most effective tool that the U.S. government has at its disposal to promote the retention of Chinese students and professionals is immigration and visa policy. I make three specific recommendations for the U.S. government to align immigration policy with the objective of retaining Chinese immigrant human capital.

First, allow international students in OPT to travel abroad and reenter the United States on multi-entry visas. Family ties in China are the top motivator for return migration among Chinese students. For this population for whom family ties are extremely important, the inability to visit family abroad for one to three years while in OPT is discouraging. It discourages international students from staying in the United States to work post-graduation and increases the likelihood of returning to China. Making the visa a multiple-entry visa can solve this dilemma. A counterargument to this recommendation might be that allowing back-and-forth travel could facilitate technology transfer and intellectual property theft by international student workers. However, this concern would equally apply to employees on H-1B visas, yet H-1B workers are allowed to enter and exit the United States multiple times. Making the student OPT visa a multiple-entry visa would pose no more risk of technology transfer than the H-1B visa program already poses.

Second, increase the number of H-1B visas available to Chinese nationals. This can be done by increasing the annual cap on H-1B visas, increasing the annual per-country cap, or eliminating the annual per-country cap. Scientific research benefits from the fact that positions in universities, nonprofit research centers, and government research centers are already exempt from the H-1B cap. However, to be successful in economic competition, the private sector must be sufficiently staffed. H-1B visas are reserved for positions that can feasibly be filled only by immigrant workers because there is a shortage of qualified U.S. workers. There have been 570,594 H-1B petitions rejected for FY 2024 because they were in excess of the cap,

[143] Doug Lederman, "U.S. Plans to Help Universities Protect Security of Research," *Inside Higher Ed*, June 28, 2022.

which means that U.S. companies likely had over 570,000 positions left unfilled going into FY 2025.[144]

Third, increase the number of green cards available through employment preference categories. The current annual cap on employment-based green cards is set at 140,000, and the per-country cap is set at 7 percent of the total. This means that each year, only about 9,800 Chinese workers in the United States can become legal permanent residents through employment preference categories. This cap has created a backlog of Chinese applicants who meet the requirements to gain a green card yet must wait years for their application to be approved. Highly skilled immigrants being kept in this limbo report having high levels of intent to migrate to a third country or to return to their countries of origin.[145] The United States can learn from its own experience with the Chinese Student Protection Act of 1992. That law exempted certain Chinese nationals from the cap and from other requirements; as a result, 54,000 Chinese immigrants took advantage of the opportunity, and return migration was lower among educated Chinese immigrants than it is today.[146] Although holding U.S. immigration status can incentivize return migration by increasing a worker's value in the Chinese labor market and by making moving to China less risky, holding a green card might not have a significant effect in encouraging return migration because there are physical presence requirements for maintaining one's green card.

Narrow Security Response

The U.S. security response to internal Chinese threats should be—and should appear to be—narrowly targeted to avoid creating a climate of fear that drives away valuable human capital. The United States should refrain from naming targeted countries in the titles of security-related bills, federal policies, or federal initiatives. The naming of the China Initiative went against tradition by specifically naming a targeted country, and this created the impression that laws would be applied unequally to people of certain national origins.[147] Although only a very small minority of researchers were targeted, the fact that more than 90 percent of defendants in China Initiative cases were of Chinese descent created a perception that this program was discriminatory, which chilled the activity of Chinese researchers in the United States.[148]

U.S. authorities should prioritize research security and research integrity cases that have clear connections to national security or economic espionage. Efforts to monitor individuals engaged in basic scientific research of which the results are published openly and of which the

144 U.S. Citizenship and Immigration Services, "H-1B Electronic Registration Process," webpage, last updated August 5, 2024.

145 Andrew Moriarty, "Per-Country Cap Reform: Priority Bill Spotlight," FWD.us, December 5, 2023.

146 Public Law 102-404, 1992; Aguilar Esteva, 2013.

147 Perez, 2022; Yu et al., 2023.

148 Xie et al., 2023; Guo, Aloe, and Hao, 2021.

topic has a very tenuous relation to national security issues should be deprioritized. Infractions by researchers who are involved in such nonsensitive research and who are not suspected of espionage or economic espionage should be addressed with lower-profile strategies. For example, the Office of the Inspector General of relevant grantmaking agencies could seek settlements with researchers and their universities instead of the DOJ issuing arrest warrants.

Laws governing grant disclosures and foreign talent program participation should be clarified, and law enforcement activities should tightly adhere to those laws. In regard to disclosure policies, several research integrity cases were dismissed because it was not clear what information was required to be disclosed in grant applications and related forms.[149] Clarifying those policies and avoiding misunderstandings that lead to high-profile cases would be better for all involved. In regard to foreign talent program participation, it should be noted that participating in foreign talent programs is not illegal under U.S. law. However, public statements by the DOJ indicate that it views law enforcement activities as a way to chill participation in Chinese talent programs. A 2021 DOJ press release quotes a U.S. attorney saying the following about the sentencing of a China Initiative defendant: "We hope Zheng's prison sentence deters others from having anything to do with China's so-called '1000 Talents Plan' or any of its variations."[150] By using federal prosecution to "deter" people from participating in legal activities, authorities foster the impression that law enforcement is not aligned with the law and that the rule of law is flexible. It creates confusion about what is legal or illegal and creates feelings of fear and resentment in targeted communities. It may be better to pass clear laws making participation in foreign talent programs illegal rather than leaving them in a gray zone.

Conclusion

The steps outlined above could help the United States retain high-skilled Chinese immigrant workers while guarding against risks to national security. Doing so would advance U.S. economic and technological development, relieve some social stress posed by unemployed and underemployed returnee youth in China, and restrict China's access to valuable human capital.

---

[149] Viswanatha and Hua, 2021.

[150] U.S. Department of Justice, "University Researcher Sentenced to Prison for Lying on Grant Applications to Develop Scientific Expertise for China," press release, May 14, 2021.

Supplementary Materials: Comparison of Data Sources and Summaries of Chinese Data on Returnee Population Profiles

Table 6.5 provides context on the data sources on return migrants referred to throughout this chapter and includes notes on the assessment of the data's reliability. Tables 6.6 and 6.7 summarize the results of multiple surveys on the attributes of returnees to China.

TABLE 6.5
Comparison of Sources on Chinese Return Migrants and Return Migration

Data Source Title	Year Conducted (or Published*)	Producer	Population of Focus	Sample Size	Reliability Notes
Insight Report on Overseas Students Returning to China to Seek Employment[a]	2022	LinkedIn China	Overseas students	868	• Nonprobability sample • Low response rate • Only LinkedIn users • 2020 survey results presented without details on methods or sample
Insight Report on Overseas Students Returning to China to Seek Employment	2020 (2022*)	LinkedIn China	Overseas students	Unknown	• Sample size and methods not provided • Only LinkedIn users
2021 China Study Abroad White Paper[b]	2015–2021	New Oriental	Overseas students and prospective overseas students	7,983	• Nonprobability sample • Includes both actual overseas students and intended overseas students
Student Migration: Evidence from Chinese Students in the US and China[c]	2014	U.S.- and China-based academics	Overseas students	472	• Nonprobability sample • Study designed to test correlations of return
Survey of Earned Doctorates[d]	2020	U.S. National Science Foundation	Overseas students	6,336	• Highly reliable annual census of doctorates earned at U.S. universities
Asian American Academic Climate Survey[e]	2021–2022	Asian American Scholar Forum	U.S. university faculty of Chinese descent	1,229	• Nonprobability sample • Response bias and social desirability bias may have produced results that exaggerate the effect of the negative climate.

Table 6.5—Continued

Data Source Title	Year Conducted (or Published*)	Producer	Population of Focus	Sample Size	Reliability Notes
Analysis of the Development of Overseas Students Three Years After Graduating[f]	2017–2019 (2021*)	MyCOS Research Institute	Returnees and domestic graduates	Unknown	• Data manipulation possible • Methods and sample size not stated
Data Analysis Report on the Group of Returned Overseas Students[g]	2019 (2021*)	Beijing Institute of Economic and Social Development	Returnees	1,016	• Data manipulation possible • Unusually high reported response rate • Details on methods unavailable
Survey on Employment of Chinese Returned Overseas Students in 2019[h]	2019 (2021*)	Center for China and Globalization; Zhaopin	Returnees	2,020	• Data manipulation possible • Nonprobability sample • Only Zhaopin.com users
2015 Blue Book for Employment in China after Returning from Study Abroad[i]	2014	Ministry of Education (China)	Returnees	Unknown	• Data manipulation possible • Details on survey methods unavailable
Report on Employment and Entrepreneurship of Chinese Returnees 2017[j]	2017	Center for China and Globalization; Zhaopin	Returnees	1,821	• Data manipulation possible • Nonprobability sample • Only Zhaopin.com users

[a] LinkedIn China, 2022.

[b] New Oriental's '2021 China Study Abroad White Paper' Officially Released: Undergraduate and Above Study Abroad Groups Are Mainstream, High School Intention Groups Rise in Percentage," 2021.

[c] Li et al., 2019.

[d] National Center for Science and Engineering Statistics, 2021.

[e] Xie et al., 2023.

[f] Cao and Zhang, 2021.

[g] Chen, Feng, and Sun, 2021.

[h] Chen and Liu, 2021.

[i] Overseas Study Service Center, 2016.

[j] Center for China and Globalization and Zhaopin.com, 2017.

TABLE 6.6

Data from the Ministry of Education of the People's Republic of China on Returned Overseas Students Circa 2015, by Degree Earned Abroad

Degree	Share of Returnee Population (%)	Average Age	Top Countries of Study (Share, %)	Top Fields of Study	Average Duration of Study Abroad (months)
Undergraduate	9.8	—	• South Korea (21.3) • United Kingdom (10.6) • United States (9.6)	• Business administration • Economics • Accounting	37
Master's	80.7	27	• United Kingdom (42.5) • United States (18.8) • Australia (10.4)	• Finance • Accounting • Business administration • Management • International business	16
Doctorate	9.5	32	• United States (29) • Japan (12.9) • United Kingdom (10)	• Chemistry • Materials science • Economics • Electrical engineering • Mechanical engineering • Computer science	46

SOURCE: Features information from Overseas Study Service Center, 2016.

NOTE: The female share of the students in this data was 59.2 percent.

TABLE 6.7

Statistics from Surveys of Returnee Populations Conducted by Chinese Research Institutes

Indicator	Percentage of Respondents in 2019 Study by Beijing Institute of Economic and Social Development	Percentage of Respondents in 2017 Study by Zhaopin.com and Center for China and Globalization
Female	45	48.3
Highest degree earned abroad		
Undergraduate	12.4	31
Master's	63.4	61.5
Doctorate	13.2	3.5
Post-doctorate	4.8	—
Other	6.2	4
Country of Study		
United Kingdom	29.7	24.9
United States	19.9	17.9
Australia	9.2	8.8

Table 6.7—Continued

Indicator	Percentage of Respondents in 2019 Study by Beijing Institute of Economic and Social Development	Percentage of Respondents in 2017 Study by Zhaopin.com and Center for China and Globalization
Japan	5.9	10.9
Other	35.3	37.5
Field of Study		
Management	26.7	47.3
Social sciences	–	10.4
Economics	19.7	
Sciences	15.7	<10
Applied sciences	26.3	16.2
Engineering	14.9	
Law	5.5	
Agricultural science	0.5	
Education	2.6	
Military science	0.1	
Medicine	2.7	
Liberal arts	11.6	10.8
Full-time work experience abroad		
None	58.4	43.9
Less than 1 year	–	28.1
1–3 years	–	18.1
3–6 years	–	6.4
More than 6 years	–	3.5
Any	41.6	56.1
Transnational links in country of study		
Naturalized citizenship	–	0.7
Residence permit	9.8	–
Own property	6.2	–
Relatives living in country of study	11.3	1.4

SOURCES: Features information from Chen, Feng, and Sun, 2021; and Center for China and Globalization and Zhaopin.com, 2017.

Abbreviations

ACS	American Community Survey
CCP	Chinese Communist Party
COVID-19	coronavirus disease 2019
DOJ	U.S. Department of Justice
FY	fiscal year
OPT	optional practical training
S&E	science and engineering
STEM	science, technology, engineering, and mathematics
ZSP	Zhongguancun Science Park

References

Aguilar Esteva, Arturo A., "Stayers and Returners: Educational Self-Selection Among U.S. Immigrants and Returning Migrants," Institute of Labor Economics, Discussion Paper No. 7222, February 2013.

Barry, Ellen, and Katie Benner, "U.S. Drops Its Case Against M.I.T. Scientist Accused of Hiding China Links," *New York Times*, January 20, 2022.

Barry, Ellen, and Gina Kolata, "China's Lavish Funds Lured U.S. Scientists. What Did It Get in Return?" *New York Times*, February 6, 2020.

Cao Chen and Zhang Lin, "The Analysis of the Development of Overseas Students After Graduating for Three Years," in Wang Huiyao and Miao Lu, eds., *Annual Report on the Development of Chinese Students Studying Abroad (2020–2021)*, Social Sciences Academic Press, 2021.

Center for China and Globalization and Zhaopin.com, *Report on Employment & Entrepreneurship of Chinese Returnees 2017*, 2017.

Center for China and Globalization and Zhaopin.com, *Report on Employment & Entrepreneurship of Chinese Returnees 2019*, 2019.

Chen, Pao-Lien, Danchi Tan, and Ruey-Jer "Bryan" Jean, "Foreign Knowledge Acquisition Through Inter-Firm Collaboration and Recruitment: Implications for Domestic Growth of Emerging Market Firms," *International Business Review*, Vol. 25, No. 1, February 2016.

Chen Siyu, Feng Dan, and Sun Wei, "Data Analysis Report on the Group of Returned Overseas Students," in Wang Huiyao and Miao Lu, eds., *Annual Report on the Development of Chinese Students Studying Abroad (2020–2021)*, Social Sciences Academic Press, 2021.

Chen Xiaoxiao and Liu Xinyao, "Survey on the Employment of Chinese Returned Overseas Students in 2019," in Wang Huiyao and Miao Lu, eds., *Annual Report on the Development of Chinese Students Studying Abroad (2020–2021)*, Social Sciences Academic Press, 2021.

Chen, Yun-Chung, "The Limits of Brain Circulation: Chinese Returnees and Technological Development in Beijing," *Pacific Affairs*, Vol. 81, No. 2, Summer 2008.

Cheng Si, "Recruiting Salaries Creep Up in 2022," *China Daily*, January 5, 2023.

Cheung, Alan Chi Keung, and Li Xu, "To Return or Not to Return: Examining the Return Intentions of Mainland Chinese Students Studying at Elite Universities in the United States," *Studies in Higher Education*, Vol. 40, No. 9, 2015.

"China Halts Publication of Youth Unemployment Report as Numbers Hit Record High," Voice of America, August 16, 2023.

"Chinese Students Back to China to Seek Jobs Hit a Record High in 2022: Survey," *Global Times*, February 14, 2023.

Depew, Briggs, Peter Norlander, and Todd Sørensen, "Flight of the H-1B: Inter-Firm Mobility and Return Migration Patterns for Skilled Guest Workers," Institute of Labor Economics, Discussion Paper No. 7456, June 2013.

Executive Order 12711, "Policy Implementation with Respect to Nationals of the People's Republic of China," Executive Office of the President, April 11, 1990.

Fedasiuk, Ryan, "The China Scholarship Council: An Overview," Center for Security and Emerging Technology, July 2020.

Filatotchev, Igor, Xiaohui Liu, Trevor Buck, and Mike Wright, "The Export Orientation and Export Performance of High-Technology SMEs in Emerging Markets: The Effects of Knowledge Transfer by Returnee Entrepreneurs," *Journal of International Business Studies*, Vol. 40, No. 6, August 2009.

Fischer, Karin, and Sasha Aslanian, "The U.S. Attracts Fewer International Students, Loses Billions in Revenue. Here's Why," NPR, August 9, 2021.

Flood, Sarah, Miriam King, Renae Rodgers, Steven Ruggles, J. Robert Warren, and Michael Westberry, "Integrated Public Use Microdata Series, Current Population Survey: Version 10.0," dataset, IPUMS, 2022.

Gaulé, Patrick, "Who Comes Back and When? Return Migration Decisions of Academic Scientists," *Economics Letters*, Vol. 124, No. 3, September 2014.

Guo, Eileen, Jess Aloe, and Karen Hao, "The US Crackdown on Chinese Economic Espionage Is a Mess. We Have the Data to Show It," *MIT Technology Review*, December 2, 2021.

Haiyang Li, Yan Zhang, Yu Li, Li-An Zhou, and Weiying Zhang, "Returnees Versus Locals: Who Perform Better in China's Technology Entrepreneurship?" *Strategic Entrepreneurship Journal*, Vol. 6, No. 3, September 2012.

Hao, Karen, and Sha Hua, "The U.S. Is Turning Away from Its Biggest Scientific Partner at a Precarious Time," *Wall Street Journal*, August 16, 2023.

He, Alex, "What Do China's High Patent Numbers Really Mean?" Centre for International Governance Innovation, April 20, 2021.

He Huifeng, "More of China's Overseas Graduates Head Home, Lured by Jobs and Convenience: Survey," *South China Morning Post*, February 13, 2023.

Higher Education Statistics Agency, "Where Do HE Students Come From?" webpage, January 31, 2023. As of:
https://www.hesa.ac.uk/data-and-analysis/students/where-from

Institute of International Education, *Open Doors 2022: Report on International Educational Exchange*, 2022.

Institute of International Education, "Open Doors Historical Data, 2000–2022," data file, 2023.

International Institute for Labour Studies, *World of Work Report 2013: Repairing the Economic and Social Fabric*, International Labour Organization, 2013.

Iredale, Robyn, Fei Guo, and Santi Rozario, eds., *Return Migration in the Asia Pacific*, Elgar Publishing, 2003.

Lederman, Doug, "U.S. Plans to Help Universities Protect Security of Research," *Inside Higher Ed*, June 28, 2022.

Lee, Amanda, and Orange Wang, "China's Youth-Unemployment Picture Still Blurry, Social and Economic Risks Remain Even as Jobless Rate Returns," *South China Morning Post*, January 17, 2024.

Li, Wei, Shengnan Zhao, Zheng Lu, Wan Yu, and Xiaojie Li, "Student Migration: Evidence from Chinese Students in the US and China," *International Migration*, Vol. 57, No. 3, June 2019.

Lin, Daomi, Jiangyong Lu, Peter Ping Li, and Xiaohui Liu, "Balancing Formality and Informality in Business Exchanges as a Duality: A Comparative Case Study of Returnee and Local Entrepreneurs in China," *Management and Organization Review*, Vol. 11, No. 2, June 2015.

Lin, Ya-Hui, Chung-Jen Chen, and Bou-Wen Lin, "The Dual-Edged Role of Returnee Board Members in New Venture Performance," *Journal of Business Research*, Vol. 90, September 2018.

LinkedIn China [领英中国], *2022 Insight Report on Overseas Students Returning to China to Seek Employment* [2022中国留学生归国求职洞察报告], 2022.

Liu, Lisong, "Return Migration and Selective Citizenship: A Study of Returning Chinese Professional Migrants from the United States," *Journal of Asian American Studies*, Vol. 15, No. 1, February 2012.

Liu, Xiaohui, Jiangyong Lu, Igor Filatotchev, Trevor Buck, and Mike Wright, "Returnee Entrepreneurs, Knowledge Spillovers and Innovation in High-Tech Firms in Emerging Economies," *Journal of International Business Studies*, Vol. 41, No. 7, September 2010.

Loudenback, Tanza, "Middle-Class Chinese People Are Buying Property in the US as a 'Safe Harbor' for Their Money," *Business Insider*, January 11, 2019.

Lu, Yixi, Li Zong, and Bernard Schissel, "To Stay or Return: Migration Intentions of Students from People's Republic of China in Saskatchewan, Canada," *International Migration and Integration*, Vol. 10, No. 3, August 2009.

Matthews, Kirstin R. W., and Daniel Morali, "Can We Do That Here? An Analysis of US Federal and State Policies Guiding Human Embryo and Embryoid Research," *Journal of Law and the Biosciences*, Vol. 9, No. 1, January–June 2022.

Ministry of Education of the People's Republic of China, "Brief Report on Chinese Overseas Students and International Students in China 2017," March 31, 2018.

Ministry of Education of the People's Republic of China, "Statistics on Chinese Learners Studying Overseas in 2019," press release, December 15, 2020.

Moriarty, Andrew, "Per-Country Cap Reform: Priority Bill Spotlight," FWD.us, December 5, 2023.

Nakashima, Ellen, and David Nakamura, "China Initiative Aims to Stop Economic Espionage. Is Targeting Academics over Grant Fraud 'Overkill'?" *Washington Post*, September 15, 2021.

National Bureau of Statistics of China, "Statistics on Graduate Students and Students Studying Abroad," in *China Statistical Yearbook 2021*, China Statistics Press, 2021.

National Center for Education Statistics, "Undergraduate Enrollment," webpage, Institute of Education Sciences, U.S. Department of Education, last updated May 2023. As of July 7, 2023: https://nces.ed.gov/programs/coe/indicator/cha

National Center for Science and Engineering Statistics, *Doctorate Recipients from U.S. Universities: 2020*, National Science Foundation, NSF 22-300, 2021.

National Center for Science and Engineering Statistics, *Doctorate Recipients from U.S. Universities: 2021*, National Science Foundation, NSF 23-300, 2022a.

National Center for Science and Engineering Statistics, "National Survey of College Graduates: 2021," dataset, National Science Foundation, NSF 23-306, 2022b.

National Science and Technology Council, *Guidance for Implementing National Security Presidential Memorandum 33 (NSPM-33) on National Security Strategy for United States Government–Supported Research and Development*, January 2022.

National Science Board, *Science and Engineering Indicators 2022: The State of U.S. Science and Engineering*, National Science Foundation, NSB-2022-1, 2022.

"New Oriental's '2021 China Study Abroad White Paper' Officially Released: Undergraduate and Above Study Abroad Groups Are Mainstream, High School Intention Groups Rise in Percentage" ["新东方《2021中国留学白皮书》正式发布：本科及以上留学群体是主流，高中意向群体占比上升"], Sohu, May 21, 2021.

Nulimaimaiti, Mia, "China's Returning Overseas Graduates Hit in the Pocket, Face Harsh Reality of Job Market," *South China Morning Post*, May 21, 2024.

O'Connor, Sean, *How Chinese Companies Facilitate Technology Transfer from the United States*, U.S.-China Economic and Security Review Commission, May 6, 2019.

Office of the United States Trade Representative, *Findings of the Investigation into China's Acts, Policies, and Practices Related to Technology Transfer, Intellectual Property, and Innovation under Section 301 of the Trade Act of 1974*, Executive Office of the President, March 22, 2018.

Overseas Study Service Center, *2015 Blue Book for Employment in China After Returning from Study Abroad* [中国留学回国就业蓝皮书2015], Ministry of Education of the People's Republic of China, 2016.

Perez, Evan, "Justice Department Ends Trump-Era China Initiative Following Bias Concerns," CNN, February 23, 2022.

Proclamation 10043, "Suspension of Entry as Nonimmigrants of Certain Students and Researchers from the People's Republic of China," Executive Office of the President, May 29, 2020.Public Law 102-404, Chinese Student Protection Act of 1992, October 9, 1992.

Ruggles, Steven, Sarah Flood, Matthew Sobek, Danika Brockman, Grace Cooper, Stephanie Richards, and Megan Schouweiler, "IPUMS USA: Version 13.0," dataset, IPUMS, 2023.

Saxenian, AnnaLee, *Regional Advantage: Culture and Competition in Silicon Valley and Route 128*, Harvard University Press, 1996.

Saxenian, AnnaLee, *The New Argonauts: Regional Advantage in a Global Economy*, Harvard University Press, 2006.

Statista, "Business Sectors with the Highest Share of Overseas Returnees Recruitment in China in 2019," webpage, December 2019. As of December 5, 2023: https://www.statista.com/statistics/1121056/china-sectors-with-highest-overseas-returnees-demand/

Sun, Wei, "The Productivity of Return Migrants: The Case of China's 'Sea Turtles,'" *IZA Journal of Development and Migration*, Vol. 2, No. 1, December 2013.

Urdal, Henrik, "A Clash of Generations? Youth Bulges and Political Violence," *International Studies Quarterly*, Vol. 50, No. 3, September 2006.

U.S. Citizenship and Immigration Services, *Characteristics of H-1B Specialty Occupation Workers: Fiscal Year 2021 Annual Report to Congress*, U.S. Department of Homeland Security, 2022.

U.S. Citizenship and Immigration Services, "H-1B Electronic Registration Process," webpage, last updated August 5, 2024. As of December 20, 2024:
https://www.uscis.gov/working-in-the-united-states/temporary-workers/h-1b-specialty-occupations/h-1b-electronic-registration-process

U.S. Department of Justice, "University Researcher Sentenced to Prison for Lying on Grant Applications to Develop Scientific Expertise for China," press release, May 14, 2021.

U.S. Government Accountability Office, *China: Efforts Underway to Address Technology Transfer Risk at U.S. Universities, but ICE Could Improve Related Data*, GAO-23-106114, November 2022.

Viswanatha, Aruna, and Sha Hua, "The U.S. Pursued Professors Working with China. Cases Are Faltering," *Wall Street Journal*, December 20, 2021.

Wadhwa, Vivek, AnnaLee Saxenian, Richard B. Freeman, Gary Gereffi, and Alex Salkever, *America's Loss Is the World's Gain: America's New Immigrant Entrepreneurs, Part IV*, March 2009.

Wang Huiyao and Miao Lu, eds., *Annual Report on the Development of Chinese Students Studying Abroad (2020–2021)*, Social Sciences Academic Press, 2021.

Weinstein, Emily S., "Chinese Talent Program Tracker," webpage, Center for Security and Emerging Technology, November 2020. As of August 3, 2023:
https://cset.georgetown.edu/publication/chinese-talent-program-tracker

Wong, Matthew, "More Chinese Students Returning Home After Overseas Study," China.org.cn, April 5, 2020.

Wu Bingcong, "Only 6.1% of Recent Undergraduates Start at More Than $10,000, and Very Happy but Underpaid Jobs Are Popular" ["仅6.1%应届本科生起薪过万，很幸福但工资不高的工作受欢迎"], Sohu, February 26, 2023.

Wu Feiyi, Niu Xiao, and Yang Jingguang, "New Features of Returnee Entrepreneurship in the New Era," in Wang Huiyao and Miao Lu, eds., *Annual Report on the Development of Chinese Students Studying Abroad (2020–2021)*, Social Sciences Academic Press, 2021.

Yu, Wan, "To Stay or to Return? Return Intentions and Return Migrations of Chinese Students During the Transition Period in the United States," *Papers in Applied Geography*, Vol. 2, No. 2, 2016.

Yu Xie, Xihong Lin, Ju Li, Qian He, and Junming Huang, "Caught in the Crossfire: Fears of Chinese-American Scientists," *Proceedings of the National Academy of Sciences*, Vol. 120, No. 27, July 4, 2023.

Zeithammer, Robert, and Ryan P. Kellogg, "The Hesitant 'Hai Gui': Return-Migration Preferences of U.S.-Educated Chinese Scientists and Engineers," *Journal of Marketing Research*, Vol. 50, No. 5, October 2013.

Zhang, Lei, "The Chinese Student Protection Act of 1992: Student Immigration and the Transpacific Neoliberal Model Minority," *Journal of Asian American Studies*, Vol. 24, No. 3, October 2021.

Zhou, Yu, and Jinn-Yuh Hsu, "Divergent Engagements: Roles and Strategies of Taiwanese and Mainland Chinese Returnee Entrepreneurs in the IT Industry," *Global Networks*, Vol. 11, No. 3, July 2011.

Zweig, David, Siu Fung Chung, and Wilfried Vanhonacker, "Rewards of Technology: Explaining China's Reverse Migration," *Journal of International Migration and Integration*, Vol. 7, No. 4, September 2006.

Zweig, David, Kang Siqin, and Wang Huiyao, "'The Best Are Yet to Come': State Programs, Domestic Resistance and Reverse Migration of High-Level Talent to China," *Journal of Contemporary China*, Vol. 29, No. 125, 2020.

CHAPTER 7

Energy and Environmental Security as Drivers for U.S.-China Economic Cooperation and Competition

Noosha Uddin

Overview

Efforts aimed at energy and environmental security are characterized by conditions of coupled, strategic interactions between the United States and China; the two countries cooperate in the development and deployment of some energy sources while competing in others. These interactions introduce both benefits and costs to both countries, as well as to countries that depend on the United States and China for trade, to the global energy market, and to international efforts to mitigate climate change.

The transition to clean energy sources provides benefits to third parties—in addition to the country that is investing in those resources—through reductions in emissions of greenhouse gases. Efforts to decarbonize at the national level result in climate benefits that extend beyond sovereign borders. Thus, the interests of the United States and of China to commercialize nuclear, solar, wind, and other alternative energy sources through bilateral strategic interactions in pursuit of their respective net-zero carbon emissions targets can contribute to energy and environmental security worldwide.

In this chapter, I address energy and environmental security as forums for competition and cooperation between the United States and China. The aim is to better understand the challenges that the United States will face to ensure that its economy meets the nation's needs.

Relations between the United States and China have been mixed since the latter's admittance to the World Trade Organization in 2001. Each country's policies regarding national interests—such as the United States' continued support of Taiwan's ability to resist a forcible takeover by China and China's refusal to condemn Russia for its invasion of Ukraine—have divided the two states. Global finance and supply chain geopolitics further complicate these dynamics; China has increased its global influence through its Belt and Road Initiative (BRI) and through financing and investments in the countries of West Asia, the Middle East and North Africa, and Sub-Saharan Africa on the sale of critical minerals.[1] For example, China has increased its engagement in metals and mining in 2022 through vertical integration investments in nickel mining in Indonesia, lithium mining in Mali, copper processing agreements in Saudi Arabia, and the commissioning of a lithium processing plant in Zimbabwe.[2] In turn, Washington has adopted policies to invest in U.S. competitiveness and innovation, align with allies and partners, and compete with China in defining future technologies and the global system.[3] Yet the interconnected nature of the global economic system—from finance to technology to energy—limits the efficacy of economic policy instruments that have been employed against China. These interconnections can result in opportunities for collaboration between the two countries that would benefit both.

One such domain is the global energy market, which has been and will continue to be critical for strategic competition between the United States and China. Fluctuations in the price and supply of liquefied natural gas (LNG), the latest of which is accelerated by Russia's invasion of Ukraine, stress the need for actionable policies that guarantee domestic energy secu-

1 For a breakdown of these investments by date, quantity (in millions of U.S. dollars), sector, and country, see American Enterprise Institute and Heritage Foundation, China Global Investment Tracker, database, July 2023.

2 Audina Nur, "Contemporary Ampere Technology (CATL) Investment in Indonesian Battery Megaproject to Be Completed in December," *Indonesia Business Post*, November 29, 2023; "Strengthening Saudi-China Ties; Major Announcement from Arab-China Business Conference," Zawya, June 13, 2023; "Chinese Mining Company Opens Lithium Processing Plant in Zimbabwe," Africanews, July 6, 2023; Christoph Nedophil Wang, *China Belt and Road Initiative (BRI) Investment Report 2023*, Griffith Asia Institute, Griffith University and Green Finance and Development Center, FISF Fudan University, February 2024; Jeffrey Kucik and Mark Kennedy, "Investment and Trade Agreements Essential to De-Risking Critical Minerals Supply Chains," Wilson Center, April 30. 2024.

3 Anthony J. Blinken, "The Administration's Approach to the People's Republic of China," speech transcript, U.S. Department of State, May 26, 2022.

rity and sustainability for both countries.[4] As the two largest emitters of greenhouse gases in the world, both the United States and China have stated that climate change is a global threat and are transitioning to alternative fuels and adopting long-term decarbonization strategies. Both are investing heavily in wind and solar power and are conducting research and development (R&D) on new nuclear technologies and other clean energy sources, although China has also been investing in conventional nuclear power plants. Existing interactions between the two countries in the production, technology, and deployment of energy, such as the renewed U.S.-China Science and Technology Agreement, can safeguard U.S. economic prosperity in the next 30 years amid what may be an increasingly bipolar or multipolar world system.[5]

In this chapter, I analyze the bilateral efforts to ensure energy and environmental security and to mitigate climate change in the complexity of coupled, strategic competition between the United States and China. I first define energy and environmental security in both U.S. and Chinese contexts and analyze the outlooks for fossil fuel and alternative energy production in the two countries. I then analyze the national policies toward energy and economic development in the next 20 to 30 years that aim to ensure energy and environmental security and that aim to reduce emissions of greenhouse gases to mitigate the effects of climate change. Incentives to reach net-zero carbon emissions drive the need to expand the production of renewable energy. However, China has also sought to maintain economic growth rates, so it has relegated efforts to combat climate change to a lower national priority despite its increasingly deleterious environmental impacts.

I use these analyses to generate energy scenarios of cooperation and competition through 2050, highlighting potential outcomes of gains and losses for both countries through their economic interactions. I conclude with policy recommendations for the United States on strategies to promote a healthy national economy while engaging with China on reducing emissions of greenhouse gases in the coming decades.

Defining Energy and Environmental Security

Energy security is defined by the International Energy Agency (IEA) as "the uninterrupted availability of energy sources at an affordable price."[6] It can take on several forms based on time-dependent scenarios. In the short term, it concerns the ability of the energy system to react promptly to sudden changes in the supply-demand balance. Long-term energy security

---

4 U.S. Energy Information Administration, "U.S. Liquefied Natural Gas Exports to China," webpage, last updated May 31, 2024c.

5 Michael McShane, "House Foreign Affairs Committee Unanimously Passes Rep. Titus's U.S.-China Science and Technology Oversight Bill," press release, Office of Congresswoman Dina Titus, March 21, 2024; Natasha Gilbert and Gemma Conroy, "US Extends Science Pact with China: What It Means for Research," *Nature*, August 25, 2023.

6 IEA, "Energy Security," webpage, undated.

scenarios concern domestic and international investments to meet economic development—and in the face of climate effects, threats to the environment. Both China and the United States have made notable efforts in this regard with their pursuit of shifting the energy mix to include clean and alternative energy sources. However, both countries have also simultaneously increased their production of fossil fuels; the United States has increased output of oil and gas primarily from fracking shales, and China has been mining more coal.

In contrast, environmental security is context dependent within the two countries. Political and social implications of the constraints on environmental resources have prompted debates among climate activists, scholars, and the scientific community since the 1980s, propelling environmental security as an important part of the national agenda. As of 2001, the U.S. Department of State has defined *environmental security* as "encompass[ing] the mitigation and prevention of energy threats, including threats to sources and supply lines, and environmental risks and related stresses that directly contribute to political and economic instability or conflict in foreign countries or regions of importance."[7] Unlike energy security, which focuses primarily on the actions of and effects of fluctuations in supply and prices on the domestic economy, environmental security transcends sovereign borders. Environmental stresses on already fragile states have the potential to undermine the economic, political, and military interests of the United States, thereby making it necessary to include environmental security in national strategic security planning.[8]

For China, the concept of environmental security is relatively new. In prioritizing a national agenda toward economic development, climate change was relegated to a secondary goal. However, as the largest energy consumer in the world, Beijing has found itself increasingly exposed to the negative opinions of the international community about its emissions of greenhouse gases. In response, the country created expert committees in 2008—such as the Military Climate Change Expert Commission within the People's Liberation Army (PLA)—to research the impact of climate change on military operations and on key economic indicators, such as the availability of food and water and the rising risk of disasters.[9] At the Copenhagen climate change summit in 2009, China pledged to reduce its carbon intensity per unit of GDP. In 2016, it signed the 2015 Paris Agreement committing to pursue a wide array of energy-saving and climate mitigation strategies.[10] These pledges signaled to the global community China's commitment to reduce emissions of greenhouse gases.

---

7 U.S. Department of State, *Environmental Security Threat Report*, October 2001.

8 Junko Mochizuki and ZongXiang Zhang, *Environmental Security and Its Implications for China's Foreign Relations*, East-West Center, Working Paper No. 116, March 2011.

9 This commission is composed of key government agencies, such as the National Development and Reform Commission, the China Meteorological Administration, the Ministry of Science and Technology, the Ministry of Foreign Affairs, and the National Natural Science Foundation of China. See Duncan Freeman, "The Missing Link: China, Climate Change and National Security," Brussels Institute of Contemporary China Studies, January 2010.

10 "China Signs Paris Agreement on Climate Change," Xinhua, April 23, 2016.

Energy security, environmental security, and national security are linked through the ways in which countries interact with one another. Competition can result in advances in new technologies to reduce emissions of greenhouse gases through the generation of clean electricity. Cooperation among countries can strengthen supply chains for critical materials required to manufacture batteries, solar panels, and other technologies used to reduce emissions of greenhouse gases. Capital costs and possible increases to national security risks may limit the extent to which these strategies are pursued, especially if the commercial market for nuclear energy expands. However, policies in pursuit of these agendas have the potential to mutually strengthen both the U.S. and Chinese economies as the two countries interact with one another in the global energy market.

Energy Outlooks for the United States and China

Electricity Generation by Energy Source

Rising electricity demand and the global push for the electrification of energy end uses that traditionally have used fossil fuels, such as engines and heat pumps, are motivating countries to take decisive actions toward ensuring supplies of electric power.[11] The expansion of clean energy technologies, especially to generate electricity, is essential for mitigating greenhouse gas emissions and their effects on climate. Although the end goal of electrification is to transition away from fossil fuels to sources of clean energy—such as solar, wind, biomass, and nuclear—current and future outlooks show continued reliance on natural gas for generating electricity in the United States and coal in China, as shown in Figure 7.1.[12] Switching from coal to natural gas does not provide a long-term answer to decarbonization, but it can lead to significant reductions in emissions of greenhouse gases and improvements in air quality.[13] The contribution of bridge fuels, such as LNG, to energy transitions in the short term can help reduce emissions along energy supply chains. Large-scale deployment of carbon capture, utilization, and storage technologies can make continued combustion of coal and natural gas feasible in the drive to net zero emissions of greenhouse gases.

Fossil Fuels

The United States' relative independence in the global energy market shapes its views on energy and environmental security. The shale boom in 2010 transformed the country into the world's top oil and gas producer and a leading exporter. Policymakers and stakeholders alike hoped that these effects would foster an era of energy independence, but because of

[11] The IEA defines electrification as "replacing technologies or processes that use fossil fuels . . . with electrically-powered equivalents" (IEA, "Electrification," webpage, last updated July 11, 2023b).

[12] The U.S. Department of Energy defines nuclear energy as a "clean energy" source (U.S. Department of Energy, "3 Reasons Why Nuclear Is Clean and Sustainable," webpage, updated June 2022a).

[13] International Energy Agency, *The Role of Gas in Today's Energy Transitions*, July 2019.

FIGURE 7.1

U.S. and Chinese Electricity Generation by Fuel in Billion Kilowatt-Hours (kWh)

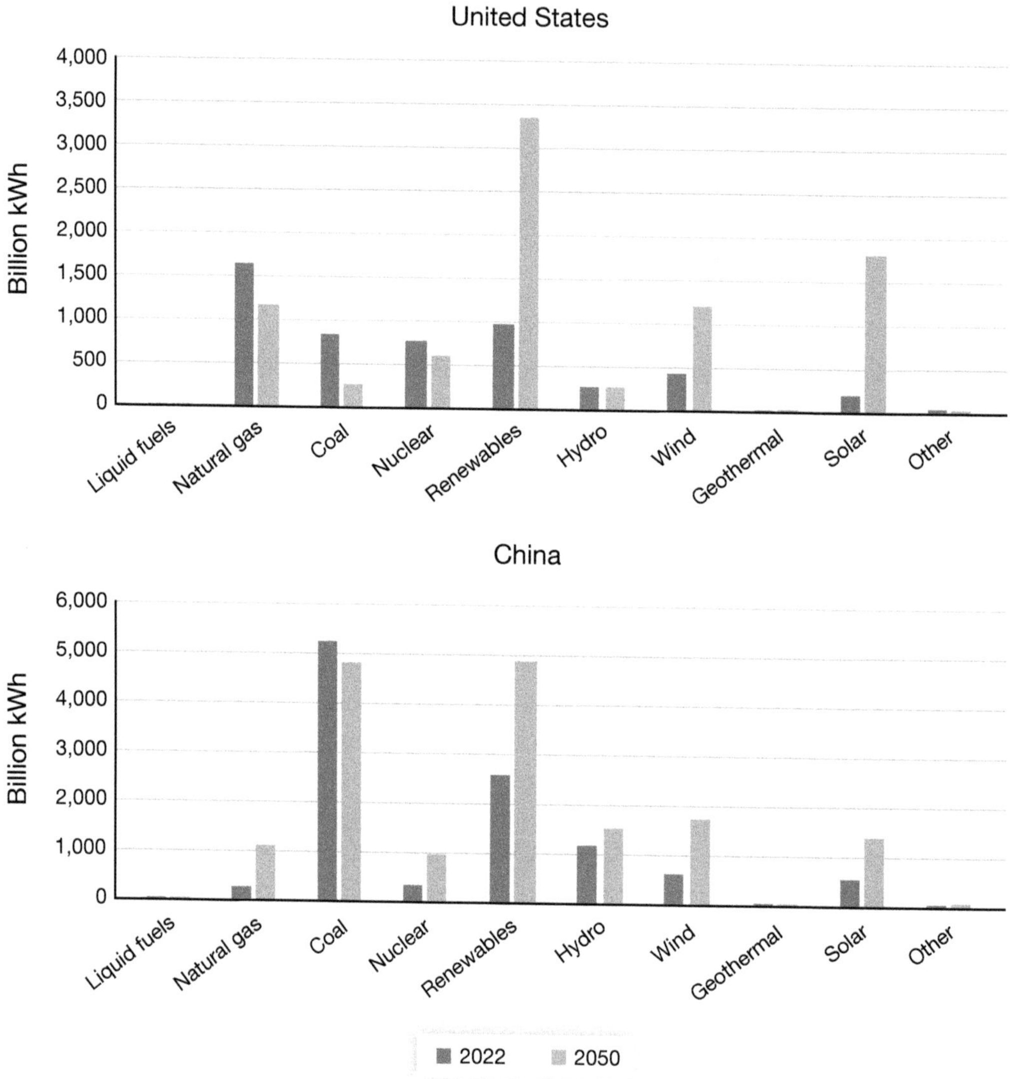

SOURCE: Author's analysis of data from U.S. Energy Information Administration, "International Energy Outlook 2023: Data Tables (2020–2050)," webpage, October 11, 2023.

NOTE: Data for 2050 are projections. As of 2022, liquid fuels make up about 11 and 13 billion kilowatt hours of total electricity generation for the United States and China, respectively. The data for 2050 reflect U.S. Energy Information Administration projections of the shares of liquid fuels decreasing to 5 and 0 billion kilowatt hours of total electricity generation for the United States and China, respectively. These figures do not appear on the graph because of the scale of the y-axis. Nuclear energy, although often categorized with renewable energy sources within policies that support a transition away from fossil fuels, is itself not a renewable energy source. Nuclear fuels, such as uranium-235 and plutonium-239, are finite materials that can only be mined from specific geological locations, making them a critical mineral in the global political economy. However, the capacity of nuclear power stations to use a relatively small amount of fuel to generate the same amount of electricity as a coal or gas power station—with a significantly lower and zero-carbon lifecycle emissions process—make it a reliable source of energy for decades to come. See National Grid, "What Is Nuclear Energy (and Why Is It Considered a Clean Energy)?" webpage, last updated August 8, 2022.

oil's status as a global commodity, the United States remains vulnerable to price shocks. As a result, policymakers under the Biden administration have since adopted strategies imposing a moratorium on new oil and gas leasing on federal lands and waters, despite the United States' production in crude oil reaching record heights in 2023.[14]

Similarly, U.S. exports of LNG have grown substantially, from 10.6 billion cubic feet per day (Bcf/d) in 2022 to 11.9 Bcf/d in 2023—a 12-percent increase—making it the largest LNG exporter that year.[15] The largest consumers of U.S. LNG were the Netherlands, France, the United Kingdom, and Spain, accounting for nearly 35 percent of all U.S. LNG exports, as a result of natural gas supply challenges after Russia cut off pipeline exports and higher prices emerged in Europe's natural gas trading hubs.[16] As with crude oil, the United States has risen as the world's largest LNG producer by installed capacity in 2022.[17] The U.S. economy benefits from the increased output from oil and gas and the downward pressure that the increase in supply has put on domestic and world market prices for these commodities.

China's official policy on energy security is driven by its needs to meet rising energy demand.[18] Decades of rapid economic growth have dramatically expanded China's energy needs, resulting in it becoming the world's largest energy consumer.[19] Although China's coal production comprises the majority of the country's current domestic energy mix, the volatility of coal prices and power shortages from supply fluctuations have threatened the stability of the supply of electricity. To improve its energy security, China depends on imports of oil and natural gas to supplement domestic supplies from several—oftentimes politically unstable—countries, such as Russia and Iraq.[20] Policies to alleviate this dependence have

---

[14] Executive Order 14008, "Tackling the Climate Crisis at Home and Abroad," Executive Office of the President, January 27, 2021; Erik Kreil, "United States Produces More Crude Oil Than Any Country, Ever," U.S. Energy Information Administration, March 11, 2024.

[15] Victoria Zaretskaya, "The United States Was the World's Largest Liquefied Natural Gas Exporter in 2023," U.S. Energy Information Administration, April 1, 2024; U.S. Energy Information Administration, "Natural Gas Monthly," webpage, updated May 31, 2024a.

[16] Victoria Zaretskaya, "Europe Was the Main Destination for U.S. LNG Exports in 2022," U.S. Energy Information Administration, March 22, 2023; Paul Bolton, *Imports of Fossil Fuels from Russia*, House of Commons Library, Research Briefing Number 9523, March 13, 2023.

[17] Scott Disavino, "US LNG Project Approvals on Track for Record New Volumes," Reuters, June 23, 2023; Zaretskaya, 2023.

[18] Becca Wasser, Howard J. Shatz, John J. Drennan, Andrew Scobell, Brian G. Carlson, and Yvonne K. Crane, *Crossroads of Competition: China, Russia, and the United States in the Middle East*, RAND Corporation, RR-A325-1, 2022; Stephan Liedtke, "China's Energy Investments in Europe: An Analysis of Policy Drivers and approaches," *Energy Policy*, Vol. 101, February 2017; Mary Hui, "Oil and Gas Exports Are Complicating the US-China Relationship," *Quartz*, June 28, 2023.

[19] China Power Project, "How Is China's Energy Footprint Changing?" Center for Strategic and International Studies, March 27, 2022.

[20] John Calabrese, "China Prioritizes Short-Term Energy Security: Implications for Sino-Middle East Relations," Middle East Institute, July 12, 2022; Oceana Zhou and Sambit Mohanty, "China's Crude Imports from Russia Hits Record as Xi, Putin Eye Stronger Energy Ties," S&P Global, March 20, 2023.

focused on expanding investments in domestic sources of energy and on integrating energy supply chains.

Renewable Energy and Policies Promoting Decarbonization

The passing of the Inflation Reduction Act (IRA) in 2022 marked a significant turning point in U.S. climate legislation by offering additional funding, programs, and incentives to energy producers to accelerate the transition to a clean energy economy by 2035.[21] Announcements of private investments in clean energy have skyrocketed as a result; since the passing of the IRA, firms along the U.S. electric vehicle (EV) supply chain have announced almost $55 billion in investments in at least 30 new battery manufacturing projects in the United States, with a projected capacity of 1,000 gigawatt-hours per year by 2030, enough to manufacture between 10 million and 13 million EVs per year.[22] In addition to the IRA, the Biden administration launched the first National Climate Task Force in 2021; its objectives are to reduce greenhouse gas emissions 50 percent or more below 2005 levels by 2030, reach 100 percent carbon-free electricity by 2035, achieve a net-zero emissions economy by 2050, and deliver 40 percent of the benefits from federal investments in climate and clean energy to disadvantaged communities.[23] These policies mark the latest attempt by the United States to create actionable goals for mitigating the effects of climate change through adding clean energy sources to the national energy mix.

Despite the national agenda to decarbonize the U.S. economy, the United States continues to produce coal and hydrocarbons. The country's energy independence in fossil fuels is key to short-term energy security, whereas a full transition to alternative energy sources is relegated to a long-term strategy. In preparation for the transition, oil and gas firms are engaging with U.S. policymakers and international agencies to implement clean energy strategies in their refining and extraction practices, despite climate experts arguing that such efforts slow true climate change solutions and practices that ensure durable environmental security.[24] For example, in an October 2021 congressional hearing on the role that fossil fuel industries play in propagating climate disinformation, top executives from Exxon Mobil, BP America, Chevron, and Shell Oil discussed the possibility of a "lower carbon future" that will be powered by the fossil fuel industry through carbon capture storage technologies that can remove

---

[21] U.S. Environmental Protection Agency, "Summary of Inflation Reduction Act Provisions Related to Renewable Energy," webpage, last updated October 25, 2023; White House, *Building a Clean Energy Economy: A Guidebook to the Inflation Reduction Act's Investments in Clean Energy and Climate Action*, version 2, January 2023.

[22] Brian Deese, "The New Climate Law Is Working. Clean Energy Investments Are Soaring," *New York Times*, May 30, 2023.

[23] White House, "President Biden's Historic Climate Agenda," webpage, undated.

[24] For more on the business and political behavior of U.S. oil and gas firms vis-à-vis decarbonization, see Jessica Green, Jennifer Hadden, Thomas Hale, and Paasha Mahdavi, "Transition, Hedge, or Resist? Understanding the Political and Economic Behavior Toward Decarbonization in the Oil and Gas Industry," *Review of International Political Economy*, Vol. 29, No. 6, 2022.

carbon dioxide emissions from their products and further enhance oil recovery.[25] These and other actions taken by fossil fuel industries are driven by corporate social responsibility initiatives—which suggest that "curbing negative externalities such as environmental degradation . . . can also improve a firm's bottom line" and can maintain the industry's status as key energy producers and suppliers—rather than by broader environmental security goals.[26]

Scaling up production in clean energy has been difficult because of fluctuations in the supply and prices of raw materials, such as critical minerals, and frequent changes in domestic environmental and economic regulations.[27] In 2022, U.S. renewable energy growth slowed "due to rising costs and project delays driven by supply chain disruptions, trade policy uncertainty, inflation, increasing interest rates, and interconnection delays," many of which are a result of lingering aftershocks of the COVID-19 pandemic and Russia's war with Ukraine.[28] To minimize the impact of these geopolitical effects, the IRA has expanded the types of projects that are eligible for financing and increased federal lending authority to support clean energy, environmental justice, job creation, and domestic manufacturing goals.[29]

Increases in renewable energy investments, both domestic and international, are an important part of China's Outline of the 14th Five-Year Plan (2021–2025).[30] The plan targets a 50-percent increase in renewable energy, establishes a 2025 renewable electricity consumption share of 33 percent, and predicts that nearly half of China's incremental electricity and energy consumption will come from renewables by 2025.[31] Despite its dependence on coal

---

[25] June Sekera and Neva Goodwin, "Why the Oil Industry's Pivot to Carbon Capture and Storage—While It Keeps On Drilling—Isn't a Climate Change Solution," *The Conversation*, November 23, 2021; "Big Oil to Attend U.S. House Climate Disinformation Hearing," Reuters, October 22, 2021.

[26] Green et al., 2022.

[27] Alberto Bettoli, Florian Heineke, Nadine Janecke, Thomas Nyheim, Andreas Schlosser, Sophia Spitzer, Christian Staudt, Holder Klärner, Raffael Winter, and Jakub Zivansky, "Renewable-Energy Development in a Net-Zero World: Disrupted Supply Chains," McKinsey & Company, February 17, 2023.

[28] Marlene Motyka, Jim Thomson, and Kate Hardin, *2023 Renewable Energy Industry Outlook*, Deloitte, 2023, p. 3.

[29] Such funding expansions have been allocated to the Title 17 Clean Energy Financing Program, the Advanced Technology Vehicles Manufacturing Loan Program, and the Tribal Energy Finance Program (Jigar Shah, "Transforming Clean Energy Financing and Supply Chains in the United States: LPO One Year After the IRA," U.S. Department of Energy, August 16, 2023.

[30] *Outline of the People's Republic of China 14th Five-Year Plan for National Economic and Social Development and Long-Range Objectives for 2035* [中华人民共和国国民经济和社会发展第十四个五年规划和 2035 年远景目标纲要], March 12, 2021, trans. by Etcetera Language Group, Inc., ed. by Ben Murphy, Center for Security and Emerging Technology, May 12, 2021.

[31] Zhou Feng, Peng Linan, and Li Jie, "China's 14th Five-Year Plans on Renewable Energy Development and Modern Energy Development," Energy Foundation China, September 5, 2022.

for more than 60 percent of domestic electricity generation and new coal-fired power plants under development, the country has made notable progress in the clean energy transition.[32]

China has added more solar power capacity than any other country year after year and is home to 70 percent of global manufacturing capacity for EV batteries. The current rate of installations for wind and solar photovoltaics (PV) places China on track to reach 1,200 gigawatts of renewable power capacity by 2025, five years ahead of what it had projected in the 14th Five-Year Plan. Much of this progress has been fueled by China's growing transition in financial lending from real estate to manufacturing, especially in clean energy production, in turn causing anxieties in U.S. and European markets pushing to reshore domestic capacity for solar and wind power equipment, batteries, heat pumps, and fuel cells.[33]

Apart from domestic energy production, China's infrastructure financing in lower-income countries through its BRI has propelled it as one of the most significant investors in global power infrastructure. The China Overseas Finance Inventory Database captures nearly 600 power plants in 87 BRI countries, of which only 18 percent are coal-fired power plants; nearly 67 percent are dedicated to renewable energy.[34] China's dominance in global markets for renewable manufacturing ultimately translates into lower global prices for wind and solar equipment and an efficient and low-cost equipment supply chain.[35] Renewable energy is only one part of the BRI's significance in Chinese energy and environmental security and has greater implications in terms of geopolitical alliances and the security of energy supply chains in the future.[36]

These investments and other policies accord with President Xi Jinping's carbon neutrality pledges from 2020 emphasizing the link between China's climate commitments, energy transition, and energy supply security.[37] Yet the speed at which China has expanded its clean

---

[32] In some cases, coal and renewable energy production coexist within the same power plant, such as at the Kubuqi power plant located in inner Mongolia, which generates 20 gigawatts of electricity split between solar (12 gigawatts), wind (4 gigawatts), and coal (4 gigawatts) (David Fickling, "How China's Renewables Boom Is Fueling Its Coal Expansion," *Financial Review*, July 17, 2023.

[33] Niels Graham, "China's Manufacturing Overcapacity Threatens Global Green Goods Trade," Atlantic Council, December 11, 2023.

[34] Lihuan Zhou, Ziyi Ma, Shuang Liu, Xinyue Ma, Kevin Acker, Margaret Myers, Deborah Brautigam, and Kevin Gallagher, China Overseas Finance Inventory Database, World Resources Institute, updated June 30, 2023.

[35] Ziyi Ma and Yu Ma, "What's After Coal? Accelerating China's Overseas Investment in Renewables," World Resources Institute, January 31, 2023; Alex Blackburne, "China's Increasingly Cheap Wind Turbines Could Open New Markets," S&P Global, September 26, 2022.

[36] By the end of 2023, China had increased BRI financing after scaling back in the years following the COVID-19 pandemic. Energy has been the main sector of China's BRI investment strategy; clean energy production (such as solar, wind, and hydropower) makes up an aggregate 34 percent of total energy engagement (Wang, 2024; Daniel Rosen, Matt Mingey, Camille Boullenois, and Laura Gormley, "China Pathfinder: Quarter 1 2024 Update," Atlantic Council, May 16, 2024).

[37] IEA, "China Has a Clean Pathway to Build a More Sustainable, Secure and Inclusive Energy Future," press release, September 29, 2021c; IEA, *An Energy Sector Roadmap to Carbon Neutrality in China*, September 2021b.

energy manufacturing capacity suggests a more pertinent national security goal to establish preeminence in the clean energy supply chain as global markets transition.[38] Despite its efforts to rapidly expand energy sources, China remains heavily dependent on fossil fuels, even at the cost of environmental security. China remains the largest producer and consumer of coal and the largest carbon dioxide emitter as of 2022.[39] Climate effects—such as coastal flooding and erosion, storm surges, and saltwater intrusion—from China's fossil fuel industries threaten the country's economically critical cities, home to one-fifth of its population and over one-third of the country's GDP.[40] Increases in LNG imports from the United States and other global actors are expected to drive up fossil fuel consumption—and greenhouse gas emissions—at a much higher rate than the expected rates of clean energy development.[41] In terms of international action, China has pledged to achieve carbon neutrality by 2060, a full decade later than the United States and the European Union, and continues to lag behind other top-carbon emitter countries in environmental protection measures.[42] Beijing's action are clear; it intends to decarbonize at its own pace, favoring economic development over environmental concerns.

Critical Minerals and Battery Storage Technologies

R&D in battery storage technologies is essential to environmental security strategies by speeding up the replacement of fossil fuels with renewable energy sources. The construction of solar PV plants, wind farms, and EVs requires minerals other than fossil fuels—most notably lithium, nickel, cobalt, and manganese, all of which are crucial to the battery performance, longevity, and density needed to help electricity grids ensure a reliable supply of energy.[43] Such systems will play an increasingly pivotal role between clean energy supplies and meeting rising electricity demand, incentivizing energy producers and nations to secure the supply of critical minerals.[44]

---

38 China holds at least 60 percent of the world's manufacturing capacity for most mass-manufactured renewable technologies, such as solar PV, wind systems, and batteries; Europe and the United States are the largest importers (IEA, *Energy Technology Perspectives 2023*, January 2023a).

39 China Power Project, 2022.

40 World Bank, "China's Transition to a Low-Carbon Economy and Climate Resilience Needs Shifts in Resources and Technologies," press release, October 12, 2022.

41 Christian Shepherd, "John Kerry Hails China's 'Incredible Job' on Renewables, Warns on Coal," *Washington Post*, July 17, 2023.

42 Laura Edwards, "4 Things to Know About China's Climate Approach," Center for American Progress, September 30, 2021; *Outline of the People's Republic of China 14th Five-Year Plan for National Economic and Social Development and Long-Range Objectives for 2035* [中华人民共和国国民经济和社会发展第十四个五年规划和 2035 年远景目标纲要], March 12, 2021, trans. by Etcetera Language Group, Inc., ed. by Ben Murphy, Center for Security and Emerging Technology, May 12, 2021, p. 94.

43 IEA, *The Role of Critical Minerals in Clean Energy Transitions*, May 2021a.

44 *Critical minerals* are defined by the U.S. Energy Act of 2020 as "any mineral, element, substance, or material designated as critical by the Secretary of the Interior, acting through the director of the U.S. Geological

Although reserves of these minerals are found all over the world, critical mineral production and processing is concentrated in a handful of countries. Figure 7.2 shows the top three extractors and processors of various critical minerals by country in 2022. There has been limited progress in diversifying these sources since 2019. Because of their wide variety of applications, bottlenecks in the supply chain of critical minerals—caused by such factors as the availability of materials, equipment, or workers; market conditions; and regulatory frameworks—can hinder capacity expansion and extend product lead-times.[45] China has become the world leader in refining and processing these minerals for use in end products, leveraging huge gains in cost reductions for renewable energy while simultaneously creating a global risk to supply chains and energy security because of its market dominance. To mitigate these risks and reduce reliance on China, some countries—such as those in the Quadrilateral Security Dialogue, made up of the United States, Australia, India, and Japan—have mapped domestic mining, refining, and processing capacities for critical minerals and their capacity and vulnerabilities in global semiconductor supply chains.[46]

The United States is rich in mineral reserves—including cobalt, copper, lithium, and rare earth elements (REEs)—yet its production and processing capacity is small, especially compared with China.[47] Raw materials mined domestically are shipped overseas, often to China, for processing before returning as end products. This international supply chain dependence has raised concerns about the defense industry's reliance on limited domestic suppliers, global supply chains vulnerable to disruption, and competitor country suppliers.[48] Similar concerns arise in the energy sector; a surge in demand for minerals by 2050 to power new clean energy technologies, coupled with rising U.S.-China tensions, could trigger measures and partnerships designed to stimulate the U.S. domestic economy and forge new global supply chains outside China.[49]

Survey" (U.S. Department of Energy, "What Are Critical Materials and Critical Minerals?" webpage, undated.)

[45] U.S. Department of Energy, *Critical Minerals Assessment*, July 2023.

[46] Zongyuan Zoe Liu, "How to Secure Critical Minerals for Clean Energy Without Alienating China," blog post, Council on Foreign Relations, May 25, 2023; Shepherd, 2023.

[47] The only REE mining and processing facility in North America is the Mountain Pass Rare Earth Mine, located in California's Mojave Desert, accounting for roughly 15 percent of the world's REE production (Jackie Benton, "Rare Earth Elements: Texas Rare Earths Show Economic Potential For State," *Fiscal Notes*, Texas Comptroller's Office, November 2021; Earth Observatory, "Mountain Pass Rare Earth Mine," National Aeronautics and Space Administration, December 25, 2022)

[48] Office of the Under Secretary of Defense for Acquisition and Sustainment and Office of the Deputy Assistant Secretary of Defense for Industrial Policy, *Assessing and Strengthening the Manufacturing and Defense Industrial Base and Supply Chain Resiliency of the United States*, U.S. Department of Defense, September 2018; Daniel F. Runde and Austin Hardman, "Elevating the Role of Critical Minerals for Development and Security," Center for Strategic and International Studies, September 2023.

[49] White House, *Building Resilient Supply Chains, Revitalizing American Manufacturing, and Fostering Broad-Based Growth: 100-Day Reviews Under Executive Order 14017*, June 2021; Christina Lu, "The U.S. Strategic Minerals Situation Is Critical," *Foreign Policy*, June 30, 2023.

FIGURE 7.2
Extractors and Processors of Various Critical Minerals by Country, 2022

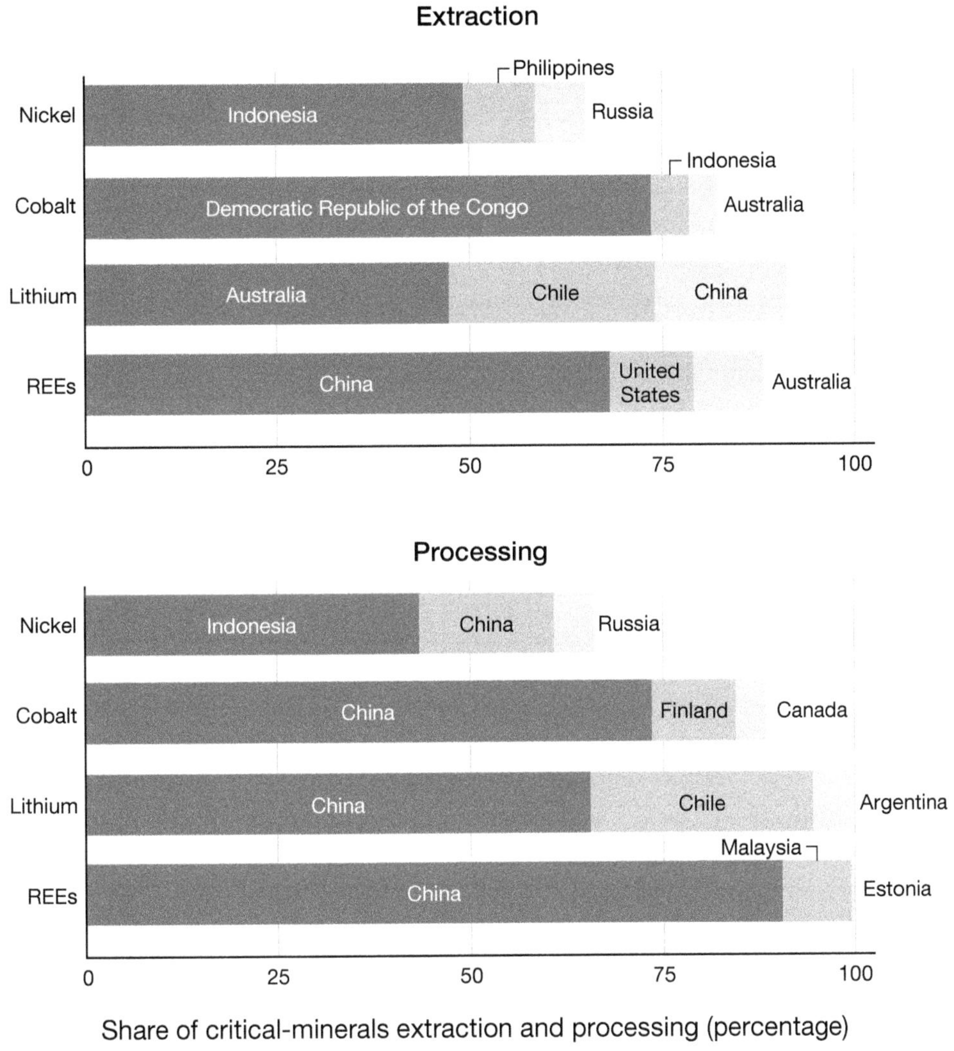

SOURCE: Adapted from "The Global Fight for Critical Minerals Is Costly and Damaging," *Nature*, July 19, 2023, which draws data from International Energy Agency, *Critical Minerals Market Review 2023*, December 2023c.

China's lead in mining, refining, and processing critical minerals is part and parcel of global concerns over supply chain bottlenecks. China's share of refining is around 35 percent for nickel, 50 to 70 percent for cobalt, and nearly 90 percent for REEs.[50] China's control over "much of the world's EV battery manufacturing, as well as the manufacturing of wind turbines, solar panels, energy storage, and electric transmission, and other applications," posi-

[50] IEA, 2021a.

tions the country as a key supplier as the world advances in the energy transition.[51] Beijing's position in the supply chain of critical minerals has made it possible for China to sign trade agreements with both allies and adversaries for these products and to ensure its competitive position in the global energy transition while also meeting economic development goals as outlined in its 14th Five-Year Plan and its previous iterations.

Although China is dominant in processing critical minerals, the extraction of critical minerals is concentrated in countries in Africa, Southeast Asia, and South America, and in Australia. Mining REEs follows potentially exploitative practices, leading some mineral-rich countries to adopt export controls and other mechanisms to capture the processing of high-value products within their borders. Methods of mining critical minerals are often environmentally damaging; the shift to the reuse and recycling of materials rather than fueling an ever-increasing demand for raw materials will be essential to critical mineral processing in the coming decades to ensure both environmental and energy security.[52] The challenge of achieving net-zero emissions will require significant scaling up of the production of and international trade in critical minerals. To remain competitive in this market, the United States and China may need to prioritize geopolitical alliances and trade agreements with mineral-rich countries to ensure a reliable supply chain.

Nuclear Power Generation and Waste Management

United States

Although solar and wind have accounted for the vast majority of clean energy capacity additions, nuclear power serves as another source of low-carbon electricity generation. Although nuclear power generates radioactive waste, it does not emit carbon dioxide or other greenhouse gases.[53] The physical footprint of nuclear facilities is also relatively small compared with renewable energy. The U.S. Department of Energy notes that a "typical 1,000-megawatt nuclear facility in the United States needs a little more than 1 square mile to operate," whereas wind farms and solar PV plants require tens to hundreds of times more space.[54] Given these advantages, countries that are invested in diversifying their energy mixes are seriously considering nuclear energy.

Outside domestic energy production, nuclear power plant manufacturers hope for export markets to grow. In 2010, the IEA and Nuclear Energy Agency estimated that additions to nuclear capacity will more than double by 2050, restoring the fuel source to its historical high of 17 percent of the global electricity supply and displacing enough coal-fired power to

[51] Rodrigo Castillo and Caitlin Purdy, *China's Role in Supplying Critical Minerals for the Global Energy Transition: What Could the Future Hold?* Brookings Institution, July 2022, p. 5.

[52] "The Global Fight for Critical Minerals Is Costly and Damaging," 2023; White House, 2021.

[53] World Nuclear Association, *Comparison of Lifecycle Greenhouse Gas Emissions of Various Electricity Generation Sources*, July 2011.

[54] U.S. Department of Energy, 2022a.

cut worldwide carbon dioxide emissions by 2.5 gigatons.[55] If implemented, such increases to nuclear energy capacity will not only promote countries already equipped with nuclear power infrastructure to diversify their domestic clean energy mix but also encourage trade with other nations at the early stages of their respective energy transitions. Expanding the global market for nuclear energy in these ways may be the most pragmatic and cleanest approach to meet decarbonization goals worldwide.

The resurgence of nuclear energy for commercial use grew out of a combined national security interest promoting collaboration among advanced nuclear nations and efforts to reduce the risk of nuclear proliferation. The George W. Bush administration's Global Nuclear Energy Partnership, later renamed the International Framework for Nuclear Energy Cooperation (IFNEC), was a comprehensive strategy "to develop a fuel services program that would provide nuclear fuel and recycling services to nations in return for their commitment to refrain from developing enrichment and recycling technologies."[56] As both a research and technology and international policy initiative, the IFNEC's mission was to expand global nuclear power in a safe and secure manner and increase the efficiency of the current nuclear fuel cycle by engaging in mutually beneficial efforts with other states in the nuclear energy supply chain.[57]

Nuclear energy can be harnessed and distributed for commercial use in one of two ways. Nuclear fission, or the process by which radioactive isotopes break apart into smaller isotopes and generate steam from released gamma photons, has been the predominant method of generating electricity; all existing commercial nuclear reactors use fission technology. Nuclear *fusion*, or the process by which two isotopes of hydrogen unite under conditions of extreme pressure and temperature, generates several times the amount of energy produced from fission.[58] However, fusion is not currently commercially viable; no prototype commercial reactors have yet been built. Fusion has not yet been used to produce power because of its volatility and the cost of constructing the necessary conditions to control such a reaction.[59] Nevertheless, the scientific and policymaking communities are engaging in the R&D of nuclear

---

[55] Peter Fairley, "Why Don't We Have More Nuclear Power?" *MIT Technology Review*, May 28, 2015; IEA and Nuclear Energy Agency, *Nuclear Energy Technology Roadmap*, OECD Publishing, 2010.

[56] U.S. Department of Energy, "The Global Nuclear Energy Partnership: Greater Energy Security in a Cleaner, Safer World," fact sheet, February 6, 2006.

[57] World Nuclear Association, "International Framework for Nuclear Energy Cooperation," updated November 7, 2016.

[58] Nuclear Information Center, "Fission vs. Fusion—What's the Difference?" webpage, Duke Energy, May 27, 2021.

[59] Three main conditions are necessary for nuclear fusion: (1) temperatures must be hot enough to allow ions to fuse together, at nearly 100 million degrees Celsius; (2) ions have to be confined together in close proximity to allow for fusion; and (3) ions must be held together in close proximity at high temperatures long enough to avoid plasma cooling (Quamrul Haider, "Nuclear Fusion: Holy Grail of Energy" in Igor Girka, ed., *Nuclear Fusion: One Noble Goal and a Variety of Scientific and Technological Challenges*, Intech Open, 2019).

fusion technology because it produces less radioactive material and reaps a nearly unlimited fuel supply. The U.S. Department of Energy's Office of Science Fusion Energy Program helps researchers coordinate across multiple disciplines involved with fusion, including plasma physics, nuclear engineering, and advanced scientific computing.[60] R&D into fusion technologies also spans borders; the United States and the United Kingdom have supported research to better understand how to sustain fusion reactions and generate power. Major advances in fusion technology in the past few years have attracted almost $4 billion in private funds aimed at building proof-of-concept fusion pilot plants by the end of the decade.[61] Whether national interest in adopting fusion technologies will expand will depend on the viability of these initial plants.

In the United States, nuclear energy has remained a key junction between military and economic development. As a result, government policy has been central to discussions of nuclear power since the 1945 Manhattan Project.[62] Federal oversight by the U.S. Atomic Energy Agency reflects mitigation strategies for the risks associated with nuclear energy generation, specifically that of nuclear fallout, as was seen in the meltdowns of the Three Mile Island Unit 2, Chernobyl, and Fukushima Daiichi power plants. Public-private partnerships between the energy sector and federal agencies have bolstered nuclear power generation through safety and environmental regulations, R&D funding, and setting national energy goals. As a result, in 2021, the United States had the highest nuclear electricity generation capacity—contributing almost 20 percent of total electricity generation for domestic use—and generates more nuclear electricity than any other country.[63] Figure 7.3 shows the locations of nuclear reactors in the United States.

Despite the importance of U.S. nuclear power in total generation, public opinion and energy industries differ in assessing the value of this energy source. Public opinion surveys show that nearly 57 percent of Americans favor more nuclear power plants to generate electricity, up from 43 percent in 2020, although they are still far more likely to favor more solar power (82 percent) and wind (75 percent).[64] Federally owned electricity providers, such as the Tennessee Valley Authority, have recognized nuclear power as the key to significantly reduc-

---

60 Matt Lanctot, "DOE Explains . . . Fusion Energy Science," webpage, U.S. Department of Energy, undated.

61 Sally M. Benson and Costa Samaras, "Parallel Processing the Path to Commercialization of Fusion Energy," Office of Science and Technology Policy, Executive Office of the President, June 3, 2022; White House, "Fact Sheet: Developing a Bold Vision for Commercial Fusion Energy," March 15, 2022.

62 Government oversight includes but is not limited to lengthy, detailed requirements on the construction and operation of all reactors and conversion, enrichment, fuel fabrication, mining, and mining facilities (World Nuclear Association, "U.S. Nuclear Power Policy," webpage, updated February 2023a).

63 France remains the country with the highest share of nuclear power (68 percent) in total national annual electricity generation; however, it is second when it comes to nuclear electricity generation capacity and third in terms of gigawatt hours generated (U.S. Energy Information Administration, "Nuclear Explained: Nuclear Power Plants," webpage, last updated August 21, 2023a).

64 Rebecca Leppert and Brian Kennedy, "Growing Share of Americans Favor More Nuclear Power," Pew Research Center, August 18, 2023.

FIGURE 7.3

Nuclear Reactors Operating in the United States

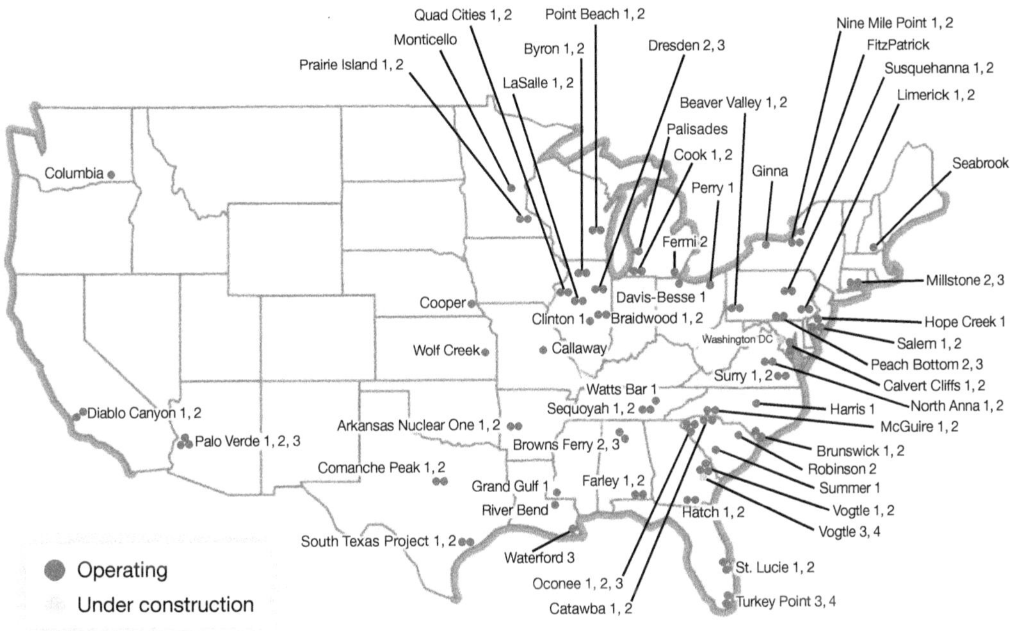

SOURCE: Adapted from World Nuclear Association, "Nuclear Power in the USA," webpage, updated August 27, 2024c.

ing carbon emissions while providing substantial amounts of power.[65] Differing opinions of political stakeholders are only one part of why nuclear energy has not been as impactful a source in the electricity sector as other renewables. While Figure 7.3 shows the locations of existing reactors in the United States, almost all U.S. nuclear power plants were built between 1967 and 1990.[66] The capital costs of building a reactor, including the time lags from planning to operations and federal regulatory limitations, deter firms from investing in conventional nuclear power plants. Policymakers are determined to promote nuclear energy by supporting R&D with the understanding that current and future solar, wind, and other renewable power generation and their baseload battery operations will not be enough to meet rising electricity demand and net-zero emissions goals in the next 20 to 30 years.[67] The IRA is the latest to

65 "The U.S. Is Divided over Whether Nuclear Power Is Part of the Green Energy Future," Associated Press, January 18, 2022.

66 Georgia Power's Vogtle 3 plant is the first new nuclear reactor built in the past 40 years; it reached 100-percent power in July 2023 (World Nuclear Association, "U.S. Operating Nuclear Reactors: Nuclear Power in the USA Appendix 1," webpage, updated August 2023e; Emily Jones, "The US Is Getting Its First New Nuclear Reactor in 40 Years," Grist, June 6, 2023).

67 This chapter does not include the capacity of geothermal energy for electricity generation or for energy and environmental security writ large.

support nuclear power through tax incentives and investments subsidies. It projects growth in nuclear energy generation to meet decarbonization goals.[68] As private investors continue research in new fission—and fusion—technologies, greater understanding and risk analyses of nuclear energy generation will be made more evident to allow for the public support of such fuels.

China

China has invested heavily in its nuclear energy program. The impetus for China's investments in nuclear power stems from nuclear power's relatively low challenges to environmental security coupled with rapidly increasing energy demand. Continued coal production has brought the highest levels of air pollution in China since before the start of the COVID-19 pandemic; widespread power outages would threaten the stability of the country's electricity grid. Logistical issues, such as difficulties in transporting coal from mines in the west and north to cities in the southeast, have compelled China to build most of its nuclear reactors along the coast. With 38 reactors in operation and 19 under construction, China has become the world's largest market for new nuclear energy production capacity, investment, construction, and maintenance.[69] China's growing investments are expected to yield nuclear capacity of 120 to 150 gigawatts by 2030, according to its National Energy Administration, making nuclear energy the source of roughly 10 percent of China's total power generation by 2035.[70] These projections reflect China's rapid ascendancy in nuclear power generation capacity, which stands third after France and the United States.

In terms of fueling existing and future reactors, Beijing's intentions are to "become self-sufficient not just in nuclear power plant capacity, but also in the production of fuel for those plants."[71] National policy reflects these intentions; the plan is to obtain uranium domestically, through Chinese equity in foreign mines (see Table 7.1), and through the open market along existing partnerships with BRI countries.[72]

Despite China's claim to be a "uranium-rich country," with roughly 2 million tons of elemental uranium (tU) available from domestic supplies, identifiable recoverable resources

---

[68] For example, the IRA includes $150 million in investments by the U.S. Department of Energy toward infrastructure improvements at the Idaho National Laboratory to accelerate the replacement of aging plant infrastructure (U.S. Department of Energy, "Biden-Harris Administration Announces $150 Million to Improve Nuclear Research and Development Infrastructure at Idaho National Laboratory," press release, October 25, 2022b; U.S. Department of Defense, "DoD to Build Project Pele Mobile Microreactor and Perform Demonstration at Idaho National Laboratory," press release, April 13, 2022).

[69] Laura Gil, "How China Has Become the World's Fastest Expanding Nuclear Power Producer," *IAEA Bulletin*, Vol. 58, No. 4, November 2017.

[70] Genevieve Donnellon-May, "Powering China's Nuclear Ambitions," *The Diplomat*, September 20, 2022.

[71] World Nuclear Association, "China's Nuclear Fuel Cycle," webpage, updated July 2023b.

[72] World Nuclear Association, 2023.

TABLE 7.1
Operating Uranium Mines in China

Mine	Province	Type	Nominal capacity (tU/year)	Started
Yining	Xinjiang	In-situ leach	850	1993
Lantian	Shaanxi	Underground, heap leach	0	1993
Fuzhou	Jiangxi	Underground, mill	350	1966
Chongyi	Jiangxi	Underground, heap leach	0	1979
Shaoguan	Guangdong	Underground, heap leach	200	2008
Tongliao	Inner Mongolia	In-situ leach	200	2015
Total			1,600	

SOURCE: Adapted from World Nuclear Association, 2023b.

total roughly 223,900 tU, of which roughly half is reasonably assured.[73] China depends on uranium imports from Central Asia, Eastern Europe, and the Middle East, which are essential for its domestic nuclear energy generation and broader environmental security goals of net-zero emissions. China's plans to build and finance 30 nuclear reactors in BRI countries over the next decade furthers China's position as a leading nuclear energy technology exporter.[74] The international implications of Chinese nuclear development within the context of BRI are vast. The larger China's share of the nuclear technology market, the more say it will have in shaping the rules and norms in nuclear governance. Chinese exports of nuclear technology have the potential to increase recipient countries' reliance on China for decades. China is not only competing against Western countries with nuclear technologies but also with Russia for sales of nuclear power plants in the Middle East and North Africa (MENA) region.[75]

Along with nuclear fuel generation comes nuclear waste management. In the United States, nuclear waste is handled and stored on site in dry casks in compliance with stringent requirements by the U.S. Nuclear Regulatory Commission, the U.S. Department of Energy, and the U.S. Environmental Protection Agency.[76] In terms of long-term storage, the Yucca Mountain Nuclear Waste Repository was to become the main disposal site for both spent

---

73 World Nuclear Association, 2023; World Nuclear Association, "Supply of Uranium," webpage, updated August 2023d.

74 Lami Kim, "Nuclear Belt and Road: China's Nuclear Exports and Its Global Implications," in Abraham M. Denmark and Lucas Myers, eds., *Essays on the Rise of China and Its Implications*, Wilson Center, 2021.

75 China is also competing with Russia for the development of new oil fields in the MENA region (Wasser, 2022).

76 Hannah Hickman, "What Happens to Nuclear Waste in the U.S.?" Nuclear Energy Institute, November 19, 2019.

nuclear fuel and other forms of high-level radioactive waste. However, cuts to federal funding and widespread opposition from state and regional officials and from Western Shoshone tribes have led to delays in the project through all presidential administrations since 2010.[77] In China, several temporary storage facilities for low- and mid-level nuclear waste are located in the Gansu, Guangdong, and Sichuan provinces.[78] Despite existing infrastructure in both countries, R&D for the future geological disposal of high-level radioactive waste, including spent nuclear fuel, is in its infancy. China is constructing its first underground research laboratory on nuclear waste management in the Gobi Desert following more than 30 years of research with the support of the International Atomic Energy Agency.[79] If nuclear energy is to provide a larger share of electric power generation in both the United States' and China's electricity mixes, the expansion of nuclear waste storage capacities will need to be prioritized in national energy strategies.

Interlinkages and Dependencies

The U.S. and Chinese economies remain closely intertwined despite the economic and political disputes between the two countries in recent years. Each country benefits from sustained growth in the other, while national policies threatening to undermine each other through trade disputes, sanctions regimes, and other coercive measures impose economic costs on both countries.[80] This dynamic is most apparent in key goods and services in which the United States or China has a comparative advantage over the other. China continues to depend on fossil fuel resources to uphold its national energy security strategies, including meeting current and expected energy demand. Beijing's policies to increase imports of LNG to reach these goals and to diversify its energy mix to mitigate the climate effects from coal create enhanced dependence on the United States, which provides as much as 40 percent of China's total LNG imports.[81] Additionally, China's imports of crude oil, of which 50 percent are from the Persian Gulf, depend on the U.S. security that is provided to shipping lanes.

[77] U.S. Nuclear Regulatory Commission, *Yucca Mountain Review Plan: Final Report*, NUREG-1804, rev. 2, July 2003; Hannah Northey, "GAO: Death of Yucca Mountain Caused by Political Maneuvering," *New York Times*, May 10, 2011.

[78] World Nuclear Association, 2024a. The nuclear disposal plant located in the Sichuan province has also made headways in high-level radioactive liquid waste disposal by turning the waste into glass as of 2021 (Fan Anqi and Deng Xiaoci, "China Makes Breakthrough in High-Level Radioactive Waste Disposal Technique, Achieves Milestone in Nuclear Industry Devt," *Global Times*, September 12, 2021).

[79] Bridget Carter and Gerald Nieder-Westermann, "China Begins Construction of Its First Underground Research Laboratory for High Level Waste Disposal," International Atomic Energy Agency, July 23, 2021.

[80] Paul Haenle and Sam Bresnick, "Why U.S.-China Relations Are Locked in a Stalemate," Carnegie Endowment for International Peace, February 21, 2022.

[81] Jessica Jaganathan and Chen Aizhu, "U.S. LNG Cargoes Heading to China After Beijing Awards Tax Waivers," Reuters, April 7, 2020.

China's growing energy demand creates a stable market for U.S. fossil fuels, making possible a long-term scenario of cooperation between both countries that also greatly benefits U.S. energy security goals.[82]

China's comparative advantage in processing critical minerals and manufacturing batteries reverses its relationship of dependency on the United States. The growth in sales of EVs by Chinese companies over the past decade has increased demand for such vital components as lithium-ion batteries, rare earth magnets, electrical steel, and power electronics—markets in which China is already prominent—creating an opportunity for a supply chain bottleneck.[83] In preparation for this scenario, the Biden administration has taken steps to promote U.S. economic competitiveness and strengthen national security by increasing domestic supplies of materials or friendshoring with other critical minerals suppliers. In June 2022, the United States and its Group of Seven (G7) partners launched the Partnership for Global Infrastructure and Investment to build clean energy supply chains and the Minerals Security Partnership to produce, process, and recycle critical minerals.[84] Beijing's position in the supply chain of critical minerals is essential to its investments in resource-rich BRI countries across Asia, Sub-Saharan Africa, and MENA, creating an additional obstacle for the United States for the same raw materials, ultimately driving up the global price of these finite resources.[85] To the extent that the United States can compete in the market for critical minerals and end products for battery storage, capabilities will be determined by the country's investments in processing and refining facilities.

Ensuring a true net-zero carbon emissions future will require nuclear energy to remain an important source of non-intermittent electricity. The United States and China have cooperated in the production, development, and deployment of civil nuclear energy in the past. The 2007 U.S.-China Bilateral Civil Nuclear Energy Cooperative Action Plan pursued joint studies of advanced nuclear technologies, including a memorandum of understanding between the U.S. Department of Energy and the Chinese Academy of Sciences on Cooperation in Nuclear Energy Sciences and Technologies, seeking to "enhance and foster common interests in nuclear energy collaboration among U.S. and Chinese scientists, laboratories, research institutes, and universities."[86] However, the United States no longer collaborates on nuclear manufacturing technologies with China. The end of U.S.-Chinese agreements to collaborate

---

[82] Ben Cahill and Sophie Coste, "Subtle Shift in U.S. LNG Export Authorizations," Center for Strategic and International Studies, July 28, 2023.

[83] U.S. Department of Energy, 2023.

[84] Bentley Allan, Noah Gordon, and Cathy Wang, "Friendshoring Critical Minerals: What Could the U.S. and Its Partners Produce?" Carnegie Endowment for International Peace, May 3, 2023.

[85] As of 2023, there was more than $15 billion of Chinese investment in metals across BRI countries in these regions (American Enterprise Institute and Heritage Foundation, 2023; Derek Scissors, *China's Global Investment Surges, Finally*, American Enterprise Institute, July 2023).

[86] Office of Nuclear Energy, "Bilateral Cooperation," webpage, U.S. Department of Energy, undated.

on commercial nuclear technologies will shift the onus of increasing civil nuclear use to meet net-zero carbon emission goals onto individual countries.

The lack of existing interlinkages between the United States and China concerning energy may rebound depending on various political and economic effects of future bilateral relations. Moreover, the current context of higher inflation and interest rates compared with the past decade could constrain policymakers' decisions as they consider the inflationary impacts of the green transition in the future. Recent research suggests that these concerns can be alleviated by opting for climate policies that would subsidize green energy sectors, which in turn are dependent on the market effects of U.S.-China relations in energy production and sales to other countries and on the supply chain and manufacturing of clean energy equipment.[87] In the following section, I illustrate possible scenarios for U.S.-China strategic interactions of cooperation and competition, including discussing the costs and benefits to both countries.

Scenarios for 2050

The United States and China have a variety of options for managing their energy relations. In this section, I explore five possible scenarios: business-as-usual, enhanced cooperation, selective delinking, complete delinking, and competition. For each scenario, I outline costs and benefits to both countries.

Business-as-Usual

Figure 7.4 illustrates a costs-and-benefits matrix for the United States and China under a business-as-usual scenario. As noted earlier, existing trade agreements between the United States and China within the global energy market are highly dependent on the export and reliability of U.S. fossil fuels to China and exports of China's refined critical minerals to the United States. Benefits to both countries through this interdependence contribute to national energy security strategies; China's position as a top critical minerals processor help expands U.S. clean energy technologies, the domestic job opportunities that come with them, and the replacement of fossil energy by renewable energy in generating electricity. The United States' position as a top oil and gas exporter helps China meet its growing demand for natural gas and petroleum. The coupled nature of U.S.-China economic relations creates mutual risks of supply chain bottlenecks, which can limit the efficacy of coercive measures imposed by both countries during times of conflict.

[87] Marco Del Negro, Julian Di Giovanni, and Keshav Dogra, "Is the Green Transition Inflationary?" Federal Reserve Bank of New York, No. 1053, revised December 2023.

FIGURE 7.4
Costs and Benefits of a Business-as-Usual Scenario in U.S.-China Global Energy Cooperation

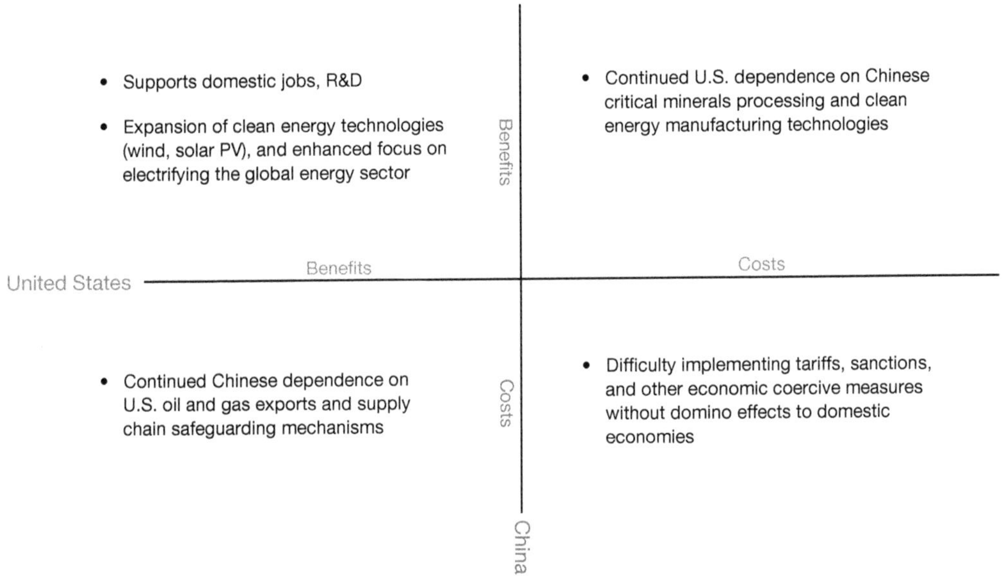

Enhanced Cooperation

Figure 7.5 illustrates a costs-and-benefits matrix for the United States and China under an enhanced cooperation scenario. Policies of enhanced cooperation suggest a shift in the mutual dependence of both U.S. and Chinese energy goods and services to include greater collaboration by the scientific and expert communities in both countries. Such collaborations may include research on the efficiencies and capacities of battery storage technology, from which the United States can benefit by upscaling domestic battery manufacturing as outlined by provisions in the IRA. Costs of continued dependence between both countries are expected to remain, however, with heightened concerns about intellectual property theft and loss of domestic manufacturing jobs.

The diffusion of knowledge about nuclear energy technologies can induce investments in such technologies by private firms, contributing to global decarbonization goals at a faster rate than energy transitions that rely solely on solar PV, wind, or other renewable energy fuel sources. Yet national security risks surrounding nuclear energy R&D and its defense applications hinder the degree to which academic collaboration will ensue, which promotes policies of information security or limiting nuclear energy research to U.S. scientists and engineers. A scenario of enhanced cooperation will most likely involve battery storage technology rather than nuclear energy because of U.S. primacy in the latter for electricity generation and for defense.

Moreover, increases in import penetration from China could lead to declines in U.S. manufacturing jobs in clean energy sectors at the cost of clean energy production investments,

FIGURE 7.5

Costs and Benefits of an Enhanced Cooperation Scenario in U.S.-China Global Energy Cooperation

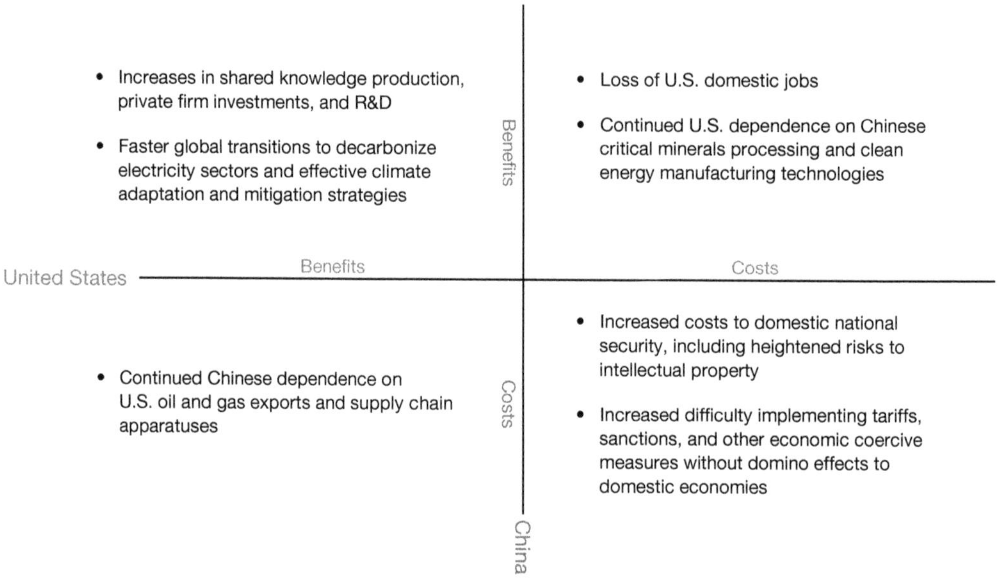

mirroring trends of import competition with China throughout the 2000s.[88] This scenario would only be credibly beneficial to the United States in the long run and beyond sovereign borders; increased investments in clean energy result in quicker transitions to decarbonize the electricity sector writ large.

Selective Delinking

Figure 7.6 illustrates the costs-and-benefits matrix for the United States and China under a selective delinking scenario. Growing concerns over China's continued dominance in the critical minerals processing market has resulted in stepped-up efforts to diversify global sources of supply, thereby making it difficult for China to use export restrictions on these products as political tools. Programs funded by the IRA and the European Union's Critical Raw Materials Act seek to encourage the development of alternative supplies locally and in friendly markets by providing investment subsidies, removing trade barriers, and creating targeted trade agreements with allies.[89] For example, the United States has already signed a

---

[88] White House, "Investing in Places Historically Left Behind: Foreign Direct Investment in U.S. Clean Energy Manufacturing," June 6, 2024b; David H. Autor, David Dorn, and Gordon H. Hanson, "The China Syndrome: Local Labor Market Effects of Import Competition in the United States," *American Economic Review*, Vol. 103, No. 6, October 2013.

[89] Yusuf Khan, "Increasing Export Restrictions on Critical Minerals Threaten Energy Transition, OECD Says," *Wall Street Journal*, April 11, 2023; Allan, Gordon, and Wang, 2023.

FIGURE 7.6

Costs and Benefits of a Selective Delinking Scenario in U.S.-China Global Energy Cooperation

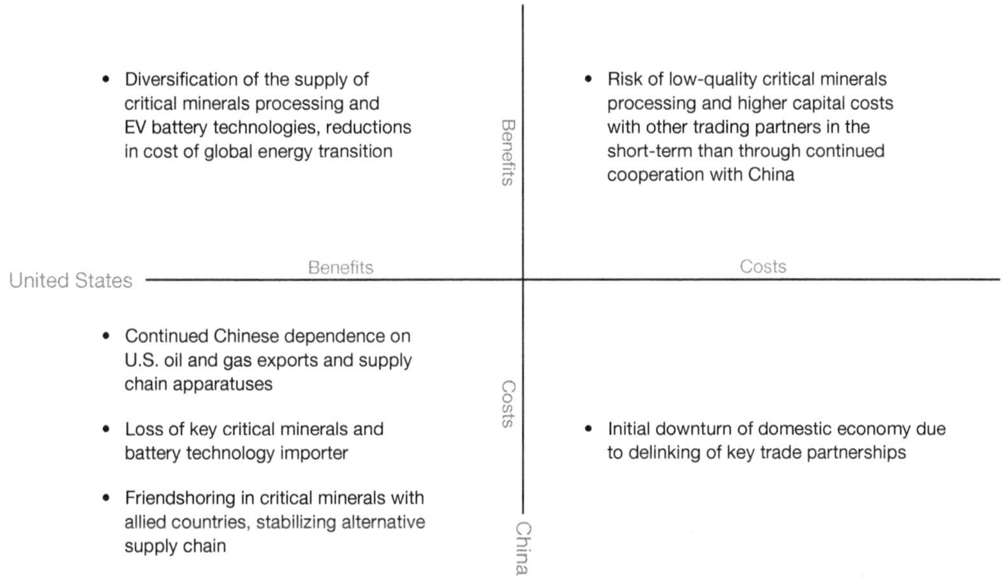

bilateral agreement with Japan to diversify critical minerals supply chains and promote the adoption of EV battery technologies that do not rely on minerals for which China is the primary supplier.[90] However, many U.S. allies, such as Chile, are caught between domestic production and refining and heavy reliance on exports to China.[91] Countries like Chile—even those with free trade agreements (FTAs) with the United States outside the G7—may be reluctant to be seen as choosing sides between the G7 and China under this scenario.

China's success at capturing key markets in clean energy supply chains has not only given the country leverage; China has also greatly reduced the costs of energy transitions in other economies through its improvements in the process technologies used to refine these materials and manufacture key components. As a result of strategic decoupling efforts, the United States may endure a period of increased costs for battery technologies and materials processing from other suppliers until friendshoring strategies expand alternative supply chains. Such shifts in the market will reduce China's influence over renewable energy equip-

---

[90] Andrew Duehren, "U.S. and Japan Strike Deal on Minerals Used in Batteries for Electric Cars," *Wall Street Journal*, March 28, 2023; Kucik and Kennedy, 2024.

[91] For example, in 2021, China consumed over 65 percent of Chilean mineral exports ($22.5 billion), making up about 6 percent of Chile's GDP (Christopher Hernandez-Roy, Henry Ziemer, and Nathaniel Laske, "De-Risking Critical Mineral Supply Chains: The Role of Latin America," Center for Strategic and International Studies, April 11, 2024).

ment markets worldwide, even as the country continues to draw on U.S. gas and oil to supply domestic energy.[92]

Complete Delinking

Figure 7.7 illustrates a costs-and-benefits matrix for the United States and China under a complete delinking scenario. It reflects an extreme case, given the downstream effects on the global economy if the United States and China were to sever their decades-long economic relationship. For example, as the United States pulls away from providing oil and gas to China, the latter will be compelled to turn to less secure sources of the same fuels, threatening its economic and energy security.[93]

Delinking can create multiple benefits for the United States and its allies in the energy market. The first Trump administration terminated collaborations on energy technologies with China—such as the U.S.-China Cooperative on Advanced Fuel Cycle Research, the U.S.-China Ten-Year Framework for Cooperation on Energy and the Environment, and the U.S.-

FIGURE 7.7
Costs and Benefits of a Complete Delinking Scenario in U.S.-China Global Energy Cooperation

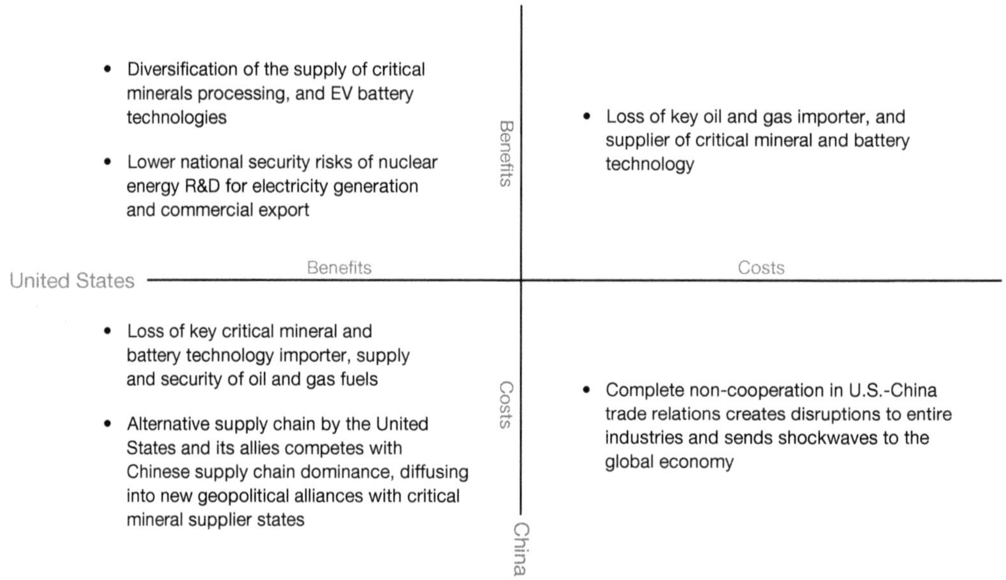

[92] U.S. exports of crude oil and other petroleum products to China increased from roughly 234 million barrels in 2022 to 357 million barrels in 2023, making the latter the second-highest importer of U.S. crude oil that year—although for China, the United States is a minor supplier of such resources compared with other trading partners (U.S. Energy Information Administration, "U.S. Exports to China of Crude Oil and Petroleum Products," dataset, May 31, 2024b).

[93] John Calabrese, "Beijing to Baghdad: China's Growing Role in Iraq's Energy Sector," Middle East Institute, June 7, 2023.

China Climate Change Working Group—to avoid national security risks regarding knowledge about nuclear energy technologies.[94] Similar policies can be adopted toward critical minerals processing and refining; diversifying the market can bring down the costs of battery storage technologies and manufacturing for clean energy fuels, thereby creating an alternative supply chain that competes with that of China. Delinking might be beneficial in the long run, but upfront costs and disruptions to entire industries that depend on U.S.-China trade can slow investments in clean energy installations.

Competition

Figure 7.8 illustrates a costs-and-benefits matrix for the United States and China under a competitive scenario. Unlike delinking, U.S-China trade competition can bolster solar PV, wind, and critical minerals processing markets by creating alternative supply chains and trade partnerships to bring prices down globally. However, competition can result in permanent restrictions on collaboration in R&D for energy technologies, which can ultimately hinder global decarbonization efforts as each bloc secures its intellectual property. Competition between the United States and China will also forge new geopolitical relationships as countries rich in REE shift sales from one country to the other as a result of the growth in refining and manufacturing capacity outside China.

FIGURE 7.8

Costs and Benefits of U.S.-China Global Energy Competition

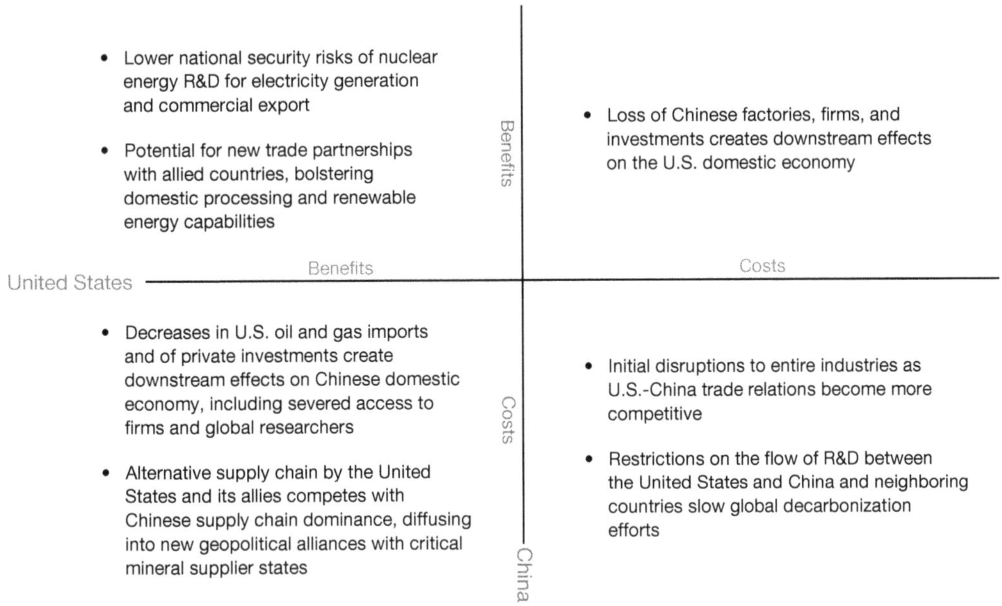

[94] Aimee Barnes, Fan Dai, and Angela Luh, "How the U.S. and China Could Renew Cooperation on Climate Change," Center on Global Energy Policy, Columbia School of International and Public Affairs, December 18, 2020.

For the United States and China, total competition can have deleterious effects on their domestic economies, like those in the complete delinking scenario. The loss of private investment between both countries can lead to downstream effects on domestic job growth and financial instability given the existing degree of interdependence. Whether these losses can be recouped in separate energy markets will depend on the rate at which R&D for battery storage, critical minerals processing, and nuclear energy generation can be applied in commercial electricity generation.

Policy Recommendations

The findings presented in this chapter and the scenario matrices of the potential costs and benefits of U.S-China strategic interactions in the energy market offer several approaches for U.S policymakers to consider as both countries take greater roles in worldwide decarbonization efforts. The following policy recommendations are actions that federal agencies may wish to consider preparing for long-term energy and environmental security strategies.

Promote Clean Energy Production for Domestic Consumption and Reallocate Fossil Fuels for Export

Private investments in clean energy technologies are at an all-time high, thanks to the IRA. In continuing to promote these policies to meet net-zero emissions goals and bring down the costs of clean energy generation, U.S. policymakers will also boost long-term domestic investments in clean energy production. However, this course of action does not ignore current and future fossil fuel developments; as with its oil and gas exports to China, the United States has an opportunity to authorize the export of bridge fuels, such as LNG, and secure geopolitical alliances with countries struggling to decarbonize.[95] The resulting energy mix in the United States will mimic those of hydrocarbon producers in the Persian Gulf, in which the domestic economy is on track for full decarbonization while fossil fuels continue to make up a sizable share of the country's exports.

[95] There is a precedent for U.S. policy on the authorization of fuel exports: In January 2024, the Biden administration announced a temporary pause on pending decisions on LNG exports to non-FTA countries so that the U.S. Department of Energy can update underlying analyses for authorizations, accounting for considerations such as potential energy cost increases for American consumers and manufacturers and the latest assessment of the impact of greenhouse gas emissions (White House, "Fact Sheet: Biden-Harris Administration Announces Temporary Pause on Pending Approvals of Liquefied Natural Gas Exports," January 26, 2024a; Emily P. Mallen, Christopher A. Treanor, Ryan Thompson, Kenneth J. Markowitz, Brian Arthur Pomper, Stephen S. Kho, Matt Kapinos, Sarah Sprinkle, and Jose Borjon, "Implications of US Department of Energy Decision to 'Pause' Authorizations of Liquefied Natural Gas Exports May Extend Beyond Delays to Pending Projects," Akin Gump Strauss Hauer & Feld LLP, January 31, 2024).

Build Up Critical Minerals Processing Capabilities in the United States and in Friendly Countries

China's dominant position in refining critical minerals has created a dependency for the United States. However, whether China remains the sole supplier in the coming decades or whether trade relations between the United States and China become more hostile depend on future geopolitical interactions. The United States can prepare for such supply chain fluctuations by building up its own processing capabilities and promoting trade agreements with REE-rich supply countries to (1) reduce dependency on Chinese imports in worst-case scenarios and (2) promote collaborations in building supply chains and hedging strategies in best-case scenarios. Although this comes at the expense of higher processing costs in the short term as the technology sector develops its minerals processing technologies, it can promote energy security and sustainability in the development of domestic clean energy technologies in the long run.

Support the Expansion of Domestic Nuclear Industries for Commercial Use

Commercial nuclear energy capacities, although in their infancy, can have long-lasting geopolitical implications, both within the U.S.-China trade dyad and beyond in terms of exports to other countries that have decided to invest in nuclear power plants. Supporting the expansion of domestic nuclear industries is the first step to meeting domestic needs for non-intermittent electricity and to break into the market currently dominated by Chinese firms.

Many Pathways Toward Energy Goals

These policy recommendations, findings, and scenario matrices suggest that there are many interlocking aspects to domestic energy and environmental security strategies and to the consequences of U.S.-China trade relations on enhancing or hindering both countries' goals for their domestic economies and for global clean energy. In taking these initial steps toward decarbonization of the domestic energy sector, and in remaining cognizant of BRI initiatives and the politics of critical mineral supply countries, the United States can be well poised to meet future challenges in the energy supply chain while retaining benefits from cooperation—where possible—with China.

Abbreviations

BRI	Belt and Road Initiative
EV	electric vehicle
FTA	free trade agreement
G7	Group of Seven
GDP	gross domestic product
IEA	International Energy Agency
IRA	Inflation Reduction Act
LNG	liquefied natural gas
MENA	Middle East and North Africa
PLA	People's Liberation Army
PV	photovoltaic
R&D	research and development
REE	rare earth elements

References

Allan, Bentley, Noah Gordon, and Cathy Wang, "Friendshoring Critical Minerals: What Could the U.S. and Its Partners Produce?" Carnegie Endowment for International Peace, May 3, 2023.

American Enterprise Institute and Heritage Foundation, China Global Investment Tracker, database, July 2023. As of June 14, 2024:
https://www.aei.org/china-global-investment-tracker

Autor, David H., David Dorn, and Gordon H. Hanson, "The China Syndrome: Local Labor Market Effects of Import Competition in the United States," *American Economic Review*, Vol. 103, No. 6, October 2013.

Barnes, Aimee, Fan Dai, and Angela Luh, "How the U.S. and China Could Renew Cooperation on Climate Change," Center on Global Energy Policy, Columbia School of International and Public Affairs, December 18, 2020.

Benson, Sally M., and Costa Samaras, "Parallel Processing the Path to Commercialization of Fusion Energy," Office of Science and Technology Policy, Executive Office of the President, June 3, 2022.

Benton, Jackie, "Rare Earth Elements: Texas Rare Earths Show Economic Potential for State," *Fiscal Notes*, Texas Comptroller's Office, November 2021.

Bettoli, Alberto, Florian Heineke, Nadine Janecke, Thomas Nyheim, Andreas Schlosser, Sophia Spitzer, Christian Staudt, Holder Klärner, Raffael Winter, and Jakub Zivansky, "Renewable-Energy Development in a Net-Zero World: Disrupted Supply Chains," McKinsey & Company, February 17, 2023.

"Big Oil to Attend U.S. House Climate Disinformation Hearing," Reuters, October 22, 2021.

Blackburne, Alex, "China's Increasingly Cheap Wind Turbines Could Open New Markets," S&P Global, September 26, 2022.

Blinken, Anthony J., "The Administration's Approach to the People's Republic of China," speech transcript, U.S. Department of State, May 26, 2022.

Bolton, Paul, *Imports of Fossil Fuels from Russia*, House of Commons Library, Research Briefing Number 9523, March 13, 2023.

Cahill, Ben, and Sophie Coste, "Subtle Shift in U.S. LNG Export Authorizations," Center for Strategic and International Studies, July 28, 2023.

Calabrese, John, "China Prioritizes Short-Term Energy Security: Implications for Sino-Middle East Relations," Middle East Institute, July 12, 2022.

Calabrese, John, "Beijing to Baghdad: China's Growing Role in Iraq's Energy Sector," Middle East Institute, June 7, 2023.

Carter, Bridget, and Gerald Nieder-Westermann, "China Begins Construction of Its First Underground Research Laboratory for High Level Waste Disposal," International Atomic Energy Agency, July 23, 2021.

Castillo, Rodrigo, and Caitlin Purdy, *China's Role in Supplying Critical Minerals for the Global Energy Transition: What Could the Future Hold?* Brookings Institution, July 2022.

China Power Project, "How Is China's Energy Footprint Changing?" Center for Strategic and International Studies, March 27, 2022.

"China Signs Paris Agreement on Climate Change," Xinhua, April 23, 2016.

"Chinese Mining Company Opens Lithium Processing Plant in Zimbabwe," Africanews, July 6, 2023.

Deese, Brian, "The New Climate Law Is Working. Clean Energy Investments Are Soaring," *New York Times*, May 30, 2023.

Del Negro, Marco, Julian Di Giovanni, and Keshav Dogra, "Is the Green Transition Inflationary?" Federal Reserve Bank of New York, No. 1053, revised December 2023.

Disavino, Scott, "US LNG Project Approvals on Track for Record New Volumes," Reuters, June 23, 2023.

Donnellon-May, Genevieve, "Powering China's Nuclear Ambitions," *The Diplomat*, September 20, 2022.

Duehren, Andrew, "U.S. and Japan Strike Deal on Minerals Used in Batteries for Electric Cars," *Wall Street Journal*, March 28, 2023.

Earth Observatory, "Mountain Pass Rare Earth Mine," National Aeronautics and Space Administration, December 25, 2022.

Edwards, Laura, "4 Things to Know About China's Climate Approach," Center for American Progress, September 30, 2021.

Executive Order 14008, "Tackling the Climate Crisis at Home and Abroad," Executive Office of the President, January 27, 2021.

Fairley, Peter, "Why Don't We Have More Nuclear Power?" *MIT Technology Review*, May 28, 2015.

Fan Anqi and Deng Xiaoci, "China Makes Breakthrough in High-Level Radioactive Waste Disposal Technique, Achieves Milestone in Nuclear Industry Devt," *Global Times*, September 12, 2021.

Fickling, David, "How China's Renewables Boom Is Fueling Its Coal Expansion," *Financial Review*, July 17, 2023.

Freeman, Duncan, "The Missing Link: China, Climate Change and National Security," Brussels Institute of Contemporary China Studies, January 2010.

Gil, Laura, "How China Has Become the World's Fastest Expanding Nuclear Power Producer," *IAEA Bulletin*, Vol. 58, No. 4, November 2017.

Gilbert, Natasha, and Gemma Conroy, "US Extends Science Pact with China: What It Means for Research," *Nature*, August 25, 2023.

"The Global Fight for Critical Minerals Is Costly and Damaging," *Nature*, July 19, 2023.

Graham, Niels, "China's Manufacturing Overcapacity Threatens Global Green Goods Trade," Atlantic Council, December 11, 2023.

Green, Jessica, Jennifer Hadden, Thomas Hale, and Paasha Mahdavi, "Transition, Hedge, or Resist? Understanding Political and Economic Behavior Toward Decarbonization in the Oil and Gas Industry," *Review of International Political Economy*, Vol. 29, No. 6, 2022.

Haenle, Paul, and Sam Bresnick, "Why U.S.-China Relations Are Locked in a Stalemate," Carnegie Endowment for International Peace, February 21, 2022.

Haidar, Quamrul, "Nuclear Fusion: Holy Grail of Energy" in Igor Girka, ed., *Nuclear Fusion: One Noble Goal and a Variety of Scientific and Technological Challenges*, Intech Open, 2019.

Hernandez-Roy, Christopher, Henry Ziemer, and Nathaniel Laske, "De-Risking Critical Mineral Supply Chains: The Role of Latin America," Center for Strategic and International Studies, April 11, 2024.

Hickman, Hannah, "What Happens to Nuclear Waste in the U.S.?" Nuclear Energy Institute, November 19, 2019.

Hui, Mary, "Oil and Gas Exports Are Complicating the US-China Relationship," *Quartz*, June 28, 2023.

IEA—*See* International Energy Agency.

International Energy Agency, "Energy Security," webpage, undated. As of July 25, 2023: https://www.iea.org/topics/energy-security

International Energy Agency, *The Role of Gas in Today's Energy Transitions*, July 2019.

International Energy Agency, *The Role of Critical Minerals in Clean Energy Transitions*, May 2021a.

International Energy Agency, *An Energy Sector Roadmap to Carbon Neutrality in China*, September 2021b.

International Energy Agency, "China Has a Clear Pathway to Build a More Sustainable, Secure and Inclusive Energy Future," press release, September 29, 2021c.

International Energy Agency, *Energy Technology Perspectives 2023*, January 2023a.

International Energy Agency, "Electrification," webpage, last updated July 11, 2023b. As of August 22, 2023:
https://www.iea.org/energy-system/electricity/electrification

International Energy Agency, *Critical Minerals Market Review 2023*, December 2023c.

International Energy Agency and Nuclear Energy Agency, *Nuclear Energy Technology Roadmap*, OECD Publishing, 2010.

Jaganathan, Jessica, and Chen Aizhu, "U.S. LNG Cargoes Heading to China After Beijing Awards Tax Waivers," Reuters, April 7, 2020.

Jones, Emily, "The US Is Getting Its First New Nuclear Reactor in 40 Years," Grist, June 6, 2023.

Khan, Yusuf, "Increasing Export Restrictions on Critical Minerals Threaten Energy Transition, OECD Says," *Wall Street Journal*, April 11, 2023.

Kim, Lami, "Nuclear Belt and Road: China's Nuclear Exports and Its Global Implications," in Abraham M. Denmark and Lucas Myers, eds., *Essays on the Rise of China and Its Implications*, Wilson Center, 2021.

Kreil, Erik, "United States Produces More Crude Oil Than Any Country, Ever," U.S. Energy Information Administration, March 11, 2024.

Kucik, Jeffrey, and Mark Kennedy, "Investment and Trade Agreements Essential to De-Risking Critical Minerals Supply Chains," Wilson Center, April 30, 2024.

Lanctot, Matt, "DOE Explains . . . Fusion Energy Science," webpage, U.S. Department of Energy, undated. As of August 21, 2023:
https://www.energy.gov/science/doe-explainsfusion-energy-science

Leppert, Rebecca, and Brian Kennedy, "Growing Share of Americans Favor More Nuclear Power," Pew Research Center, August 18, 2023.

Liedtke, Stephan, "China's Energy Investments in Europe: An Analysis of Policy Drivers and Approaches," *Energy Policy*, Vol. 101, February 2017.

Liu, Zongyuan Zoe, "How to Secure Critical Minerals for Clean Energy Without Alienating China," blog post, Council on Foreign Relations, May 25, 2023.

Lu, Christina, "The U.S. Strategic Minerals Situation Is Critical," *Foreign Policy*, June 30, 2023.

Ma, Ziyi, and Yu Ma, "What's After Coal? Accelerating China's Overseas Investment in Renewables," World Resources Institute, January 31, 2023.

Mallen, Emily P., Christopher A. Treanor, Ryan Thompson, Kenneth J. Markowitz, Brian Arthur Pomper, Stephen S. Kho, Matt Kapinos, Sarah Sprinkle, and Jose Borjon, "Implications of US Department of Energy Decision to 'Pause' Authorizations of Liquefied Natural Gas Exports May Extend Beyond Delays to Pending Projects," Akin Gump Strauss Hauer & Feld LLP, January 31, 2024.

McShane, Michael, "House Foreign Affairs Committee Unanimously Passes Rep. Titus's U.S.-China Science and Technology Oversight Bill," press release, Office of Congresswoman Dina Titus, March 21, 2024.

Mochizuki, Junko, and ZongXiang Zhang, *Environmental Security and Its Implications for China's Foreign Relations*, East-West Center, Working Paper No. 116, March 2011.

Motyka, Marlene, Jim Thomson, and Kate Hardin, *2023 Renewable Energy Industry Outlook*, Deloitte, 2023.

National Grid, "What Is Nuclear Energy (and Why Is It Considered a Clean Energy)?" webpage, last updated August 8, 2022. As of July 27, 2023:
https://www.nationalgrid.com/stories/energy-explained/what-nuclear-energy-and-why-it-considered-clean-energy

Northey, Hannah, "GAO: Death of Yucca Mountain Caused by Political Maneuvering," *New York Times*, May 10, 2011.

Nuclear Information Center, "Fission vs. Fusion—What's the Difference?" webpage, Duke Energy, May 27, 2021. As of August 20, 2023:
https://nuclear.duke-energy.com/2021/05/27/fission-vs-fusion-whats-the-difference-6843001

Nur, Audina, "Contemporary Amperex Technology (CATL) Investment in Indonesian Battery Megaproject to Be Completed in December," *Indonesia Business Post*, November 29, 2023.

Office of Nuclear Energy, "Bilateral Cooperation," webpage, U.S. Department of Energy, undated. As of July 26, 2023:
https://www.energy.gov/ne/bilateral-cooperation

Office of the Under Secretary of Defense for Acquisition and Sustainment and Office of the Deputy Assistant Secretary of Defense for Industrial Policy, *Assessing and Strengthening the Manufacturing and Defense Industrial Base and Supply Chain Resiliency of the United States*, U.S. Department of Defense, September 2018.

Outline of the People's Republic of China 14th Five-Year Plan for National Economic and Social Development and Long-Range Objectives for 2035 [中华人民共和国国民经济和社会发展第十四个五年规划和 2035 年远景目标纲要], March 12, 2021, trans. by Etcetera Language Group, Inc., ed. by Ben Murphy, Center for Security and Emerging Technology, May 12, 2021.

Rosen, Daniel, Matt Mingey, Camille Boullenois, and Laura Gormley, "China Pathfinder: Quarter 1 2024 Update," Atlantic Council, May 16, 2024.

Runde, Daniel F., and Austin Hardman, "Elevating the Role of Critical Minerals for Development and Security," Center for Strategic and International Studies, September 2023.

Scissors, Derek, *China's Global Investment Surges, Finally*, American Enterprise Institute, July 2023.

Sekera, June, and Neva Goodwin, "Why the Oil Industry's Pivot to Carbon Capture and Storage—While It Keeps On Drilling—Isn't a Climate Change Solution," *The Conversation*, November 23, 2021.

Shah, Jigar, "Transforming Clean Energy Financing and Supply Chains in the United States: LPO One Year After the IRA," U.S. Department of Energy, August 16, 2023.

Shepherd, Christian, "John Kerry Hails China's 'Incredible Job' on Renewables, Warns on Coal," *Washington Post*, July 17, 2023.

"Strengthening Saudi-China Ties: Major Announcement from Arab-China Business Conference," Zawya, June 13, 2023.

U.S. Department of Defense, "DoD to Build Project Pele Mobile Microreactor and Perform Demonstration at Idaho National Laboratory," press release, April 13, 2022.

U.S. Department of Energy, "What Are Critical Materials and Critical Minerals?" webpage, undated. As of December 10, 2023:
https://www.energy.gov/cmm/what-are-critical-materials-and-critical-minerals

U.S. Department of Energy, "The Global Nuclear Energy Partnership: Greater Energy Security in a Cleaner, Safer World," fact sheet, February 6, 2006.

U.S. Department of Energy, "3 Reasons Why Nuclear Is Clean and Sustainable," webpage, updated June 2022a. As of June 10, 2024:
https://www.energy.gov/ne/articles/3-reasons-why-nuclear-clean-and-sustainable

U.S. Department of Energy, "Biden-Harris Administration Announces $150 Million to Improve Nuclear Research and Development Infrastructure at Idaho National Laboratory," press release, October 25, 2022b.

U.S. Department of Energy, *Critical Minerals Assessment*, July 2023.

U.S. Department of State, *Environmental Security Threat Report*, October 2001.

U.S. Energy Information Administration, "Nuclear Explained: Nuclear Power Plants," webpage, last updated August 21, 2023a. As of August 22, 2023:
https://www.eia.gov/energyexplained/nuclear/nuclear-power-plants.php

U.S. Energy Information Administration, "International Energy Outlook 2023: Data Tables (2020–2050)," webpage, October 11, 2023b. As of June 11, 2024:
https://www.eia.gov/outlooks/ieo/data.php

U.S. Energy Information Administration, "Natural Gas Monthly," webpage, updated May 31, 2024a. As of June 12, 2024:
https://www.eia.gov/naturalgas/monthly

U.S. Energy Information Administration, "U.S. Exports to China of Crude Oil and Petroleum Products," dataset, May 31, 2024b. As of June 14, 2024:
https://www.eia.gov/dnav/pet/hist/LeafHandler.ashx?n=pet&s=mttexch1&f=a

U.S. Energy Information Administration, "U.S. Liquefied Natural Gas Exports to China," webpage, last updated May 31, 2024c. As of June 12, 2024:
https://www.eia.gov/dnav/ng/hist/ngm_epg0_eng_nus-nch_mmcfm.htm

U.S. Environmental Protection Agency, "Summary of Inflation Reduction Act Provisions Related to Renewable Energy," webpage, last updated October 25, 2023. As of December 10, 2023:
https://www.epa.gov/green-power-markets/
summary-inflation-reduction-act-provisions-related-renewable-energy

"The U.S. Is Divided over Whether Nuclear Power Is Part of the Green Energy Future," Associated Press, January 18, 2022.

U.S. Nuclear Regulatory Commission, *Yucca Mountain Review Plan: Final Report*, NUREG-1804, rev. 2, July 2003.

Wang, Christoph Nedophil, *China Belt and Road Initiative (BRI) Investment Report 2023*, Griffith Asia Institute, Griffith University and Green Finance and Development Center, FISF Fudan University, February 2024.

Wasser, Becca, Howard J. Shatz, John J. Drennan, Andrew Scobell, Brian G. Carlson, and Yvonne K. Crane, *Crossroads of Competition: China, Russia, and the United States in the Middle East*, RAND Corporation, RR-A325-1, 2022. As of December 10, 2023:
https://www.rand.org/pubs/research_reports/RRA325-1.html

White House, "President Biden's Historic Climate Agenda," webpage, undated. As of July 17, 2023:
https://www.whitehouse.gov/climate

White House, *Building Resilient Supply Chains, Revitalizing American Manufacturing, and Fostering Broad-Based Growth: 100-Day Reviews Under Executive Order 14017*, June 2021.

White House, "Fact Sheet: Developing a Bold Vision for Commercial Fusion Energy," March 15, 2022.

White House, *Building a Clean Energy Economy: A Guidebook to the Inflation Reduction Act's Investments in Clean Energy and Climate Action*, version 2, January 2023.

White House, "Fact Sheet: Biden-Harris Administration Announces Temporary Pause on Pending Approvals of Liquefied Natural Gas Exports," January 26, 2024a.

White House, "Investing in Places Historically Left Behind: Foreign Direct Investment in U.S. Clean Energy Manufacturing," June 6, 2024b.

World Bank, "China's Transition to a Low-Carbon Economy and Climate Resilience Needs Shifts in Resources and Technologies," press release, October 12, 2022.

World Nuclear Association, *Comparison of Lifecycle Greenhouse Gas Emissions of Various Electricity Generation Sources*, July 2011.

World Nuclear Association, "International Framework for Nuclear Energy Cooperation," updated November 7, 2016.

World Nuclear Association, "U.S. Nuclear Power Policy," webpage, updated February 2023a. As of October 15, 2024:
https://world-nuclear.org/information-library/country-profiles/countries-t-z/usa-nuclear-power-policy.aspx

World Nuclear Association, "China's Nuclear Fuel Cycle," webpage, updated July 2023b. As of August 18, 2023:
https://world-nuclear.org/information-library/country-profiles/countries-a-f/china-nuclear-fuel-cycle.aspx

World Nuclear Association, "Nuclear Power in the USA," webpage, updated August 2023c. As of August 23, 2023:
https://world-nuclear.org/information-library/country-profiles/countries-t-z/usa-nuclear-power.aspx

World Nuclear Association, "Supply of Uranium," webpage, updated August 2023d. As of September 12, 2023:
https://world-nuclear.org/information-library/nuclear-fuel-cycle/uranium-resources/supply-of-uranium.aspx

World Nuclear Association, "U.S. Operating Nuclear Reactors: Nuclear Power in the USA Appendix 1," webpage, updated August 2023e. As of August 28, 2023:
https://world-nuclear.org/information-library/country-profiles/countries-t-z/appendices/nuclear-power-in-the-usa-appendix-1-us-operating-n.aspx

Zaretskaya, Victoria, "Europe Was the Main Destination for U.S. LNG Exports in 2022," U.S. Energy Information Administration, March 22, 2023.

Zaretskaya, Victoria, "The United States Was the World's Largest Liquefied Natural Gas Exporter in 2023," U.S. Energy Information Administration, April 1, 2024.

Zhou Feng, Peng Linan, and Li Jie, "China's 14th Five-Year Plans on Renewable Energy Development and Modern Energy Development," Energy Foundation China, September 5, 2022.

Zhou, Lihuan, Ziyi Ma, Shuang Liu, Xinyue Ma, Kevin Acker, Margaret Myers, Deborah Brautigam, and Kevin Gallagher, China Overseas Finance Inventory Database, World Resources Institute, updated June 30, 2023. As of August 18, 2023:
https://datasets.wri.org/dataset/cofi

Zhou, Oceana, and Sambit Mohanty, "China's Crude Imports from Russia Hits Record as Xi, Putin Eye Stronger Energy Ties," S&P Global, March 20, 2023.

CHAPTER 8

What *Is* a Chinese Privately Owned Enterprise? Implications for the United States in a Strategic Competition

Steven W. Popper

Overview

If the United States is to ensure that its economy meets the nation's needs under conditions of coupled, strategic competition, it needs to better understand the basis of that competition and the character of its competitors. Assumptions about how Chinese privately owned enterprises (POEs) will conduct business and operate as economic entities may be misplaced if such firms are categorically regarded as operating according to the same rules of thumb, incentive structures, and practices as their Western counterparts. They may well not. This, in turn, makes their behavior more uncertain; left unexamined, these differences might result in unexpected effects on strategic competition, supply chain security, industrial structure, intellectual property ownership, and regulatory and trade matters.

In this chapter, I lay out the principal issues regarding the forms and nature of POEs in China to determine how they differ from those in advanced market economies. The issue that most impairs the ability to perceive what constitutes a Chinese POE is the deeply rooted concept that economic ownership equates to control over decisions. A first pass through available evidence suggests that differences from Western firms do, in fact, exist. There are three factors that may make China a special case and the Chinese POE an appropriate focus of greater attention and scrutiny. The first is the intentionality and strategy that underlies senior decisionmaking in China and the resultant influence on firm behavior. The second is the omnipresence and univalent political authority of the Chinese Communist Party and the means by which it blurs the line demarcating where the party-state ends and the firm begins. The third is the sheer scale of resources available to China as it implements policy.

In viewing the Chinese POE, external governments and planners implicitly presume a familiar organizational type understood to be the analogue to a POE in an advanced market economy. This analogy is probably less well-grounded than it should or could be. It is worth taking the trouble to improve such understanding.

The purpose of this chapter is to raise to the level of active consideration the following simple question: *What is a Chinese privately owned enterprise* (POE)?

China has moved away from a system in which trade, manufacturing, and service industries were constituted almost entirely by state-owned enterprises (SOEs). Many of China's present international champions are now POEs, such as Huawei, Alibaba, Baidu, and Tencent (to name only the most generally familiar). Regulatory and policy bodies in the United States and elsewhere are wary of such large firms' Chinese origin but largely relegate them to the same familiar business and legal categories as occupied by non-Chinese private firms. But in what ways does the Chinese POE resemble its developed economy analogues, and in what ways does it differ? If differences exist, do we need to recognize them?

If the United States is to ensure that its economy meets the nation's needs under conditions of coupled, strategic competition, it needs to better understand the basis of that competition and the character of its competitors. Assumptions about how Chinese POEs will grow, target markets, develop goods and services, follow market signals, allocate investments, develop innovative goods and services, acquire capital and intellectual property (IP) assets, engage employees, and operate as economic entities may be misplaced if they are categorically regarded as operating according to the same rules of thumb, incentive structures, and accounting and legal practices as their Western counterparts. They may well not. This, in turn, makes their behavior more uncertain. In particular, Chinese POEs may not be fully at liberty to take business decisions independently of the geostrategic implications of their actions. As suppliers of goods and services to the United States, the default assumption of similarity should be queried and its implications examined. Left unexamined, there might be unexpected effects on strategic competition, supply chain security, industrial structure, and IP ownership, as well as regulatory and trade matters.

In this chapter, I lay out the principal issues regarding the forms and nature of POEs in China to determine how they differ from those found in the countries of the Organisation for Economic Cooperation and Development (OECD), the organization whose members are generally the advanced Western, market-based economies. I conjecture where these differences might affect U.S. interests in realms varying from strategic competition to innovation, trade, and the U.S. industrial base. I make a case for delving more deeply into considering the following:

- How do POEs differ from private firms in OECD member states?
- What are the important consequences for firm behavior, innovation, the effects on U.S. domestic industrial structure, and national security that arise from these differences?
- How may the U.S. partner nations and international agencies ensure the facilitation of trade and realize benefits from cooperation with China while measuring and monitoring effects and applying appropriate regulatory and policy tools?

Laying out and exploring these questions is a first step toward acquiring the knowledge and tools necessary to support recommendations for the U.S. government and international agencies. The purpose of this chapter is not to resolve these questions; its value is in raising them.

A Changed Global Business Environment

In a recent meeting between RAND economic analysts and Chinese university-based political economists, the Chinese delegation asked its American counterparts to explain the U.S. purpose and intended goals in pursuing an economic strategic competition with China. The U.S. interlocutors were mildly taken aback. The question is not often posed in these terms. That such a framing was not readily familiar to the RAND attendees should not come as a surprise. A more common rendering of the state of mind of most U.S. agencies, actors, and analysts is that they have only belatedly come to realize that they do, in fact, find themselves well into a strategic competition with the People's Republic of China (PRC) across the world's markets. Their stance appears generally more one of reactive scrambling than of active calculation.

There are several reasons for this. A widely held, if implicit, presumption since China's admission to the World Trade Organization (WTO) was that aspects of Chinese state behavior, as well as those of its myriad economic units—and certainly China's rapidly growing number of POEs—would increasingly come to resemble those of other WTO signatories, at least in the economic dimension.[1] Clearly, China would be able to tap the immense latent power of its gigantic domestic market. But at the same time, foreign firms would be granted increasing access to this market, thus enhancing their own sources for growth and global market penetration.

This motive force for change seemed inescapable for a China that was coming to embrace the market mechanism. From the earliest days of instruction in economic studies, observers from the United States and other market economies outside the PRC were taught that economic decisionmaking and activities are separate from political or institutional concerns. If this lesson was not taught directly, it nevertheless could be inferred indirectly by virtue of the absence of political and institutional considerations from core curricula in neoclassical economics. And, of course, the Cold War with the Soviet Union and its partners was successfully concluded in the developed West's favor. The liberal democratic order and its handmaiden, the Washington Consensus, seemed ascendant. This could only be ever more the case as time went on.

That was then.

But this is now.

1 "Full Text of Clinton's Speech on China Trade Bill," *New York Times*, March 9, 2000.

Coercive forfeiture and covert theft of foreign IP continues and has contributed to Chinese commercial success, both foreign and domestic.[2] In important respects, a variety of local rules, both formal and informal, meant that Chinese markets did not open to foreign firms in the manner that many had expected. Subventions in various guises, whether from the national or regional governments, have allowed Chinese firms to gain substantial dominance in several key global markets.[3] This ability to grab large market shares has affected supply and technology dominance by these firms in such sectors as fifth generation (5G) communications, solar energy systems, and electrical battery supply. This would be sufficient to raise concern. But a recently more aggressive "wolf warrior" approach to global geopolitics,[4] combined with an increasingly central Chinese Communist Party (CCP) desire to see military-civil fusion take hold and a greater and more active involvement by private-sector players in enhancing the capabilities of the People's Liberation Army (PLA),[5] sow confusion in forums more accustomed to thinking of economic and political and national security affairs being divided into two spheres of activities that are only tangentially connected. The good business for Western firms of being able to sell high-end semiconductors and advanced marine and aerial engines into the lucrative Chinese market has come, in retrospect, to be seen possibly less as an opportunity for the canny and more as a trap for the unwary.

The apparent disparity between the presumptions of 30 years ago around China's rise to economic prominence and the realities of today require review.[6] The frame of reference within which this rise is examined should be tuned to better accord with both emerging realities and fundamental U.S. and U.S.-partner interests if policy, both active and reactive, is to serve those interests well. To achieve this outcome will require changing the reflexive posture toward actors and activities that might be at greater disparity with "business as usual" than was once supposed.

Doing so should not be perceived as "China bashing." The intended realization is not one of viewing China as an implacable foe nor its rise as necessarily a zero-sum game played at others' expense. Indeed, the world benefits from accommodating such a rapid ascension into

---

[2] For example, theft of Japanese high-speed train designs by its joint venture partner and wind turbine designs from a U.S. company played a role in launching these industries in China (Carlos Tejada, "Beg, Borrow or Steal: How Trump Says China Takes Technology," *New York Times*, March 22, 2018; Keith Bradsher, "How China Obtains American Trade Secrets," *New York Times*, January 15, 2020).

[3] At the time of this writing in September 2023, the European Union (EU) has just announced a probe into how direct state support and other practices affect the pricing on the European market of electric vehicles manufactured in China (Philip Blenkinsop, "EU to Investigate 'Flood' of Chinese Electric Cars, Weigh Tariffs," Reuters, September 13, 2023).

[4] Peter Martin, "Understanding Chinese 'Wolf Warrior Diplomacy,'" transcript of interview conducted by Joanna Nawrotkiewicz, National Bureau of Asian Research, October 22, 2021.

[5] Elsa B. Kania and Lorand Laskai, *Myths and Realities of China's Military-Civil Fusion Strategy*, Center for a New American Security, January 2021.

[6] A recent survey of this shift in U.S. policy opinion can be found in Bob Davis, "Broken Engagement," *The Wire: China*, July 14, 2024.

the ranks of the leading economic powers. The raising from poverty of the greatest part of the Chinese population within a generation is an achievement of truly historical importance. To have this rise be accepted so peacefully and comparatively seamlessly into the global economic order is itself an achievement. Scientific discovery or technology development, for example, that may now be fostered in China will either be of direct benefit to many—owing to the limited ability to fully appropriate all the advantage that such knowledge conveys; hence the public support for research and development (R&D) in almost all countries—or indirectly useful when embodied in goods and services available for purchase.

But this evolution might not necessarily continue to be seamless. The magnitude of China's rise and development could all too easily lead to misjudgments, misgivings, and misunderstandings profound enough to raise points of confrontation or even risk potential conflagration. Therefore, there is need for all parties to take the trouble to gain an understanding of the other's constraints, conceptions, interests, and intentions.

A Question of Perspective

The global economic order is as much framed around a set of norms as it is by formal regulatory or governance bodies. These norms arose over time but largely have rested on assumptions about the nature of the actors—such as firms, governments, and banks—from whose interactions they evolved. The norms are so deeply ingrained that many of these assumptions have become invisible. The easy presumption, in the absence of evidence to the contrary, is that a government is a government, a bank a bank, and a firm a firm wherever it might be domiciled.

In particular, there is an implicit assumption in the minds of governments, regulators, and competing firms that business decisions by publicly held private firms (those that are listed on equity markets) will be made primarily on the basis of business considerations and shareholder interests—at least in the ideal. Of course, political and public considerations may enter in, but these, too, can be seen as being part of the balance made when assuring the bottom line over the long as well as the short term. Countries may seek to support their national champions, such as Japan's Ministry of International Trade and Industry did in the 1970s or several European states collaborated in doing by forming Airbus.[7] But such instances have been more exceptional than common, are of relatively small scale and highly focused, and tend to characterize early-stage behavior as a market-entry strategy rather than a standard practice.

There are several reasons to hypothesize that the generally presumed separation of the economic from the political, in retrospect, may have been less true for China in the past and even less so along its current trajectory. The establishment, capitalization, and regulation of firms; activities geared toward advancing their placement in global markets; and framing

[7] Dylan Gerstel and Matthew P. Goodman, *From Industrial Policy to Innovation Strategy: Lessons from Japan, Europe, and the United States*, Center for Strategic and International Studies, September 2020.

their purposes and forms has seen a fusion of strategic intentions with business activity as a matter of policy. This is neither mysterious nor sinister. China naturally viewed itself as a late developer and so as being vulnerable in several dimensions. China has needed to overcome several disadvantages: from rising above poverty to escaping the middle-income trap; from industrializing to becoming the world's workshop; from mastering *extensive* growth (growth from additions of labor and capital) by using, above all, its prodigious labor resources to breaking into the realm of *intensive* growth characterized by innovation and productivity gains. But given the nature of China's domestic political system and the recent aspirations of its political elites to achieve greater geopolitical weight externally, this orientation has carried into the present. Indeed, with the consolidation of power by CCP General Secretary and President of China Xi Jinping, the tangency of interests has fused into doctrine.

Specific outcomes resulting from this marriage of economic development with geopolitical strategic purpose (from Huawei's prospective 5G market dominance to the preponderance of Chinese presence in the supply chains for batteries, solar panels, critical metals, and other raw materials) have now brought this tangency into the open. There are two principal reasons why these trends were difficult to perceive during their gestation. These reasons both involve unquestioned prior assumptions about the appropriate frame of reference to use in translating perceptions into accurate analyses of trends and events that were not readily perceived heretofore.

The first of these has been alluded to above. The neoclassical economic perspective that prevails in most Western countries has proven to be a powerful tool since the start of the 20th century. Yet, it possesses some inherent blind spots. I have already discussed its tendency to compartmentalize the observation of strictly economic outcomes some distance away from the political consequences that may also accrue to actors because of those outcomes. The accumulation of wealth, to use a simple example, translates not infrequently into greater political heft.[8] But it is only rarely that any resulting recursive effect on the economic system's structure as a consequence of that increased power is accounted for.

The neoclassical lens has most routinely been engaged in the evaluation of comparative statics. *Comparative statics* is the comparison of two economic equilibria characteristic of the competitive, prospectively steady-state market conditions that are in place prior to and then following some supply or demand shock or the implementation of regulatory, fiscal, or other market-affecting policy. The attention paid to the two bookending equilibria contrasts with the relatively less scrutiny placed on characterizing the dynamic, time-step pathway traversing the two equilibrium states. Indeed, the equilibrium focus reduces inquiry into how the nature of potentially alternative dynamic pathways themselves might well determine the nature of the post-shock equilibrium that eventuates. In this way, the near-Newtonian tools

[8] Recent antitrust practice within the U.S. government has mostly focused on short-term consumer benefits. If costs decrease with no diminution of service or product quality, the growth of monopoly power in markets has generally been viewed as incurring less societal cost than had been the view of earlier generations of regulators in the trust-busting Progressive era or that of the New Deal.

of economic analysis on which policy planners and the officials to whom they report often rely are not tuned to observe the dynamics of change that might affect equilibrium end states (if equilibrium ever truly exists for more than a fleeting moment). Dynamic pathways involving complex patterns of influence among economic and non-economic variables are not well accounted for.

The second grand assumption was the convenient pigeonholing of Chinese institutional forms into categories long familiar in Western economies. The privately held corporation is a familiar form whose modern roots date back at least to medieval Italy. Therefore, a privately owned and operated firm originating in China is for practical purposes conceived of as residing in the same intellectual box as a German *aktiengesellschaft*, French *société anonyme*, or U.S. corporation ("Inc."). Behaviors by Chinese firms that may not have been completely explicable in market terms, associations with government (both regulatory and financial) that go beyond what is common with Western-economy counterparts, and apparent consonance (if not direct coordination) of POE actions with large-scale national leadership objectives have come as a latter-day surprise.

This is an issue that is brought home most forcefully by the competition with China but also goes beyond China. We may need to consider the accuracy and effectiveness of the perspective being applied to the problem of how to operate under—and frame policies appropriate to—conditions of strategic competition. It is in this spirit that the question is posed: "What is a Chinese POE?" Although important in itself, the question can also serve as a single focal point around which larger questions can be framed regarding what systemic differences exist between the Chinese economy and those more typical of the developed West. This is a necessary precursor to then asking what stance U.S. regulatory, trade, investment and other policies should take for the purpose of achieving national goals within a geopolitically strategic competitive environment.

The Nature of the Privately Owned Firm

If equating Chinese POEs implicitly with Western-style private corporations might be in error, why does the mistake arise? A partial explanation is that people have grown unused to the idea of different economic systems. The apparent triumph at the end of the Cold War of the liberal economic order—as exemplified by the general understanding of the term *Washington Consensus*—has led to a decreased sensitivity to the real differences that exist across economies. Even the market systems of, for example, the United States, France, Japan, South Korea, and Germany differ noticeably from each other in several aspects. But when it comes to the nature of privately held or publicly traded firms, such differences are relatively small. It is convenient to treat them as being largely equivalent for most purposes.

The differences in economic institutions and processes across systems may be rooted in fundamentally different simple models. In the ideal *command* economy, an omniscient central planner determines the allocation of resources that will lead to production of outputs in accord with the objectives of the political leadership.[9] In the ideal *market* economy, the butcher, the baker, the candlestick maker, the grower of grain, and their myriad anonymous peers make atomized individual decisions by observing or anticipating price signals. Of course, neither ideal ever existed as anything other than pure conceptions. The economy of the Soviet Union for most of its existence had numerous market elements, particularly in the allocation of labor, while all market economies have many major price makers in addition to the price-taking small producers and consumers. All economic systems have examples of both markets and hierarchies.[10] But at the level of policy discourse, the simple ideal models hold large sway.

I advance the hypothesis that the ideal model of the Chinese economy is neither that of command nor market; rather, it is that of a **connected** *guan xi* economy.[11] This is not entirely unfamiliar. France in the 1950s through 1970s produced *indicative* national plans.[12] These plans were not based on principles of command but rather were predicated on the presumed value of providing more explicit (as opposed to indirectly market-derived) general information on sectoral intentions and the sense of government policy direction to mostly independent (but also some important state-owned) producers. Japan had similar intentions during the same period—as did other countries, such as India—to engage in some degree of indicative planning.[13] Although there are echoes of the same approach to national direction in China today, two elements would appear to take the system beyond that of an indicative planned economy to that of a connected economy.

The first distinguishing factor is that such an economic system as that of the PRC, which has made a transition from a preponderant reliance on formal command signals to a high reliance on signals coming from markets, will likely contain more than just vestiges of the earlier system, especially when it comes to the informal institutions and interactions that also are features of any economic system. The second is that, unlike France, Japan, or India in the mid-20th century, China's connected economy sits within a system of unipolar domestic

---

9 Gregory Grossman, "Notes for a Theory of the Command Economy," *Soviet Studies*, Vol. 15, No. 2, 1963.

10 Oliver E. Williamson, *Markets and Hierarchies: Analysis and Antitrust Implications: A Study in the Economics of Internal Organization*, Free Press, 1975.

11 This term is often translated as *relationship*, but it has a richer context. *Guan xi* can describe mutually beneficial business or private connections as well as connote a network of reciprocal obligations of long standing. At times in the West, it is presented as a mysterious, inscrutable concept sufficient to explain the business and politics of China in a manner that smacks of Orientalism. But the long-standing historical associations of guan xi that reach into the imperial past and continue in the interstices between economic and political actors and institutions in present-day China make it an apt way of characterizing a connected economy lying between command and market.

12 Charles P. Kindleberger, "French Planning," in Max F. Milikan, ed., *National Economic Planning*, National Bureau of Economic Research, 1967.

13 Kazuo Sato, "Indicative Planning in Japan," *Journal of Comparative Economics*, Vol. 14, No. 4, December 1990; Bela Balassa, "Indicative Planning in Developing Countries," *Journal of Comparative Economics*, Vol. 14. No. 4, December 1990.

political power. The government retains the ability to impinge directly or indirectly, inflict punishments or grant rewards both formally and informally, and operate with no judicial check on its powers.

Both effects have been strongly in play during the period of Xi's dominance and its continuation. Not only is a power monopoly present in today's PRC in a way unmatched by other practitioners of indicative planning (Congress Party–led India could best be described as mostly oligarchic in character, and even Prime Minister Narendra Modi's present-day India still has a very long way to go in coming even close to the exclusive power of the CCP), but Xi has directed a development pathway built on mechanisms of economic direction that conflict on several levels from the institutions of Western economic producers.

SOEs remain in the Chinese economic system and have even seen a revival of the ideological and policy favor previously shown to them by the highest party levels in earlier periods of China's development.[14] There is a literature on the ownership and governance structures of SOEs and the changes in both over time. Understandably, relatively few of the studies stem from the most recent years of the Xi era, during which much CCP party work has been devoted to SOEs.[15] A general conclusion drawn by Beck and Brødsgaard is that, whereas in the past there may have been two parallel structures of SOE corporate governance and CCP personnel management, in the Xi era, it is possible to perceive the creation of a hybrid model that brings "the Party out of the shadows."[16]

It is less common to find similar discussions of Chinese POEs. During the 20 years prior to Xi's ascendant control in 2013, there was a considerable push even in the state-owned sector to look toward Western norms and "best practices" for guidance on enterprise forms, structures, and process.[17] The presumption that POEs would adopt similar approaches is understandable. Indeed, that is precisely what they did. Therefore, the relative scarcity of work on POEs similar to that performed by analysts looking at SOEs is not surprising.

Despite the apparent similarities of POEs to Western firms, however, there may well be dissimilarities that have important implications. The literature on SOEs can provide indications of where such dissimilarities might be found. This is ever more the case because it is clear from senior CCP statements that there is a growing desire to bring POEs more

---

14 Daisuke Wakabayashi, Chang Che, and Claire Fu, "In Xi's China, the Business of Business Is State-Controlled," *New York Times*, October 17, 2022.

15 Among these studies are Kasper Ingerman Beck and Kjeld Erik Brødsgaard, "Corporate Governance with Chinese Characteristics: Party Organization in State-Owned Enterprises," *China Quarterly*, Vol. 250, June 2022; Zhang Jide and Liu Suhan, "The Select of Strategic Investor from the Perspective of China Unicom's Mixed Ownership Reform" ["从中国联通混合所有制改革看战略投资者的选择"], *Accounting Research* [会计研究], Vol. 7, 2018; and Wendy Leutert, "Firm Control: Governing the State-Owned Economy Under Xi Jinping," *China Perspectives*, Nos. 1–2, 2018.

16 Beck and Brødsgaard, 2022, p. 490.

17 Henry Paulson's personal chronicle of those years provides fascinating insights into how this process proceeded at all levels of Chinese policy and business thought. See especially Chapter 17. Henry M. Paulson, Jr., *Dealing with China: An Insider Unmasks the New Economic Superpower*, Twelve, 2016.

directly under the party's influence despite the differences in ownership regimes.[18] Many of the mechanisms formally within SOEs do not necessarily exist in POEs (although there may be more direct influence found in POEs that are publicly listed or in other mixed ownership companies that themselves have a large measure of SOE ownership), but there are many indications emanating from the CCP in recent years that there is interest in finding other means to make certain that such enterprises are paying heed to the lines of public interest outlined by the party or are conforming in both form and action to the ideal of "socialism with Chinese characteristics."[19]

To see where this may make a difference in incentives, operations, and business decisions, it is necessary to take a more detailed look both inside the POE and at how it interacts with other relevant bodies. There are several explanations for why firms exist and what roles they play. One of the oldest is that a firm is an institution for reducing transaction costs that would otherwise be incurred through market-based activity. A firm is a willing association, defined by "incomplete" employment contracts that substitute for what would otherwise be myriad complete contracts, and is a supplier to itself for a variety of goods and services.[20] In fact, an independent firm in a market economy is itself a microcosmic hierarchy in many respects.[21]

Firms as small-level decisionmakers within markets have their actions affected by market failures. But as hierarchies, there is also potential for organizational failures within firms. Oliver Williamson posited that, beyond reduced transactions costs, firms can deal with uncertainty or complexity in an adaptive fashion, develop an internal language that is common to those who share the interests of the firm, and promote convergent expectations. They can also more easily audit the performance of subgroups to ensure that opportunism does not affect actions and can settle disputes when they do arise.[22] Information impactedness (uncertainty combined with asymmetric possession of information); in the presence of opportunism, bounded rationality (the fact that economic actors and managers are not omniscient);[23] and small-number conditions, however, also favor the shift to hierarchy (firm) over market.[24] As Williamson explains,

> In principle, the adjustment process [to a new equilibrium based on a common set of expectations] could be shortened by having one of the autonomous parties to the exchange temporarily serve as the decision maker for all: he would declare who is to adapt and how.

---

[18] Wakabayashi, Che, and Fu, 2022.

[19] Scott Livingston, *The Chinese Communist Party Targets the Private Sector*, Center for Strategic and International Studies, October 8, 2020.

[20] Ronald H. Coase, "The Nature of the Firm," *Economica*, Vol. 4, No. 16, November 1937.

[21] James G. March and Herbert A. Simon, *Organizations*, 2nd ed., Wiley-Blackwell, 1993.

[22] Williamson, 1975, pp. 25, 29.

[23] Jonathan Bendor, "Bounded Rationality," in Neil J. Smelser and Paul B. Baltes, eds., *International Encyclopedia of Social & Behavioral Sciences*, Pergamon, 2001.

[24] Williamson, 1975, p. 33.

> The risk of giving such an assignment to an autonomous party is that he will refer to his private gains rather than to a collective calculus in making a recommendation. To the extent that internal organization mitigates such opportunistic behavior, without incurring offsetting costs, a shift from market to hierarchy will promote efficient adaptation.[25]

Williamson considers firm formation, organization, and behavior within a market-based system operating in the absence of a uniquely—and exclusively—authoritative political actor. Such an actor, similarly confronted by issues of limited information and the near certainty of private firm managers privileging private gains over serving a public purpose, will certainly wish to remove uncertainty by ensuring that a corrective in the form of formal or informal lines of influence between the public policy authorities and the POE actor will be present. Although the formal channels might be less well-defined than is the case in an SOE for which a state entity is the principal owner, the incentive for the party-state to exert informal control might be all that much greater in the case of the POE because of the differential in information possessed by its managers compared with that held by the party in its self-appointed role as guardian of the public interest. The traditions and legal basis on which the PRC is predicated, particularly that of party primacy, would raise less difficulty than elsewhere for public officials to ascribe greater weight to the public good than the private benefit of firm owners.

A Yardstick for Measuring Differences

Before moving from theory to present realities, it is useful to lay out where differences between Chinese POEs and their non-Chinese counterparts might lie. Doing so is also to lay out a substantial enterprise of empirical research. The scope of this chapter is insufficient to treat all aspects of this discussion. Instead, I will continue with a brief presentation of several findings that appear in the literature. The intent is to substantiate the case for further analysis.

The factor that most impairs the ability to perceive what constitutes a POE is the deeply rooted concept that economic ownership equates to control over decisions. There are several types of control, ranging from agency over the operations of daily production to making longer-term decisions regarding designs, products, data, and algorithms. But control also includes having agency over more-strategic decisions regarding corporate finance, partnerships, and alliances; exerting influence; and preparing for and anticipating change.

Of course, even in the world outside China, the connection between ownership and control over decisions has its limitations. Conflicts of interest between owners (perhaps company shareholders) and their agents (a firm's senior managers) are well known. Regulatory policies and legislative actions may limit the range of uses to which owners may apply their assets. But a controlling interest in a publicly traded or privately owned firm generally holds deci-

[25] Williamson, 1975, p. 26.

sive sway in determining the strategies and activities of the firm. In China, this calculation becomes much more difficult to track or even to perceive.

We can look across two categories of potential difference between Chinese POEs and private firms in the OECD. The first set relates to the structure of the firm (roughly its *genotype* in biological terms) and its relation to the system that surrounds it. In this perspective, a preliminary list of sources of difference might include the following:

1. firm organization, decision processes, and ownership structure
2. control over management decisions
   a. *de jure* control—limited but more formalized, explicit (firm management, labor unions, board membership, internal party organs)
   b. *de facto* control (external local, regional, national party organs)
3. the nature and setting of managerial incentives
4. limitations on the sphere of managerial control.

There is a similar list of prospective differences in the observed behavior of a Chinese POE (its *phenotype* to continue the biological analogy). A preliminary list of possible sources of observable differences in firm actions might include the firm's

1. market behavior
2. relationship to the PRC and CCP
3. relationships to potential business partners
4. relationships to non-PRC state actors.

A first pass through the available evidence suggests that points of difference do, in fact, exist. I briefly treat a few of these topics in the following sections.

Organization and Structure

Party Organizations

Intra-firm CCP organizations (cells or units) are distinct from company trade unions. Their recent increase may be an indicator of the CCP's institutional expansion of its purview to include private businesses and even foreign firms.[26] As of 2018, the party reported that 1.88 million firms not included on the roster of SOEs had established party cells and accounted for over 73 percent of all nonstate firms.[27] In 2018, the securities regulator set rules for mandatory party units in firms listed on domestic exchanges "and required companies to

26 Margaret M. Pearson, Meg Rithmire, and Kellee S. Tsai, *The State and Capitalism in China*, Cambridge University Press, 2023, p. 23.

27 Organization Department of the CPC Central Committee [中共中央组织部], "2017 Inner-Party Statistical Bulletin of the Communist Party of China," ["2017年中国共产党党内统计公报"], Xinhua, June 30, 2018.

provide the 'necessary conditions'" for activities in support of or in response to CCP priorities and directives to occur.[28]

In 2020, the CCP called for an increase in party ideological work and influence in the private sector.[29] In fact, the party favors having its organizations within POEs (and SOEs as well) as a way to push back on Western ways of management and ideology within firms.[30] This in itself provides a strong indicator of a difference in POE structure from non-Chinese private firms, the very intention of which is to affect enterprise management, decisionmaking, and, presumably, economic behavior. The benefits are not one-sided: Companies report that having CCP organizations within their structure facilitates communication with the government, helps align the companies with government policy, trains and socializes new employees, provides employee services (such as loans and medical services), and provides career coaching.[31] The number of such internal party organizations has continued to grow significantly among China's top POEs.[32]

Ownership

A good deal of privatization occurred through purchases of stakes in SOEs or the middle ground "collectively owned enterprises" that could arise from the state selling its shares.[33] Furthermore, when the state bails out a POE, it often takes an ownership stake. In the case of Mengniu Dairy and its infamous melamine scandal, an SOE bought 20 percent of the company's shares and became its largest shareholder, thus effectively nationalizing it while retaining the label of POE.[34] POEs benefit from government investment and oversight to the extent that this aids in accessing credit and financing more generally and dealing with bureaucracies. POEs can access credit more easily with a government stake in their ownership than can POEs lacking government involvement.[35]

---

28 Pearson, Rithmire, and Tsai, 2023, p. 24.

29 Livingston, 2020.

30 Christopher Marquis and Kunyuan Qiao, *Mao and Markets: The Communist Roots of Chinese Enterprise*, Yale University Press, 2022, p. 225.

31 Marquis and Qiao, 2022, pp. 227–228.

32 Daniel H. Rosen, Nargiza Salidjanova, Rachel Lietzow, Josh Lipsky, Jeremy Mark, and Niels Graham, *Running Out of Road: China Pathfinder Annual Scorecard*, Atlantic Council and Rhodium Group, October 2023, p. 21.

33 Marquis and Qiao, 2022, pp. 214–215.

34 "Poisoned Milk Scandal Widens in China, Top Dairies Implicated," CBC News, September 19, 2008.

35 Marquis and Qiao, 2022, p. 220.

Lines of Control over Management Decisions

There is variation among firms. The shift toward greater state and party involvement is more visible in larger firms and has less impact on small- and medium-sized enterprises.[36] In a 2023 book on state and capitalism in China, the authors do not treat this as a swing back to the state away from the "market"; rather, the political imperative dictates "the embrace of public and private ownership and the use of market mechanisms to bolster political control."[37] In 2020, the party signaled its wish to increase party influence over POE decisions in a manner similar to the effort to do so among SOEs the half-decade before. A Central Committee opinion called for POEs to "improve their corporate governance structure and explore the establishment of a modern enterprise system with Chinese characteristics."[38]

In a speech by Ye Qing, Vice Chairman of the All-China Federation of Industry and Commerce, Ye elaborated that referring to "Chinese characteristics" meant giving the firm's local party group control over human resource decisions, the right to conduct company audits, and monitor "internal behavior." He asked that the CCP clarify its role in corporate governance structures.[39] The existence and advancement since 2012 of state-owned capital investment companies that use various avenues to invest in POEs is viewed as a means to advance state industrial policy goals and provide capital to nonstate firms with "strong growth potential."[40] In both POEs and SOEs, there have been efforts enacted in legislation in 2015, 2017, and 2020 to create more direct involvement in enterprise governance (such as the transformation of the focus of intra-firm party committees from being on trade unions and welfare to more general managerial issues).[41]

Incentives

The influence of internal, regional, and national CCP organs on the behavior and incentives of POE managers is not solely coercive. That is, the existence of these channels also holds potential for gaining private advantages beyond those obtainable in the traditional market or through formal means. In a 2019 paper published by the National Bureau of Economic Research, the authors suggest that regular contacts and interactions exist that might work to the benefit of the individual POE and its managers.[42] This raises the question of whether this mechanism—in addition to those that more directly align firm actions with party and state

[36] Pearson, Rithmire, and Tsai, 2023, p. 4.

[37] Pearson, Rithmire, and Tsai, 2023, p. 58.

[38] Livingston, 2020, p. 1.

[39] Livingston, 2020.

[40] Pearson, Rithmire, and Tsai, 2023, p. 20.

[41] Beck and Brødsgaard, 2022, p. 503.

[42] Chong-En Bai, Chang-Tai Hsieh, and Zheng Michael Song, *Special Deals with Chinese Characteristics*, National Bureau of Economic Research, Working Paper 25839, May 2019.

authorities—might also create distortions of incentives that affect POE behavior, decisions, and development.

The assertion is that POE success often depends, in part, on gaining an understanding with a local government or party leader that will allow the POE to circumvent formal rules or obtain favorable access to resources.[43] Such deals are not unheard of in other rapidly developing economies, but it is usually judged that the dead-weight loss to the economy as a whole outweighs the benefits that might accrue from the success of firms that can cut such deals. The authors argue, however, that the informal institutionalization of this type of access in China may have a lasting effect that overcomes the usual costs of such extra-market transactions.[44] This point would then suggest that the phenomenon might be more than just an artifact of this stage of China's economic transition.

One reason to expect persistence is that the "enormous administrative capacity" of Chinese authorities can help firms with special deals. Benefits may include "exemptions to regulations, lobbying the central government for the right to break rules, improving local infrastructure, providing land (and to a lesser extent credit) at below market prices, and blocking entry of other firms that threaten the profits of the favored firms."[45] Some of this might lower welfare, but the exemptions to inefficient regulations might be growth-enhancing.[46] In either case, both sides of the transaction *believe* the actions to be justified, and, therefore, the informal dealmaking is likely to continue.

Beyond this, local political leaders themselves have incentives to put their thumbs on the scales:

> Local leaders may support private firms simply out of a sense of duty or because local leaders that show competence in supporting private business are recognized and promoted. The benefits can also be entirely monetary, ranging from tuition payments for their child to (hidden) equity stakes in favored private firms held by family members. Because of the high-powered incentives to support private firms, a large and increasing number of Chinese firms benefit from the special deals.[47]

The authors cite the example of Shanghai and the joint venture with General Motors: "The commercial goal of selling more GM Buicks and Chevrolets in China becomes a political and economic campaign to enhance the power and might of the City of Shanghai. Think of it as Shanghai Inc. with the Mayor as the Chairman and CEO."[48]

---

[43] Bai, Hsieh, and Song, 2019, p. 3.

[44] Bai, Hsieh, and Song, 2019.

[45] Bai, Hsieh, and Song, 2019, p. 3.

[46] Bai, Hsieh, and Song, 2019, p. 3.

[47] Bai, Hsieh, and Song, 2019, pp. 3–4.

[48] Michael J. Dunne, *American Wheels, Chinese Roads: The Story of General Motors in China*, John P. Wiley, 2011, p. 11, as cited in Bai, Hsieh, and Song, 2019, p. 3.

Finally, local governments actively support private firms and compete to attract them:

> Competition between local governments is crucial in limiting the predatory power of protected firms. A local government can block competitors of favored firms in its locality but has no ability to do so in other cities. Competition also gives firms options when faced with incompetent or predatory local governments.[49]

Thus, the authors suggest that this system—certainly well within the sphere of the long tradition of guan xi connection as a fact of business life in China—is potentially beneficial and, by inference, will be maintained. Again, although no firm inside or outside China can remain indifferent to at least understanding the interests of local authorities, the incentive structure within Chinese POEs may be pulled in this direction to an extent that would be unfamiliar in most OECD countries. And once more, the unique and unchallenged power of the CCP as political authority will accentuate these tendencies in China.

It is worth considering the other side of the coin. These include what might be the less obvious costs—in addition to the sought-for benefits—to closer associations between POEs and government entities. Data on corporate returns on assets have shown a gradual decline across China's SOEs, POEs, and shareholding enterprises from at least 2013, albeit at different rates.[50] Interestingly, those of Hong Kong, Macau, Taiwan, and foreign enterprises remained fairly consistent, at about 10 percent over the nine years before the Chinese economy fell off a cliff during the COVID-19 pandemic. The decline was more gradual for SOEs, from about 5 percent in 2013 to a bit under 4 percent by mid-2020. But returns on assets for POEs declined from triple the SOE rate in 2013 (Xi's first year as president) to about double in 2020. Data since then show a collapse of any meaningful difference among enterprise types; these rates are indistinguishable from each other into early 2023. Clearly, many factors are at play. But at least one of them could possibly be a change in the nature and processes of corporate decisionmaking within POEs over the period.

More discussion is available in the literature on the structural (genotype) differences between Chinese POEs and other nations' private firms than is available on the behavioral (phenotype) differences. This is where further research might be the most profitable. This section ends with a few points along these lines.

Relationship of Company to State and Party

The nature of this relationship is increasingly dictated by legal behavioral constraints. Several recent laws—most distinctly the National Security Law of 2015 and National Intelligence Law of 2017—make clear that all enterprises, including POEs, are intended to be important components in a newly securitized party-state economy. In other words, POEs are mandated

[49] Bai, Hsieh, and Song, 2019, p. 4.

[50] Rosen et al., 2023, p. 25.

by law to behave in a prescribed manner and may not, as U.S. firms that received government demands to make data and other security information available have done in several instances, use the courts to resist such appeals. The same might be said of the increasingly prominent role that POEs are required to play as part of a major campaign to make knowledge and capabilities contained in China's private sector available to SOEs. That is a behavior not at all in character with those of non-Chinese firms even in countries in which the equivalent of state-owned production entities exists.

Market Behavior

The principal difference in market activity by Chinese firms is an observed or imputed willingness to undercut competitors' pricing because of access to funding or guarantees (whether formally or informally) that are usually not available to non-Chinese enterprises. The charge is most frequently laid at the door of SOEs for which state ownership is clear and the tendency toward preferential treatment—and more—by the state is well-documented. The question of such behaviors by POEs is less well-documented. But the not-infrequent incidence of obscured state ownership stakes in such firms through the SOEs and the preferential access that some receive from local officials seeking to groom unicorns and champions makes this area one for potentially fruitful scrutiny for signs of POE behavior that might differ from what might be expected of a non-Chinese private firm.

Role as Instrument of CCP's "Visible Hand"

The biggest challenge may not lie in the behavior of any one or several POEs. Rather, the fact that they are treated by the Chinese polity as active, semiautonomous agents (given the various strictures under which they operate) taking part in a larger strategic design (as laid out in various CCP initiatives, such as Made in China 2025) makes them both awkward to categorize and regulate by foreign trading partners and more formidable competitors in the mass than are their non-Chinese counterparts.[51]

The recent concern over Chinse electric vehicle (EV) exports to the EU market is a case in point. It is possible that individual Chinese car component suppliers or original equipment manufacturers of EVs sold in Europe might have been recipients of various forms of state benefaction, such as an ability to engage in low-ball pricing strategies, receipt of beneficial state subsidies or informal bank preferences, or even having benefited from unauthorized technology transfers from willing or unwilling non-Chinese manufacturers that assemble in or receive components from China. But the EU documents do not base their concern on such overt examples of shadowy or illegal behavior. Rather, the problem is that, in the mass, Chinese firms (both POEs and SOEs) appear poised not only to gain a large share of the

[51] "'Made in China 2025' Plan Unveiled," *China Daily*, May 19, 2015.

EU market but to displace long-standing domestic manufacturers. This fact, and the intent behind it, are a principal concern:[52]

> Beyond competition, the investigation is also about politics, says Ilaria Mazzocco, a senior fellow at the Center for Strategic and International Studies and the coauthor of a recent report on China's EV exports. "I think it's coming as a response to concerns that Europe is too dependent on China" she says, "and that the benefits of decarbonization are maybe flowing to China rather than staying in the European Union."[53]

But some of the earlier discussion of relationship between POEs and the PRC state and party will be very much on the table as well: "The burden will be on China to demonstrate that the price of Chinese EVs is not subsidized. That will be a hard lift, since it's well known that continued state support has been a big factor in the success of China's EV industry."[54]

This suggests a consideration beyond those of the simple genotype or phenotype of the individual POE. To extend the biological metaphor further beyond the individual, an ecology of firms that have institutional connections with the Party and state not usually seen elsewhere may, in the aggregate, lead to outcomes that would not be expected as a result of the normal rent-seeking activity of individual private firms.[55]

Rent-seeking may lead to market dominance by one or several private-sector firms, whether privately owned or publicly traded. Depending on regulatory policy and the nature of the market (as well as of the good or service being offered), oligopoly or near monopoly may arise. But there is usually no political entity that retains latent de facto or de jure influence or control over firm actions, the interests of which may extend into the economic sphere but for which expanded market share accrues strategic, geopolitical benefits for that state actor. Some analogues come close: the designs for the global automobile market by Japan's Ministry of International Trade and Industry, the expansion of soft power through entertainment services by South Korea, the U.S. share of global oil markets prior to and during the World War II. The comparisons might be stronger or weaker, but in each instance the examples affected single-sector industrial niches.

---

[52] When Volkswagen and various Japanese manufacturers first put a serious dent into the U.S. domestic automobile market in the wake of the 1973 oil embargo, there was similar concern for local manufacturers. In neither case, however, was there either the fact or the suspicion of such increased presence being part of a larger geopolitical intent by either Japan or West Germany. Nor was either state suspected of being capable of coordinating or supporting the prospect of gaining dominance in the U.S. market.

[53] Zeyi Yang, "Europe Is About to Crack Down on Chinese Electric Cars," *MIT Technology Review*, September 26, 2023.

[54] Yang, 2023.

[55] *Rent-seeking* is a term that describes a situation in which an entity, such as a private firm, expends resources to receive some type of transfer or benefit—such as a license, a subsidy, or the right to a monopoly—generally from the government. The expenditure of the resource and the transfer can both be socially costly although privately beneficial (Robert D. Tollison, "The Economic Theory of Rent Seeking," *Public Choice*, Vol. 152, No. 1–2, July 2012).

The generality of institutional and other linkages, both formal and informal, between the Chinese state and the vast majority of Chinese POEs suggests that there might be effects in the aggregate that are not of concern in the case of most individual POEs. This is not intended to put a modern face on the Yellow Peril histrionics of the late 19th century or the slightly more nuanced bashing of Japan, Inc. in the 1980s. The intent, rather, is to bring to the level of explicit policy attention something that might otherwise be off the scope if each POE is taken on its own merits and judged by its individual actions: an institutional connection of exceptional scale with the apparatus of a Chinese state that retains both exclusive political authority and interests that go beyond the rent-seeking seen as the usual focus of private firm managers' activities, decisionmaking, and behaviors. Those interests go beyond those of the market but might follow a pathway through the market. Other state actors should at least build cognizance of whether and how those interests might affect their own.

Conclusion

The evidence surely substantiates an intent by the Chinese state and party authorities to gain more influence over the management and actions of POEs. Measures have been promulgated to facilitate that end. Two questions remain:

- How successful are efforts by the state and party to bring about a different form of POE, one that is designed not so much for operating in a market economy but in a connected economy?
- Are there outcomes in the form of changed firm behaviors, outputs, and development trajectories that differ from those exhibited by private-sector firms outside of China?

Many of the tendencies that have been discussed are similar to instances found elsewhere: from government support in nurturing national champion firms and the presence of a political dimension in enterprise decisionmaking to blurred lines with asymmetric information between principals and agents and conflicting incentives between public authorities and private interests.

There are three factors that may make China a special case and the Chinese POE an appropriate focus of greater attention and scrutiny.

The first of these is the intentionality and strategy that underlies PRC senior decisionmaking. A remnant of the Marxist heritage that might have waned somewhat in the decades after Mao, at least in the public presentation of the CCP, has come much more recently to the fore under Xi: an awareness of and attention to the political dimension of all actions (public and private) in the economic sphere. Industrial organization, enterprise growth and regulation, marketplace behavior, finance and capital formation, R&D and innovation, employment relations, global trade, and other aspects carry political implications that affect the large policy directions set by a leadership that looks increasingly toward strategic geopolitical considerations. These considerations may well be as much generated by China's own sense of insecurity with respect to its domestic economy and global supply chains as anything else.[56]

The predisposition by the party to implement these intentions might in practice amount to little more than inflicting an efficiency loss on the economy and private-sector economic agents. But it could just as easily provide a coherence that governments and regulators outside China are not used to considering. The tendency for foreigners to view a POE, its actions, and its results solely on its own account and not as part of a greater whole might be to miss the greater consequences that might ensue from individual foreign government actions (or inactions) that are not usually perceived as potentially having more than local effect.

The second distinguishing factor is the omnipresence and univalent political authority of the CCP. China's courts of law, in both theory and practice, are accessory arms for enforcing that authority. When political campaigns are trumpeted, as currently is that of bringing POEs to greater account for their actions and making them more active contributors toward meeting the goals of the senior leadership, such campaigns have a coverage and ubiquity that is outside the realm of experience of most external observers. The outlook of this uniquely authoritative party and state apparatus is to blur the line demarcating where the party-state ends and the firm begins.[57] This is especially true as reflected in such policies as those in the 2017 National Intelligence Law that tend to elevate economic activities to the level of national security.[58]

The third factor is the matter of scale. Other nations may also seek to engage in industrial policies to support their industries to the same extent that China is prepared to do, but few lack the means to do so even if political support is widely achievable. In a 2022 comparative study of state industrial policies, researchers found that China's potential and actual commitments were enormous.[59] In 2019, funding for what the researchers classify as industrial policy amounted to at least 1.73 percent of GDP, some $250 billion to $400 billion (depending on exchange rates).[60] This amount is greater than the share spent on national defense in that year: "As a share of GDP, China spends over twice as much as South Korea," the second largest spender in the sample.[61]

---

56 Margaret M. Pearson, Meg Rithmire, and Kellee S. Tsai, "China's Party-State Capitalism and International Backlash: From Interdependence to Security Dilemma Dynamics," *International Security*, Vol. 47, No. 2, Fall 2022, p. 149.

57 Pearson, Rithmire, and Tsai, 2022, p. 136.

58 Pearson, Rithmire, and Tsai, 2022, p. 148.

59 Gerard DiPippo, Illaria Mazzocco, and Scott Kennedy, *Red Ink: Estimating Chinese Industrial Policy in Comparative Perspective*, Center for Strategic and International Studies, May 2022.

60 As the researchers noted, "[a]lternative data and assumptions, including for China's below-market credit, subsidies to non-listed private firms, government guidance funds, and state-owned enterprise net payables, would result in larger aggregate estimates" (DiPippo, Mazzocco, and Kennedy, 2022, p. 2).

61 DiPippo, Mazzocco, and Kennedy, 2022, p. 2.

These three factors, along with the discussion presented in this chapter, suggest the value of, at the very least, bringing a new perspective to thinking about and treating Chinese POEs at the level of policy and regulation. By the very nature of their mechanisms, markets and the individuals who participate in those markets will be unaware of and will not feel justly responsible for some of the larger considerations that may be attached to trading, partnering with, or investing in POEs. Only public bodies, such as government agencies, can take on this challenge and provide the means for understanding its dimensions. Perhaps it is time to begin looking to gain greater perspective on the unprecedented challenges that might be just over the next hill.

The argument presented in this chapter is not that there will necessarily be large or perhaps unrecoverable consequences ensuing from relations and trade with Chinese POEs. Although possible, that suggestion would require analysis beyond the scope of this chapter to detail where such harms might be found. Rather, the United States and U.S. partner nations should recognize that such a possibility exists. Making the all-too-convenient assumption that there is nothing extraordinary about such firms could potentially create an opening for tangible harms to ensue, whether originally intended by the trading entities or not.

In viewing the Chinese POE, external governments and economic actors are dealing with an organizational form that they believe they understand—but probably do not as well as they should or could. It is worth taking the trouble to improve that understanding.

This chapter is dedicated to the memory of the late Professor Gregory Grossman,
University of California, Berkeley
(1921–2014)

Abbreviations

5G	fifth generation
CCP	Chinese Communist Party
EU	European Union
EV	electric vehicle
GDP	gross domestic product
IP	intellectual property
OECD	Organisation for Economic Co-operation and Development
PLA	People's Liberation Army
POE	privately owned enterprise
PRC	People's Republic of China
R&D	research and development
SOE	state-owned enterprise
WTO	World Trade Organization

References

Bai, Chong-En, Chang-Tai Hsieh, and Zheng Michael Song, *Special Deals with Chinese Characteristics*, National Bureau of Economic Research, Working Paper 25839, May 2019.

Balassa, Bela, "Indicative Planning in Developing Countries," *Journal of Comparative Economics*, Vol. 14. No. 4, December 1990.

Beck, Kasper Ingerman, and Kjeld Erik Brødsgaard, "Corporate Governance with Chinese Characteristics: Party Organization in State-Owned Enterprises," *China Quarterly*, Vol. 250, June 2022.

Bendor, Jonathan, "Bounded Rationality," in Neil J. Smelser and Paul B. Baltes, eds., *International Encyclopedia of Social & Behavioral Sciences*, Pergamon, 2001.

Blenkinsop, Philip, "EU to Investigate 'Flood' of Chinese Electric Cars, Weigh Tariffs," Reuters, September 13, 2023.

Bradsher, Keith, "How China Obtains American Trade Secrets," *New York Times*, January 15, 2020

Coase, Ronald H., "The Nature of the Firm," *Economica*, Vol. 4, No. 16, November 1937.

Davis, Bob, "Broken Engagement," *The Wire: China*, July 14, 2024.

DiPippo, Gerard, Ilaria Mazzocco, and Scott Kennedy, *Red Ink: Estimating Chinese Industrial Policy in Comparative Perspective*, Center for Strategic and International Studies, May 2022.

Dunne, Michael J., *American Wheels, Chinese Roads: The Story of General Motors in China*, John P. Wiley, 2011.

"Full Text of Clinton's Speech on China Trade Bill," *New York Times*, March 9, 2000.

Gerstel, Dylan, and Matthew P. Goodman, *From Industrial Policy to Innovation Strategy: Lessons from Japan, Europe, and the United States*, Center for Strategic and International Studies, September 2020.

Grossman, Gregory, "Notes for a Theory of the Command Economy," *Soviet Studies*, Vol. 15, No. 2, 1963.

Kania, Elsa B., and Lorand Laskai, *Myths and Realities of China's Military-Civil Fusion Strategy*, Center for a New American Security, January 2021.

Kindleberger, Charles P., "French Planning," in Max F. Milikan, ed., *National Economic Planning*, National Bureau of Economic Research, 1967.

Leutert, Wendy, "Firm Control: Governing the State-Owned Economy Under Xi Jinping," *China Perspectives*, Nos. 1–2, 2018.

Livingston, Scott, *The Chinese Communist Party Targets the Private Sector*, Center for Strategic and International Studies, October 8, 2020.

"'Made in China 2025' Plan Unveiled," *China Daily*, May 19, 2015.

March, James G., and Herbert A. Simon, *Organizations*, 2nd ed., Wiley-Blackwell, 1993.

Marquis, Christopher, and Kunyuan Qiao, *Mao and Markets: The Communist Roots of Chinese Enterprise*, Yale University Press, 2022.

Martin, Peter, "Understanding Chinese 'Wolf Warrior Diplomacy,'" transcript of interview conducted by Joanna Nawrotkiewicz, National Bureau of Asian Research, October 22, 2021.

Organization Department of the CPC Central Committee [中共中央组织部], "2017 Inner-Party Statistical Bulletin of the Communist Party of China" ["2017年中国共产党党内统计公报"], Xinhua, June 30, 2018.

Paulson, Henry M., Jr., *Dealing with China: An Insider Unmasks the New Economic Superpower*, Twelve, 2016.

Pearson, Margaret M., Meg Rithmire, and Kellee S. Tsai, "China's Party-State Capitalism and International Backlash: From Interdependence to Security Dilemma Dynamics," *International Security*, Vol. 47, No. 2, Fall 2022.

Pearson, Margaret M., Meg Rithmire, and Kellee S. Tsai, *The State and Capitalism in China*, Cambridge University Press, 2023.

"Poisoned Milk Scandal Widens in China, Top Dairies Implicated," CBC News, September 19, 2008.

Rosen, Daniel H., Nargiza Salidjanova, Rachel Lietzow, Josh Lipsky, Jeremy Mark, and Niels Graham, *Running Out of Road: China Pathfinder Annual Scorecard*, Atlantic Council and Rhodium Group, October 2023.

Sato, Kazuo, "Indicative Planning in Japan," *Journal of Comparative Economics*, Vol. 14, No. 4, December 1990.

Tejada, Carlos, "Beg, Borrow or Steal: How Trump Says China Takes Technology," *New York Times*, March 22, 2018.

Tollison, Robert D., "The Economic Theory of Rent Seeking," *Public Choice*, Vol. 152, No. 1–2, July 2012.

Wakabayashi, Daisuke, Chang Che, and Claire Fu, "In Xi's China, the Business of Business Is State-Controlled," *New York Times*, October 17, 2022.

Williamson, Oliver E., *Markets and Hierarchies: Analysis and Antitrust Implications: A Study in the Economics of Internal Organization*, Free Press, 1975.

Yang, Zeyi, "Europe Is About to Crack Down on Chinese Electric Cars," *MIT Technology Review*, September 26, 2023.

Zhang Jide and Liu Suhan, "The Select of Strategic Investor from the Perspective of China Unicom's Mixed Ownership Reform" ["从中国联通混合所有制改革看战略投资者的选择"] *Accounting Research* [会计研究], No. 7, 2018.

CHAPTER 9

A Requiem for the Global Trade Order?

King Mallory

Overview

In this chapter, I analyze the history of the evolution of China's economic reforms. I describe the unique features of the Chinese system of economic management and the unanticipated distortions that that system's emergence caused to the global trading regime under the rules of the General Agreement on Tariffs and Trade and its successor, the World Trade Organization. I then investigate the shortcomings of and potential fixes and additions to the global trading regime. I describe and evaluate three different policy options going forward and assess methods by which these options might be implemented. I suggest that U.S. policymakers consider a standalone cooperatively negotiated multilateral competitive neutrality framework as a means by which to (1) address trade distortions created by China's unique system of economic management; (2) steer U.S.-China relations out of a zero-sum trajectory into a mutually beneficial one; (3) simultaneously provide benefits to all trading nations; and (4) resuscitate a global trade order that has significantly boosted global standards of living and reduced global poverty over the past 70 years.

China's economy underwent a remarkable growth trajectory between 1978 and 2023. That path resulted in a unique system of economic management. The party-state oversaw a complex set of mechanisms that provided more control over the economy than was available in almost any other country. Because of the size to which China's economy had grown and China's role in global trade, the aid that China provided to its enterprises caused overcapacity and enabled predatory pricing and other anticompetitive behaviors on those enterprises' part in global markets. Although five different models of economic management were anticipated when the World Trade Organization (WTO) was created in 1995 (as discussed later), the system of economic management that China put in place in 2003, after its 2001 WTO accession, had not been anticipated. The General Agreement on Tariffs and Trade (GATT)-WTO trading regime was therefore only partially able to address the distortions of world trade caused by China's newfound prominence in global trade, economic policies, and system of economic management.

Frustrated by this fact and a series of rulings against it by the WTO's Dispute Settlement Body (DSB), in 2017–2018 the United States imposed tariffs on 49 percent of Chinese imports. By refusing to consider replacement candidates to serve on the DSB's Appellate Body, the United States crippled that organ. The failure of the Doha Round of multilateral trade negotiations in 2007 had already inflicted serious damage on the WTO's ability to update global trade rules. The United States' 2017–2018 decisions effectively hamstrung the WTO's ability to regulate global trade. The global trading system began to disintegrate. Nations sought to address new challenges to international trade through bilateral agreements and a series of large regional free trade agreements (FTAs) instead.

In this chapter, I analyze the history of the evolution of China's economic reforms. I describe the unique features of the Chinese system of economic management and the unanticipated distortions that the system caused to the GATT-WTO trading regime. I investigate shortcomings of and potential fixes and additions to that regime. I close by describing and evaluating three options for dealing with the international trading regime going forward and assess methods by which these options might be implemented.

Between 1948 and 2017, the GATT-WTO trading regime contributed to a 30-fold increase in gross world output. Surmounting a 5-billion-person increase in world population, the regime enabled an eightfold increase in the global standard of living and a 43-percent reduction in extreme poverty.[1] Yet events that transpired in 2007 and 2017–2018 effectively hamstrung that regime. As the United States enters a new period of competition with China, policymakers are faced with the decision of whether to preside over a requiem for the global trade order or attempt to revive it. Doing nothing appears fraught with potential peril. At least two other options appear to be available:

1. Make small fixes within the system of the WTO.
2. Make significant additions and improvements to that system.

It appears that only the latter course can address the systemic and probably unintended effects on international trade of practices brought on by China's unique system of economic management. In addition to a series of potential incremental fixes to the GATT-WTO trade regime, one possible improvement is to institute a standalone multilateral competitive neutrality framework (MCNF) in parallel or in addition to that regime (described in detail later in the chapter). Unlike fixes to the existing regime, such a framework—properly implemented—has the potential to successfully address the effects of China's unique system of economic management on the global trade system in a politically meaningful time frame.

An MCNF could do so while also potentially providing a win-win outcome for all trading nations. It might therefore be welcomed by WTO member states, particularly those in the developing world. There are also signs that such a framework might be welcomed by economic reformers in China. Furthermore, there is a good chance that partners in Australia and Europe may be receptive toward such a framework. That is not to say that implementing an MCNF would be simple or straightforward. This is particularly true because an MCNF cannot work without an enforcement mechanism; in turn, a taxing and politically costly rehabilitation of the WTO's DSB would be required for an MCNF to be viable.

An MCNF could be implemented in either a cooperative or noncooperative, compellent manner. There is a real prospect that, given the political will, an MCNF might be able to resuscitate the GATT-WTO trade regime through the former path. An attempt at reanimation of this kind is in both the U.S. and Chinese national interests. Such an effort could have the additional benefit of redirecting U.S.-China competition into a more constructive direction, one that provides positive results for all nations involved.

[1] J. Bradford DeLong, *Estimates of World GDP, One Million B.C.–Present*, University of California, Berkeley, 1998; United Nations, "How Certain Are the United Nations Global Population Projections?" Population Facts, No. 2019/6, December 2019; Michail Moatsos, "Global Extreme Poverty: Present and Past Since 1820," in Organisation for Economic Co-operation and Development (OECD), *How Was Life?* Vol. II, *New Perspectives on Well-Being and Global Inequality Since 1820*, OECD Publishing, 2021, p. 2; Kym Anderson, "Contributions of the GATT/WTO to Global Economic Welfare: Empirical Evidence," *Journal of Economic Surveys*, Vol. 30, No. 1, February 2016.

China's Unique Economic Structure Emerges

China's trajectory over the past 45 years has been remarkable. In the 18 years before his death in 1976, Mao Zedong, Chairman of the Chinese Communist Party (CCP), implemented two misconceived policies: the Great Leap Forward (1958–1961) and the Cultural Revolution (1966–1976). They led to more than 30 million Chinese deaths and left China's economy in ruins.[2]

But then, between 1978 and 1982 under the leadership of Deng Xiaoping (1978–1989), the People's Republic of China (referred to as *China* in the rest of this chapter) started to open its economy to the world. State contracting for production down to the household level boosted agricultural productivity. State-owned enterprises (SOEs) were permitted both greater management control and to retain a share of profits once they had exceeded their production quotas. Labor that was less productively employed on the land became free to move to coastal special economic zones, where it was put to more productive and better use. Between 1983 and 1986, SOEs were allowed to sell excess production at market prices, control corporate funds, and set prices. In exchange, they were expected to pay corporate tax and fund themselves from retained earnings or bank loans instead of relying on government appropriations. Between 1987 and 1992, China further implemented a contract responsibility system that gave SOEs full control over their operations if they hit contractual profit targets.[3]

But in spring 1989, protests demanding greater freedom broke out in Beijing's Tiananmen Square and in cities throughout China. They were brutally repressed on June 4 of that year. The protests elevated a conservative CCP faction under the leadership of Premier Li Peng (1987–1998) to political primacy. Under Li Peng's leadership, China briefly tacked away from economic reform. Li Peng placed greater reliance on the state's role in the economy. Economic growth stalled. It was only rebooted after Deng Xiaoping undertook a tour of southern Chinese cities in 1992 during which he encouraged further reforms.[4]

Starting in the mid-1990s, as China prepared for accession to the WTO, the country embarked on another round of economic reform under the leadership of Premier Zhou Rongji (1998–2003). China's state-owned banks (SOBs) were recapitalized. They partnered with foreign investors and were listed on domestic and international stock markets. The share of financial system assets that they controlled declined. At the same time, the state-owned sector was consolidated significantly, reducing the number of SOEs by 65 percent. Notwith-

---

[2] Jonathan D. Spence, *The Search for Modern China*, 3rd ed., W.W. Norton & Company, 2013; Jonathan D. Spence, *Mao Zedong*, Viking, 1999; Edgar Snow, *Red Star over China*, Grove Press, 1961; John Delury, *Agents of Subversion : The Fate of John T. Downey and the CIA's Covert War in China*, Cornell University Press, 2022, p. 278.

[3] Nicholas R. Lardy, *Markets over Mao: The Rise of Private Business in China*, Peterson Institute for International Economics, 2014; Ezra F. Vogel, *Deng Xiaoping and the Transformation of China*, Harvard University Press, 2011; Ting-Wei Chiang, "Chinese State-Owned Enterprises and WTO's Anti-Subsidy Regime," *Georgetown Journal of International Law*, Vol. 49, No. 2, 2018.

[4] Desmond Shum, *Red Roulette: An Insider's Story of Wealth, Power, Corruption, and Vengeance in Today's China*, Simon & Schuster, 2021.

standing the implications for political stability, between 1998 and 2004, 30 million Chinese workers—mostly from the state sector—became unemployed as a result of these reforms. China weathered the 1997 Asian financial crisis relatively unscathed. However, the crisis sensitized Chinese leaders to the importance of economic security to a greater extent than theretofore.[5]

Overall, the results of China's economic reforms were outstanding. China achieved double digit economic growth rates. More than 800 million people in China were able to lift themselves out of poverty. They achieved a $10,000 per annum standard of living (or GDP per capita), on par with that of other upper-middle-income countries. However, rapid economic change and unemployment caused social tensions. With WTO membership achieved, under the presidency of Hu Jintao (2002–2012), China began to turn away from economic reform once again. In pursuit of a more "harmonious socialist society," Hu Jintao rolled back some of the previous economic reforms. He also implemented a fundamental reorganization of the way in which China's economy was managed. The reforms were designed to support continuing economic growth while guaranteeing the future control of the CCP. Importantly, this restructuring had implications that were not anticipated when China negotiated its accession to the WTO.[6]

Leaders in Beijing's Zhongnanhai government quarter responded to the 2008 global financial crisis with $586 billion in debt-financed government spending—a massive fiscal stimulus program. SOEs were the principal vehicles by which this stimulus was delivered. For Chinese leaders, the crisis was a turning point; they saw it as an affirmation of the superiority of China's socialist market economic model. However, by 2016, China's total outstanding debt stood at 264 percent of national income (GDP), unusually high compared with countries in China's economic peer group. The decreases previously achieved in the high levels of SOE indebtedness were reversed. Starting in 2012, under the leadership of CCP General Secretary and later President Xi Jinping (2013–present), a noticeable change in strategy took place. China became more assertive on the international stage. It doubled down on favoring state-led growth under the leadership of the CCP over private sector–led growth and further economic liberalization.[7]

---

[5] Lardy, 2014.

[6] Nicholas R. Lardy, *The State Strikes Back: The End of Economic Reform in China?* Peterson Institute for International Economics, 2019, pp. 102, 116, 119, 140; World Bank Group, "The World Bank in China," webpage, last updated April, 2024; Max J. Zenglein, and Anna Holzmann, *Evolving Made in China 2025: China's Industrial Policy in Quest for Global Tech Leadership*, Mercator Institute for China Studies, July 2019, p. 19; Henry M. Paulson Jr., *Dealing with China: An Insider Unmasks the New Economic Superpower*, 1st ed., Twelve, 2015, p. 172; Mark Wu, "The 'China, Inc.' Challenge to Global Trade Governance," *Harvard International Law Journal*, Vol. 57, No. 2, Spring 2016.

The share of financial system assets controlled by the largest SOBs gradually declined from 70 percent in 1986 to 60 percent in 1995 and 25 percent by the end of 2016. There were approximately 120,000 state industrial firms in 1995. By 2000, the number had fallen to 42,000 because of the reforms introduced by Zhou Rongji. China left GATT in 1951, after the CCP seized power (Wu, 2016).

[7] Lardy, 2019, pp. 10, 108, 148; Wu, 2016, p. 277.

China launched initiatives designed to reshape the international system to be more reflective of its newfound economic influence. In 2013, Xi announced the Belt and Road Initiative (BRI), a state-led global infrastructure program. He also announced the formation of a supporting Asian Infrastructure Investment Bank (AIIB). By 2023, a decade later, the BRI had grown to encompass close to $1 trillion in financial commitments by China (mostly loans) to 150 participant countries. Ninety-six countries had subscribed for a total of $1 billion in AIIB share capital.[8]

In 2015, two years after BRI was announced, faced with increasingly uncompetitive Chinese real wage levels compared with China's immediate neighbors and with declining real economic growth rates as it rebalanced its economy away from investment toward consumption, China announced the Made in China 2025 (MIC25) initiative. Targeting ten priority sectors, MIC25 was not a further economic reform program.[9] Instead, it was a top-down state-led blueprint to establish a strong national innovation system, backed by a forceful industrial policy and massive state financing. MIC25 was designed to "propel China through the middle-income trap and transform the nation into a globally competitive manufacturing superpower largely independent of foreign technology."[10]

Private Western companies, basing their strategies and operations on free-market economic principles, and lacking the massive state backing of Chinese SOEs, felt threatened by MIC25. It targeted an 80 percent to 90 percent dominant global market share in key emerging technologies, such as new energy vehicles and information technology products for vehicles, threatening to displace Western private companies entirely. MIC25 included an aggressive strategy by which to acquire hard-to-get Western proprietary technologies, the most extreme forms of which included theft and coercion. SOEs in four of the ten priority sectors targeted

---

8 Lardy, 2019, p. 27. The BRI was first announced by Xi in September and October 2013 during visits to Kazakhstan and Indonesia. According to the World Bank,

> China proposed the Belt and Road Initiative (BRI) in 2013 to improve connectivity and cooperation on a transcontinental scale. . . . [P]rojects in all sectors that are already executed, in implementation, or planned are estimated to amount to USD 575 billion. . . . If completed, BRI transport projects could reduce travel times along economic corridors by 12%, increase trade between 2.7% and 9.7%, increase income by up to 3.4% and lift 7.6 million people from extreme poverty. (World Bank Group, "Belt and Road Initiative," 2018)

9 The ten priority sectors were next-generation information technology, high-end computerized machines and robots, aviation and space equipment, maritime engineering equipment and high-technology ships, advanced railway transportation equipment, energy-saving and new vehicles, energy equipment, agricultural equipment, new materials, and biomedicine and high-performance medical equipment.

10 Zenglein and Holzmann, 2019, p. 19. See also Paulson, 2015, p. 314; Zenglein and Holzmann, 2019, pp. 19–20; Lardy, 2019, p. 10.

> [The] "middle-income trap" [is] a phrase economists use to describe what happens to developing countries that make it to the middle-income range only to watch as their relative cost advantages erode before they can compete effectively with developed countries on innovation and higher-quality services and manufacturing. The bottom falls out of their once-booming growth rates, and they can no longer climb the wealth ladder. (Paulson, 2015, p. 314)

by MIC25 enjoyed an 80-percent share of total sectoral revenue or higher in China.[11] They were likely to benefit from massive Chinese state aid to their international expansion plans. In a defensive response to these developments, countries began to impose restrictions on international trade and financial transactions with China.[12]

By 2023, China was one of the largest economies in the world.[13] It was the principal trading partner for more than 100 countries, accounting for 80 percent of world GDP. Close to 11 million private firms were producing approximately 75 percent of China's national income. However, because of the large role of the state, China remained a nonmarket economy. Six features placed China's economy in a class of its own:

1. the degree of control exercised by the CCP
2. the state's remaining control over significant industrial sectors of the economy
3. the state's control over financial institutions and other financing vehicles
4. the role of China's central economic planning agency
5. the networked hierarchy of China's economy
6. the intertwined nature of private enterprise and the party-state.[14]

China's economy is exceptional because of the dual roles played by the CCP and the state. The 86-million-member CCP operates independently of the state. It has its own investigative, detention, and disciplinary apparatus and controls appointments to and within key state agencies that oversee economic management. Furthermore, the CCP controls promotions within and the appointment of the top management and chief executive officers of state-owned enterprises. Every organization—including SOEs, private companies, and foreign firms—with more than three CCP members also has its own party committee. And CCP committees within each SOE play a large role in major company decisions. Taken together, these features endow the state-party system with a level of influence over the economy that is unparalleled in other countries.[15]

---

[11] The four sectors targeted by MIC25 were telecommunications, shipbuilding, aviation, and high-speed railways.

[12] Zenglein and Holzmann, 2019, pp. 8, 12–13; Chad P. Bown, *The U.S.-China Trade Conflict After 40 Years of Special Protection*, Peterson Institute for International Economics, Working Paper 19-7, April 2019, p. 20; OECD, *Excess Capacity in the Global Steel Industry and the Implications of New Investment Projects*, OECD Science, Technology and Industry Policy Papers No. 18, OECD Publishing, 2015; OECD, *Measuring Distortions in International Markets: The Semiconductor Value Chain*, OECD Trade Policy Papers No. 234, OECD Publishing, 2019.

[13] Its specific rank depends on whether GDP is adjusted for differences in price levels between countries or not.

[14] Wu, 2016, pp. 270–284.

[15] Wu, 2016, pp. 280–282. Formally, the Organization Department of the CCP nominated, and nominally independent SOE boards confirmed, candidates for the top three management positions at SOEs.

With over 111,000 SOEs, China is an extreme outlier in terms of the size of state-owned nonfinancial assets relative to GDP. Oil production remains an oligopoly composed of three companies under state control.[16] Three-fifths of SOEs are controlled by a government agency formed in 2003, the State-owned Assets Supervision and Administration Commission of the State Council (SASAC). The remainder, accounting for more than half of state-owned assets, are controlled at the subcentral provincial, local, or municipal levels of government. Profit maximization is just one of SASAC's goals. The goals include the pursuit of China's broader national interest and make China's model of deploying state assets and exercising economic oversight unique.[17]

The banking system remains under government control, with negligible private competition. Central Huijin Investment Ltd., a wholly owned subsidiary of China's sovereign wealth fund China Investment Corporation, is the controlling shareholder of China's top four state-owned banks.[18] It also holds majority shares in nine of China's second-tier commercial banks. Through Central Huijin, the party-state has a larger pool of funds available than any comparable country, which it can direct in pursuit of its policy goals.[19]

As in many other economies, China retains a state planning commission. Renamed the National Development and Reform Commission (NDRC) in 2003, it is responsible for the five-year plan; it oversees setting prices for commodities whose prices have not yet been liberalized (such as electricity); it manages China's strategic petroleum reserve; and it enforces China's anti-monopoly law. The NDRC's power to mobilize resources was shown in 2008–2009 when it was able organize a $586 billion fiscal stimulus in response to the global financial crisis in short order.[20]

Unlike the conglomerates known as *keiretsu* (*zaibatsu* before World War II) of Japan or the *chaebol* of South Korea, China's economy is characterized by nested corporate group structures. These "networked hierarchies" are interlinked by a series of "institutional bridges." While not impeding competition, they facilitate the exchange of information and reduce frictions in policy implementation.[21]

---

[16] These companies are China National Petroleum Company, Sinopec, and China National Offshore Oil Corporation.

[17] Lardy, 2019, pp. 107, 129, 137, 145, 152; Wu, 2016, pp. 271–273.

[18] The four banks are China Construction Bank, Industrial and Commercial Bank of China, Bank of China, and the Agricultural Bank of China.

[19] Wu, 2016.

[20] "The Precarious Position of the WTO," *Strategic Comments*, Vol. 29, No. 1, February 14, 2023; Wu, 2016, pp. 301, 305, 311; Ines Willemyns, "Disciplines on State-Owned Enterprises in International Economic Law: Are We Moving in the Right Direction?" *Journal of International Economic Law*, Vol. 19, No. 3, September 2016. China's NDRC is thought by some scholars to have a conflict of interest because it is at the same time responsible for developing national champion companies while administering the country's anti-monopoly legislation.

[21] Wu, 2016, pp. 274–279, 282–284.

Only a handful of China's economic sectors are still dominated by SOEs, and much of China's economy remains uncaptured by the crony capitalism that is characteristic of many other countries. However, the boundary between state and private ownership of enterprises remains blurred. The extent of the linkages between the two sectors set China apart from any other economy. In summary, "the Party-state oversees a more complex set of formal mechanisms for controlling important economic activity than its counterparts in any other major economy in the world."[22]

China provides state aid from its SOEs to downstream enterprises through a variety of means, just one of which is in the form of subsidies (see Box 9.1 for an account of more than 30 other such forms of aid).[23] Chinese state aid to enterprises of this kind sometimes causes excess production capacity in the industries that receive the aid. Because of the large size of China's economy and its large role in global trade, that overcapacity depresses prices in those industrial sectors throughout the world. Sometimes, Chinese state aid to enterprises also allows firms to price their products below marginal cost, a behavior that economists term *predatory pricing*.[24] These two developments—overcapacity and predatory pricing—disadvantage Chinese firms' private international competitors and sometimes have driven them out of business entirely. Another concern is that the state-funded overseas expansion of Chinese SOEs has not always been carried out with purely commercial objectives in mind. Sometimes, because of the soft-budget constraint that Chinese enterprises enjoy thanks to state aid, Chinese enterprises pursue other additional goals, such as control of nat-

[22] Wu, 2016, pp. 274–279, 282–284. Quote is on p. 284.

[23] A subsidy has a very particular meaning under the Agreement on Subsidies and Countervailing Measures (ASCM) and under U.S. law (Title VII of the Tariff Act of 1930). A *subsidy* is defined as a "financial contribution" from a government and that provides a benefit. The forms that a subsidy can take include the following:

- a direct transfer of funds (e.g., a grant, loan, or infusion of equity)
- a potential transfer of funds or liabilities (e.g., a loan guarantee)
- forgone government revenue (e.g., a tax credit)
- the purchase of goods, or the provision of goods or services (other than general infrastructure).

Under the ASCM, actions can only be taken against subsidies that are "specific." A *specific subsidy* is one that is only given to one company or to a special group of companies.

[24] Ordinarily, unsubsidized enterprises that engage in predatory pricing first price their product below marginal cost to gain market share or drive competitors out of the market. They then raise their prices to recoup the profits lost after they originally set prices below marginal cost. Continuing state subsidies to enterprises can create a management perception that the SOEs they run enjoy "soft budget constraints." Consequently, unlike their private-sector counterparts, SOE managers may not necessarily feel the need to recoup forgone profits after engaging in predatory pricing. In such cases, they can engage in a form of predatory pricing termed *non-recoupment predation*. Enterprises benefiting from state aid can use non-recoupment predation to lower their prices, boost their production at the expense of their unsubsidized competitors, and benefit from the lower costs accruing from consequent greater economies of scale in a manner that their unsubsidized competitors cannot. This behavior has caused products to be overproduced, has caused prices in the international market for those products to fall, and has driven unsubsidized international competitors of those products out of business. Examples include solar panels, steel, aluminum, and auto parts.

BOX 9.1

Types of State Aid to Chinese State-Owned Enterprises

Enterprises that receive state aid enjoy several privileges and immunities that are not available to their purely private counterparts. Those advantages include subsidies, concessionary financing, preferential tax and regulatory treatment, in-kind benefits, advantages in public procurement and capital structure, and information asymmetries.

Subsidies can take the form of a direct transfer of funds from government to the favored enterprise. They can also take the form of the government directly or indirectly providing goods or services to the enterprise for less than adequate remuneration. Examples include low-cost land purchases, below-cost electricity, and below-cost raw materials.

Concessionary financing involves providing loans on nonmarket terms, predominantly in the form of loans at below-market rates of interest. Such loans can be provided to the favored business either directly by the government or by SOBs. Favored enterprises can also be the beneficiaries of government guarantees of their debt, whether explicit or implicit. Alternatively, they may receive outright exemptions from bankruptcy laws or from activities to resolve failed or failing financial institutions.[a] Governments can also provide enterprises with equity infusions or bailouts on nonmarket or below-market terms.[b]

Preferential tax and regulatory treatment can involve the government applying a lower effective tax rate to favored enterprises. Tax incentives, income tax reductions or exemptions, exemptions from or rebates on value-added tax, reductions in social insurance payments, and reductions in import and export tariff rates have all been used. Preferential treatment can also involve lowered compliance and disclosure requirements for the favored enterprise (e.g., nonperforming loan reporting requirements); de facto or de jure full or partial exemptions from national competition law; exemptions from local ordinances, such as zoning regulations;[c] grandfathering state-aided companies when new, stricter regulations are implemented; and restrictive licensing regulations.

In-kind benefits come in the form of free or below-market rate land usage rights and government-granted rights of way. Public procurement can be arranged by the government in such a way as to give preference to state-favored businesses over private local or foreign entities (e.g., through no-bid contracts) or by funding overpriced projects. Captive equity results from the fact that the favored businesses take the form of unincorporated, unlisted statutory corporations or quasi-corporations. Equity ownership in such enterprises is difficult to convey from one owner to another and is therefore captive. Information asymmetries occur because the management of favored enterprises are frequently politically appointed and have better lines of communication to government officials than do the managers of their private counterparts. This can lead to the former receiving competitive advantages derived from better and more-complete access to key market-moving information. Such managers can also exploit their greater proximity to government officials successfully to lobby the government to adopt restrictive regulations that make market entry by competitors more costly or prohibitive.

Only a small fraction of the vehicles by which state aid is provided to enterprises listed above fall within the purview of the GATT-WTO regulatory regime. Import and export tariffs are regulated. So are direct subsidies. But indirect subsidies from upstream SOEs to other enterprises for less-than-adequate compensation remain a gray area. Most of the 30 other types of state aid, described above, are not regulated by the GATT-WTO trade regime. State aid to enterprises is thus only marginally subject to the rules of the post-war global trade order; it skirts those rules. Without violating those rules' letter, state aid violates their spirit—maximizing the gains available from trade and efficient resource allocation to promote the highest standard of living achievable for all nations through fair, open, and rules-based competition.

SOURCES: Antonio Capobianco and Hans Christiansen, *Competitive Neutrality and State-Owned Enterprises: Challenges and Policy Options*, OECD Publishing, OECD Corporate Governance Working Papers No. 1, 2011; Chiang, 2018; Alicia García-Herrero and Gary Ng, "China's State-Owned Enterprises and Competitive Neutrality," Policy Contribution, No. 5, February 2021; Willemyns, 2016; OECD, *The Size and Sectoral Distribution of State-Owned Enterprises*, OECD Publishing, 2017; Lardy, 2019; Bown, 2022a.

[a] For example, Italy's national airline while under bankruptcy protection received large loans or transfers from the government (International Monetary Fund [IMF], "State Owned Enterprises: The Other Government," in *Fiscal Monitor: Policies to Support People During the COVID-19 Pandemic*, April 2020).

[b] South Africa's government-owned power company, Eskom, received a rolling government bailout of 2⅓ percent of GDP over three years. (IMF, 2020; IMF, OECD, World Bank, and WTO, *Subsidies, Trade and International Cooperation*, 2022).

[c] The U.S. Postal Service, an SOE, is exempt from local planning ordinances.

ural resources, acquisitions of technology, or political or diplomatic objectives. Significant frictions between China and its major trading partners, ensue. Those frictions have had an impact on multilateral trading arrangements.[25]

The Challenge China Poses to the Global Trade Order

On October 28, 1929, after the Dow Jones Industrial Average had risen six-fold during the decade of the Roaring Twenties, an increase in reserve requirements imposed on banks by the U.S. Federal Reserve System (the Fed) caused the U.S. stock market to crash. The gold standard, then in force, obliged international central banks to raise interest rates in response to the Fed's actions, tipping the global economy into recession. In the United States, the Fed intervened to boost the money supply, temporarily containing the stock market crisis. However, on June 17, 1930, U.S. President Herbert Hoover signed the Smoot-Hawley Tariff Act

[25] U.S. International Trade Administration, "Trade Guide: WTO Subsidies Agreement," webpage, undated-b; Capobianco and Christiansen, 2011, pp. 17, 20, 24; Chiang, 2018, p. 852; Willemyns, 2016, p. 670, footnote 64; Bown, 2019a, p. 17; IMF, 2020.

into law. Designed to protect farmers, it raised import tariffs by 20 percent. The legislation unleashed a series of retaliatory tariff increases by U.S. trading partners that caused international trade to fall by 65 percent. The Smoot-Hawley Tariff Act is widely credited with exacerbating the Great Depression, which assumed full force when the United Kingdom exited the gold standard on September 21, 1931, precipitating a series of commercial bank failures. The Great Depression ended a decade after the stock market crash, only after U.S. GDP had fallen by 15 percent and unemployment had reached 23 percent.[26]

After the conclusion of World War II, both the United States and the United Kingdom agreed on the need to prevent a repeat of the protectionism that had had such negative effects on economic growth, standards of living, and employment during the interwar years. Unable to agree on terms for a more ambitious International Trade Organization, a group of 23 states accounting for 60 percent of world trade at the time agreed to a more limited General Agreement on Tariffs and Trade (GATT). Its goals were to reduce discrimination in trade through a set of rules and to reduce tariffs. GATT entered into force on January 1, 1948, on a provisional basis that was to remain provisional for 47 years until the conclusion of the Uruguay Round of trade negotiations in 1995.[27]

GATT was successful in reducing tariffs and in boosting trade. By the time the 1986 Uruguay Round negotiations to replace it with a successor organization began, 88 countries had joined. However, GATT suffered from at least three shortcomings:

1. Although it reduced tariffs, GATT did not prevent the emergence of new barriers to trade. One form that they took was government-imposed import quotas termed *voluntary export restraints* (VERs). At one point, VERs constrained up to 12 percent of total U.S. imports (primarily automobiles and textiles).
2. There were gaps in the types of trade that GATT covered. As the U.S. economy transformed itself after World War II, exports of services and of intellectual property assumed greater importance. Neither was well covered under GATT.
3. GATT lacked an arbitration mechanism by which to resolve trade disputes.[28]

[26] Unemployment peaked at 33 percent in other countries. In recognition of the deleterious impact of the Smoot-Hawley Tariff Act, in 1934, the U.S. Congress delegated authority to negotiate trade agreements and reciprocal tariff reductions to the President of the United States. See Gary Richardson, "The Great Depression," webpage, Federal Reserve History, November 22, 2013; Gary Richardson, Alejandro Komai, Michael Gou, and Daniel Park, "Stock Market Crash of 1929," webpage, Federal Reserve History, November 22, 2013; Chad P. Bown and Soumaya Keynes, *Why Trump Shot the Sheriffs: The End of WTO Dispute Settlement*, Peterson Institute for International Economics, Working Paper 20-4, March 2020, p. 6; Corporate Finance Institute, "Smoot-Hawley Tariff Act," webpage, undated; and Kristie M. Engemann, "Banking Panics of 1931–33," webpage, Federal Reserve History, November 22, 2013.

[27] Donald M. McRae, "General Agreement on Tariffs and Trade," United Nations, 2021.

[28] Bown, 2020, pp. 3–5.

Because of these shortcomings, and because it was increasingly unable to achieve its goals through GATT, the United States began to impose trade remedies (such as antidumping duties) on its trading partners unilaterally and with increasing frequency.[29] It was in part to address these shortcomings and this behavior that the 1986–1994 Uruguay Round of international trade negotiations established the WTO. The WTO dismantled the 1974 Multifiber Arrangement (MFA) that had imposed quotas limiting textile trade. It restrained import quotas, such as the VERs. It also sought to make tariffs more attractive by imposing a three-year waiting period before countries could retaliate against safeguard tariffs imposed to defend against surging imports. GATT rules had allowed countries to retaliate immediately.[30]

The WTO included a Dispute Settlement Body (DSB). Countries involved in a trade dispute would first try to resolve the matter bilaterally. If that was not possible, an ad hoc three-member WTO panel would rule on the matter. Should one or more of the states party to the WTO refuse to accept the panel's ruling, they could appeal to the WTO's Appellate Body, which had the final word. The Appellate Body consisted of seven members serving four-year terms, which were renewable once. The Appellate Body was obliged to rule on appeals within 90 days of their receipt.[31]

In 1995, at the conclusion of the Uruguay Round of trade negotiations, four agreements designed to address some of GATT's shortcomings entered into force:

1. The General Agreement on Trade in Services (GATS)
2. The Agreement on Subsidies and Countervailing Measures (ASCM)
3. The Agreement on Agriculture
4. The Agreement on Trade-Related Aspects of Intellectual Property Rights.[32]

Between 2001 and 2008, WTO member states participated in a further Doha Round of multilateral trade negotiations. The negotiations were ambitious and sought to implement significant further improvements to international trade. They included efforts to improve market access, particularly in agriculture and information technology, and to improve the regulation of trade in services. The Doha Round also included an embedded development

---

[29] A product is considered *dumped* if it is exported to another country at a price below the normal price of a like product in the exporting country. Antidumping measures are unilateral remedies (the imposition of antidumping duties on the product in question) that the government of the importing country may apply after a thorough investigation has determined that the product is, in fact, being dumped and that sales of the dumped product are causing material injury to a domestic industry that produces a like product. See International Trade Administration, "Trade Guide: WTO Anti-Dumping Agreement," webpage, undated-a.

[30] The 1995 WTO Agreement on Textiles and Clothing replaced the MFA and slowly phased out volume limits on those products. Less-developed countries (LDCs) were not happy with the abolition of the MFA. China's textile exports surged as a result pushing LDC textile industries out of the international market. See Bown and Keynes, 2020, pp. 2–5; Bown, 2019, p. 8.

[31] Bown, 2020, pp. 5, 6, 23.

[32] Chiang, 2018, p. 846.

agenda, which was to provide "special and differential" treatment for LDCs and was designed to improve LDC access to patented medicines. The Doha Round further sought to reform the WTO's rules, to improve its DSB, and to link trade rules to multilateral environmental agreements. The negotiations foundered in 2007 on the rocks of agricultural subsidies by rich farm nations and of opening access to industrial and agricultural markets in other countries.

The failure of the Doha Round of trade negotiations marked another turning point. It undermined one of the key pillars of the multilateral trading regime represented by GATT and its successor, the WTO:[33] the ability to convene and conclude periodic multilateral negotiations by which to update the rules of international trade. Those rules were not updated in the following 15 years (2007–2023), a period of significant change during which China rose to prominence in global trade.[34]

On the heels of the failure of the Doha Round and under the WTO's auspices, governments concluded three additional international trade agreements that achieved some of the goals sought during the Doha Round, albeit in a piecemeal fashion. In 2011, 21 states concluded the Government Procurement Agreement (GPA). In 2017, a Trade Facilitation Agreement was concluded that might lower the costs of trade by 10–18 percent, disproportionately benefiting LDCs. And in 2022, an Agreement on Fisheries Subsidies was concluded with the aim of curbing the depletion of global fish stocks caused by overfishing.[35]

When it was first signed in 1947 and updated in 1994, GATT's rules were conceived under the assumptions that (1) states party to the agreement would be free-market economies and (2) their enterprises would principally be driven by the objective of maximizing profits. The rules therefore did not include specific provisions relating to enterprises receiving state aid and engaging in asset-maximizing, market share–maximizing or other non-profit-maximizing strategies. The GATT text does not mention SOEs, and it lacks any specific disciplinary measures that are applicable to them. It does place restrictions on related but different state trading enterprises (STEs),[36] to avoid their use to circumvent rules governing international trade.[37] Key elements of GATT did, however, apply to SOEs receiving state aid:

---

[33] Hereinafter referred to as the *GATT-WTO trading regime* or the *global trade order.*

[34] Ian F. Ferguson, *World Trade Organization Negotiations: The Doha Development Agenda*, Congressional Research Service, RL32060, December 12, 2011; Jagdish Bhagwati, "The Broken Legs of Global Trade," Project Syndicate, May 29, 2012; Bown, 2019a, p. 20.

[35] "The Uncertain Future of the World Trade Organization," *Strategic Comments*, Vol. 27, No. 2, April 23, 2021.

[36] The WTO's "Understanding on the Interpretation of Article XVII of the General Agreement on Tariffs and Trade 1994" provides the working definition of STEs, which states that they are "[g]overnmental and non-governmental enterprises, including marketing boards, which have been granted exclusive or special rights or privileges, including statutory or constitutional powers, in the exercise of which they influence through their purchases or sales the level or direction of imports or exports" (WTO, "Understanding on the Interpretation of Article XVII of the General Agreement on Tariffs and Trade 1994," undated-c).

[37] Chiang, 2018, p. 846; Willemyns, 2016, pp. 663, 669; Przemyslaw Kowalski, Max Büge, Monika Sztajerowska, and Matias Egeland, *State-Owned Enterprises: Trade Effects and Policy Implications*, OECD Pub-

> The principle of national treatment [was] a core element of the legal framework of the General Agreement on Tariffs and Trade (GATT, Article III). It require[d] signatory governments to treat imported goods equally to like domestically produced goods and ha[d] the consequence of protecting foreign producers supplying a market from behind-the-border barriers, including when their products compete[d] with products of SOEs of the importing country or [were] procured or handled by SOEs. The same could be said about most-favored nation (MFN) and other principles; countries [could not] normally discriminate between their trading partners, independent of their ownership status. . . .
>
> GATT Article VI, as developed in the "Anti-Dumping Agreement", allow[ed] governments affected by dumping to defend their domestic industries by taking targeted anti-dumping measures in cases where imports from foreign producers—SOEs or POEs [privately owned enterprises]—[were] priced below the normal value and cause[d] injury, or [had] the potential to cause injury, to a domestic industry producing the like product.[38]

The Uruguay Round of trade negotiations (1986–1994) assumed that not all countries joining the WTO would be free-market economies. Negotiators instead anticipated four additional and different types of participating economies:

1. command economies, such as the Soviet Union
2. economies in transition, such as those in Eastern Europe, after the fall of communism
3. corporatist economies, often encountered in Latin America or Europe
4. economies led by integrated conglomerates, such as the keiretsu/zaibatsu and chaebol models of economic organization encountered in Japan and South Korea, respectively.

The economy that emerged in China, after its 2001 accession to the WTO and after Hu Jintao's 2003 reorganization of economic management (described previously), did not conform to any of these anticipated models.

All WTO signatories were parties to the GATS, and the GATS does include an MFN obligation. However, the national treatment obligation that eliminated behind-the-border barriers to trade only applied to trade in member states' services on an opt-in basis. GATS also included a provision whereby member states could expressly stipulate that the agreement only applied to POEs, thereby exempting the member states' SOEs. Although Article XVI of GATS obliges members to negotiate multilateral measures by which to address trade-distorting subsidies of services, no such measures were agreed in the almost 30 years that

---

lishing, OECD Trade Policy Papers No. 147, 2013, pp. 39–40; Lardy, 2019, pp. 90, 104, 105.

[38] Kowalski, 2013, pp. 77, 79. *Dumping* is, in general, a situation of international price discrimination, in which the price of a product when sold in the importing country is less than the price of that product in the market of the exporting country (World Trade Organization, "Technical Information on Anti-Dumping," webpage, undated-b).

elapsed after the agreement's signature. In short, "services—an important sector with significant SOE presence—was not efficiently disciplined by existing WTO subsidy rules."[39]

Purchases by governments and SOEs accounted for between 10 and 25 percent of countries' GDP. Government preference to national enterprises and SOEs in procurement could shield domestic companies from local and international competition, deter market entry, and artificially inflate prices. The GPA was concluded in 2011 in part to address these issues. The GPA had 42 signatories. However, neither Brazil, Russia, India, Indonesia, China, or South Africa was party to the agreement, somewhat limiting its utility. As part of its 2001 WTO accession protocol, China did, however, commit to join the GPA.[40]

The 1994 ASCM was perhaps the multilateral agreement that gained the most traction when it came to addressing overcapacity and predatory pricing by enterprises that received state aid. Through the ASCM, the WTO regulated subsidies regardless of the form of ownership of the entity receiving them. The ASCM applied three criteria by which to determine whether a measure should be treated as a subsidy:

1. It had to involve a financial contribution or an income or price support.
2. It had to be made by a government body, public body or a private body entrusted or directed by a government or public body.
3. A benefit had to be conferred.

WTO disciplinary action under the ASCM became complicated when attempts were made to apply it to China's unique model of economic management. What was to happen when it was unclear what constituted a *public body*, when SOEs were conveyors as opposed to receivers of subsidies, or when the subsidies did not take the form of plain financial contributions but rather that of raw materials or materiel provided for less-than-adequate compensation? All three of these questions applied to aid that the Chinese party-state provided to its enterprises.[41]

In 2006, the U.S. Department of Commerce decided to treat Chinese SOEs as "public entities" and used that decision to impose countervailing duties on Chinese SOEs receiving state aid. Increasing numbers of countries expressed interest in making use of this avenue by which to institute more equal terms of trade. However, in 2011, a ruling by the WTO Appellate Body significantly circumscribed this avenue of redress by restricting complainants' ability to consider Chinese SOEs as public bodies.[42]

---

[39] Kowalski, 2013, p. 79. See also Kowalski, 2013, pp. 78, 79, 84; and Willemyns, 2016, p. 667.

[40] Kowalski, 2013, pp. 90-91.

[41] Chiang, 2018, p. 863; Kowalski, 2013, pp. 39, 68; Chad P. Bown, *Trump Ended WTO Dispute Settlement. Trade Remedies Are Needed to Fix It*, Peterson Institute for International Economics, Working Paper 22-1, January 2022; Chad P. Bown and Melinda Kolb, "Trump's Trade War Timeline: An Up-to-Date Guide," Peterson Institute for International Economics, November 17, 2022.

[42] Wu, 2016.

The ASCM suffered from other shortcomings. China observed the ASCM's subsidy notification requirement in the breach. As shown, the ASCM's definition of what constituted a subsidy was arguably too narrow. If it was provided at all, redress under ASCM was only provided post facto once the damage of overcapacity, predatory pricing, and other anticompetitive behaviors had already been wrought. The ASCM relied on countries bringing cases against providers of state aid for adjudication by the WTO. The onus of acting against state aid that had systemic global economic effects thus rested on the shoulders of individual countries. Remediation in the case of single countries only diverted subsidized goods and services to other countries, leaving the systemic trade diversion and trade deflection effects of state aid to enterprises unaddressed.[43]

When China negotiated its accession to the WTO, special safeguard anti-dumping provisions were applied to China for ten years, expiring in 2011. China also agreed to be treated as a nonmarket economy for 15 years post accession, expiring in 2016. Both provisions were designed to provide protection against large systemic economic shocks that might result from China's accession to the WTO. China's accession resulted in relatively unfettered access for Chinese exports to the U.S. market. The ensuing "China shock" had a profound influence on U.S. manufacturing communities, on U.S. society, and on the U.S. political landscape. As the special safeguards that were applied to China on its WTO accession neared expiration, WTO shortcomings—particularly in addressing the way in which China provided aid to its enterprises—became acute. The United States started applying unilateral trade remedies against China, such as anti-dumping duties, with increasing frequency. In 2016, a new administration was elected in the United States. It started to adopt a much more hardline stance on the rules of international trade in general and the rules of trade with China in particular.[44]

In 2017–2018, in a series of actions (documented in detail by Chad Bown), the United States, targeting China, imposed escalating import tariffs on solar panels, washing machines, steel, aluminum, automobile parts and other products. China was quick to retaliate, imposing tariffs on U.S. agricultural and other goods. U.S. allies were negatively affected by these tariffs and launched legal actions against the United States at the WTO, as did China. The United Sates subsequently exempted some allies from the tariffs, sometimes permanently, sometimes temporarily, and sometimes only in exchange for new quotas imposed on allies' exports (VERs). When all was said and done, by the end of 2018, the U.S.-China trade dispute

[43] Chiang, 2018, pp. 845, 847, 856, 864–869; Chad P. Bown and Jennifer A. Hillman, *WTO'ing a Resolution to the China Subsidy Problem*, Peterson Institute for International Economics, Working Paper 22-1, October 2019; Capobianco, 2011, p. 11; Willemyns, 2016, p. 670; Bown, 2022, p. 16. The systemic effects that were unaddressed were *trade deflection*, whereby Chinese exports to third countries rose because of the imposition of tariffs on exports to the United States, and *trade diversion*, whereby U.S. imports of the same products from third countries rose in response to the imposition of tariffs (Bown, 2019, p. 16).

[44] Wu, 2016, p. 286; David H. Autor, David Dorn, and Gordon H. Hanson, *The China Shock: Learning from Labor Market Adjustments to Large Changes in Trade*, National Bureau of Economic Research, Working Paper 21096, January 2016; Bown and Hillman, 2019, p. 3; Bown, 2020, p. 18.

had caused tensions with more than half of the United States' allies. The dispute resurrected VERs previously thought near dead. It had a negative impact on U.S. farmers, forcing the United States to provide them with even further subsidies as compensation for losses caused by Chinese tariffs. It did cause manufacturing production to be relocated to the United States but at an average cost of $650,000 per new job created. And the dispute had a disproportionately negative economic impact on LDCs. In total, $250 billion of $504 billion in Chinese exports to the United States (49 percent) ended up subject to the higher tariffs. China's retaliation covered approximately $110 billion in U.S. exports to China, or 70 percent of goods exported to China from the United States.[45]

A new feature of the 2017–2018 dispute was that the United States justified its application of some of the tariffs to Chinese products by applying Section 232 of the U.S. Trade Expansion Act of 1962. That act permitted such tariffs based on the threat that imports might pose to U.S. national security. Article XXI of the GATT reserved for member states the legal authority to restrict trade in goods to protect members' "essential" security interests. Prior to the 2017–2018 U.S.-China trade dispute, Article XXI had been invoked only sparingly. The United States' use of Section 232 of the Trade Expansion Act of 1962 in 2017–2018 reflected its frustration with the rulings of the WTO's Appellate Body:

> Perhaps most concerning to the [United States] was the sheer number of successful challenges that had been mounted to its use of antidumping duties. . . . a series of WTO legal decisions made it harder for the United States to use tools that it thought that it had negotiated to keep . . . tools that the United States traditionally used were becoming increasingly ineffective.[46]

Soon additional voices that had been skeptical of the WTO's Appellate Body from the very outset of the WTO joined those in the United States, leveling several criticisms at its members:

- They were not adequately reviewed for bias when appointed.
- They were inadequately prepared.
- They met in secret.
- Instead of interpreting existing trade law evenhandedly, they had a proclivity to legislate from the bench and to view their rulings as establishing legal precedents.

[45] The U.S. friends and allies negatively affected included Argentina, Australia, Brazil, the 27 member states of the European Union (EU), India, Japan, Mexico, South Korea, Taiwan, Turkey, and the United Arab Emirates. "[U.S.] subsidy payments to farmers ballooned from just over $4 billion in 2017 to more than $20 billion in 2020 (Anne Schechinger, "Under Trump, Farm Subsidies Soared and the Rich Got Richer," Environmental Working Group, February 24, 2021). See also Bown, 2019a, pp. 3, 12; and Bown, 2022.

[46] Bown and Keynes, 2020, pp. 2, 11–12. One condition of U.S. WTO accession was that the United States retain the right to apply anti-dumping duties. Article 17.6 of the Anti-Dumping Agreement states that the WTO dispute resolution mechanism should show deference to domestic authorities in trade remedy investigations.

- They were unelected international bureaucrats advancing their own substantive agendas.
- They failed to process appeals within the prescribed 90 days.
- They remained at WTO to finish their existing cases after their terms of office expired.
- Their decisions superseded those of governments, compromising states' sovereignty.[47]

Eventually, U.S. policymakers concluded that the WTO's DSB did not show adequate deference toward U.S. policy and deprived the U.S. government of the flexibility needed to protect U.S. citizens against unfair or excessive imports. The WTO was also deemed unequal to the task of tackling the systemic challenges to global trade posed by China. The U.S. administration took the steps against China that it did in 2017–2018 because other approaches were not resolving the problems created by Chinese state aid to enterprises. As a matter of national policy, the United States deliberately pushed the global trade order to its breaking point. When two billets on the Appellate Body became vacant in late 2017, the U.S. administration made it clear that it would block all future candidates for the posts until its concerns about the GATT-WTO trade regime had been addressed.[48]

After a new administration was elected in 2020, it largely chose to continue the tariffs that had been imposed on Chinese imports by its predecessor. In February 2021, the new administration reiterated the U.S. position toward the Appellate Body by once again blocking candidates to fill its empty billets, thereby preventing the Appellate Body from functioning. The following August, the U.S. President signed the Inflation Reduction Act into law.[49] The legislation caused further tension between the United States and its allies, particularly the EU. It provided significant subsidies to the U.S. semiconductor and electric vehicle industries—subsidies very similar to those provided to Chinese SOEs under industrial policies of which the United States had previously been so critical.[50]

In December 2021, the WTO issued four adverse DSB panel reports on the complaints made against the United States by China, Norway, Switzerland, and Turkey because of its 2017–2018 actions under Section 232. The new U.S. administration responded that the United States would ignore the WTO panel reports because issues of national security were not within the purview of the WTO.

In the intervening years since the 2007 collapse of the Doha Round of international trade negotiations spelt the end of the WTO's ability to periodically update international trade rules, many new challenges to international trade had emerged. In addition to challenges nominally within the scope of the WTO's rulemaking powers, such as subsidies and anti-

[47] Bown and Keynes, 2020, pp. 13–15; "The Precarious Position of the WTO," 2023.

[48] Bown and Keynes, 2020, pp. 2, 3, 6, 14, 15, 18.

[49] Public Law 117-169, Inflation Reduction Act of 2022, August 16, 2022.

[50] Bown, 2019, pp. 3, 12; Bown, 2022; Bown and Kolb, 2022.

dumping cases, those challenges consisted of developments both new and old. For example, there were questions relating to how to handle

- exchange rate manipulation by member states[51]
- the domicile of data and international data flows
- international cyber-commerce
- cross-border strategic investments
- the application of national competition laws to large internationally active SOEs.[52]

The Appellate Body was increasingly forced to try to legislate from the bench to maintain the relevance of international trade rules to those challenges and to the changing international trade system. The United States' 2017 and 2021 actions relating to the Appellate Body closed the sole remaining avenue by which to update the GATT-WTO global trading regime, leaving the postwar GATT-WTO trading regime effectively moribund.[53]

Bereft of a functioning global body, nations increasingly turned to bilateral FTAs and large regional FTAs, such as the Transatlantic Trade and Investment Partnership (T-TIP) or the Comprehensive and Progressive Agreement for Trans-Pacific Partnership (CPTPP). Those FTAs sought to update the rules of international trade for areas in which the WTO had been unable or unwilling to act (e.g., state aid to SOEs or conflicts of interest in applying national competition law). They also sought to address the question of how to resolve disputes. The Trans-Pacific Partnership (TPP)—the progenitor of the CPTPP—for example, provided for a dispute resolution mechanism outside of and in parallel to that provided by the WTO.[54]

[51] Beginning in 2001, China's central bank had to begin purchasing foreign exchange to maintain the peg of the renminbi to the U.S. dollar. In the absence of official exchange market intervention, the currency of a country with a trade surplus would tend to automatically appreciate. The supply of foreign currency in the exchange market would exceed the demand, causing the foreign currency to fall in value and the domestic currency to appreciate. But in China, the central bank purchases of foreign exchange cut off this adjustment mechanism. These purchases started modestly in 2001–2002 but quickly rose to average almost 10 percent of GDP in 2004–2006 and then peaked at 14 percent of GDP in 2007 (Lardy, 2019, p. 30).

[52] China's NDRC is thought to have a conflict of interest because it was at the same time responsible for developing national champion companies while administering the country's antimonopoly legislation ("The Precarious Position of the WTO," 2023, p. 4; Wu, 2016, pp. 301, 305, 311; Willemyns, 2016, p. 664).

[53] The three key pillars of that order were the WTO's ability to convene multilateral trade negotiations, vitiated by the 2008 failure of the Doha Round; the WTO's rulemaking authority; and the WTO's DSB ("The Uncertain Future of the World Trade Organization," 2021, p. 4; "The Precarious Position of the WTO," 2023, pp. 2, 3; Bown and Keynes, 2020, p. 14).

[54] Wu, 2016, pp. 315, 318, 321; Willemyns, 2016, p. 669.

Three Global Trade Order Policy Options

With the global trade order hamstrung, there appear to be at least three paths forward available to policymakers:

1. Do nothing.
2. Work within the WTO system to reform it.
3. Make the needed fixes by concluding a standalone agreement negotiated by a subset of WTO members that others are permitted but not required to join.[55]

Do Nothing

For a long time, national laws, bilateral investment treaties (BITs), bilateral FTAs, and large plurilateral regional FTAs, such as T-TIP and CPTPP, have coexisted in parallel with the GATT-WTO trading regime. One possible path forward is to do nothing at the global level and continue to manage international trade and investment issues at each of these available subordinate levels. National competition and investment law would be used to handle the anticompetitive and technology acquisition behaviors of SOEs. FTAs (whether bilateral or regional) and BITs would be used to discipline other aspects of state aid to enterprises that the global system has proved unable to address.[56]

Work Within the WTO System to Fix It

At the most fundamental level, working within the WTO system to reform it would require that both the WTO's capability to negotiate updates to multilateral trade rules and its ability to resolve trade disputes be repaired. Three paths appear available:

1. implementing small fixes approved by a WTO Ministerial Conference or General Council
2. amending one or more existing international trade agreements
3. signing additional treaty text(s) in a new comprehensive undertaking required of all WTO members.[57]

The high evidentiary burden that had to be met in proving the existence of a subsidy when pursuing relief through the WTO was a recurring challenge. This was particularly true for nonmarket economies, such as China, for which it was difficult to establish true prices. One

---

[55] Bown, 2019, p. 20; Bown, 2022, p. 6; Wu, 2016, p. 312.

[56] Wengxiao Wang, Peter Draper, Dessie Ambaw, Andreas Freytag, Naoise MacDonagh, and Keith Wilson, *Industrial Subsidies, Market Competition, Global Trade and Investment: Towards a Research Agenda*, University of Adelaide, Working Paper 01, April 2020, p. 9; Willemyns, 2016, p. 670.

[57] Wu, 2016, pp. 308–309, 312.

approach to rectifying this imbalance would be to "establish a set of rebuttable presumptions for countries that believe they have suffered as a result of another member's subsidies."[58] Such a move would not require a change in the WTO rules, could be decided at the WTO Ministerial Conference or General Council level, and would shift the burden of proof in subsidy cases to the subsidizing member. However, given the number of additional fixes to the GATT-WTO trade regime that appear to be required, it is unlikely that this move on its own would restore the WTO's DSB to full credibility, authority, and function. Because the DSB was created by Annex II of the 1994 Marrakesh Agreement establishing the WTO, reanimating the DSB would in all probability require changes to the WTO treaty text. Potential changes to that text might include the following:

- tightening the requirements for confirmation to service on the DSB's Appellate Body
- adding a rotating door provision that only permits service on the body after a fixed number of years have elapsed since certain prior types of activity and that stipulates a cooling off period of a number of years before such activities are permitted after exiting the body
- strictly enforcing Appellate Body members' terms of service
- increasing resources for the Appellate Body or, alternatively, including a materiality hurdle whereby the Appellate Body only considers cases that have a potentially global impact, deferring in all other cases to DSB panel decisions[59]
- extending the 90-day deadline for resolving appeals or having a hard deadline after which a case is closed if it has not yet been resolved
- limiting the DSB's remit to one of strict textualism: defining each DSB decision as unique to the countries in question and therefore ineligible for consideration as precedent.[60]

The ASCM is another prime candidate for making changes to existing trade agreement text to revive the GATT-WTO trade regime. Putative changes might be divided into those aiming to fix existing shortcomings and those aiming to add improvements to the existing treaty regime.

Potential fixes include those designed to provide greater transparency, better definitions of terms, and improved remedies for infractions. It seems undisputed both that better data on subsidies are required and that the WTO's subsidy notification process has failed. One proposed change to the treaty text "would establish administrative penalties for failure to

[58] Bown and Hillman, 2019, p. 18.

[59] The instigation of the DSB was followed by a fourfold increase in unfair trade cases filed between nations. In the 19 years between 1995 and 2016, WTO members filed over 500 formal disputes against one another (about 26 per year). During the 46 years of GATT's existence (1948–1994), they filed 300 (about seven per year) (Bown and Keynes, 2020, p. 10).

[60] "The Uncertain Future of the World Trade Organization," 2021, p. 5; Bown and Hillman, 2019, pp. 2, 18–19.

notify, ranging from a bar on chairing WTO bodies to a fine paid into the WTO budget for use in technical assistance, with penalties ratcheting up over time."[61] In January 2020, the United States, the EU, and Japan proposed amendments to the ASCM that would create greater precision about and broaden the definition of subsidies. The amendments would do so by expanding the list of prohibited subsidies that distort capacity, shifting the burden of proof onto subsidizing countries to show that their subsidies are doing no harm.[62] Alternative approaches that have been suggested include creating a narrowly defined category of nonactionable subsidies and creating a red, amber, and green light system for subsidies, such as that used under the Agreement on Agriculture. The terms *public body* and *financial contribution* would have to be redefined to accommodate China's unique institutional structure and to capture indirect in-kind aid provided to enterprises for less-than-adequate compensation. Another proposal is for states that lose subsidy cases to be obliged to repay the entire amount of the subsidy provided—presumably to the plaintiff(s) or to the WTO. Another fix that could be made by working within the GATT-WTO trading regime is to attempt to hold China to its commitment to join the 1994 Government Procurement Agreement.

If the ASCM treaty is to be renegotiated, several improvements to that text have been suggested. Prime among those is including a definition of subsidies on services and a stipulation that such subsidies should be subject to the same or similar disciplines as those applicable to subsidies for goods. The WTO prohibitions applicable to China regarding export taxes and tax rebates might be extended to all WTO member states. And the ASCM might establish minimal bankruptcy law and competition law requirements for states party to the agreement. A clear definition and boundary level for government subsidies to research and development might also be set. Most ambitiously, where WTO panels or the WTO Appellate Body have ruled on the legality or actionability of specific subsidies, such rulings might be consolidated into an updated ASCM treaty.[63]

At least three other avenues by which to work within the WTO system to fix it appear to exist:

1. extending the GPA to all 164 WTO member states
2. extending the GATS to cover SOEs

---

[61] Bown and Hillman, 2019, p. 19.

[62] The "[p]roposals by the EU, Japan, the United States, and others [aimed] to (i) make the WTO better able to monitor members' activities; (ii) create sanctions to encourage members to comply with notification requirements; (iii) expand technical assistance to developing-country members that lack capacity to make adequate notifications; and (iv) encourage members to make counter-notifications to fill gaps. In contrast, many other [WTO] members called for actions to build capacity rather than punitive measures, emphasizing that some developing members struggle to comply with existing obligations" (IMF, OECD, World Bank, and WTO, 2022, p. 22).

[63] IMF, OECD, World Bank, and WTO, 2022; Bown, 2022, p. 15; Wang, 2021, p. 13; Gary Horlick and Peggy A. Clarke, *Rethinking Subsidy Disciplines for the Future*, International Centre for Trade and Sustainable Development and World Economic Forum, January 2016, p. 4; Bown and Kolb, 2022, pp. 2, 5, 15–18.

3. making national treatment mandatory under GATS.

However, none of those avenues appear easy or straightforward. In fact, some—if not all—may be completely infeasible because of likely recalcitrance from several WTO member states.

The years that have elapsed since the Doha Round of multilateral trade negotiations until the time of this writing (2008–2025) have been the longest period that the multilateral trade regime has gone without an update to its rules. As described, the absence of revisions has led to efforts to update those rules piecemeal through large regional FTAs (such as CPTPP or T-TIP) and to attempts by the DSB to legislate from the bench. The failure of the global Doha Round negotiation process appears traceable to two proximal causes: (1) an overly ambitious agenda of revisions and (2) an overly large number of negotiating parties.

Given this experience, it seems clear that any attempt to reboot the process of negotiating global trade rules should limit itself to a modest agenda and to taking a series of small incremental steps rather than one large one. It is worth remembering that GATT was negotiated by just 23 nations that accounted for 60 percent of global trade at the time. By contrast, in 2023, the WTO had 164 member states. The existence of so many potential negotiating parties would likely severely complicate any future attempt to reach global agreement on updating trade rules. In descending order of likely arduousness, at least three potential paths by which to achieve a revived global dispute settlement mechanism appear viable:

1. Institute a new body authorized to negotiate on behalf of all WTO members whose limited membership is carefully designed to represent all the major stakeholders.
2. Negotiate new rules with a subset of WTO members that others are permitted but not required to join.
3. In a bow to pragmatism and reality, devise a process and criteria by which new rules agreed as part of the conclusion of large multilateral FTAs can, with time, become incorporated into the WTO rules and international trade law.[64]

Table 9.1 summarizes the fixes that can be achieved by working within the WTO system.

Conclude a Standalone Agreement

The two policy options discussed so far have involved either doing nothing or working within the GATT-WTO system fix it. The latter option would involve working to amend or supplement existing treaty texts on the assumption that the system can in fact be fixed with some dispatch. A further, alternative, third (and perhaps more realistic) option is to defer such fixes to the GATT-WTO regime to a later date. A new agreement that would implement an MCNF would first be created as a standalone solution in addition and in parallel to the GATT-WTO

[64] Wu, 2016; Bown, 2020, p. 8.

TABLE 9.1
Fixes Working Within the WTO System

Area of Applicability	Fixes
Systemwide	• Institute a new multilateral negotiating regime. • Rehabilitate the dispute resolution mechanism.
ASCM	• Cure systemic effects, including trade deflection and trade diversion. • Redefine subsidies to include indirect and nonfinancial ones. • Clarify the applicability of the agreement on subsidies to SOEs ("public bodies"). • Rehabilitate the subsidy notification regime. • Extend restrictions on the Chinese tax regime to all member states.
GATS	• Conclude agreement on subsidies to the service industry. • Extend to include mandatory coverage of member states' SOEs. • Extend national treatment so as to be mandatory for all signatories.
GPA	• Broaden to include all WTO member states.

regime. Only thereafter would changes to the GATT-WTO regime that would fix that regime and subsume the agreed MCNF within it be attempted. This approach would allow negotiators to avoid the establishment of an MCNF being held hostage to reaching agreement on a potential legion of changes to the existing world trading regime that negotiators might want addressed first.

Chinese policymakers might be willing to consider such a standalone agreement because Chinese state aid to enterprises imposes significant costs on China. Anywhere between one-quarter and two-fifths of Chinese SOEs lost money in 2019. Among all industrial companies in China, SOEs' share of loss-making companies was twice that of the rest. Subcentral SOEs, which accounted for more than half of all state-owned assets in China, underperformed compared with firms controlled by the central government. Subcentral SOEs persistently lost more money. Several hundred were so-called zombie firms that made losses three years in a row. In 2016, 6.5 percent of all Chinese SOEs (2,041 companies) were so-called zombie firms.[65]

State ownership is associated with lower returns on capital. As Nicholas Lardy, an expert on China's economy, expounds in detail, "over past decades [Chinese] SOE performance . . . deteriorated and the gap with private companies . . . widened by several measures: profits and losses, dependence on subsidies, return on assets (ROA), leverage, [and] interest coverage."[66] SOE losses were sometimes covered by additional borrowing, the proceeds being used to pay

[65] Lardy, 2019, pp. 80, 82, 148, 149–150, 152.

[66] Lardy, 2019, pp. 76–77.

the principal and interest on previous loans. Consequently, SOEs were more indebted than private companies. Other Chinese SOE financial health indicators were weaker than those of their private counterparts. As a result, although the balance sheets of private Chinese companies had improved, state firms were more exposed to economic shocks.[67]

The costs to China of its continuing preference of SOEs were at least twofold: (1) forgone economic growth and (2) excessive financial risk exposure. As Lardy points out, the "wide heterogeneity in firm performance within industries and across ownership types indicate[d] resource misallocation."[68] And as "China remain[ed] a capital scarce economy . . . its misallocation ha[d] a larger negative effect on economic growth" than it did in other economies.[69] Lardy estimated that the market exit of "zombie" firms alone might lift Chinese economic growth one time by 2 percentage points. Eliminating the dispersion in marginal returns to capital between state and private firms might lift China's GDP by 5 percent. Convergence between state and private firm performance might raise China's long-term growth potential between 0.7 and 1.2 percentage points per year. As China's annual economic growth rate has subsided from the double-digit rates of the early 2000s, the value of this forgone growth has started to become material. It amounts to $1.255 trillion in forgone one-time economic gains. The annual cost of forgone recurring economic growth lies between $125 billion and $214 billion. As a perpetuity (a type of financial instrument), the forgone recurring economic growth cost China between $3.115 trillion and $5.340 trillion, or potentially as much as 30 percent of China's GDP.[70]

Chinese SOEs enjoy an implicit state guarantee against defaulting on their debts and against bankruptcy. With high leverage and low interest coverage ratios, there is a chance that subcentral SOEs, which account for 40 percent of the total number, might prove to be poten-

---

[67] The returns on assets of private Chinese construction companies, for example, were more than five and one-half times that of state-owned construction companies. In close to three-quarters of the service sector, the returns on assets of registered private firms were close to two and one-half times that of SOEs. Furthermore, because SOEs received subsidies, SOE returns on assets were probably overstated. In 2007, before the massive government stimulus program that was mounted in response to the 2008 global financial crisis, Chinese SOEs carried one and one-half times more debt than their private-sector counterparts. Chinese SOE's interest burden was three and one-half times that of their private counterparts. See Lardy, 2019, pp. 76–77.

[68] Lardy, 2019, p. 75.

[69] Lardy, 2019, pp. 108.

[70] Lardy, 2019, pp. 75, 108, 150; Kensaku Ihara and Frances Cheung, "China Economists Expect 5.4% GDP Growth in 2023: Survey," *Nikkei Asia*, April 6, 2023; Ruchir Sharma, "'Boomy' Talk about the Chinese Economy Is a Charade," *Financial Times*, May 21, 2023.

The value of Chinese GDP in 2023 was $17.8 trillion (National Bureau of Statistics of China, "National Data," webpage, undated). 0.02 of Chinese 2023 GDP of $17.8 trillion = $356 billion. 0.05 of $17.8 trillion = $890 billion, for total one-time gains of $1,255 billion. 0.007 of $17.8 trillion = $124.6 billion. 0.012 of $17.8 trillion = $213.6 billion. The present value of a perpetuity of $124.6 billion discounted at a rate of 4 percent = $3,115 billion. The present value of a perpetuity of $213.6 billion discounted at a rate of 4 percent = $5,340 billion. $5,340 billion divided by $17.8 trillion = 0.3.

tial sources of financial instability in China. This turned out to be the case in 1997 both for Guangdong Enterprises (GE) and for Guangdong International Trust and Investment Company (GITIC). Heavily indebted, both local government finance vehicles (LGFVs) proved unable to roll over their short-term loans (i.e., get them refinanced). To contain the damage resulting from incompetence, greed, and theft on local CCP officials' part, the CCP was forced into a messy, time-consuming, and expensive $6 billion debt restructuring. China's 2023 debt-to-GDP ratio suggests that the risk of a repeat performance is not inconsiderable.[71]

Financial risk accumulated in China after the global financial crisis. Starting in 2012, at the CCP's direction, the share of loans by SOBs to SOEs and to local government financial institutions burgeoned. In a phenomenon that economists term *crowding out*, China's more productive private firms were squeezed out of access to credit. In essence, in China—a capital-scarce country—the CCP instituted a massive misallocation of capital. After the centrally controlled SOBs were recapitalized in the 1990s, controls were instituted that made it difficult for local CCP official "dirt emperors" to lean on those banks to make loans to loss-making local SOEs. The same was not true of second-tier city and rural commercial banks that were in capture to those officials. Local officials successfully pressured city and rural banks to extend credit to local zombie SOEs. As a result, "increased lending by local financial institutions to local zombie SOEs account[ed] for a large share of the increase in the credit outstanding" in China.[72]

China's SOBs failed to impose a hard budget constraint on loss-making SOEs. The large flow of credits started to pose a systemic risk to China's financial system. As an indication of the accumulation of risk at provincial and local level financial institutions (and in a deviation from international best practice), Chinese financial regulators allowed banks to categorize loans that were more than 90 days overdue (ordinarily categorized as "non-performing") as "overdue but not impaired" or as "special mention loans."[73]

China's slow growth and accumulation of domestic debt since the 2008 global financial crisis prompted fears that these debt burdens could cause a major financial crisis. In 2018, the China Banking and Insurance Regulatory Commission required the 200 plus banks that had availed themselves of these regulatory loopholes to recategorize "overdue but not impaired loans" as "non-performing." The potential impact at the subcentral level of China's financial

---

[71] There is a risk that such LGFVs might take on too much debt. Should the sponsoring government's income fall (e.g., through lack of real estate sales proceeds) or should the government alternatively prove unable to raise additional debt with which to service existing interest and principal payment obligations, these vehicles, like those in Guangdong, could become insolvent. Every Chinese province had an International Trust and Investment Company of its own (Paulson, 2015, p. 86; Delury, 2022, p. 442).

[72] Lardy, 2019, pp. 10–11, 19, 39, 64, 128, 141, 152–153.

[73] A bank's deposits constitute its liabilities—deposits owed to savers. Loans represent assets—assets that borrowers have to repay to the bank. The difference between the larger amount of loans outstanding (assets) and deposits (liabilities) is the bank's shareholders' equity. If the value of loans outstanding that are nonperforming and that must consequently be written down in value on the balance sheet is large enough, a bank's liabilities (deposits) can exceed its assets (loans), making it insolvent and headed for bankruptcy.

system was significant enough that city and rural commercial banks were allowed to delay implementation of this regulation by one year to have time to shore up or restructure their balance sheets.

For many years, the CCP encouraged real estate development. With time, huge levels of debt were taken on by private real estate developers. Eventually, developers found themselves unable to service these debts' principal and interest payments. Large insolvencies, such as that of the Evergrande Group or Country Garden, ensued. Because Chinese local governments have depended on real estate sales to such developers to raise the revenue with which to service and pay off LGFV debt, the 2022–2023 financial crisis caused by overleverage and massive insolvencies in China's real estate sector had knock-on effects on the already precarious finances of China's provincial, local, and municipal governments.[74]

For much of the 2018–2023 period, the U.S. national security community's focus was on the military threat presented by the consequences of China's economic growth. The community appears to have underestimated the economic security threat that might be posed by a Chinese financial crisis and the ensuing global ramifications.[75]

The recategorization in bank loans ordered in 2018 was but one indicator of tensions that existed within the Chinese leadership at two different levels (at least). One set of tensions was between the center and the periphery. Central government attempts to institute best management practices ran into efforts by local dirt emperors to stymie those reforms. The $6 billion GE and GITIC restructurings showed that the consequences of local-level incompetence, subversion, and theft could be extreme. The second set of tensions within the CCP elite was between conservative and reformist philosophies of economic management. As shown, since Mao's death, the pendulum has alternatingly swung to provide primacy to each in turn.[76]

Between 1978 and 1989, by force of miserable circumstance, reformers had the upper hand under Deng Xiaoping. After the 1989 Tiananmen Square massacre, the conservatives gained the upper hand under Li Peng. Economic growth slowed until Deng's 1992 southern tour relaunched the process of reform, culminating in Zhou Rongji's reforms of the late 1990s. Social tension unleashed by the 30 million that became unemployed gave conservatives under the leadership of President Hu Jintao and Premier Wen Jiabao (2003–2013) more influence. The 2008 global financial crisis also lent conservatives newfound confidence in China's socialist market economic model. They doubled down on the state-led strategy, expanding further their primacy in economic policy.

---

[74] Chen Leng and Edward White, "Xi Jinping Tightens Financial Sector Control as New Super-Regulator Takes Shape," *Financial Times*, October 25, 2023; Stephen Roach, "China's 'Whack-a-Mole' Economic Playbook Leads to Confusion," *Financial Times*, August 21, 2023; Joe Leahy, Sun Yu, Chan Ho-him, "Does Xi Jinping Need a Plan B for China's Economy?" *Financial Times*, October 25, 2023; Sharma, 2023; Sun Yu, "China's Local Governments Stuck with Bill for Neighborhood Surveillance," *Financial Times*, May 1, 2023.

[75] Lardy, 2019, pp. 25, 69, 90, 126–127; Roach, 2023; James Kynge, "China Has Fallen into a Psycho-Political Funk," *Financial Times*, August 11, 2023.

[76] Shum, 2021.

Applying Competitive Neutrality as a Potential Standalone Solution

The Australian Competitive Neutrality Framework

Competitive neutrality exists when (1) enterprises of all types face the same set of rules and (2) no contract with the state gives competitive advantage to any market participant.[77] In 1995, in response to a period of lengthy economic malaise, the Commonwealth of Australia's states and territories agreed to introduce a competitive neutrality framework (CNF) by which to address the distortionary effects of state aid to enterprises on the national economy. They introduced five key principles designed to ensure competitive neutrality within Australia's borders:

1. taxation neutrality
2. debt neutrality
3. regulatory neutrality
4. commercial rates of return
5. prices reflecting costs.[78]

Each of these principles was designed to address the myriad ways in which states can provide economically distortionary aid to enterprises (over 30 have previously been described, see Box 9.1).

The Australian CNF required that, where governments of states and territories provided services through market mechanisms that allow actual or potential competition from the private sector, competition should be fair. It stipulated that governments not use their powers to the advantage of their own businesses over the private sector. The CNF did not apply to nonprofit, nonbusiness activities. Nor did it require governments to restructure the delivery of social programs or to remove community service obligations (CSOs) from government businesses. Australia's CNF applied only to government business entities (GBEs), non-GBE companies and authorities, department or agency business units, or other organizations engaging in business activities with revenues more than 10 million Australian dollars and then only when the benefits exceeded the costs.[79]

The CNF required corporatization of government businesses, where incorporation under corporate law was considered desirable. Where it was not, the CNF required accounting separation of CSO and business activities. It further required tax neutrality—removing taxation exemptions and benefits from government businesses. Alternatively, taxation-equivalent regimes could be established if they were cost-effective. Debt neutrality subjected government businesses to similar borrowing costs to those faced by private-sector businesses. Gov-

[77] García-Herrero and Ng, 2021, p. 1.

[78] Australian Government, *Commonwealth Competitive Neutrality Policy Statement*, June 1996.

[79] The Australian CNF defined a business as an organization that charged users for goods and services, faced the presence of an actual or potential competitor, and enjoyed managerial independence (Australian Government, 1996, pp. 5, 7, 8, 9–11).

ernment businesses had to pay market rates of interest or compensate the Australian government through a government borrowing levy that considered any below-market rates paid plus any implicit or explicit government debt guarantee. The CNF required that government businesses meet preset financial targets, setting prices to fully cover their costs, and paying commercial rates for capital (set at the long-term bond rate plus an appropriate premium for risk). It also required that SOEs pay a commercial dividend rate. Regulatory neutrality meant subjecting, where appropriate, all identified organizations to the same regulatory environment as private-sector businesses. The Australian CNF also included a complaints mechanism. The mechanism would ensure that the government would respond to complaints that Commonwealth organizations were not complying with the CNF or to complaints that other additional organizations should be required to comply with the CNF.[80]

In 2005, a decade after its inception, the performance of Australia's CNF was reviewed by the Australian government. In 2022, the government of New South Wales conducted a further review. Both found that the CNF had been a major contributor to a surge in productivity in Australia's states and territories that had underpinned 13 years of continuous economic growth, one of the longest phases of economic expansion on Australian record. The CNF helped to bring unemployment to its lowest levels in three decades. It benefited high- and low-earners in both city and rural areas. The CNF contributed to the highest growth in real Australian per capita income on record in the 20th century and to increased tax revenues. It contributed to a significant reduction in the costs and prices of many goods and services. It also stimulated innovation; improved customer service responsiveness, quality, and reliability; and expanded customer choice.[81]

At the same time, there were areas for improvement. The CNF caused unemployment in public utilities and in other previously protected infrastructure sectors. The protected milk farming sector suffered, while the overall dairy farming industry improved slightly. The CNF's public interest test was not always consistently applied. The fact that the CNF placed the onus of keeping government aid on those seeking to retain it remained a bone of contention. No measures were put in place to lock in gains and to guard against backsliding. Nor were any steps taken to facilitate adjustments required by the policy or to address its adverse distributional effects. New regulatory arrangements that arose because of the CNF's implementation were not always scrutinized in advance to ensure that benefits continued to exceed the costs. There was a constant need for better cost accounting and reporting. The framework's complaints procedure could have been simpler, and there were no penalties for noncompliance with the policy. A single policy applicable to both state and local governments

[80] Australian Government, 1996, pp. 16–18, 20.

[81] Electricity sector average real prices fell by 19 percent. Reductions in rail freight rates of between 8 and 42 percent were achieved. Real port charges fell by up to 50 percent. Telecommunications charges fell by more than 20 percent in real terms. And the average price of milk fell by 5 percent (Productivity Commission, *Review of National Competition Policy Reforms*, Commonwealth of Australia, Report No. 33, February 2005, pp. xii, xv, xvii, xviii, xix, xx, 33; Independent Pricing and Regulatory Tribunal, *Competitive Neutrality in NSW: Draft Report*, December 2022).

would also have been helpful. The framework's overall success was enabled by the flexibility that states and territories were allowed in implementing it and by the fact that states and territories shared in the dividends from meeting their agreed reform commitments via payments from the central government.[82]

China's Potential Interest in Competitive Neutrality

An incident in March 2019 indicated that China's state-led 2015 MIC25 strategy was controversial. "Lou Jiwen (2013–16), the former minister of finance . . . publicly criticized MIC25 for its unrealistic aims and overall inefficiency. He even called the initiative a 'waste of taxpayer's money.'"[83] Prior to the 2008 global financial crisis and Xi Jinping's subsequent doubling down on the state-led economic growth model, reformers within another Chinese bastion of neoliberal economic thought, the People's Bank of China, recognized the need to address the issue of state aid to enterprises and to adopt a more neutral attitude toward private companies and SOEs. In October 2018, Central Bank Governor Yi Gang (2018–present) stated that China would consider applying the principle of competitive neutrality to China's SOEs.[84] This statement unleashed a policy debate within the CCP. Premier Li Keqiang (2013–2023) subsequently endorsed that debate formally during the March 2019 National People's Congress meeting.[85] Former Vice President Wang Qishan (2018–2023)—a key reformer under Premier Zhou Rongji—reportedly predicted an impending further slowdown in economic growth under Xi's state-led approach to economic development. Wang is reported to have expressed the belief that Xi's approach would, at some point, cause the "music to stop" and force another round of SOE privatization in China.[86] Economic reform appears to retain a constituency within the CCP's leadership.[87]

Applying Competitive Neutrality More Broadly

As an issue, the policy of adopting competitive neutrality toward enterprises is far from limited to Australia or China. State aid to enterprises is a global phenomenon that causes significant economic costs.[88] The IMF recommended a series of best practices to contain the finan-

---

[82] Productivity Commission, 2005, pp. xxii, xxiii, xxiv, xxv; Independent Pricing and Regulatory Tribunal, 2022, p. 7.

[83] Zenglein and Holzmann, 2019, p. 30.

[84] Wengxiao et al. 2021, p. 12.

[85] Zenglein and Holzmann, 2019, p. 46.

[86] Shum, 2021, p. 174.

[87] Shum, 2021, p. 173; Zenglein and Holzmann, 2019, pp. 30, 46; IMF, OECD, World Bank, and WTO, 2022, p. 3; Wang, 2021, p. 15; Bown and Hillman, 2019, p. 2.

[88] "SOEs operate in virtually every country in the world. In some, they number in the thousands (China, Germany, Italy, Russia, Sweden, Ukraine) and are owned by national or subnational governments. SOEs owned by subnational governments such as local bus, sewer, and water services, often outnumber SOEs owned by the central government. SOEs are among the largest corporations in some advanced economies

cial risks and drag that SOEs impose on economic growth and government finances.[89] Some overlapped with the prescriptions of Australia's CNF. The IMF recommended that SOEs

- be corporatized, if possible
- be consolidated under an autonomous government agency or holding company
- install professional management
- have private minority shareholder oversight
- have a professional board of directors
- undergo regular assessments of performance
- be publicly listed
- be subject to regular audits of their financial statements.[90]

The fact that China, to one degree or another, had already adopted all these suggestions by 2023 serves as a further indicator that an appetite for adopting a policy of competitive neutrality toward enterprises had survived in pockets of Zhongnanhai.[91]

Ruminating on the piecemeal set of options available to address the adverse impacts of state aid to enterprises at the international level, the IMF suggested that "a more cooperative

(France, Italy, Norway) and comprise one-third or more of the largest firms in several emerging markets (China, India, Indonesia, Malaysia, Russia, Saudi Arabia, United Arab Emirates)" (IMF, 2020, p. 48).

89 As a general proposition, "SOEs . . . have low productivity, distort competition, and can be plagued by corruption" (IMF, 2020, p. 66). Cross-country evidence showed that they were less productive than private firms in the same sectors. Because they enjoyed implicit government guarantees against debt default and bankruptcy, SOEs often faced soft budget constraints. These allowed them to take on large amounts of debt that could pose a risk to public sector finances, on occasion requiring government bailouts on the order of one-fifth of GDP. The large profits generated because of their role as some of the largest enterprises in certain economies provided strong incentives for corruption. SOE officials received 80 percent of total bribes in foreign bribery cases. See IMF, 2020, pp. 52, 54, 56, 58, 65, 66.

90 IMF, 2020, pp. 49–53; OECD, 2017.

91 "By the end of 2016, [Chinese] authorities had corporatized more than 92 percent of the subsidiaries of 101 central state firms . . . A new push on corporatization was . . . confirmed by Premier Li Keqiang in March 2017 in his speech to the National People's Congress. Shortly thereafter, in July 2017, the State Council formally announced plans to complete the corporatization of all central state firms, except those in the financial and cultural sectors, by the end of 2017" (Lardy, 2019, p. 116). However, that initiative did not account for 40 percent of SOEs under subcentral control that accounted for over 50 percent of state-owned assets in China. As previously related, established in March 2003, SASAC was charged with improving the performance of China's largest nonfinancial state firms. SASAC eventually assumed consolidated control over 60 percent of all Chinese SOEs. Formally, the Organization Department of the CCP had long nominated, and nominally independent SOE boards had long confirmed, candidates for the top three management positions at SOEs. During the privatizations carried out under Zhou Rongji's reforms of the late 1990s, the Chinese government secured strategic investors as minority shareholders in many initial public offerings of stock of SOEs. "Under the regulations set by [SASAC], each firm was also supposed to generate a 6 percent return on equity every year. Smart SOE bosses hit the target because they understood that if they came in too low, they'd get sacked, but if their return was too high, foes would angle to get their jobs" (Shum, 2021, p. 141). See also Lardy, 2019, pp. 107, 116, 129, 137, 145, 152; and Paulson, 2015, pp. 31, 78, 152, 160–164, 170, 362.

solution would be a multilateral agreement on general principles to ensure a level playing field between SOEs and private firms."[92] Drawing on the decades-long experience of its European and Australian allies, the United States might therefore propose instituting a separate, standalone MCNF. This MCNF might work in parallel and in addition to the GATT-WTO trade regime until such a time as changes were put in place to the governing instruments of the WTO needed to ensure that competitive neutrality could function within that broader framework. To incentivize movement away from state aid to enterprises, the mechanism might enforce criteria according to which enterprises receiving state aid were subjected to differing levels of import tariff surcharges under a sliding scale, whereby the import tariff surcharge declines to zero as layers of state aid are removed (see Box 9.2).

However attractive such a scheme might appear on paper, each of the three potential global trade policy options outlined above (do nothing; work within the WTO system to reform it; or make the needed fixes by concluding a standalone agreement, such as an MCNF, negotiated by a subset of WTO members that others are permitted but not required to join) enjoys potential advantages, disadvantages, and implementation challenges. I examine these next.

Assessing the Options and Their Implementation

The advantage of a "do nothing" policy approach to the global trade order is that it is politically a seemingly low-cost option. Relatively limited amounts of domestic political capital need to be expended to follow this course. For this reason, it is the most likely outcome. It offers the option of pursuing national trade and investment interests at multiple levels: that of national investment and competition law, that of bilateral FTAs and BITs, and that of large plurilateral regional FTAs, such as CPTPP and T-TIP. The heavy lifting involved with other approaches in reaching consensus among 164 WTO member states can be sidestepped through coalitions of the willing. That in turn can allow countries to address pressing new developments in the international trade and investment arena whose resolution has proved elusive under the GATT-WTO trade regime. The "do nothing" approach offers the promise of fewer or no adverse DSB rulings against large trading nations, such as the United States and China. It further provides such nations greater leeway to lean on smaller trading nations, which is afforded to them by dint of their economic power.

The "do nothing" approach also harbors several significant disadvantages and potential future costs. In recent years, regional FTAs have clearly targeted China, creating antagonism. There is a chance that the global trade order might disintegrate further into a greater number of competing and adversarial regional FTAs, each with its own rules and dispute resolution mechanisms (e.g., the Regional Comprehensive Economic Partnership, which includes China). It is conceivable that future tariff disputes within and between such entities could proliferate and escalate, much as global trade was affected by the Smoot-Hawley Tariff Act.

[92] IMF, 2020, p. 68.

BOX 9.2

Possible Features of a Multilateral Competitive Neutrality Framework

The exact form that an MCNF would take on would be the result of intergovernmental negotiations. In a deliberate move, the possible features of such a framework outlined below are high quality and aspirational. The framework suggested does not focus on state ownership. It would apply to any enterprise that receives state aid. It would also apply to any level of government that provides aid to enterprises: supranational, national, regional, provincial, local, or municipal.

It is important to recognize from the outset that state aid to enterprises is often used by LDCs that have small economies and low exposure to international trade. They can be excluded from the strictures of an MNCF. To create greater transparency and allow reliable calculation of the cost-effectiveness of applying an MCNF, all enterprises identified to the MNCF administration by a complaints mechanism as receiving state aid and that compete with other enterprises would be subject to a requirement to disclose all state aid received annually. Enterprises that fail to comply would automatically be subject to a high import tariff surcharge when importing goods to MNCF member states. A somewhat lower automatic surcharge would apply to those in compliance. Enterprises would be able to reduce this surcharge further, along a sliding scale that ends at zero, depending on their ability to document progress along one or more of the following dimensions:

- *Tax neutrality.* Tax-exemption benefits have been neutralized either by the application of taxation equivalent regimes or by the passage of legislation abolishing them.
- *Debt neutrality.* Any outstanding arrears of debt have been cleared. Concessionary finance benefits have been equalized by applying borrowing costs equal to those paid by business of the same risk in the same industry in free financial markets. Implicit or explicit state debt guarantees have been neutralized by the payment of debt guarantee charges to the state at market-determined rates. SOEs are subject to a no-bailout provision or regular statutory insolvency processes.
- *Regulatory neutrality.* Amendments to legislation, regulations, or administrative actions have removed all preferences received from the state.
- *Market returns.* The enterprises' shareholders and bondholders are earning commercial rates of return that at a minimum equal the ten-year median return on capital for enterprises in their industry. The enterprise also pays a commercial dividend that at least matches the median for its industry.
- *Full-cost pricing.* The enterprise can document that the prices that it charges for its business activities reflect full cost attribution. Where enterprises have businesses with and without market power, separate books are kept for each line of business, and the enterprise can document that no cross-subsidization has taken place.
- *Competitive tendering and contracting.* The enterprise can document that it was freely able to choose between in-house or state-aided suppliers of goods and services and external commercial contractors in performing core functions. It can document that (1) in-house tenders or those from state-aided enterprises were prepared in iso-

lation from those in the enterprise responsible for evaluating tenders and awarding contracts and (2) the tenders received reflected full cost attribution, including taxation, return on capital, and all relevant overheads.

- *Transparency and corporate governance.* The enterprise is overseen by an autonomous agency or holding company. It has a well-defined and documented policy mandate that is subject to regular review. It has audited financial statements that are fully integrated into the country's public accounts. It can document that it has reincorporated from a statutory corporation or quasi-corporation to a standard national corporate form. It has minority private shareholders, professional managers with independent decisionmaking authority, and a professional board of directors with independent directors all selected at arm's length. It has fiscal and financial targets to which management is held accountable, it has progressed from unlisted to listed status, and it has transformed from majority government ownership to a point in which the government no longer holds a blocking minority of shares or can influence the enterprise's decisions.

SOURCES: Australian Government, 1996; Capobianco, 2011; Kowalski, 2013; Willemyns, 2016; Chiang, 2018; IMF, 2020.

Were a future financial crisis in China to unleash severe global economic consequences, such as those experienced during the Great Depression, then a beggar-thy-neighbor race to the bottom on tariffs might ensue, serving only to exacerbate the crisis. It might also have a similar severe impact on global growth, standards of living, and employment.

In the unlikely event that nations choose to play by the rules of differing agreements, there is also the risk of conflicting judgments, in which one regional FTA dispute resolution body rules for and another rules against the same claimant. This in turn raises the prospect that nations might engage in venue shopping, trying to have a trade case adjudicated under the regional FTA regime that they deem most likely to judge in their favor. Faced by the differing requirements of differing trading regimes, multinational trading enterprises might experience diseconomies of scale as they are forced to tailor their products to the requirements of each regional FTA regime. This would cause less efficient use of resources, reduced profits, and reduced national standards of living. Future global economic growth would be impaired.

As a reminder of the stakes, thanks in large part to the GATT-WTO trading regime put in place at the end of World War II, between 1940 and 2019, gross world product increased almost 30-fold. The global standard of living (GDP per capita) increased eightfold. Extreme poverty was reduced from 52 percent to just under 9 percent. And China was one of the greatest beneficiaries. Further disintegration of the global trade order of the kind outlined above threatens to reverse this progress. It could facilitate renewed global conflict. The Great Depression—whose depth is believed to have been exacerbated by the actions of U.S. Senators Smoot and Hawley and U.S. President Hoover—was a contributing factor to the rise of fascism and to unleashing a global war that lasted six to eight years and caused between 69 to 84 million deaths through military violence, disease, and famine.[93]

Working within the WTO system to fix the global trade order offers the prospect of appearing less discriminatory, particularly toward China. Because all 164 WTO member states would be involved in constructing a new negotiating mechanism, equitable future negotiating solutions and a mechanism by which to regularly update multilateral trade rules might be assured under this approach. This approach would also involve negotiating a functioning, refurbished dispute settlement mechanism. That, in turn, would lend credibility and authority to a reanimated GATT-WTO trade regime. This implementation would build on and extend existing international trade law. It also potentially offers a couple of relatively quick and easy fixes:

1. China's accession to the GPA
2. fixing the WTO's DSB by "establish[ing] a set of rebuttable presumptions for countries that believe they have suffered as a result of another member's subsidies," through a decision at the Ministerial Conference or at the General Council level.[94]

However, small fixes of that kind will probably not be sufficient to address the systemic trade deflection and trade diversion effects caused by state aid to enterprises. Rehabilitating the WTO's DSB and agreeing on a new multilateral mechanism by which to periodically update international trade rules would be taxing and would require a large amount of time. The large number of states that would be party to such negotiations almost guarantees that no more than a least common denominator outcome would be achieved. A large domestic political price would likely have to be paid to gain acquiescence to any global agreement reached.

Putting a standalone MCNF in place would be just as time-consuming and complicated. In recognition of the fact that lower-income countries provide their enterprises with state aid, such a framework would have to define threshold levels of economic activity below which it would not apply. Developed nations, such as the United States, have many subnational SOEs that might be adversely affected should that threshold be set too low. Conversely, an MNCF could adversely affect large Western firms that are national champions and that receive direct and or indirect government subsidies (e.g., large aerospace conglomerates). Implementing an MCNF would be of little value in the absence of an authoritative, credible, and effective enforcement and dispute resolution mechanism. The politically taxing rehabilitation of the

93 DeLong, 1998; United Nations, 2019; Moatsos, 2021, p. 2; Anderson, 2016. The length and cumulative death toll of World War II depends on whether one considers the German 1939 invasion of Poland or the 1937 Marco Polo bridge incident between China and Japan as the starting point of the war.

94 Bown and Hillman, 2019, p. 18; "The Uncertain Future of the World Trade Organization," 2021.

multilateral dispute resolution mechanism would appear to be a prerequisite were this option to be pursued.[95]

A standalone MCNF also might offer several potential benefits. An MCNF could address the many ways that state aid to enterprises confers unfair competitive advantages. By focusing on state aid to enterprises, it neatly sidesteps a definitional quagmire associated with state ownership (see Box 9.3). By applying import surcharges on a global basis, the MCNF could solve a shortcoming that bilateral dispute resolution under the auspices of the WTO does not appear to be able to cure. Under the WTO dispute resolution regime, even once a country has been sanctioned because of an adverse DSB ruling in a bilateral trade dispute, overcapacity and predatory pricing caused by state aid continue to cause systemic trade deflection and trade diversion impacts on other countries. Instead of curing problems ex post facto, an MCNF might be able to address the anticompetitive effects of state aid to enterprises ex ante—*before* the damage is done to competing firms and industries. Progress toward competitive neutrality can also be measured.[96]

Rather than proposing a coercive vehicle that singles out China by punishing it alone for state aid to its enterprises, an MCNF can be framed as a nondiscriminatory public good that potentially provides a cooperative, win-win (pareto superior) solution for all participants in global trade. It could benefit many countries, by virtue of the systemic long-term improvements in economic efficiency and standards of living that its proper implementation could bring. An MCNF therefore appears to be a relatively easy concept to promote to potentially skeptical lower-income WTO member states. Both the EU and Australia have long experience in implementing similar regulatory regimes. They are therefore likely to be receptive to such an initiative and to be willing to bring their experience to bear in negotiating and implementing it. And there are indications that such a framework might find support among reform-minded leaders in China. China could become a prime beneficiary of such a framework because—properly implemented—it could boost that nation's economic growth significantly over the long term. There is therefore a chance that an MCNF could be put in place by working cooperatively with China. An MCNF thus represents a potential means to replace the current zero-sum game in the U.S.-China competition for global leadership with a poten-

[95] "Most subsidies appear to be provided by sub-central government entities, although separate data on the value of production affected are not available. Official notifications to the WTO show extensive subcentral subsidy programs. Of those reporting subcentral subsidies, information for 2018 shows that Australia, Canada, China, the EU, India, and the United States reported the largest shares of subsidy programs at the subcentral level (EU data refer to programs at the EU level as well as to incentives by a range of individual member states, some of which are provided at subnational level). A large number of the reported subsidies by these economies were provided at the sub-central level, for example, by U.S. states [approximately 90 percent] or Chinese provinces [approximately 81%]" (IMF, 2022, p. 13). See also Bown, 2022, p. 17.

[96] Progress can be measured by calculating the differences in interest expense to total debt, effective tax rate, and return on assets between national enterprises that have been favored by state aid and those that have not (García-Herrero and Ng, 2021).

BOX 9.3

Challenges Involved with the Term *State-Owned Enterprise*

According to the OECD,

> [a] state-owned enterprise is any corporate entity recognised by national law as an enterprise and in which the central level of government exercises ownership and control. This includes joint stock companies, limited liability companies and partnerships limited by shares. In addition, statutory corporations, whose legal personality is established through specific legislation, should be considered as SOEs if they engage in economic activities, either exclusively or together with the pursuit of public policy objectives. An economic activity is one that involves offering goods or services on a given market and which could, at least in principle, be carried out by a private operator to make profits. Quasi-corporations, which are autonomous commercial activities carried out inside the general government sector, should be considered as SOEs if they are financially autonomous and charge economically significant prices.[a]

This definition is fraught with potential issues.

Which state? Does the definition of ownership apply only to central national government? Or should it also apply to supranational organizations or regional, local, and municipal governments? Many subcentral or sub-federal SOEs exist; even smaller SOEs can have distortive economic effects.[b]

What kind of ownership? Majority ownership of an enterprise's equity capital is but one of many indications of influence or control. Sometimes a golden share or blocking minority share (25 percent in many countries) will suffice. Rules and procedures other than shareholder rights can be used to exercise control.[c] A political party may, for example, have the right to appoint management or dictate the enterprise's business decisions.

What kind of enterprise? The beneficiaries of state economic aid can take on many forms. Both incorporated enterprises and unincorporated statutory or quasi-corporations exist. The former can have their stock listed and traded on a public exchange or not. Does the definition of SOE encompass all the above?

What kind of activities? Is the entity in question purely pursuing a government-mandated nonprofit (universal) public service obligation or policy goal? Or is it also operating on a for-profit basis? Is the government-mandated service that is being provided unique, thus conferring market power on the entity in question? Does the entity have other commercial activities? Is it using rents extracted from a government-mandated activity that confers market power to cross-subsidize the cost of another activity in which it competes commercially with entities that do not receive similarly favorable government treatment?[d]

SOURCES: OECD, 2017; IMF, 2020; Lardy, 2019; IMF, 2022; Capobianco, 2011.

[a] OECD, 2017, p. 11.

[b] According to the IMF, "SOEs owned by subnational governments, such as local bus, sewer, and water services, often outnumber SOEs owned by the central government" (IMF, 2020, p. 48). In

China, the majority of SOEs are administered by local governments. In the United States up to 90 percent of SOEs are administered at the sub-federal level.

[c] "For example, the German state of Lower Saxony has only 20 percent of the voting rights of Volkswagen but, legally, also has a veto right over key decisions such as factory closures, mergers and acquisitions" (IMF, 2020, p. 50).

[d] "For example, Deutsche Post (and its predecessors) over a period of 25 years until 2000 used profits from its letter delivery monopoly to cross-subsidize below-cost selling in the market for business parcel delivery" (IMF, 2020, p. 50).

tial win-win solution that redirects U.S.-China competition into a more productive channel that could provide positive results for many nations.

There appear to be at least four scenarios under which the options of either fixing or adding to the GATT-WTO trade regime might be implemented, each of which would involve negotiations of differing scales and complexity:

1. cooperative global negotiations among all 164 WTO member states
2. cooperative negotiations between China and a coalition of the willing
3. noncooperative negotiations involving the United States and the EU
4. noncooperative negotiations involving the United States and its allies.

Cooperative Global Negotiations

Were negotiations to involve both (1) additions to the GATT-WTO trade regime, such as the proposed MCNF, and (2) fixes made by changes to that regime, there is a chance that WTO member states might agree to multilateral negotiations to bring those changes about. However, an additional MCNF is no small step, of the kind recommended above. That said, the smaller fixes recommended are not likely to be deemed worth the effort without bigger-step improvements to the GATT-WTO regime. Cooperative global negotiations are likely to be taxing, time-consuming, and fraught with the risk of a collapse, such as that experienced during the Doha Round. Such a further failure of global negotiations might represent the death knell of the GATT-WTO trade regime. As mentioned, if agreement were to be reached, there is also a significant risk that only a least common denominator result could be achieved—that transformational change would prove elusive. However, it seems that, even if only for diplomatic appearances' sake, this is an implementation scenario that—at least at the outset—may almost have to be pursued. Charges of an attempt at great-power condominium would likely be made were any of the other implementation scenarios discussed to be pursued on their own.

Cooperative Negotiations Between China and a Coalition of the Willing

Which states might join such a coalition? The EU and Japan have already volunteered to join the United States. To provide balance between Europe and Asia, furnish a counterbalance within Asia to China, and draw on Australia's unique CNF experience, it seems that such a coalition might consist of China, the United States, the EU, Japan, South Korea, and Australia. Among them, these six entities accounted for 59 percent of global 2022 merchandise trade—close to the 60 percent of global trade controlled by the 23 founding members of GATT.[97] An agreement among these six parties might therefore be sufficient to create an accomplished fact. Other trading nations might find themselves compelled to acquiesce to the revisions to the GATT-WTO regime agreed by such a coalition by virtue of its combined market power.

Noncooperative Negotiations Involving the United States and the EU

China might balk at the idea of reform to the GATT-WTO trade regime. The United States and the EU accounted for almost 37 percent of global 2022 merchandise trade—over 2.5 times that of China at 14 percent. Their combined market power would be nowhere near that which would be mobilized by a cooperative negotiation with China of the kind described above, but, given the right circumstances, it might be sufficient to compel other nations into acquiescing to revisions to the GATT-WTO trade regime.[98]

Noncooperative Negotiations Involving the United States and Its Allies

This is another potential implementation scenario. It might occur were the EU, for some reason, to refuse to cooperate, forcing the United States to look to alternative partners. In 2017, the United States had 65 treaty, de facto, and major non–North Atlantic Treaty Organization allies. Together they accounted for 58 percent of global 2022 merchandise trade—four times that of China and more than China, the EU, Japan, and the United States combined (Figure 9.1). Agreement among such a coalition might be sufficient to compel other nations to acquiesce to revisions to the GATT-WTO regime. However, forging such a coalition might be time-consuming and taxing. The other negative considerations attached to multilateral negotiations already mentioned above might also come into play under such an implementation scenario.[99]

---

97 WTO, "Statistics on Merchandise Trade," webpage, undated-a.

98 WTO, undated-a. The right circumstances might include further widespread Chinese acts of economic predation and coercion or a Chinese conflict with or a blockade of Taiwan.

99 King Mallory, Luke J. Matthews, Michael J. McNerney, Kaleb J. Redden, Adrienne M. Propp, Mark Toukan, Omair Khan, and Jonathan Welburn, *U.S. Alliance and Partner Networks: A Network Analysis of*

FIGURE 9.1

Potential Negotiators' Share of 2022 World Trade

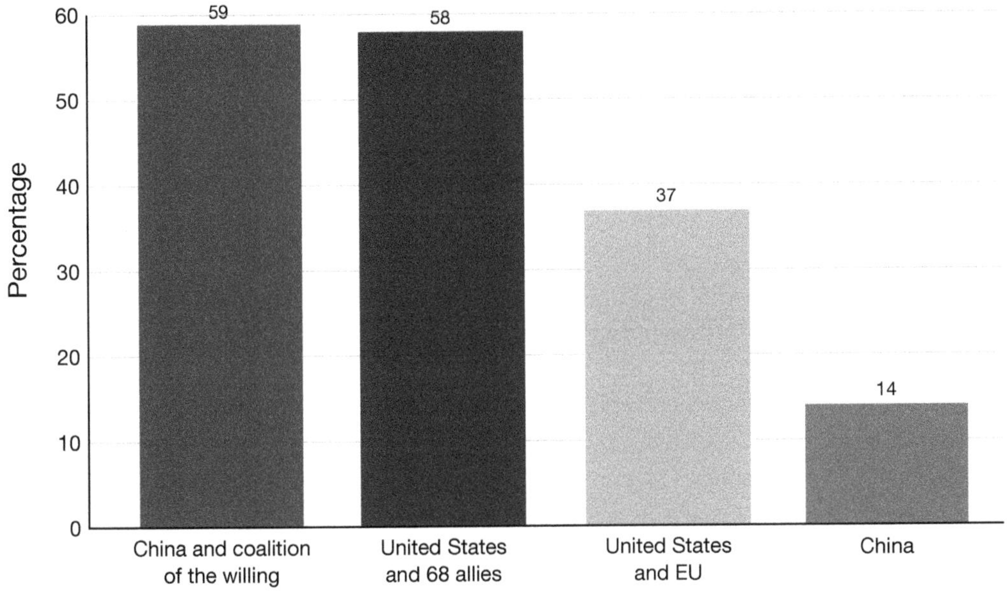

SOURCE: Features information from WTO, WTO Stats Dashboard—Merchandise Trade, database, undated-d.

Although not impossible, the noncooperative implementation scenarios are less appealing than the cooperative ones. That is because they involve aspects of compellence or control.[100] Combinations of the cooperative and compellent implementation scenarios are possible. One such combination would involve China, the EU, Japan, and the United States first negotiating fixes and additions to the GATT-WTO regime. The remaining WTO member states might then be offered two options:

1. a one-time up or down vote to accede to the agreement
2. acceding piecemeal to the agreement after the passage of some time (which many states chose to do after the 1947 signature of GATT).

Their Health and Strength, RAND Corporation, RR-A1066-1, 2024; WTO, undated-a.

100 "*Control* involves the deliberate use of force (political, economic, or military) to restrict an adversary's strategic choices; it depends originally on judgments about the opponent's strategy, but those judgments eventually become irrelevant as the adversary runs out of options. . . . *Compellence* involves persuading an adversary that it *must* act for fear of the consequences if it does not. A compellent threat is intended to persuade the opponent to give up something of value. It is a strategy designed to make others act in ways they consider harmful to themselves but that benefit the compellor" (King Mallory, *New Challenges in Cross Domain Deterrence*, RAND Corporation, PE-259-OSD, April 2018, p. 3). See also Glenn H. Snyder, *Deterrence and Defense; Toward a Theory of National Security*, Princeton University Press, 1961, pp. 2, 4; and Lawrence Freedman, *Deterrence*, Polity Press, 2004, pp. 26, 27, 409, 100, 109, 110.

Conclusion

China's economy underwent a remarkable trajectory over the past 45 years. That path resulted in a unique system of economic management in China in which the party-state oversaw a complex set of mechanisms that yielded more control over the economy than in the overwhelming majority of other countries. Because of the size to which China's economy has grown and China's role in global trade, the aid that China has provided to its enterprises (including subsidies) has caused overcapacity and enabled predatory pricing and other anticompetitive behaviors on those enterprises' parts in global markets that have damaged competing private businesses.

Although five different models of national economic management were anticipated when the WTO was created, the system that China put in place in 2003 after its 2001 WTO accession was not anticipated. The GATT-WTO trading regime was therefore only partially able to address the distortions of world trade caused by China's newfound prominence. Frustrated by this fact and a series of adverse rulings by the WTO's DSB, in 2017–2018, the United States imposed tariffs on 49 percent of its imports from China. By refusing to consider replacement candidates for the WTO's Appellate Body, the United States also caused the WTO's DSB to cease to function. The failure of the Doha Round of multilateral trade negotiation in 2007 had already inflicted serious damage on the WTO's ability to update global trade rules. The United States' 2017–2018 decisions effectively hamstrung the WTO's ability to regulate global trade. The global trading system began to disintegrate. Nations sought to address new challenges to trade through a series of large regional FTAs.

As the United States engages in a period of competition with China, policymakers are faced with the decision of whether to preside over a requiem for the global trade order (the most likely outcome) or attempt to resuscitate it. Doing nothing appears fraught with potential perils. At least two other options appear available: (1) make small fixes within the system of the WTO or (2) make significant improvements to that system.

It is likely that only the latter course can address the systemic effects on international trade of China's economic policies and unique system of economic management. One possible such improvement is to institute an MCNF in parallel or in addition to the existing GATT-WTO trading regime. Such a framework may have the potential to successfully address the systemic impacts of China's unique system of economic management. At the same time, it could provide a win-win outcome for all trading nations. Such an amendment to the international trading regime might therefore be welcomed by WTO member states, particularly lower-income countries. There are also signs that such a framework might be welcomed by economic reformers in China. Trade partners in Europe are also likely to be receptive. An MCNF can be implemented in a noncooperative, compellent manner. However, there may be a real prospect that, given the political will to do so, the GATT-WTO trade regime can be resuscitated in a cooperative fashion. A cooperative attempt at revival is in both the U.S. and Chinese national interest. It could also direct U.S.-China competition into a more constructive channel that provides positive results for all nations involved.

Abbreviations

AIIB	Asian Infrastructure Investment Bank
ASCM	Agreement on Subsidies and Countervailing Measures
BIT	bilateral investment treaty
BRI	Belt and Road Initiative
CCP	Chinese Communist Party
CNF	competitive neutrality framework
CPTPP	Comprehensive and Progressive Agreement for Trans-Pacific Partnership
CSO	Community Service Obligations
DSB	Dispute Settlement Body
EU	European Union
FTA	free trade agreement
GATS	General Agreement on Trade in Services
GATT	General Agreement on Tariffs and Trade
GBE	government business entity
GDP	gross domestic product
GE	Guangdong Enterprises
GITIC	Guangdong International Trust and Investment Company
GPA	Government Procurement Agreement
IMF	International Monetary Fund
LDC	less-developed country
LGFV	local government finance vehicle
MCNF	multilateral competitive neutrality framework
MFA	Multifiber Arrangement
MIC25	Made in China 2025
NDRC	National Development and Reform Commission
OECD	Organisation for Economic Co-operation and Development
POE	privately owned enterprise
PRC	People's Republic of China
SASAC	State-owned Assets Supervision and Administration Commission
SOB	state-owned bank
SOE	state-owned enterprise
STE	state trading enterprise
TPP	Trans-Pacific Partnership
T-TIP	Transatlantic Trade and Investment Partnership
VER	Voluntary Export Restraint
WTO	World Trade Organization

References

Anderson, Kym, "Contributions of the GATT/WTO to Global Economic Welfare: Empirical Evidence," *Journal of Economic Surveys,* Vol. 30, No. 1, February 2016.

Australian Government, *Commonwealth Competitive Neutrality Policy Statement*, June 1996.

Autor, David H., David Dorn, and Gordon H. Hanson, *The China Shock: Learning from Labor Market Adjustments to Large Changes in Trade*, National Bureau of Economic Research, Working Paper 21096, January 2016.

Bhagwati, Jagdish, "The Broken Legs of Global Trade," Project Syndicate, May 29, 2012.

Bown, Chad P., *The 2018 US-China Trade Conflict After 40 Years of Special Protection*, Peterson Institute for International Economics, Working Paper 19-7, April 2019.

Bown, Chad P., *Trump Ended WTO Dispute Settlement. Trade Remedies Are Needed to Fix It*, Peterson Institute for International Economics, Working Paper 22-1, January 2022.

Bown, Chad P., and Jennifer A. Hillman, *WTO'ing a Resolution to the China Subsidy Problem*, Peterson Institute for International Economics, Working Paper 22-1, October 2019.

Bown, Chad P., and Soumaya Keynes, *Why Trump Shot the Sheriffs: The End of WTO Dispute Settlement 1.0*, Peterson Institute for International Economics, Working Paper 20-4, March 2020.

Bown, Chad P., and Melinda Kolb, "Trump's Trade War Timeline: An Up-to-Date Guide," Peterson Institute for International Economics, November 17, 2022.

Capobianco, Antonio, and Hans Christiansen, *Competitive Neutrality and State-Owned Enterprises: Challenges and Policy Options*, OECD Publishing, OECD Corporate Governance Working Papers No. 1, 2011.

Chiang, Ting-Wei, "Chinese State-Owned Enterprises and WTO's Anti-Subsidy Regime," *Georgetown Journal of International Law,* Vol. 49, No. 2, 2018.

Corporate Finance Institute, "Smoot-Hawley Tariff Act," webpage, undated. As of April 18, 2023:
https://corporatefinanceinstitute.com/resources/economics/smoot-hawley-tariff-act/

DeLong, J. Bradford, *Estimates of World GDP, One Million B.C.–Present*, University of California, Berkeley, 1998.

Delury, John, *Agents of Subversion: The Fate of John T. Downey and the CIA's Covert War in China*, Cornell University Press, 2022.

Engemann, Kristie M., "Banking Panics of 1931–33," webpage, Federal Reserve History, November 22, 2013. As of April 18, 2023:
https://www.federalreservehistory.org/essays/banking-panics-1931-33

Ferguson, Ian F., *World Trade Organization Negotiations: The Doha Development Agenda*, Congressional Research Service, RL32060, December 12, 2011.

Freedman, Lawrence, *Deterrence*, Polity Press, 2004.

García-Herrero, Alicia, and Gary Ng, "China's State-Owned Enterprises and Competitive Neutrality," *Policy Contribution*, No. 5, February 2021.

Horlick, Gary, and Peggy A. Clarke, *Rethinking Subsidy Disciplines for the Future*, International Centre for Trade and Sustainable Development and World Economic Forum, January 2016.

Ihara, Kensaku, and Frances Cheung, "China Economists Expect 5.4% GDP Growth in 2023: Survey," *Nikkei Asia*, April 6, 2023.

IMF—*See* International Monetary Fund.

Independent Pricing and Regulatory Tribunal, *Competitive Neutrality in NSW: Draft Report*, December 2022.

International Monetary Fund, "State-Owned Enterprises: The Other Government," in *Fiscal Monitor: Policies to Support People During the COVID-19 Pandemic*, April 2020.

International Monetary Fund, Organisation for Economic Co-operation and Development, World Bank, and World Trade Organization, *Subsidies, Trade and International Cooperation*, 2022.

International Trade Administration, "Trade Guide: WTO Anti-Dumping Agreement," webpage, undated-a. As of May 9, 2023:
https://www.trade.gov/trade-guide-anti-dumping

International Trade Administration, "Trade Guide: WTO Subsidies Agreement," webpage, undated-b. As of May 9, 2023:
https://www.trade.gov/trade-guide-wto-subsidies

Kowalski, Przemyslaw, Max Büge, Monika Sztajerowska, and Matias Egeland, *State-Owned Enterprises: Trade Effects and Policy Implications*, OECD Publishing, OECD Trade Policy Papers No. 147, 2013.

Kynge, James, "China Has Fallen into a Psycho-Political Funk," *Financial Times*, August 11, 2023.

Lardy, Nicholas R., *Markets over Mao: The Rise of Private Business in China*, Peterson Institute for International Economics, 2014.

Lardy, Nicholas R., *The State Strikes Back: The End of Economic Reform in China?* Peterson Institute for International Economics, 2019.

Leahy, Joe, Sun Yu, and Chan Ho-him, "Does Xi Jinping Need a Plan B for China's Economy?" *Financial Times*, July 17, 2023.

Leng, Chen, and Edward White, "Xi Jinping Tightens Financial Sector Control as New Super-Regulator Takes Shape," *Financial Times*, October 25, 2023.

Mallory, King, *New Challenges in Cross Domain Deterrence*, RAND Corporation, PE-259-OSD, April 2018. As of October 11, 2024:
https://www.rand.org/pubs/perspectives/PE259.html

Mallory, King, Luke J. Matthews, Michael J. McNerney, Kaleb J. Redden, Adrienne M. Propp, Mark Toukan, Omair Khan, and Jonathan Welburn, *U.S. Alliance and Partner Networks: A Network Analysis of Their Health and Strength*, RAND Corporation, RR-A1066-1, 2024. As of October 10, 2024:
https://www.rand.org/pubs/research_reports/RRA1066-1.html

McRae, Donald M., "General Agreement on Tariffs and Trade," United Nations, 2021.

Moatsos, Michail, "Global Extreme Poverty: Present and Past Since 1820," in Organisation for Economic Co-operation and Development, *How Was Life?* Vol. II, *New Perspectives on Well-Being and Global Inequality Since 1820*, OECD Publishing, 2021.

National Bureau of Statistics of China, "National Data," webpage, undated. As of December 23, 2024:
https://data.stats.gov.cn/english/easyquery.htm?cn=C01

OECD—*See* Organisation for Economic Co-operation and Development.

Organisation for Economic Co-operation and Development, *Excess Capacity in the Global Steel Industry and the Implications of New Investment Projects*, OECD Science, Technology and Industry Policy Papers No. 18, OECD Publishing, 2015.

Organisation for Economic Co-operation and Development, *The Size and Sectoral Distribution of State-Owned Enterprises*, OECD Publishing, 2017.

Organisation for Economic Co-operation and Development, *Measuring Distortions in International Markets: The Semiconductor Value Chain*, OECD Trade Policy Papers No. 234, OECD Publishing, 2019.

Paulson, Henry M., Jr., *Dealing with China: An Insider Unmasks the New Economic Superpower*, 1st ed., Twelve, 2015.

"The Precarious Position of the WTO," *Strategic Comments*, Vol. 29, No. 1, February 14, 2023.

Productivity Commission, *Review of National Competition Policy Reforms*, Commonwealth of Australia, Report No. 33, February 2005.

Public Law 117-169, Inflation Reduction Act of 2022, August 16, 2022.

Richardson, Gary, "The Great Depression," webpage, Federal Reserve History, November 22, 2013. As of April 18, 2023:
https://www.federalreservehistory.org/essays/great-depression

Richardson, Gary, Alejandro Komai, Michael Gou, and Daniel Park, "Stock Market Crash of 1929," webpage, Federal Reserve History, November 22, 2013. As of April 18, 2023:
https://www.federalreservehistory.org/essays/stock-market-crash-of-1929

Roach, Stephen, "China's 'Whack-a-Mole' Economic Playbook Leads to Confusion," *Financial Times*, August 21, 2023.

Schechinger, Anne, "Under Trump, Farm Subsidies Soared and the Rich Got Richer," Environmental Working Group, February 24, 2021.

Sharma, Ruchir, "'Boomy' Talk About the Chinese Economy Is a Charade," *Financial Times*, May 21, 2023.

Shum, Desmond, *Red Roulette: An Insider's Story of Wealth, Power, Corruption, and Vengeance in Today's China*, Simon & Schuster, 2021.

Snow, Edgar, *Red Star over China*, Grove Press, 1961.

Snyder, Glenn H., *Deterrence and Defense; Toward a Theory of National Security*, Princeton University Press, 1961.

Spence, Jonathan D., *Mao Zedong*, Viking, 1999.

Spence, Jonathan D., *The Search for Modern China*, 3rd ed., W.W. Norton & Company, 2013.

"The Uncertain Future of the World Trade Organization," *Strategic Comments*, Vol. 27, No. 2, April 23, 2021.

United Nations, "How Certain Are the United Nations Global Population Projections?" Population Facts, No. 2019/6, December 2019.

Vogel, Ezra F., *Deng Xiaoping and the Transformation of China*, Harvard University Press, 2011.

Wang, Wengxiao, Peter Draper, Dessie Ambaw, Andreas Freytag, Naoise MacDonagh, and Keith Wilson, *Industrial Subsidies, Market Competition, Global Trade and Investment: Towards a Research Agenda*, University of Adelaide, Working Paper 01, April 2020.

Willemyns, Ines, "Disciplines on State-Owned Enterprises in International Economic Law: Are We Moving in the Right Direction?" *Journal of International Economic Law*, Vol. 19, No. 3, September 2016.

World Bank Group, "Belt and Road Initiative," March 29, 2018.

World Bank Group, "The World Bank in China," webpage, last updated April 2024. As of April 18, 2023:
https://www.worldbank.org/en/country/china/overview

World Trade Organization, "Statistics on Merchandise Trade," webpage, undated-a. As of December 23, 2024:
https://www.wto.org/english/res_e/statis_e/merch_trade_stat_e.htm

World Trade Organization, "Technical Information on Anti-Dumping," webpage, undated-b. As of April 25, 2023:
https://www.wto.org/english/tratop_e/adp_e/adp_info_e.htm

World Trade Organization, "Understanding on the Interpretation of Article XVII of the General Agreement on Tariffs and Trade 1994," undated-c.

World Trade Organization, WTO Stats Dashboard—Merchandise Trade, database, undated-d. As of 12/30/2022:
https://stats.wto.org/dashboard/merchandise_en.html

WTO—*See* World Trade Organization.

Wu, Mark, "The 'China, Inc.' Challenge to Global Trade Governance," *Harvard International Law Journal*, Vol. 57, No. 2, Spring 2016.

Yu, Sun, "China's Local Governments Stuck with Bill for Neighborhood Surveillance," *Financial Times*, May 1, 2023.

Zenglein, Max J., and Anna Holzmann, *Evolving Made in China 2025: China's Industrial Policy in Quest for Global Tech Leadership*, Mercator Institute for China Studies, July 2019.

CHAPTER 10

Conclusion: Seeking Reward in a Complex Relationship

Daniel Egel and Howard J. Shatz

The U.S. and Chinese economies are deeply intertwined. At the same time, the United States and China are strategic competitors, if not adversaries.[1] The closest historical analogy is the relatively large shares of trade that occurred between Germany and its adversaries before World War I. However, in the post–World War II era, the close U.S.-Chinese economic ties in the context of tense security relations is highly unusual.[2] During the Cold War, the United States and the Soviet Union were strategic adversaries, but their economies were largely separate by design and by the choice of the Soviet Union. In the 1970s, 1980s, and early 1990s, the United States' closest economic competitor was Japan, as exemplified by a series of fiction and nonfiction books.[3] Yet the two countries were treaty allies and security partners.

The United States' relationship with China poses challenges largely because of the realities of international economic exchange when separated from national security issues: International trade brings economic gains from employing comparative advantage, which results in greater economic efficiency, more affordable goods and services, and higher returns to labor and capital in the aggregate.[4] Also, international investment, particularly foreign direct investment, improves economic efficiency by capturing economies of scale through expanded

1 White House, *National Security Strategy of the United States of America*, December 2017; White House, *National Security Strategy*, October 2022.

2 The U.S. public has recognized that, while China poses a military or security threat, interactions with it can also bring economic benefits (Bonny Lin, Howard J. Shatz, Nathan Chandler, Cristina L. Garafola, Eugeniu Han, Andy Law, King Mallory, and Zev Winkelman, *Bridging the Gap: Assessing U.S. Business Community Support for U.S.-China Competition*, RAND Corporation, RR-A1417-1, 2022).

3 Shintaro Ishihara, *The Japan That Can Say No: Why Japan Will Be First Among Equals*, Simon & Schuster, 1991; Michael Crichton, *Rising Sun*, Alfred A. Knopf, 1992.

4 Brad McDonald, "Back to Basics: Why Countries Trade," *Finance and Development*, Vol. 46, No. 4, December 2009.

markets and the diffusion of technologies.[5] These benefits are not shared equally across and within societies. A challenge for U.S. policymakers at least since the 1950s has been to design policies—not wholly successfully—to ensure that gains are more equally distributed, especially to those who lose jobs because of trade.[6]

Although much of the focus of U.S. policy is on China's strengths, it must also be recognized that China has numerous, mounting weaknesses. A rising China may be of concern to the United States, but so might a declining China.

In this concluding chapter, we first draw together the findings of the previous chapters. We then discuss the challenges facing China. Next, we draw from the preceding chapters to lay out major policy questions to be answered as the United States, and the world, try to move toward greater supply chain assurance and an improved trading system in which all economies can thrive on a basis that they find both fair and beneficial.

The Many Dimensions of U.S.-China Economic Interactions and Competition

The previous chapters explored a broad range of topics related to U.S.-China economic interactions and competition, the basic empirical patterns of which were outlined in Chapter 1. Several patterns emerge regarding conceptual differences, evaluation of policy approaches to competition, empirical interactions, and policy directions.

Conceptual Differences

One of the challenges of evaluating U.S.-China competition and creating effective policies to ensure a healthy U.S. economy that meets the nation's needs over the long term is that, in many ways, the U.S. and Chinese economies are strikingly different in how they operate. The chapters in this report explore two conceptual differences, the first related to economic security and the second to private enterprises.

China appears to have a much broader conception of economic security than does the United States. China's concept of economic security overlaps with other aspects of national security—such as politics, governance, and the military—and it has become central to the

5 Theodore H. Moran and Lindsay Oldenski, *Foreign Direct Investment in the United States: Benefits, Suspicions, and Risks with Special Attention to FDI from China*, Peterson Institute for International Economics: August 2013; Gary Clyde Hufbauer, Theodore H. Moran, and Lindsay Oldenski, with Martin Vieiro, *Outward Foreign Direct Investment and US. Exports, Jobs, and R&D: Implications for US Policy*, Peterson Institute for International Economics, 2013.

6 Jeffrey D. Sachs and Howard J. Shatz, "Trade and Jobs in U.S. Manufacturing," Brookings Papers on Economic Activity, No. 1, 1994; David H. Autor, David Dorn, and Gordon H. Hanson, "The China Syndrome: Local Labor Market Effects of Import Competition in the United States," *American Economic Review*, Vol. 103, No. 6, October 2013.

legitimacy of the Chinese Communist Party (CCP). China's economic security concept reflects concerns about subjugation and control by foreign powers and the CCP's reliance on economic growth. It has led to significant involvement of the government and party in the economy and to efforts to shape and lead international rule-setting. Most important, the strong overlap between economic and political security underpins resistance to foreign pressure to change its own economic system.

This government involvement in the economy extends to the realities of private companies in China and how they might differ from private companies in the United States and, more generally, the Western, market-oriented economies. Thinking of Chinese and Western privately owned enterprises as similar may be misplaced if such firms are categorically regarded as operating according to the same rules, incentives, and practices.

Three factors may make China a special case and the Chinese private enterprise an appropriate focus of greater attention and scrutiny. The first is the intentionality and strategy that underlies senior decisionmaking in the government of the People's Republic of China and the resultant influence on firm behavior. The second is the omnipresence and univalent political authority of the CCP and the means by which these features blur the line demarcating where the party-state ends and the firm begins. The third is the sheer scale of resources available to China as it implements policy, especially in the way that the government and party can subsidize and otherwise support private enterprises.

These conceptual differences mean that an agreed-on set of rules—such as those that governed the Western-dominated international trading system from the end of World War II until the rise of China's economy—might have very different consequences for the behavior of Chinese firms versus Western firms. What might appear to be a level playing field or a setting for fair competition based on cost and quality might in fact be quite different, and firms from one jurisdiction might have some form of nonmarket advantage over firms from another jurisdiction.

Evaluation of Policy Approaches to Competition

These differences, or at least their outcomes, are not unfamiliar to policymakers. Chapters 3 and 5 explored policy responses and potential policy responses to this evolving form of competition. Over the past 20 years, particularly following the global financial crisis, the United States has sought to influence the trajectory of China's economic engagement with the United States and the world. Although initially focused on cooperative economic measures, the United States has relied increasingly on coercive economic measures.

Coercive economic measures have included sanctions, tariffs, and law enforcement actions and have been instituted with more frequency since 2018. Coercive measures can have substantial consequences for the Chinese economy, but they can also have negative unintended consequences for the U.S. economy and for U.S. allies and partners. The effects of cooperative measures are more diffuse and difficult to measure, but such cooperative measures have been associated with several positive outcomes and have few downsides.

Many questions remain about whether to lean forward with coercive or cooperative measures. More work assessing the strategic effects of coercive economic measures is needed (such as whether they fulfill their goals), as is more work assessing the longer-term effects (such as whether they cause China to reshape its economy in ways that might be unfavorable to U.S. interests). Likewise, the causal effects of cooperative measures are uncertain.

One way to approach this problem is by theoretical modeling. Recent policy-oriented research has considered bureaucratic constituencies, individual and group psychology, and the powerful groups that a leader needs behind him to remain in power—a so-called selectorate. Agent-based modeling of how these groups might respond to coercive versus cooperative measures—and in particular how their responses might change national policy—could provide insight into the direction of future U.S. policy.

The model created for this report (Chapter 5) found that sanctioning a particularly powerful group backfired, further concentrating the power of that group and leading to unfavorable economic results. In contrast, scenarios with cooperative economic intervention that benefited groups more inclined to foster and benefit from international trade were more effective at bringing a more diverse group of elites into positions that could influence Chinese policy.

Far from the final word, this initial proof-of-concept agent-based model shows the potential to assess policy interventions as they relate to resource allocation and international trade with Chinese elites. Future work is needed to validate the model and its representation of a large and complex political system, but its results suggest that there are numerous pathways to inform policy decisions related to U.S.-China economic competition, and that considering the consequences of policies on different interest groups within China merits attention.

Empirical Interactions

One of the challenges of crafting policy related to U.S.-China economic competition is that the U.S.-China relationship is complex, and the level of exchange and interaction is enormous. Chapters 4, 6, and 7 described different aspects of this relationship: the intertwining of production networks; Chinese students and professionals in the United States and their return migration; and the energy relationship.

The global economy has become increasingly interconnected since the mid-1990s, largely because of an increasing reliance on China as a supplier of inputs for many countries (Chapter 4). Although China has become a supplier to the world, it has increasingly drawn supplies for its production from South America, Africa, and the Middle East rather than the United States, Asian economies, and the European Union. Despite those trends, the United States and China remain the largest single-country suppliers of inputs worldwide. And although China's rapid growth in relevance for the global economy is unquestioned, the United States still supplies a higher share of foreign value-added required to produce a dollar of global output than does China.

Furthermore, in a world of global production networks, regional economic relationships remain important. Despite the shifts toward Chinese production in the past two decades, regional economic relationships remain vital to production networks. For example, the United States still relies heavily on production from Mexico and Canada. For China, even though its reliance on production from other Asian economies has fallen since the 1990s, these economies are still China's largest source of foreign production. The European Union relies intensively on production from Middle Eastern and African countries, as well as from the United States. Thus, although globalization has led to more cross-regional integration—especially with China's role in global production networks—regional relationships are still key to production networks.

It is not only in goods trade that economies are intertwined, but in services trade. Education is one form of services trade, and foreign students in the United States are an important type of U.S. export (Chapter 6). Chinese students constitute a large share of foreign students, and many of these Chinese students stay to work and contribute to the U.S. economy. Importantly for the growth and productivity of the U.S. economy, Chinese migrants play an important role in the U.S. science, technology, engineering, and mathematics (STEM) workforce. Although many might stay, becoming immigrants, many also go home.

The migration of high-skilled Chinese students, workers, and entrepreneurs from the United States and China bears on bilateral economic competition in many ways. The presence of high-skilled Chinese scholars and workers can help ensure that the U.S. economy meets the nation's needs. Attracting and retaining such high-skilled students and workers benefits the United States while depriving China of their skills, giving the United States an advantage. In many ways, the migration avenues allowing flows of high-skilled Chinese people to the United States are a source of U.S. strength. On the other hand, return migration to China could provide economic benefits to China; the experience and expertise these individuals gained in the United States benefits China's economy and strengthens China as a strategic competitor. Return migration could also be beneficial to the United States, for example, by strengthening ties between industries in both countries and encouraging fruitful cross-border collaborations. Return migration can also be a cause for concern over intellectual property transfer or even theft.

Three conclusions emerge from an examination of high-skilled return migration on the Chinese economy. First, although returnees are competitive in the Chinese labor market, many are discontented with their opportunities in China. Second, although the CCP has hailed returnees as the driving force behind China's mass entrepreneurship strategy, they tend to flounder in China's start-up scene without support from local partners and networks. Third, although returnees appear to facilitate technology transfer from developed countries to Chinese small- and medium-enterprises, they play only a minor role in China's technology transfer efforts.

Faced with these costs and benefits, U.S. policy could be directed at retaining highly skilled Chinese immigrants—particularly those in STEM fields—while narrowly tailoring the security response to focus, for example, on research security and research integrity cases that have clear connections to national security or economic espionage. These efforts can support U.S. economic growth and technological advancement and mitigate risks posed by foreign nationals.

Another way that the U.S. and Chinese economies are intertwined is through energy (Chapter 7). The two countries cooperate in the development and deployment of some energy sources—particularly wind and solar—while competing in others, such as when Chinese or U.S. companies compete for oilfield rights or when China or the United States aim to develop critical mineral supplies. Just as China is a supplier of green technologies to the United States, U.S. companies supply liquefied natural gas and petroleum to China. These interactions introduce both benefits and costs to both countries, to countries that depend on the United States and China for trade, to the global energy market, and to international efforts to mitigate climate change.

The United States and China have a variety of options for managing their relations concerning energy. These options include business-as-usual, enhanced cooperation, selective delinking, complete delinking, and competition. With both countries seeking energy security and environmental security, the United States would benefit by building critical mineral processing capabilities at home and in friendly countries and by supporting the expansion of the domestic nuclear industry for commercial use, but also by continuing to cooperate with China where both countries find such cooperation to be beneficial.

Policy Directions

A final area explored in the chapters of this report was potential policy directions. Although each chapter discussed policy implications, Chapters 4 and Chapter 9 each had a much deeper focus on policy; Chapter 4 presented a discussion on policy toward production network assurance—or, in other terms, safeguarding supply chains—and Chapter 9 presented a discussion on policy to rescue the rules-based global trading system.

There have been enormous benefits from economic *integration*, but also costs; likewise, there will be costs and benefits of economic *de-integration*, something many countries of the world are moving toward. First, such trade strategies as friendshoring can be challenging and costly. Friendshoring, or shifting trade away from potential adversaries and toward allies, could improve production network assurance by limiting undesirable exposure in the production network. But deviating from those linkages will likely be costly, at least in the short term.

Second, selective decoupling could improve production network assurance at lower cost. Economic decoupling is a costly and complex process, but countries can identify their strengths and vulnerabilities in trade relationships. Building on this knowledge, they could benefit through clear plans for decoupling to de-integrate only part of the economy and prioritize production network assurance with minimal disruption.

Finally, investments in technology, trade with allies, and alternative goods are critical to limiting the cost of production network assurance in the long run. Production network assurance is always costly in the short run, but the right kind of investments could lower the cost of production network assurance in the long run. Improving cost competitiveness through production technology, enhancing market access with allies, and increasing opportunities for alternative goods and suppliers as substitutes could help countries transition from a globalization model aimed at cost minimization to one aimed at production network assurance. Beyond just trade policy, using investments in technology to lower the cost of production network assurance calls for broad-based technological collaborations among allies.

Even with technology advances that change production processes, trade will remain important. Much of the friction in the global trade order stems from the distortions of world trade caused by China's unique system of economic management. Certainly, policymakers could choose to make no reforms to global trade and investment rules, letting the global trade order decline, perhaps slowly, perhaps suddenly. But there are other options. Policymakers could make a variety of small reforms, especially among like-minded countries. Or they could make significant additions and improvements to that system.

One possible improvement is to institute a standalone multilateral competitive neutrality framework in parallel or in addition to any smaller changes being made. Such a framework would require that firms receiving state aid and that compete with other enterprises disclose all state aid received annually. Enterprises that fail to comply would be subject automatically to a high import tariff surcharge when their goods are imported to members states that have adopted the multilateral competitive neutrality framework. A somewhat lower automatic surcharge would apply to those in compliance. Enterprises would be able to reduce this surcharge further, along a sliding scale that ends at zero, depending on their ability to document progress along several dimensions related to subsidization.

An important virtue of such a solution is that such a framework—properly implemented—has the potential to successfully address the effects of China's unique system of economic management on the global trade system in a politically meaningful time frame. Furthermore, the framework is country neutral; many countries provide state aid. And such a framework might also be welcomed by economic reformers in China who recognize the potentially ruinous outcomes of their country's extensive system of subsidies.

The U.S.-China economic relationship is complex because (1) the economies are different, large, and intertwined and (2) policy measures might have unexpected consequences because of this complexity. Trade and production network assurance are but two of many areas that can benefit from new policy thinking. There are many more measures worth exploring than those discussed above. The degree to which the economies are intertwined suggests that one factor that should be taken into account when constructing policies to ensure the long-term health of the U.S. economy is the long-term health of the Chinese economy. We turn to that next. Following that section, we lay out major policy questions.

China's Economic Fragility

The Chinese economy and Chinese citizens' confidence in the ability of China's government to manage the economy are fragile. One sure sign of this decreased confidence is increased capital exit, especially among wealthy Chinese.[7] Wealthy individuals seeking ways to get their money to safer jurisdictions is a sign of falling confidence in CCP rule.

There are growing indications that China's economic might is beginning to stall:

- China now confronts serious, long-term demographic challenges, with the working-age population of people ages 15 to 64 expected to start going into absolute decline in 2028, and the overall population expected to go into absolute decline starting in 2033.[8]
- Years of unproductive investment in infrastructure and housing, fueled by borrowing, have raised China's debt-to-GDP ratio to almost 288 percent of GDP in 2023, raising the risk of a significant growth slowdown as borrowing entities find it difficult to pay back those loans.[9]
- China's rapid economic growth has resulted in environmental degradation threatening the health and well-being of the population.[10] Although there have been recent improvements on some dimensions, environmental degradation remains a serious problem.[11]

These challenges are likely to persist—and might intensify—in the decades to come.

Demographic Challenges

China's population is aging rapidly; the median age of 39 in 2023 will rise to nearly 51 by 2050. Rapid aging will—all things being equal—drive an estimated 17-percent contraction in the Chinese economy relative to the United States by 2050; China's labor force is projected to shrink by 22 percent while that of the United States grows by 4 percent.[12] This development reflects a dramatic reversal of past trends for China, the economic rise of which was driven in

7 "How to Sneak Billions of Dollars out of China," *The Economist*, December 14, 2023.

8 U.S. Census Bureau, International Database, last updated August 2023.

9 Xia Yining and Han Wei, "China's Debt-to-GDP Ratio Climbs to Record 287.8% in 2023," *Nikkei Asia*, January 30, 2024; Chris Anstey, "China's Debt Mountain Is Even Bigger Than Feared," Bloomberg, January 6, 2024; Stella Yifan Xie, "Fueled by Long Credit Binge, China's Economy Faces Drag from Debt Purge," *Wall Street Journal*, June 11, 2023.

10 Yanzhong Huang, *Toxic Politics: China's Environmental Health Crisis and Its Challenge to the Chinese State*, Cambridge University Press, 2020.

11 Lindsay Maizland, "China's Fight Against Climate Change and Environmental Degradation," Council on Foreign Relations, May 19, 2021; Yanzhong Huang, "China's Battle Against Air Pollution: An Update," blog post, Council on Foreign Relations, April 24, 2024.

12 We estimate the long-term contraction of the economy based on a standard Cobb-Douglas model of GDP with an alpha—the exponent representing the capital share of the economy—of one-third.

part by a rapid expansion of the national labor force (85 percent growth from 1980 to 2020) and the urban labor force in particular (340 percent growth from 1980 to 2020).[13]

Demographic trends shift slowly; absent a dramatic increase in immigration, the only option for China to offset a shrinking population is to increase productivity.[14] However, China's efforts to do so will be hampered by the already diminishing returns to capital investment, slowing efficiency gains, and U.S.-led attempts to constrain the adoption and diffusion of artificial intelligence through export controls on semiconductors and semiconductor manufacturing equipment.[15]

Financial Challenges

China's growth in recent decades has been sustained by a massive increase in domestic debt. To date, this debt has not meant systemic financial instability.[16] However, much of this debt has flowed to *nonproductive* investments (i.e., the rate of return on these investments is less than the cost of capital) incurred by local governments and state-owned enterprises.[17] As a result, China's economy looks increasingly like that of Japan in the early 1990s, which preceded three decades of slow growth in that country.[18]

Unwinding China's current economic circumstances will require China to reverse the "secular decline in productivity growth" that it has faced since the mid-2000s.[19] Efforts to

---

[13] Xin Meng, "Labor Market Outcomes and Reforms in China," *Journal of Economic Perspectives*, Vol. 26, No. 4, Fall 2012.

[14] The United States is increasingly dependent on immigration for its own population growth (Congressional Budget Office, *The Demographic Outlook: 2023–2053*, January 24, 2023).

[15] Loren Brandt, John Litwack, Elitza Mileva, Luhang Wang, Yifeng Zhang, and Luan Zhao, *China's Productivity Slowdown and Future Growth Potential*, World Bank Group, Policy Research Paper 9298, June 2020.

[16] Keith Bradsher, "Why China Has a Giant Pile of Debt," *New York Times*, July 8, 2023; Zhiwu Chen, "How China Keeps Putting Off Its Lehman Moment," *New York Times*, March 26, 2023. China's debt consists of household debt (63.5 percent of GDP at the end of 2023), debt held by nonfinancial businesses (168.4 percent), and government debt (55.9 percent) (Xia and Han, 2024). Government debt might actually be much higher. The International Monetary Fund uses a concept called *augmented government debt*, which includes "debt of local government financing vehicles and other off-budget entities," and that amounted to 116 percent of GDP in 2023 (International Monetary Fund, *People's Republic of China: 2023 Article IV Consultation—Press Release; Staff Report; and Statement by the Executive Director for the People's Republic of China*, IMF Country Report No. 24/38, February 2024, p. 14 of the *Staff Report for the 2023 Article IV Consultation*, dated December 19, 2023).

[17] Michael Pettis, "The Only Five Paths China's Economy Can Follow," *China Financial Markets* blog, April 27, 2022.

[18] "Could China Become Like Japan in the Early 1990s? A Symposium of Views," *International Economy*, Winter 2023; Robin Wigglesworth, "China's Japanification," *Financial Times*, August 18, 2023.

[19] International Monetary Fund, *People's Republic of China: 2022 Article IV Consultation—Press Release; Staff Report; and Statement by the Executive Director for the People's Republic of China*, IMF Country Report No. 23/67, February 3, 2023.

address this challenge, given China's historical dependence on foreign innovation for its growth in productivity, will be undermined by increased hostility with the West and the underlying risks of "geo-economic fragmentation."[20]

Environmental Challenges

China has been the greatest source of global air pollution for more than a decade, a consequence of urbanization and its continued reliance on coal for energy.[21] China's contribution to global pollution, especially emissions of greenhouse gases, has been exacerbated by investments abroad funded by China's Belt and Road Initiative, which have included coal-fired power plants. One estimate suggests that the Belt and Road Initiative might increase global temperatures by 0.7 degrees Celsius.[22] China's air pollution is having internal consequences, including—by one measure—causing some 1.4 million premature deaths per year.[23] The net economic impact of global climate change on China (including impacts to agriculture; natural disasters, particularly in economically important coastal areas; and health) is estimated to be 0.5 to 2.3 percent of China's annual GDP (approximately $100 billion to $400 billion) per year.[24]

China has committed to carbon neutrality by 2060 and accounts for roughly 50 percent of all global investments in green energy.[25] "Climate diplomacy" has emerged as a key focus of Chinese diplomatic initiatives.[26] However, making the domestic reform necessary to achieve carbon neutrality without sacrificing economic growth is anticipated to be difficult.[27]

Risks to the United States

The gradual weakening of the Chinese economy relative to the U.S. economy may already be starting. Although this outcome is desired by many policymakers and analysts, its implications for the global economy and U.S. national security are poorly understood. With eco-

[20] On China's dependence on foreign innovation, see Jialu You and Hang Xiao, "Can FDI Facilitate Green Total Factor Productivity in China? Evidence from Regional Diversity," *Environmental Science and Pollution Research*, Vol. 29, February 25, 2022. On broader challenges, see International Monetary Fund, 2023, p. 4.

[21] Maizland, 2021.

[22] "Chinese Belt and Road Plan 'May Result in 2.7C Warming,'" Climate Home News, September 2, 2019.

[23] "China Must Raise Air Quality Standards as Smog Persists, Task Force Says," Reuters, April 23, 2022.

[24] World Bank Group, *China Country Climate and Development Report*, October 2022, p. 3.

[25] "Global Low-Carbon Energy Technology Investment Surges Past $1 Trillion for the First Time," BloombergNEF, January 26, 2023.

[26] Chris Qihan Zou, "China's Climate Diplomacy Surge," *The Diplomat*, May 6, 2023.

[27] Andrew S. Erickson and Gabriel Collins, "Competition with China Can Save the Planet," *Foreign Affairs*, May/June 2021.

nomic weakness, the Chinese government could take a more benign turn, reducing expenditures on security, putting a greater emphasis on markets and integration with the global economy (and less on self-sufficiency), boosting consumption, and reducing its unproductive investments. Alternatively, it could continue to follow the path it has appeared to have chosen starting in 2021, expanding manufacturing and exports for the purpose of shoring up employment and growth, but with the risk of creating greater trade frictions internationally.[28] More concerning, a weakening China might turn belligerent, both as a means to shore up domestic support and because it might perceive that its opportunity for achieving a core interest—namely, reunification with Taiwan—is receding as it grows economically weaker relative to its potential adversaries.[29]

Like China, Japan also experienced rapid growth with, or partly because of, overinvestment. Its population has also aged rapidly. Yet it has remained a peaceful member of the global community. It has strengthened security ties with the United States. It has also remained a major global economy with positive, albeit slow, growth. Although Japan offers one optimistic model for China, the average income of China's citizens is far below that of Japan during its own period of slow growth. Furthermore, rather than being a potential adversary of the United States, Japan has been a treaty ally of the United States since 1951, with the treaty renewed in 1960, limiting any risk of conflict with the United States to shore up domestic support.[30]

Policy Questions

If the United States and China were geopolitical or security partners, these many forms of economic entwinement might cause frictions but would largely be unremarkable and accepted. The mutual gains from trade and investment are enormous.

However, the United States and China are geopolitical and security rivals to the point in which war between the two is possible.[31] Both countries face risks. The United States relies on China for inputs into its defense industrial production; the exact nature and amount of this dependence on supply chains incorporating goods from China is not known. China could withhold these inputs in times of war. Materials and goods controlled by China are also important for civilian production; withholding them could damage U.S. economic performance. China too relies on the United States for inputs, particularly semiconductors based on

[28] Michael Pettis, "The Global Constraints to Chinese Growth," *Financial Times*, November 6, 2023.

[29] Michael Beckley and Hal Brands, "How Primed for War Is China?" *Foreign Policy*, February 4, 2024.

[30] Treaty of Mutual Cooperation and Security Between Japan and the United States of America," January 19, 1960.

[31] Beckley, 2024; Phil Stewart and Idrees Ali, "How the US is Preparing for a Chinese Invasion of Taiwan," Reuters, January 31, 2024; Timothy R. Heath, Sale Lilly, and Eugeniu Han, *Can Taiwan Resist a Large-Scale Military Attack by China?* RAND Corporation, RR-A-1658-1, 2023.

U.S. designs, semiconductor manufacturing equipment, software, and other forms of intellectual property. China also relies on the United States as a market for its exports; if access to U.S. markets were to be disrupted, unemployment and economic difficulties in China could result, leading to internal unrest.

There is no easy answer to the challenge of maintaining gains from trade and investment while reducing tensions. But several principles emerge from the chapters in this report.

Recognize the Challenge

China is not a benign player in the international economy. It plays by rules that differ from those of the advanced industrial countries of the West. It ties economic performance to security in a manner that goes well beyond what Western market economies do. By virtue of its economic system, it can damage Western economies, such as by building vast capacity in some industries with subsidies, thereby underpricing Western rivals that must live within market disciplines. Recognizing that China follows different rules means that the terms of its participation in the global system should be adjusted to take account of those differences. Reshaping those terms will require cooperation by the advanced market economies.

Recognize That Separating from the Chinese Economy Will Be Costly

The global system with China at the core of global manufacturing has evolved because China has proved to be an effective producer of goods that are low cost, adjusted for their quality, increasing the overall efficiency of the global economy. China has also boosted its manufacturing prowess through a wide array of subsidies that other countries might find hard to match.[32] The evolution of the system leading to Chinese dominance in many manufacturing sectors might not have properly priced in risk, especially costly unexpected events (which are certain to occur, although specific events are almost impossible to predict), such as the COVID-19 pandemic, in which personal protective equipment became unavailable. In a future pandemic, political disagreements could result in pharmaceutical precursors being withheld.

Changing this system will be costly. If companies need to move production, they will move to higher-cost or less efficient locations. If companies cease joint innovation activities, they might not innovate as much. If companies need to stop selling certain goods to China, they will have lower profits that might result in less employment, research and development, or investment. During the initial stages of U.S. measures to compete with and counter China, from 2017 to 2021, companies broadly agreed with the strategic direction of these

---

[32] Frank Bickenbach, Dirk Dohse, Rolf J. Langhammer, and Wan-Hsin Liu, *Foul Play? On the Scale and Scope of Industrial Subsidies in China*, Kiel Institute for the World Economy, Kiel Policy Brief No. 173, April 2024.

policies, but it was also evident that these measures were having negative consequences for their businesses.[33]

The central, immediate policy challenge will be allocating these costs. Options include subsidies by the federal government, especially if companies are forced to adjust to safeguard national security, or instituting regulations that in effect impose these costs on companies, either directly or indirectly. Raising costs to companies will make them less competitive in global markets, which could slow U.S. economic growth. There is a potentially larger policy challenge, and that is how to envision and guide a revised or new economic system that will solve the problems of the current system without creating even larger problems.[34]

This is not to argue that no measures should be taken. All evidence suggests that the United States and its allies and partners need to take actions to safeguard their security and the health of their economies, but these actions will impose costs.

Choose Carefully

Recognizing that disengaging from China, at least partially, will be costly, the United States and its allies and partners will benefit from being highly selective in how they engage and how they disengage. Guiding production into lower-cost locations other than China rather than to the United States or other wealthier countries should serve to keep the cost of separation lower than otherwise. It should also serve to build resilience by ensuring that production of important items is not concentrated in one geographic location. Concentrating all production even in the United States could be riskier than making sure it is distributed more broadly.

Even if China has a near monopoly on an item, the cost of moving production out of China might not outweigh the cost of a disruption if production can be reestablished easily elsewhere within a few weeks. This is to say that the characteristics of the manufacturing processes and industrial realities of production make a great deal of difference in whether a dominant position in production is efficient and low risk or efficient but high risk.

There is no reason to think that governments, especially when political considerations enter into decisionmaking, will choose actions that are low cost compared with the benefits those actions provide. This suggests that governments should set broad, enforceable principles that can guide the actions of the private sector and let the private sector determine the best specific courses of action.

Maintain Dialogue and Aim for Ways to Find Mutual Benefit

Tensions between the two biggest single-country economies have not proved beneficial for either; both have taken steps that are inefficient and hurt their own economies. Although

[33] Lin et al., 2022.

[34] "Complexity and the Economy—W. Brian Arthur on Perpetual Formation and Combinatorial Evolution," Athenarium, undated.

it is easy to point to increased U.S. tariffs as an economic mistake, one must also point to China's flock of intelligence and national security laws, as well as its own efforts to indigenize its supply chains and output of high-technology goods and its takeover and smothering of Hong Kong.

In the face of these tensions, efforts at dialogue have proved beneficial, not least to forestall relations getting worse. But there may also be points of agreement regarding steps each can take to enhance economic exchange through which economic benefits will exceed security costs. Furthermore, dialogue and engagement more broadly throughout China could smooth relations in ways that are mutually beneficial.

The China Challenge

The China challenge is more than just about safeguarding U.S. security interests. Even with slower rates of growth, China will remain an important and highly influential economy. Furthermore, most countries around the world will want to engage with it economically, either as a source of goods, a market for their exports, or a source of finance and infrastructure construction services. In short, the China challenge is not just protecting against risks, but also about benefiting from economic engagement.

This report has focused on the U.S.-China economic relationship. It must also be recognized that, even without the challenge from China, domestic U.S. policies can have enormous consequences on U.S. economic performance. Such policies include those related to education and skill-building, the allocation of the federal government budget, fiscal balance, regulatory policy, urban public safety, and energy policy.

And although China looms large in global economic discussions, the United States remains the dominant economy in terms of income, wealth, productivity, innovation, and finance—all sources of enormous power.

Accordingly, as detailed in the other reports that were completed for this project, U.S. economic success will depend not only on how the United States manages its relationship with China but on how it creates its own vision for economic success and develops policies that bring that about.[35]

[35] Steven W. Popper, Richard Silberglitt, Fabian Villalobos, Khrystyna Holynska, Krystyna Marcinek, Nadia Almasalkhi, and Jack Lashendock, *Build Thee More Stately Mansions: Participatory Foresight and the Mid-Century U.S. Economy*, RAND Corporation, RR-A1947-2, 2025; David R. Frelinger, Jenny Oberholtzer, Stephen M. Worman, and Kate Giglio, *Rising Tide: Designing a Game of International Economic Competition*, RAND Corporation, RR-A1947-3, 2025; David A. Shlapak, Colin Levaunt, and Gregory Smith, *Coupled Competition: A Prototype Game to Explore the U.S.-China Relationship*, RAND Corporation, RR-A1947-4, 2025.

Abbreviations

CCP	Chinese Communist Party
GDP	gross domestic product
STEM	science, technology, engineering and mathematics

References

Anstey, Chris, "China's Debt Mountain Is Even Bigger Than Feared," Bloomberg, January 6, 2024.

Autor, David H., David Dorn, and Gordon H. Hanson, "The China Syndrome: Local Labor Market Effects of Import Competition in the United States," *American Economic Review*, Vol. 103, No. 6, October 2013.

Beckley, Michael, and Hal Brands, "How Primed for War Is China?" *Foreign Policy*, February 4, 2024.

Bickenbach, Frank, Dirk Dohse, Rolf J. Langhammer, and Wan-Hsin Liu, *Foul Play? On the Scale and Scope of Industrial Subsidies in China*, Kiel Institute for the World Economy, Kiel Policy Brief No. 173, April 2024.

Bradsher, Keith, "Why China Has a Giant Pile of Debt," *New York Times*, July 8, 2023.

Brandt, Loren, John Litwack, Elitza Mileva, Luhang Wang, Yifeng Zhang, and Luan Zhao, *China's Productivity Slowdown and Future Growth Potential*, World Bank Group, Policy Research Paper 9298, June 2020.

Chen, Zhiwu, "How China Keeps Putting Off Its Lehman Moment," *New York Times*, March 26, 2023.

"China Must Raise Air Quality Standards as Smog Persists, Task Force Says," Reuters, April 23, 2022.

"Chinese Belt and Road Plan 'May Result in 2.7C Warming,'" Climate Home News, September 2, 2019.

"Complexity and the Economy—W. Brian Arthur on Perpetual Formation and Combinatorial Evolution," Athenarium, undated.

Congressional Budget Office, *The Demographic Outlook: 2023–2053*, January 24, 2023.

"Could China Become Like Japan in the Early 1990s? A Symposium of Views," *International Economy*, Winter 2023.

Crichton, Michael, *Rising Sun*, Alfred A. Knopf, 1992.

Erickson, Andrew S., and Gabriel Collins, "Competition with China Can Save the Planet," *Foreign Affairs*, May/June 2021.

Frelinger, David R., Jenny Oberholtzer, Stephen M. Worman, and Kate Giglio, *Rising Tide: Designing a Game of International Economic Competition*, RAND Corporation, RR-A1947-3, 2025. As of June 23, 2025:
https://www.rand.org/pubs/research_reports/RRA1947-3.html

"Global Low-Carbon Energy Technology Investment Surges Past $1 Trillion for the First Time," BloombergNEF, January 26, 2023.

Heath, Timothy R., Sale Lilly, and Eugeniu Han, *Can Taiwan Resist a Large-Scale Military Attack by China?* RAND Corporation, RR-A-1658-1, 2023. As of February 9, 2024: https://www.rand.org/pubs/research_reports/RRA1658-1.html

"How to Sneak Billions of Dollars out of China," *The Economist*, December 14, 2023.

Huang, Yanzhong, *Toxic Politics: China's Environmental Health Crisis and Its Challenge to the Chinese State*, Cambridge University Press, 2020.

Huang, Yanzhong, "China's Battle Against Air Pollution: An Update," blog post, Council on Foreign Relations, April 24, 2024.

Hufbauer, Gary Clyde, Theodore H. Moran, and Lindsay Oldenski, with Martin Vieiro, *Outward Foreign Direct Investment and US Exports, Jobs, and R&D: Implications for US Policy*, Peterson Institute for International Economics, 2013.

International Monetary Fund, *People's Republic of China: 2022 Article IV Consultation—Press Release; Staff Report; and Statement by the Executive Director for the People's Republic of China*, IMF Country Report No. 23/67, February 2023.

International Monetary Fund, *People's Republic of China: 2023 Article IV Consultation—Press Release; Staff Report; and Statement by the Executive Director for the People's Republic of China*, IMF Country Report No. 24/38, February 2024.

Ishihara, Shintaro, *The Japan That Can Say No: Why Japan Will Be First Among Equals*, Simon & Schuster, 1991.

Lin, Bonny, Howard J. Shatz, Nathan Chandler, Cristina L. Garafola, Eugeniu Han, Andy Law, King Mallory, and Zev Winkelman, *Bridging the Gap: Assessing U.S. Business Community Support for U.S.-China Competition*, RAND Corporation, RR-A1417-1, 2022. As of May 8, 2025: https://www.rand.org/pubs/research_reports/RRA1417-1.html

Maizland, Lindsay, "China's Fight Against Climate Change and Environmental Degradation," Council on Foreign Relations, May 19, 2021.

McDonald, Brad, "Back to Basics: Why Countries Trade," *Finance and Development*, Vol. 46, No. 4, December 2009.

Moran, Theodore H., and Lindsay Oldenski, *Foreign Direct Investment in the United States: Benefits, Suspicions, and Risks with Special Attention to FDI from China*, Peterson Institute for International Economics: August 2013.

Pettis, Michael, "The Only Five Paths China's Economy Can Follow," *China Financial Markets* blog, April 27, 2022.

Pettis, Michael, "The Global Constraints to Chinese Growth," *Financial Times*, November 6, 2023.

Popper, Steven W., Richard Silberglitt, Fabian Villalobos, Khrystyna Holynska, Krystyna Marcinek, Nadia Almasalkhi, and Jack Lashendock, *Build Thee More Stately Mansions: Participatory Foresight and the Mid-Century U.S. Economy*, RAND Corporation, RR-A1947-2, 2025. As of June 23, 2025:
https://www.rand.org/pubs/research_reports/RRA1947-2.html

Sachs, Jeffrey D., and Howard J. Shatz, "Trade and Jobs in U.S. Manufacturing," Brookings Papers on Economic Activity, No. 1, 1994.

Shlapak, David A., Colin Levaunt, and Gregory Smith, *Coupled Competition: A Prototype Game to Explore the U.S.-China Relationship*, RAND Corporation, RR-A1947-4, 2025. As of June 23, 2025:
https://www.rand.org/pubs/research_reports/RRA1947-4.html

Stewart, Phil, and Idrees Ali, "How the US is Preparing for a Chinese Invasion of Taiwan," Reuters, January 31, 2024.

Treaty of Mutual Cooperation and Security Between Japan and the United States of America, January 19, 1960.

U.S. Census Bureau, International Database, last updated August 2023. As of July 23, 2024:
https://www.census.gov/programs-surveys/international-programs/about/idb.html

White House, *National Security Strategy of the United States of America*, December 2017.

White House, *National Security Strategy*, October 2022.

Wigglesworth, Robin, "China's Japanification," *Financial Times*, August 18, 2023.

World Bank Group, *China Country Climate and Development Report*, October 2022.

Xia Yining and Han Wei, "China's Debt-to-GDP Ratio Climbs to Record 287.8% in 2023," *Nikkei Asia*, January 30, 2024.

Xie, Stella Yifan, "Fueled by Long Credit Binge, China's Economy Faces Drag from Debt Purge," *Wall Street Journal*, June 11, 2023.

Xin Meng, "Labor Market Outcomes and Reforms in China," *Journal of Economic Perspectives*, Vol. 26, No. 4, Fall 2012.

You, Jialu, and Hang Xiao, "Can FDI Facilitate Green Total Factor Productivity in China? Evidence from Regional Diversity," *Environmental Science and Pollution Research*, Vol. 29, February 25, 2022.

Zou, Chris Qihan, "China's Climate Diplomacy Surge," *The Diplomat*, May 6, 2023.

www.ingramcontent.com/pod-product-compliance
Ingram Content Group UK Ltd.
Pitfield, Milton Keynes, MK11 3LW, UK
UKHW051335010925
7672UKWH00049B/1072

9 781977 415066